THUS SPOKE ZARATHUSTRA

FRIEDRICH NIETZSCHE (1844–1900) was born in Röcken, Saxony, and educated at the universities of Bonn and Leipzig. At the age of only 24 he was appointed Professor of Classical Philology at the University of Basle, but prolonged bouts of ill health forced him to resign from his post in 1879. Over the next decade he shuttled between the Swiss Alps and the Mediterranean coast, devoting himself entirely to thinking and writing. His early books and pamphlets (*The Birth of Tragedy, Untimely Meditations*) were heavily influenced by Wagner and Schopenhauer, but from *Human, All Too Human* (1878) on, his thought began to develop more independently, and he published a series of ground-breaking philosophical works (*The Gay Science, Thus Spoke Zarathustra, Beyond Good and Evil, On the Genealogy of Morals*) which culminated in a frenzy of production in the closing months of 1888. In January 1889 Nietzsche suffered a mental breakdown from which he was never to recover, and he died in Weimar eleven years later.

GRAHAM PARKES is Professor of Philosophy at the University of Hawaii. He is the editor of *Nietzsche and Asian Thought* (1991), author of *Composing the Soul: Reaches of Nietzsche's Psychology* (1994), and co-translator of Georges Liébert's *Nietzsche and Music* (2004).

OXFORD WORLD'S CLASSICS

*For over 100 years Oxford World's Classics have brought
readers closer to the world's great literature. Now with over 700
titles—from the 4,000-year-old myths of Mesopotamia to the
twentieth century's greatest novels—the series makes available
lesser-known as well as celebrated writing.*

*The pocket-sized hardbacks of the early years contained
introductions by Virginia Woolf, T. S. Eliot, Graham Greene,
and other literary figures which enriched the experience of reading.
Today the series is recognized for its fine scholarship and
reliability in texts that span world literature, drama and poetry,
religion, philosophy and politics. Each edition includes perceptive
commentary and essential background information to meet the
changing needs of readers.*

OXFORD WORLD'S CLASSICS

FRIEDRICH NIETZSCHE

Thus Spoke Zarathustra
A Book for Everyone
and Nobody

Translated with an Introduction and Notes by
GRAHAM PARKES

OXFORD
UNIVERSITY PRESS

OXFORD
UNIVERSITY PRESS

Great Clarendon Street, Oxford OX2 6DP

Oxford University Press is a department of the University of Oxford.
It furthers the University's objective of excellence in research, scholarship,
and education by publishing worldwide in

Oxford New York

Auckland Cape Town Dar es Salaam Hong Kong Karachi
Kuala Lumpur Madrid Melbourne Mexico City Nairobi
New Delhi Shanghai Taipei Toronto

With offices in

Argentina Austria Brazil Chile Czech Republic France Greece
Guatemala Hungary Italy Japan Poland Portugal Singapore
South Korea Switzerland Thailand Turkey Ukraine Vietnam

Oxford is a registered trade mark of Oxford University Press
in the UK and in certain other countries

Published in the United States
by Oxford University Press Inc., New York

© Graham Parkes 2005

The moral rights of the author have been asserted
Database right Oxford University Press (maker)

First published as an Oxford World's Classics paperback 2005

British Library Cataloguing in Publication Data

Data available

Library of Congress Cataloging in Publication Data

Data available

Typeset in Ehrhardt
by RefineCatch Limited, Bungay, Suffolk
Printed in Great Britain by
Clays Ltd., St. Ives plc., Suffolk

ISBN 0–19–280583–5   978–0–19–280583–6

1

For Helen

CONTENTS

ABBREVIATIONS

The following abbreviations are used in the references to Nietzsche's works (references to individual books are to part and/or paragraph numbers):

B	*Friedrich Nietzsche: Sämtliche Briefe, Kritische Studienausgabe*, ed. Giorgio Colli and Mazzino Montinari, 8 vols. (Munich, 1986); references are to dates
BGE	*Beyond Good and Evil*
EH	*Ecce Homo*
HA	*Human, All Too Human*
JS	*The Joyful Science*
SE	*Schopenhauer as Educator*
W	*Friedrich Nietzsche: Sämtliche Werke, Kritische Studienausgabe*, ed. Giorgio Colli and Mazzino Montinari, 15 vols. (Munich, 1980); references are to volume and section numbers
WS	*The Wanderer and His Shadow* (in *HA*)

INTRODUCTION

Thus Spoke Zarathustra—A Book for Everyone and Nobody: the sub-title, at first puzzling, is also telling. The work is for 'nobody' insofar as it's an intensely personal piece of philosophizing: 'There is in this book an incredible amount of personal experience and suffering that is comprehensible only to me—many pages strike me as almost *blood-thirsty*' (*B* Aug. 1883). So why did Nietzsche bother to make public his personal experience? And to what extent is the result philosophy, whose practitioners have traditionally aimed at impersonality, gener-ality, or even universality? The answer lies in Nietzsche's unusual understanding of philosophy and the philosopher, as exemplified in his most unusual book: *Thus Spoke Zarathustra*.

Nietzsche knew that what is personal may after all touch others, though the process remains obscure. 'Strange!' he wrote in 1880, 'I am dominated at every moment by the thought that my history is not only a personal one, that I am doing something for many people when I live like this and work on and write about myself this way' (*W* 9: 7 [105]). A few years later he says this about the way philosophers can transform life-experience into thought: 'We must constantly give birth to our thoughts out of our pain, and nurture them with every-thing we have in us of blood, heart, fire, pleasure, passion, agony, conscience, fate, and catastrophe. Life to us—that means constantly transforming everything we are into light and flame, as well every-thing that happens to us' (*JS* Preface, 3). Such light and flame can illumine the way for others through the medium of the written page, as long as the style is sufficiently vibrant.

Then the life that is saved in the book is immortal since it survives its author's death with a strange autonomy: 'It seeks out readers for itself, ignites new life, delights, terrifies, engenders new works, becomes the soul of plans and actions' (*HA* 208). If the word 'instructs' is notably absent from this list of capabilities, this is because Nietzsche follows Goethe's well-known dictum: 'I hate everything that merely instructs me, without amplifying or directly enlivening my activity.' It is his concern with imbuing *Zarathustra*'s pages with the most vital life that enables a presentation of the personal to transform the reader's experience: 'Whoever has *lived* in this book returns to the world with an altered face and vision' (*B* 22 Feb. 1884). Dozens of Nietzsche's letters testify to a passionate desire to reach other people and change their minds.

We can see, then, how *Zarathustra* might be a book for someone other than the author, but this hardly makes it a book 'for everyone'. Martin Heidegger reads the 'for everyone' helpfully as 'for every human being as a human being, for each one whenever and insofar as one becomes for oneself worthy of thinking about in one's essential nature'.[1] But how many of us become that for ourselves? Nietzsche does claim, in a letter written while he was composing the third part of the book (*B* 13 Feb. 1883), that the work is 'accessible to anyone'—but since he is writing to his publisher, and authors seldom proclaim minimal market for their books, a little scepticism might be appropriate. Nonetheless, the publication history of *Zarathustra* suggests that the book has a remarkably broad appeal: just as it was the author's favourite among his works, it has also been the most popular among general readers (if not among Nietzsche scholars).

Heidegger reads the 'for nobody' of the subtitle as meaning 'for nobody among the inquisitive types who . . . merely intoxicate themselves with isolated fragments and particular aphorisms from this book'. This makes sense in view of Zarathustra's calling aphorisms 'mountain peaks' or 'summits', which suggests a vast mass of supporting material (thoughts, ideas, images) to be negotiated before they can be adequately understood. This takes work—or, to put it more encouragingly: *Zarathustra* is a text that richly repays the effort of repeated readings over time.

For a deeper understanding of the book, Nietzsche reminds us, we need to appreciate its context: 'To have the prerequisite for understanding *Zarathustra, all* my earlier writings must be genuinely and profoundly understood; also the *necessity* of the sequence of these writings and the development expressed in them' (*B* 29 Aug. 1886). Even if one restricts the requirement to his published works it is still exacting, in view of the seven books that appeared before *Zarathustra: The Birth of Tragedy, Untimely Observations, Human, All Too Human, Assorted Opinions and Maxims, The Wanderer and His Shadow,*

---

[1] Martin Heidegger, 'Who is Nietzsche's Zarathustra?', in David B. Allison (ed.), *The New Nietzsche* (Cambridge, Mass.: MIT Press), 64.

Dawn of Morning, and *The Joyful Science*.[2] Nietzsche explicitly refers to these last two as 'commentaries on *Zarathustra* written in advance of the text' (*B* 7 Apr. 1884).

If all this doesn't enlighten sufficiently, one can turn to Nietzsche's next book, *Beyond Good and Evil*, which he wrote as an explication of *Zarathustra*, since so few readers appeared to have understood the earlier text. In a letter to the historian Jacob Burckhardt, whose colleague Nietzsche had been at the University of Basel, he wrote: 'It says the same things as my *Zarathustra*, but differently, very differently' (*B* 22 Sept. 1886). Lastly, there is an indispensable discussion of *Zarathustra* in one of Nietzsche's last works, *Ecce Homo* (1888).

The nineteenth century was a time of fervent Orientalism in Europe, with especial interest in Zoroastrianism. Zoroaster is the Greek name for the Persian prophet Zarathustra, whose dates are unknown but who probably flourished some time between the twelfth and sixth centuries BCE. In the fifty years before Nietzsche's book appeared, over twenty major studies of the *Zend-Avesta* (the sacred text attributed to Zarathustra) and/or its author were published in German.[3] Having been a classical philologist, with friends who were Orientalists, Nietzsche was well aware of this interest in Zarathustra in academic circles and beyond. Later, in *Ecce Homo*, he remarks that no one has ever asked him 'what the name "Zarathustra" means in [his] mouth' (*EH* 'Why I Am a Destiny', 3). A notebook entry penned a few weeks after he was first struck by the thought of eternal recurrence, which became the basic idea of *Zarathustra*, reads as follows:

Midday and Eternity
Hints toward a New Life

Zarathustra, born by Lake Urmi, left his home in his thirtieth year, went to the province of Aria and wrote the *Zend-Avesta* during ten years of solitude in the mountains. (*W* 9: 11 [195])

---

[2] *Untimely Observations* was first published in four separate parts: *David Strauss the Confessor and Writer*, *The Use and Disadvantage of History for Life*, *Schopenhauer as Educator*, and *Richard Wagner in Bayreuth*. *Assorted Opinions and Maxims* was first published as a supplement to *Human, All Too Human*, and *The Wanderer and His Shadow* was subsequently published together with *Assorted Opinions and Maxims* as Volume 2 of *Human, All Too Human*.

[3] Hushang Mehregan, 'Zarathustra im Awesta und bei Nietzsche: eine vergleichende Gegenüberstellung', *Nietzsche-Studien*, 8 (1979), 292.

This sentence is a paraphrase of a passage from the cultural historian Friedrich von Hellwald concerning the Persian prophet.[4] Somewhat modified, it later becomes the opening sentence of *Thus Spoke Zarathustra*. Hellwald also writes that Zarathustra was the first to come up with the idea of a 'moral order to the world'. As Nietzsche later puts it: 'The transposition of morality into metaphysics . . . is *his* doing.' And so the reason for the choice of protagonist is this: 'Zarathustra *created* this disastrous error, morality; consequently he must be the first to *recognize* this' (*EH* ibid.).

Like many a philosophical masterpiece, *Zarathustra* engages in a dialogue with earlier texts, though the range in this case goes beyond the philosophical to include the Homeric epics, the fragments of Heraclitus, Plato's dialogues, the Luther Bible, Goethe's *Faust*, Hölderlin's *Hyperion*, Emerson's *Essays*, and Wagner's *Ring of the Nibelungen* and *Parsifal*. As a schoolboy, Nietzsche was a voracious reader, and these literary texts were a formative influence on him. Friedrich Hölderlin was, along with Goethe, Germany's greatest poet; but it was his epistolary novel *Hyperion*, whose protagonist is a romantic idealist devoted to the regeneration of his native Hellenic culture, that most fascinated the young Nietzsche. It is not generally appreciated that Ralph Waldo Emerson, 'the Sage of Concord', became so popular in Europe during his lifetime that his essays were regularly translated into German not long after their publication in Boston. At 17 Nietzsche recognized a wise mentor and kindred spirit in Emerson, whose powerfully eloquent prose style and ideas about fate, history, and the soul exerted a lasting influence on him as a thinker and writer.[5] And since *Zarathustra* is a masterpiece of literature as well as philosophy (the author calls it a poetic composition), the figure of its protagonist is formed through deliberate associations with Homer's Odysseus, Plato's Socrates, some Old Testament prophets, the Jesus of the Gospels, Byron's Manfred, Goethe's Faust, Hölderlin's Hyperion, and Wagner's Siegfried and Parsifal.

[4] Friedrich von Hellwald, *Culturgeschichte in ihrer natürlichen Entstehung bis zur Gegenwart* (Augsburg, 1874), 128. See Thomas H. Brobjer, *Nietzsche's Knowledge of Philosophy* (Urbana, Ill.: University of Illinois Press, 2005).

[5] For a brief account of the influence of Goethe, Byron, Hölderlin, and Emerson on the young Nietzsche see ch. 1 of my *Composing the Soul: Reaches of Nietzsche's Psychology* (Chicago and London: University of Chicago Press, 1994).

A consideration of this last influence highlights the musical and operatic nature of the text. Roger Hollinrake has argued persuasively that *Zarathustra* is in several respects a response to Wagner, and particularly to the 'system of thought' developed in *The Ring* and to *Parsifal*. He writes: '*Zarathustra* was planned as a whole and from the outset as a reply to Wagner, embodying in its own literary idiom just those qualities Nietzsche believed that Wagner, the artist, theorist, and messianic leader, had betrayed.'[6] To mention just the main points of the argument: while working on *Zarathustra* Nietzsche writes of his aim to 'become Wagner's heir'; Nietzsche saw Wagner and himself as distinctively 'dithyrambic artists'; the assault on Christianity (especially in the Fourth Part) is just as much 'a protest against the messianic pretensions of the second Bayreuth Festival', and Zarathustra's general deprecation of pity is primarily aimed against Wagner's doctrine of pity in *Parsifal*.

As far as the literary style of *Zarathustra* is concerned, Nietzsche emphasizes two sources in particular: 'The language of Luther and the poetic form of the Bible as the basis for a new German *poetry*: that is *my* invention!' (*W* 11: 25 [173]). But he also sees these sources as being superseded: 'With *Zarathustra* I believe I have brought the German language to its culmination. After *Luther* and *Goethe* there was still a third step to be made' (*B* 22 Feb. 1884). Many scholars believe that Nietzsche managed to make that step. Much of the language in *Zarathustra* does resonate grandly with—though it sometimes parodies—Luther's Bible, which sounds slightly less archaic to the contemporary German ear than the King James Version does to ours.

Origins

Like Jean-Jacques Rousseau and Henry David Thoreau before him, Nietzsche did his best thinking while walking in the open air, so that *place* was of the utmost importance to him as a philosopher. 'Nobody is free to live wherever he wants, and whoever has great tasks to accomplish has an especially narrow range of choice. The influence

---

[6] Roger Hollinrake, *Nietzsche, Wagner, and the Philosophy of Pessimism* (London and Boston: Allen & Unwin, 1982), p. ix.

of climate on the metabolism goes so far that a blunder in regard to place can alienate us from our task altogether' (*EH* 'Why I Am So Clever', 2). Nietzsche's strong physical constitution had been weakened by his contracting dysentery and diphtheria while serving as a medical orderly in the Franco-Prussian War in 1870. As he became older his system became ever more sensitive to the physical environment. During the last decade of his productive life, he travelled continually—packing his trunk and moving somewhere else four times a year, with every change of the seasons—all for the sake of being in the right place for his task of thinking and writing. More than with any other philosopher, Nietzsche's works show the influence of the places in which they were thought out and written down.

Although the first part of *Zarathustra* came to him while he was living in Rapallo, a fishing village on the Ligurian coast just east of Genoa, Nietzsche writes that 'the birthplace' of this book is 'the Engadin' and 'sacred Sils' in south-eastern Switzerland (*B* 3 Sept. 1883, 25 July 1884). This aphorism from *The Wanderer and His Shadow*, written shortly after his first visit to the Engadin in 1879, conveys a vivid sense of his feelings for the place that gave rise to *Zarathustra*:

In many places in nature we discover ourselves again. . . . How fortunate the one who can have this experience right *here*, in this constantly sunlit October air, in this happy and mischievous play of the breezes from morning till night, in this purest daylight and temperate coolness, in the totally graceful and genuine character of the hills, lakes, and forests of this high plateau . . . how fortunate the one who can say: 'There is surely much that is grander and more beautiful in nature, but *this* is intimately familiar to me, related by blood, and even more.' (*WS* 338)

Nietzsche didn't return to the Engadin till two years later, when the power of the place helped produce the thought that was the seed from which the book was to grow:

The basic conception of *Zarathustra*, the *thought of eternal recurrence*, the highest formula of affirmation that can ever be attained, dates back to August of 1881: it was sketched on a piece of paper with the inscription '6000 feet beyond human beings and time'. That day I was walking through the woods by Lake Silvaplana; I stopped at a powerful pyramidal block of stone not far from Surlei. The thought came to me there. (*EH* 'Why I Write Such Good Books: *Thus Spoke Zarathustra*', 1)

The basic idea of *Zarathustra*, then, is affirmative in the extreme and struck Nietzsche at a place so special that he characterizes it unambiguously. The block of stone is massive, about 3 metres tall, and stands right on the shore of the lake, slightly overhanging the water. Beyond the opposite shore looms the majestic peak of Mount Julier, which rises another 5,000 feet above the valley floor and whose pyramidal shape frames and echoes the contours of the 'eternal recurrence' rock. Given what we know about Nietzsche's hiking habits in the Sils-Maria area, he would have been walking briskly for at least forty-five minutes before coming upon this place, breathing deeply the sweet but somewhat rarefied air of the high Alpine valley. Under such conditions on an August day, in such a place, resolute pessimists could be subject to affirmative thoughts.

A year-and-a-half later Nietzsche was living on 'the graceful, quiet Bay of Rapallo':

My health was not the best, the winter cold and unusually rainy. . . . In spite of this, and almost as proof of my proposition that everything decisive originates 'in spite of' something, it was from this winter and these unfavourable circumstances that my *Zarathustra* originated.—In the mornings I would climb the magnificent road to Zoagli uphill in a southerly direction, looking out over pine trees and far out to sea. In the afternoons, as far as my health permitted, I would walk around the whole Bay of Santa Margherita as far as Portofino. . . . It was on these two paths that the whole first part of *Zarathustra* came to me, and above all Zarathustra himself, as a type: or rather, *he came over me there*. (*EH* ibid.)

A contemporary letter confirms the al fresco origins of the book's first part: 'All of it was conceived in the course of strenuous hiking: absolute certainty, as if every sentence were being called out to me' (*B* 10 Apr. 1888).

Later that year: 'In the summer [of 1883], having returned to the sacred place [Sils-Maria] where the first lightning of the Zarathustra-thought had struck me, I found the second part of *Zarathustra*. Ten days were sufficient; in no case, neither with the first nor with the third and last part, did I need longer' (*EH* loc. cit. 4). The landscape of this sacred place—with its lakes lined by pines and firs, flower-studded alpine meadows, majestic mountain peaks snow-capped all year round, tall waterfalls and rushing torrents, and everywhere spectacularly shaped, sized, and coloured rocks—permeates the text of *Zarathustra* and especially chapters in the Second Part.

And at the end of the year: 'The following winter, under the halcyon sky of Nizza [Nice] which at that time shone into my life for the first time, I found the third part of *Zarathustra*—and was finished. Scarcely one year for the entire work.' Nietzsche needed clear skies if he was to be fully creative, being exquisitely sensitive to changes in atmospheric pressure and humidity. But he also needed to be by the sea: 'I could only have composed the final verses of my *Zarathustra* on this coast, in the home of *gaya scienza*' (*B* 7 Apr. 1884). And it was just along the coast, in Menton as well as Nice, that he composed the Fourth Part of the book, in the winter of 1884–5.

If Nietzsche did indeed write the first three parts of *Zarathustra* in ten days each, then, given the book's depth of thought and intricacy of imagistic structure, we have a classic case of inspiration—as he himself observes at length:

Retaining only the smallest remnant of superstition one can still hardly reject the idea of being a mere incarnation, a mere mouthpiece, a mere medium. The concept of revelation, in the sense that suddenly and with indescribable certainty and subtlety something becomes *visible* and audible, something that shakes one to the depths and bowls one over, simply describes the fact of the matter. . . . A rapture whose enormous tension discharges itself now and again in floods of tears, in which one's walking pace involuntarily quickens or slows down. . . . Everything happens involuntarily in the highest degree, yet in a tempestuous feeling of freedom, of being unconditioned, of power, of divinity. . . . The involuntariness of the images and parables is the most remarkable thing of all; one no longer has any conception of what an image or a parable is: everything offers itself as the closest, the most appropriate, the simplest expression. (*EH* loc. cit. 3)

Nietzsche goes on to emphasize the somatic dimension to this Dionysiac effusion. Describing the composition of a chapter in the Third Part during the steep climb from sea-level to high cliffs along the coast from Nice, he writes: 'Suppleness of the muscles was always greatest for me when the creative forces flowed most fully. The *body* is inspired: let us leave the "soul" out of it. . . . I was often seen dancing; at that time I could hike in the hills for seven or eight hours without a trace of weariness' (*EH* loc. cit. 4).

Nietzsche was well aware that this outflow of creativity was possible only on the basis of his long pondering of the ideas: 'The *whole* of *Zarathustra* is an explosion of forces that have been accumulating for decades' (*B* 6 Feb. 1884). He was also aware of the dangers of such tremendous creative exhilaration: 'With explosions like this it is easy for the originator to blow up along with them.' These periods of exhilaration were clearly what made life worth living for Nietzsche, despite the grimness of their context: 'Aside from these ten-day work-periods, the years during and above all *after Zarathustra* were a time of incomparable distress. One pays dearly for being immortal: one dies for it several times during one's life' (*EH* loc. cit. 5). But a refusal to take himself too seriously also helped. Shortly after the idea of eternal recurrence struck, he wrote in letters to friends: 'I really should be in Paris at the big exhibition on electricity, partly to learn the latest, and partly as one of the exhibits. . . . In this respect I'm perhaps more sensitive than any other human being, to my great misfortune!' (*B* 21 Aug., 28 Oct. 1881).

The Overhuman

One reason why scholars of Nietzsche's work tend to devote less time to *Zarathustra* than his other books is its apparently unphilosophical form. Whereas the standard philosophical text advances arguments within the context of a clearly articulated conceptual framework, *Zarathustra* presents an imagined life within a larger play of images, by means of what the author calls a 'return of language to the nature of imagery' (*EH* loc. cit. 6). Concepts—the root of the word means 'to grasp'—enable the mind to get a grip on at least some aspects of the world by excluding what they don't grasp, through a logic of negation and opposition. Images, when deployed by a thinker as careful as Nietzsche, also operate according to a certain logic; but the ways in which they work are more complex. Whereas a treatise that articulates ideas or theories in terms of concepts asks that the reader assent to (or refute) their validity, a text like *Zarathustra* invites the reader to follow a train of thought through fields of imagery, and to participate in a play of imagination that engages the whole psyche rather than the intellect alone.

There is consequently very little standard philosophical vocabulary in *Zarathustra*: the term 'being' (*Sein*) is used rarely, and even 'nature' appears only once. Nevertheless, it is generally agreed that *Zarathustra* does contain three major philosophical ideas: the Over-human (*Übermensch*), will to power, and the eternal recurrence of the same.

In the first section of the chapter 'Why I Write Such Good Books' in *Ecce Homo*, Nietzsche tells us that the word *Übermensch* as used in *Zarathustra* refers to 'a type that has turned out in the best possible way, by contrast with "modern" human beings, with "good" human beings, with Christians and other nihilists'. The mention of 'other nihilists' suggests that the Overhuman is far from the type that dismisses this transitory world of ours as meaningless or worthless. But the term *Übermensch* is hard to translate. 'Superman' conjures up unfortunate associations with musclebound blue-suited heroes and overemphasizes the 'above' connotation of the 'over' (*über*) at the expense of the 'across'. 'Overman' is therefore better—but since *Mensch* is rendered in the present translation as 'human' or 'human being', 'Overman' fails to convey the relations Zarathustra keeps emphasizing between the human and the Overhuman: 'I want to teach humans the meaning of their Being: that is the Overhuman, the lightning from the dark cloud of the human' (Prologue, 7). Leaving *Übermensch* untranslated, on the grounds that it is almost an English word, fails in the same way.

'Overhuman' also serves to emphasize that the *Übermensch* is attained through an *overcoming* of the human—as intimated by the word's first occurrence, in Zarathustra's first words to the people: '*I teach to you the Overhuman*. The human is something that shall be overcome' (Prologue, 3). Part of what this means is that the Over-human emerges from our going beyond the human perspective and transcending the anthropocentric worldview. This is made clear by the three repetitions of the exhortation, 'Behold, I teach to you the Overhuman!' followed by declarations of the Overhuman's kinship with the natural elements: it is 'the sense of the earth', 'this sea', and 'this lightning'. And in exhorting his audience to prepare the way for the Overhuman, Zarathustra says: 'I love him who works and invents to build a house for the Overhuman and prepare for it *earth* and *animal* and *plant*' (Prologue, 4, emphasis added). Prepare those three because the way to overcome the human is to acknowledge and emu-late the nonhuman nature—mineral, animal, vegetal—of which we consist and on which we depend.[7] A notebook entry reads: 'N.B. The highest human being is to be conceived in the image of nature' (*W* 11: 25 [140]).

Given the powerful presence of the natural world throughout the narrative of *Zarathustra*, it is not surprising that the Overhuman should be reached through retaining or regaining the connection with the animal aspects of the human and with the site of natural functions that is the body. It is important to maintain the tension 'between beast and Overhuman' in crossing over to the latter (Prologue, 4), and those who despise the body are 'no bridges to the Overhuman' (1. 4). It is a psychological rather than a political goal— 'There where the state *ceases*' is where one finds 'the rainbow and the bridges of the Overhuman' (1. 11)—though it can be reached through the medium of friendship (1. 14). It is also for Zarathustra the primary goal of procreation and marriage (1. 18, 20). Rather than claiming to have attained the condition of the Overhuman himself, Zarathustra simply proclaims the possibility, which will take time to be realized: 'You lonely ones of today, who withdraw to the side, you shall one day be a people: out of you, who have chosen yourselves, shall a chosen people grow:—and out of them the Overhuman' (1. 22). But Zarathustra's father (Nietzsche often refers to Zarathustra as 'my son') later remarks on his extreme kindness (even toward 'his opponents, the priests') and adds: 'Here the human is overcome at every moment, the concept "Overhuman" had become the highest reality here' (*EH* loc. cit. 6).

Since it seems that a condition for the possibility of the appearance of the Overhuman is 'the death of God', it's often assumed that this advent heralds the disappearance of the Divine. The book's First Part does indeed end with the resounding cry, '*Dead are all Gods: now we want the Overhuman to live*'—but this is only a provisional teaching of Zarathustra's that will soon be superseded. At this early stage he would rather his disciples rid themselves of all belief in supernatural beings than move too soon to a more salutary polytheism—from which they might relapse into some other form of 'monotonotheism'. A careful reading of the last three parts of the

---

[7] For a discussion of Nietzsche's unusual interest in the mineral realm especially, see my essay 'Staying Loyal to the Earth: Nietzsche as an Ecological Thinker', in John Lippitt (ed.), *Nietzsche's Futures* (Basingstoke: Macmillan, 1998), 167–88.

book reveals that for Zarathustra the world, seen clearly and rightly understood, is 'a dance-floor for divine accidents' and 'a Gods' table for divine dice and dice-throwers' (3. 4). There is a new kind of religion here—what has been aptly called Nietzsche's 'Dionysian pantheism'.[8]

Will to Power

Will to power is a difficult idea that has been widely misunderstood, but two common misconceptions are easily dispensed with: the 'will' of will to power is not the kind of willpower exerted by the human 'I' or ego; nor is the 'power' any kind of brute force exercised by human beings. An immediate prototype of the idea of a transpersonal or cosmic will is to be found in Schopenhauer, who argues in *The World as Will and Representation* that the entire world is basically will, as manifested in phenomena such as gravity, magnetism, and the life-force that drives plants, animals, and human beings. The human will is simply a more highly developed form of the basic force of the universe. Though Nietzsche's idea of will to power is more complex, he follows Schopenhauer in understanding will cosmically and non-anthropocentrically. In *Zarathustra* (2. 12) no lesser authority than Life herself tells the protagonist that all life is 'will to power', and in aphorism 36 of *Beyond Good and Evil* (the *locus classicus* for the idea) Nietzsche suggests that not just life but the entire world 'would be precisely "will to power" and nothing besides'.[9]

For Nietzsche, brute force is the crudest, most vulgar form of power, and one quite restricted in its range. A tyrant can exercise power over others by imprisoning, torturing, and killing them, but this power comes to an end with the tyrant's death. (If henchmen continue his work, it is then their own power they are exercising, not his.) At the other end of the spectrum is the power of ideas. Socrates and Jesus had no physical power over others—indeed both were undone by others' physical power over them—but their ideas have been enormously powerful and far-reaching. Indeed some of their power accrued just because their formulators were prepared to die

[8] See my essay, 'Nature and the Human "Redivinized": Mahāyāna Buddhist Themes in *Thus Spoke Zarathustra*', in John Lippitt and James Urpeth (eds.), *Nietzsche and the Divine* (Manchester: Clinamen Press, 2000), 181–99.

[9] For a more comprehensive treatment of this idea see ch. 8 of my *Composing the Soul*.

for them: as Life says to Zarathustra, 'Much is valued by the living more highly than life itself; but out of this very valuing there speaks—will to power!' (2. 12)

While their executioners are of no significance today, Socrates and Jesus continue to affect people's lives all over the world, millennia after their deaths. Their ideas are compelling insofar as they interpret the world in a new way, offering a different understanding of existence. To the extent that they give powerful interpretations of human existence they are engaging in philosophy, which Nietzsche characterizes in *Beyond Good and Evil* as 'the most spiritual will to power' (*BGE* 9). They stand at the opposite, higher end of the spectrum from powerful tyrants. As Emerson puts it (in 'The American Scholar'): 'Not he is great who can alter matter, but he who can alter my state of mind.'

The first mention of will to power in *Zarathustra* is in the chapter 'On the Thousand and One Goals', where Zarathustra says: 'A tablet of things held to be good hangs over every people. Behold, it is the tablet of its overcomings; behold, it is the voice of its will to power' (1. 15). A people's will to power is expressed in its interpretations of the world, especially in terms of value judgements of good and evil: 'What the people believes to be good and evil betrays to me an ancient will to power' (2. 12).

After *Zarathustra* Nietzsche extends the idea of will to power beyond life to all existence, in a famous thought experiment that invites the reader to understand the drives (*Triebe*—which for him constitute our psychical life as human beings) as being what the whole world consists in. But rather than making a metaphysical or ontological assertion concerning the ultimate nature of the universe, he writes at the end of aphorism 36 of *Beyond Good and Evil* just this:

Supposing, finally, that we were to succeed in explaining our entire drive-life as the development and ramification of one basic form of will—namely, of will to power . . . supposing one could find in this the solution to the problem of procreation and nourishment—it is *one* problem—one would then have the right to determine all effective force univocally as: *will to power*. The world seen from within, the world determined and defined in its 'intelligible character', would be precisely 'will to power' and nothing besides.

This hypothesis offers an image of the human being, body and soul, as a configuration of drives situated within the larger world as an encompassing field of interpretive forces.

The following year, in an addition to *The Joyful Science*, Nietzsche suggests that 'all existence is essentially interpreting existence'—an idea that brings him close to Chinese Daoist and Japanese Buddhist ways of thinking.[10] If all existence is interpreting, then all phenomena are expressing through their existence: '*This* is what it means to be'—or rather 'become'. A rock asserts itself as a paradigm of elemental solidity. Where vegetation prevails is the claim: *these* processes, we plants, are what sun and earth, water and air, really are becoming. Trees interpret the elements most magnificently over time. Animals supervene, intimating: *this* is what vegetation can become, as they incorporate and assimilate denizens of the plant realm. And humans, presenting themselves as the ultimate embodiment of mineral, vegetal, and animal, represent the grandest interpretation of all—and among humans philosophers represent 'the most spiritual will to power'.

Eternal Recurrence

It was seven years after his epiphany on the shore of Lake Silvaplana that Nietzsche called eternal recurrence 'the basic conception of *Zarathustra*' and 'the highest formula of affirmation that can ever be attained'. The first mention of the idea is in a notebook entry with the heading 'The Recurrence of the Same' and dated 'Beginning of August 1881'. The final paragraph reads:

The new *gravity: the eternal recurrence of the same*. The infinite importance of our knowing, erring, of our habits, ways of living for all that is to come. What do we do with the *rest* of our life—we who have spent the largest part of it in the deepest ignorance? We teach the teaching— that is the most powerful means by which to *incorporate* it into ourselves. Our kind of blissfulness, as teacher of the greatest teaching. (*W* 9: 11 [141])

To the extent that each of our actions at every moment changes the world, in this moment and with effects that ramify throughout all

---

[10] *JS* 374. See the essays on China and Japan in Graham Parkes (ed.), *Nietzsche and Asian Thought* (Chicago and London: University of Chicago Press, 1991).

subsequent moments, the question 'What do we do with the *rest* of our life?' takes on considerable weight. A profound change has taken place in Nietzsche's life, and he realizes that if others can be induced to ask themselves this question, the change may well be of infinite importance for all that is to come.

A letter written shortly afterwards to his friend Heinrich Köselitz begins:

Now then, my dear, good friend! The August sun is above us, the year moves along, it becomes more still and peaceful on the mountains and in the forests. On my horizon thoughts have arisen the like of which I have never seen before—but I will let nothing be known of them and shall maintain myself in an unshakable silence. Now I shall have to live for at least a *few* years longer! (*B* 14 Aug. 1881)

But Nietzsche didn't maintain his unshakable silence for long: a year later he published *The Joyful Science*, at the end of which he introduced the thought of eternal recurrence (though not by name). Here is the classic formulation of the idea:

The Greatest Weight.—What if, one day or night, a daemon were to slide up after you in your loneliest loneliness and say to you: 'This life, as you now live and have lived it, you will have to live again and innumerable times over; and there will be nothing new in it, but every pain and every pleasure and every thought and sigh and all the unspeakably small and large things in your life must come back to you, and all in the same order and sequence—and likewise this spider and this moonlight between the trees, and likewise this moment and I myself. The eternal hourglass of existence will be turned over again and again—and you with it, you tiny speck of dust!'—Would you not throw yourself down and gnash your teeth and curse the daemon who talked this way? Or have you once experienced a tremendous moment in which you would answer him: 'You are a God and never have I heard anything more divine!' If this thought were to gain power over you, it would transform you as you are, and perhaps crush you. The question in each and every thing, 'Do you want this once more and innumerable times more?' would lie upon your actions as the greatest weight! Or how well disposed to yourself and to life would you have to be, to *long for nothing more* than this ultimate eternal confirmation and seal?— (*JS* 341)

Rather than proclaiming a metaphysical truth or proposing a theory of the universe, this aphorism invites us to engage in a thought experiment—'What if . . .?'—that could transform us as we are. The daemon's question concerns 'This life, as you now live and have lived it'. What we are asked to contemplate the eternal recurrence of is only our life *up to this moment*—it might change drastically in the next moment, depending on how we respond to the question. The main point is the choice and the choice is real: this is no fatalism, since the future is opened up by the thought.

The daemon offers two alternatives: we might curse him for burdening our existence every moment with such a weighty question, or else bless him for revealing such a divine prospect. Most people would no doubt prefer to continue living 'in the deepest ignorance' and not to have to shoulder the burden of choosing: the daemon warns that the weight could be lethally crushing. But it could also be transformative, especially if we have experienced a tremendous moment in which we were so well disposed to ourselves and to life that we could say: 'Yes, I want this once more and innumerable times more.' But this requires our also reliving eternally our life up to that moment, with 'nothing new in it . . . and all in the same order and sequence'. In *Zarathustra* we see the protagonist entertain a similar prospect, but in the company not of a daemon but a dwarf—the Spirit of Heaviness, Zarathustra's Devil and arch-enemy (3. 2).

Several notebook entries from the period after the initial epiphany shed helpful light on this difficult idea. A passage that is the prototype for 'The Greatest Weight' begins: 'The world of forces undergoes no diminution: for otherwise in an eternity of time it would have become weak and collapsed' (*W* 9: 11 [148]). Nietzsche speculates here (and elsewhere in the unpublished notes) that in a closed system containing a constant, finite sum of forces, every possible configuration of those forces will recur, given an infinite extent of time. Much scholarly ink has been spilled about this intriguing speculation, but since its plausibility doesn't underwrite the presentation of eternal recurrence in *Zarathustra* there is no need to rehearse the relevant studies here. An idea that does figure in this passage and the later text, however, is that of 'the whole interconnection of all things'. Toward the final climax of the book, Zarathustra sings: 'Did you ever say Yes to a single joy? Oh, my friends, then you said Yes to *all* woe as well. All things are chained together, entwined, in love—' (4. 19. 10). This is why affirming eternal recurrence is tantamount to *amor fati*, love of fate, since it involves saying Yes to everything that has contributed to any single moment of one's life that one wants to affirm.

The thought of eternal recurrence is not to be taken as something to think about intellectually (Can it be true? Does everything really recur?), but rather as a possibility that can inform and clarify our existential choices: 'Rather than looking towards distant unknown bliss and *blessings* and *reprieves*, simply live in such a way that we would want to live again and want to live *that way* for eternity!—Our task steps up to us at every moment' (*W* 9: 11 [161]). The beauty of this idea is that while the prospect of eternal recurrence prompts one to substitute for mindless activity, and acts performed solely out of a sense that they are socially required, things one genuinely wants to do, it prescribes no specific content. The choice is up to the individual in his or her loneliest loneliness.

There is nevertheless a strong sense in *Zarathustra* of the worth of creative activity, as prefigured in another contemporary note:

We want to experience a work of art again and again! One is to form one's life in such a way that one has the same wish with respect to its individual parts! This is the main idea! Only at the end will the *teaching* of the repetition of all that has been be presented, after the tendency has been implanted to *create* something that can *flourish* a hundred times more powerfully in the sunshine of this teaching! (*W* 9: 11 [165])

Zarathustra frequently refers to himself as a 'creator' and one who seeks fellow creators. In the wake of the death of the one Creator God, the task of creation devolves on human beings, who will not, however, create *ex nihilo* but rather in interaction with the forces of nature and history. When all transcendent sources of value turn out to be empty, creation of new values becomes an urgent task and one that requires destruction of the old values. The necessity for concomitant creation and destruction is at the core of what Nietzsche calls 'the Dionysian', a crucial feature of eternal recurrence, where what must be willed is the recurrence of everything that has led up to the present moment.

Nietzsche explains how Zarathustra can shoulder the heavy burden of fate and yet be 'the lightest':

Zarathustra is a dancer—[which is] how he who has the hardest, most terrible insight into reality, who has thought the 'most abysmal thought', nevertheless finds in that no objection to existence, nor even to its eternal

recurrence—but rather one more reason for *being himself* the eternal Yes
to all things . . . that is the concept of Dionysus. (*EH* ibid. 6)

The Story of Zarathustra

Thus Spoke Zarathustra is, as its title suggests, a book of speeches
rather than a treatise or collection of writings. Like Plato's Socrates,
Zarathustra is not a writer but a speaker, one of Nietzsche's voices
heard in an abundance of direct speech. The speeches are embedded
in a dramatic narrative, as in a *Bildungsroman*, where the protagonist
is progressively educated and shaped by the circumstances he
encounters. But while most books in this genre begin with the hero's
childhood or youth, the drama of *Zarathustra* starts when he is
already forty years old. The primary dramatic element in the narrative concerns his changing relationships with the various audiences
for his speeches and also with figures like his Wisdom and Life.

Zarathustra has lived with his eagle and serpent in a cave high in
the mountains for ten years, during which time he has gathered
much wisdom, which he now wants to share with the world by going
down to 'become human again'. He descends the mountain and
addresses a crowd assembled in the market-place on the topic of the
Overhuman—but is greeted with rude incomprehension. He realizes
he must instead find companions to whom he can impart his teachings, and who can become 'creator, harvesters, and celebrants' with
him. He succeeds in attracting some disciples, but they eventually
begin to disappoint him by failing to understand the depth and
subtlety of his teachings and by becoming mere followers. Near the
end of the book's Second Part he delivers a crucial speech 'On
Redemption' to an audience of cripples and beggars, in which he
shows how will to power can be transformed so as to will eternal
recurrence. But he himself can't yet will this way, and so he leaves his
disciples and returns to his solitude.

At the beginning of the Third Part, Zarathustra travels by ship
from the Isles of the Blest across the sea, enjoying revelatory visions
while on board. On reaching the mainland he journeys through several towns, a large city, and a town he had visited before called The
Motley Cow, making the occasional speech to a general audience on
the way, before finally returning to his cave in the mountains. There
he enjoys his solitude again and delivers several speeches to an

imagined audience in preparation for going back down to his disciples for a third time. He eventually manages to confront the thought of eternal recurrence, after which he talks about both confrontation and thought with his eagle and serpent. After an ecstatic conversation with his own soul, he sings a song to the feminine figure Life and then a final, Dionysian song to celebrate his marriage to her as Eternity.

When Nietzsche finished the Third Part of *Zarathustra* in January 1884, he announced the completion of the book as a whole in numerous letters to family and friends, referring in a letter to his publisher to 'this third act of my drama (or rather the finale of my symphony)' (*B* 18 Jan. 1884). But ten months later he writes to his sister: 'If all goes well, I shall need a publisher and printer for the fourth part of *Zarathustra* in January' (*B* 15 Nov. 1884). He even goes on to talk about 'the now unavoidable fifth and sixth parts (it cannot be helped, I must help my son Zarathustra to his beautiful *death*, or else he will give me no peace)'. But writing to an old friend three months later, he announces the existence of 'a fourth (and last) part of *Zarathustra*, a kind of sublime finale, which is not at all meant for the public' (*B* 12 Feb. 1885). In April of 1885 forty-five copies of the Fourth Part were published privately at Nietzsche's own expense and sent only to his closest friends. And so when the first edition of the complete *Zarathustra* appeared the following year, it was in three parts, with no mention of a fourth. Subsequent letters to his friends express a vehement desire never to have the Fourth Part made public. Nevertheless, those responsible for publishing new editions of Nietzsche's works after his mental collapse in 1889 saw fit to include it in the new edition of *Zarathustra* three years later.[11]

While working on the Fourth Part, Nietzsche considered calling it 'Zarathustra's Temptation', and later describes its theme as 'the overcoming of pity' (*EH* 'Why I Am So Wise', 4). Faced with a group of 'superior humans' representing the best types that the modern age can produce, Zarathustra still finds them wanting. His task is then to avoid allowing pity for them to distract him from his true 'work': preparing the ground for the Overhuman. In the morning of

---

[11] For a detailed account of the status of the Fourth Part, see Laurence Lampert, *Nietzsche's Teaching: An Interpretation of* Thus Spoke Zarathustra (New Haven and London: Yale University Press, 1986), Appendix. This superb study by Lampert is invaluable for an understanding of *Zarathustra* (and much else in Nietzsche).

the day on which the action takes place, these superior humans arrive severally in Zarathustra's domain: two kings, a scientist, an old sorcerer (and greatest living poet), the last pope, the ugliest man, a voluntary beggar, and Zarathustra's own shadow. In the central chapter, 'At Midday', the protagonist regains his solitude for a while, and in an exquisitely mystical moment he experiences the perfection of the world just as it is.

In the evening they all eat a 'Last Supper' together in Zarathustra's cave, and the superior humans celebrate an 'Ass Festival', after which even the ugliest man is able to love life and the earth enough to want them all over again. This prompts a last, profoundly Dionysian song from Zarathustra in which all opposites are brought into coincidence. But the next morning the superior humans are startled by the lion's roar into raising again their 'cry of need'—which is a sign to Zarathustra that they are not yet able to will eternal recurrence after all. And so he prepares to leave them in order to go down again and resume his work.

The Musicality of Zarathustra

Writing at the end of his career about the genesis of *Zarathustra*, and of the day in August 1881 when its basic idea first struck him, Nietzsche says: 'If I count back a few months from that day, I find as an omen a sudden and profoundly decisive change in my taste, above all in music. One can perhaps count the whole of *Zarathustra* as music—certainly a rebirth in the art of *hearing* was a precondition for it' (*EH 'Thus Spoke Zarathustra'*, 1). To understand how *Zarathustra* can be taken as music, it helps to have some biographical background.[12]

Nietzsche grew up in a distinctly musical milieu: his father played the piano, childhood friends were musical, and piano lessons from an early age developed his own talent on that instrument. When an illness once deprived him of piano playing, he wrote to his mother from boarding school: 'Everything seems dead to me when I can't hear any music' (*B* 27 Apr. 1863). During his teens and twenties he

---

[12] An excellent study in this context is Georges Liébert, *Nietzsche and Music* (Chicago: University of Chicago Press, 2004).

wrote prolifically for piano and voice, producing close to a hundred compositions.[13]

As a young teacher of classics at the University of Basel, Nietzsche followed the example of the ancient Greeks in reading aloud whatever he was writing. According to one of his students: 'He would declaim [what he had written] in order to experience its cadence, its accent, its tonality and metrical movement, also in order to test out the clarity and precision of the idea expressed.'[14] Then, a few years before composing *Zarathustra*, he wrote: 'I read thinkers by assimilating their music to my passions and I sing their melodies after them: I know that behind all those cold words there moves a soul of desire, and I hear it singing, for my own soul sings when it's moved' (*W* 9: 7 [18]). During his time in Basel he was often invited to stay with Wagner and his family in their house on Lake Lucerne, where a common after-dinner activity was to read aloud works of literature and manuscripts that he and Wagner were writing at the time.

In one of his earliest sketches for *Zarathustra*, Nietzsche envisages the First Part's being written 'in the style of the first movement of Beethoven's *Ninth Symphony*' (*W* 9: 11 [197]). And on finishing that part, he writes to his composer friend Köselitz: 'With this book I have stepped into a new *Ring*'—the allusion to Wagner's masterpiece suggesting the added dimension of opera (*B* 1 Feb. 1883). Two months later, when he asks Köselitz, 'Under which rubric does this *Zarathustra* really belong?' he reverts to the symphonic in answering his own question: 'I almost believe that it comes under "symphonies". What is certain is that with it I have crossed over into another world' (*B* 2 Apr. 1883). No lesser a symphonist than Gustav Mahler corroborates: 'His *Zarathustra* was born completely from the spirit of music, and is even "symphonically" constructed.'[15] And after finishing the Third Part Nietzsche frequently refers to it as 'the finale of my symphony', and points out that its connection with the beginning of the First Part gives the work the structure of a circle— though not, he hopes, a vicious one (*B* 30 Mar. 1884). He thereby affirms the recurrence of the ring after all.

[13] See Curt Paul Janz (ed.), *Der musikalische Nachlass / Friedrich Nietzsche* (Basel: Bärenreiter Verlag, 1976).

[14] See Curt Paul Janz, *Nietzsche Biographie*, 3 vols. (Munich and Vienna: Carl Hanser Verlag, 1978), i. 475.

[15] As quoted by Bernard Scharlitt, 'Gespräch mit Mahler', *Musikblätter des Anbruchs*, 2 (1920), 310.

In the book he wrote after *Zarathustra*, Nietzsche writes in the context of listening with 'the *third* ear' about 'the *art* in every good sentence':

A misunderstanding of its tempo, for example—and the sentence itself is misunderstood! Let there be no doubt about the rhythmically decisive syllables . . . let us lend a subtle and patient ear to every *staccato*, every *rubato*, let us divine the meaning in the sequence of vowels and diphthongs and how delicately and richly they can take on colour and change colour as they follow each other. (*BGE* 246)

This is good advice for reading *Zarathustra* in particular: Nietzsche later draws special attention to 'the tempo of Zarathustra's speeches' and their 'delicate slowness'—'from an infinite fullness of light and depth of happiness drop falls after drop, word after word'—as well as the necessity of '*hearing* properly the tone that issues from his mouth, this halcyon tone' (*EH* Preface, 4).

In the original German text most of the paragraphs in Zarathustra's speeches are around two-and-a-half lines long, with some two lines and others three or four. (The obvious prototypes are the Zarathustrian Gâthas, which are in five- or six-line stanzas,[16] and the Book of Psalms, where the verses are shorter.) The length seems to correspond with a kind of 'mental breath' on Zarathustra's—and also the reader's—part: after a full inhalation at the beginning, the thought seems to come naturally to an end after a steady exhalation over a period of two-and-a-half lines.[17] Nietzsche's punctuation further enhances the text's musicality: the exclamation-mark in *Zarathustra* (of which there is a profusion) may helpfully be read as analogous to a *forte* in a musical score, and the dash (a favourite mark of Laurence Sterne's, whom Nietzsche greatly admired) often plays the part of the *fermata* in music—especially as a means of extending a pause for reflection on the part of the reader.[18]

---

[16] For an English translation that strictly observes the metre, see Lawrence H. Mills, *Zarathustrian Gâthas in metre and rhythm* (Chicago: Open Court, 1903).

[17] 'A periodic sentence in the ancient sense is above all a physiological whole, insofar as it is encompassed by one whole breath' (*BGE* 247).

[18] Walter Benjamin offers an illuminating analogy with Jugendstil architecture and design: 'Zarathustra has appropriated from Jugendstil primarily its tectonic elements rather than its organic motifs. The pauses especially, which are characteristic of his rhythms, are an exact counterpart to the basic tectonic phenomenon of this style, which is the predominance of the hollow form over the filled.' *The Arcades Project* (Cambridge, Mass., and London: Harvard University Press, 1999), 557.

Repetition is a key element in most kinds of music, and repetition is rife throughout *Zarathustra*—not only repetition of words and phrases, but of entire sentences and even paragraphs. The motto that precedes the Second Part is a repetition of one-and-a-half sentences from the last section of the previous part, just two pages earlier. Nietzsche comments in a letter to Köselitz: 'From this motto there emerge—it is almost unseemly to say this to a musician—different harmonies and modulations from those in the first part. The main thing was to *swing oneself up to the second level*—in order from there to reach the *third*' (*B* 13 July 1883). There are also striking repetitions of vowel and consonant sounds (something very common in Wagner's librettos, and especially in *Siegfried*). In a letter to Erwin Rohde, Nietzsche writes: 'My style is a *dance*; a play of symmetries of all kinds and an overleaping and mocking of these symmetries. This goes as far as the choice of vowels' (*B* 22 Feb. 1884). Nietzsche also uses repetition of consonants to great effect: the first page-and-a-half of the Second Part builds to a climax where Zarathustra speaks of his speech as 'the roaring of a stream out of towering cliffs', of his love as 'overflowing in torrents', and his soul as 'rushing down into the valleys' (2. 1). The imagery is vivified by a flood of initial 's' and 'sh' sounds—though such a stream of sibilants is sadly impossible to reproduce in English.

Nietzsche had to ignore Rousseau when he wrote in a letter to the conductor Hermann Levi, 'Perhaps there has never been a philosopher who was so fundamentally a musician as I am' (*B* 20 Oct. 1887)—though *Zarathustra* must still qualify as the most musical work of philosophy in the western tradition. Hardly surprising from an author who wrote of 'life as music' and 'the music of life' (*JS* 372), and who said near the end of his career: 'Life without music is nothing but an error, exhausting toil, exile' (*B* 15 Jan. 1888).

Afterlife

After his death in 1900 Nietzsche's reputation grew and spread throughout Europe and beyond, to make him one of the most powerful influences on twentieth-century culture. Of *Zarathustra* especially it was true that 'it sought out readers for itself, ignited new life, delighted, terrified, engendered new works, became the soul of plans and actions' (*HA* 208). The idea of the *Übermensch* and Zarathustra's call for the destruction of old values and creation of new ones had special appeal for revolutionary movements in almost all the arts in the early twentieth century. To the extent that people sensed the death of God, there was a readiness for a teaching that affirmed human life on sacred earth. In philosophy *Zarathustra* was an influence on such figures as Martin Buber, Martin Heidegger, Karl Jaspers, Karl Löwith, Walter Benjamin, Pierre Klossowski, and Gilles Deleuze; and in psychology, on Sigmund Freud and C. G. Jung. In the fields of literature, painting, and architecture the book was received with great enthusiasm by many artists who were to set the cultural tone of the new century.[19]

The particular attention Nietzsche has received from the music world no doubt has to do with his association with Wagner, together with the fact that he himself wrote music as well as some excellent poetry. His writings have inspired the composition of more music than the work of any other philosopher: by 1975 over 170 composers had created some 370 musical settings of ninety texts by Nietzsche.[20] Among these, there are eighty-seven pieces that are settings of excerpts from *Zarathustra* or are explicitly inspired by the text as a whole. The best-known are Richard Strauss's *Also Sprach Zarathustra* (1896), the fourth movement of Gustav Mahler's Symphony No. 3 (1902), and the massive choral work by Frederick Delius, *A Mass of Life* (1907), which contains eleven substantial excerpts from the text. Other composers impressed by *Zarathustra* were Arnold Schoenberg, Anton von Webern, Paul Hindemith, Carl Orff, Hugo Wolf, and Alexander Scriabin.

Nietzsche's ideas also received attention from the National Socialists in Germany, thanks to some malicious editorial work after his death on the part of his anti-Semitic sister Elisabeth, who ultimately ingratiated herself with Hitler. To make Nietzsche's philosophy appear compatible with Nazism requires selective extraction of ideas from their contexts, since he was vehemently opposed not only to

---

[19] e.g. Franz Kafka, Thomas Mann, Hermann Hesse, Hugo von Hoffmansthal, August Strindberg, Paul Valéry, André Malraux, W. B. Yeats, James Joyce, D. H. Lawrence, George Bernard Shaw, H. L. Mencken, and Eugene O'Neill in literature; Edvard Munch, Otto Dix, Emil Nolde, and other German Expressionists in painting; and Henry van de Velde, Peter Behrens, and Le Corbusier in architecture.

[20] David S. Thatcher, 'Musical Settings of Nietzsche-Texts: an Annotated Bibliography', *Nietzsche-Studien*, 4 (1975), 284–323; 5 (1976), 355–83.

nationalism and socialism (German nationalism in particular) but also to anti-Semitism. As far as *Zarathustra* is concerned, one has to ignore half of what the protagonist says about contempt and violence and cruelty in order to render these themes sinister or disturbing. For Zarathustra, despising belongs together with loving: to avoid emitting resentment all around us we have to learn to love ourselves— and for that we need first to know ourselves, which inevitably leads to despising ourselves (thanks to the dark side of human nature in which we all participate). Similarly, the violence and cruelty Zarathustra speaks about are first of all to be directed toward oneself: he has to learn how to hammer himself into shape, a difficult and painful task, before he can earn the right to be hard on others. All of this is anathema to the Nazis, whose basic practice is to project their own shadow-side onto easily identifiable groups of 'others'.[21]

Overall, the most remarkable feature of *Zarathustra*'s reception is its more or less global reach. It was not long after Nietzsche's mental collapse in 1889 that his ideas reached Japan. An essay appeared there in 1898 under the title 'The Reception of Nietzsche's Thought in Relation to Buddhism'.[22] The author makes the insightful suggestion that 'even though Nietzsche himself did not exactly greet Buddhism with enthusiasm, one can say that in the ideal of the *Übermensch* he comes close to the idea of the Buddha'. Two famous novelists of the period, Natsume Sōseki and Mori Ōgai, were especially impressed by *Zarathustra*. In his marginalia to an English translation, Sōseki remarked a number of parallels with the Buddhist and Confucian traditions: 'This is oriental. Strange to find such an idea in the writings of a European.' And in his novel *Seinen* (Youth), Ōgai aptly compares contemporary modernizers in Japan with the 'last humans' excoriated in Zarathustra's Prologue. In 1913 the philosopher Watsuji Tetsurō published a magisterial study of Nietzsche that influenced several generations of Japanese thinkers, and notably

---

[21] On despising and loving, see Prologue, 3 and 5; 1. 17; 3. 5, 14; and for hardness and cruelty 2. 2, and *BGE* 61–2, 225.

[22] For a more detailed treatment of this topic see my essays 'The Early Reception of Nietzsche's Philosophy in Japan', in Parkes (ed.), *Nietzsche and Asian Thought*, 177–99, and 'Nietzsche and East Asian Thought: Influences, Impacts, and Resonances', in Bernd Magnus and Kathleen Higgins (eds.), *The Cambridge Companion to Nietzsche* (Cambridge: Cambridge University Press, 1996), 356–83. In his introduction to the first English translation of *Zarathustra* (1896), Alexander Tille compared the text to the Buddhist *Tripitaka* (the Pali Canon scriptures concerning the teachings of the Buddha).

members of the well-known 'Kyoto School' of philosophy. *Zara-thustra* was the first complete work of Nietzsche's to be translated into Japanese, in 1911, and since then no fewer than five further translations have been published.

The first (partial) translation into Chinese appeared in 1919, by Lu Xun, who went on to be one of China's best-known writers. Many of the intellectuals involved in the revolutionary New Culture and May Fourth movements, which got under way in 1915, were deeply influenced by Nietzsche's 'culture criticism' and iconoclasm. Lu Xun maintained his interest in Nietzsche and sponsored the first full translation of *Zarathustra*, which was published in 1936. Since then no fewer than nine further complete translations have appeared in China—a figure that is all the more amazing since none were published in the twenty years following the Communist takeover in 1949. Given the size of print-runs in China, it is probable that more copies of *Zarathustra* have been sold in Chinese than in any other language.[23]

The enthusiastic reception of Nietzsche in Asia derives in part from his having had some acquaintance with Indian philosophy (through books on Hindu and Buddhist thought), Chinese philo-sophy (one Confucian and one Daoist text), and Japanese culture (through one of his best friends).[24] But whatever the extent of influence *ex oriente*, the Asian reception of his work suggests that his attempts to 'think *more orientally* about philosophy' and to look at the world with a 'trans-European' and even an 'Asiatic and trans-Asiatic eye' met with some success.[25] At any rate, the resonances between themes in *Zarathustra* and in Buddhist, Confucian, and Daoist philosophies are undeniable, and are surely the major ground for the book's enthusiastic reception in Asia. While Nietzsche's claim that with *Zarathustra* he has 'given humanity the greatest gift that has been given to it so far' (*EH* Preface, 4) may be some-what overstated, the book is surely one of the most cosmopolitan philosophical texts ever written.

[23] See Cheung, Chiu-yee, *Nietzsche in China (1904–1992): An Annotated Bibli-ography* (Canberra: Australian National University, 1992), and Shao, Lixin, *Nietzsche in China* (New York: Peter Lang, 1999).

[24] See Thomas H. Brobjer, *Nietzsche's Knowledge of Philosophy* (Urbana, Ill.: Uni-versity of Illinois Press, 2005), cha. 6. For Nietzsche's Japanophile friend, see my 'Nietzsche and East-Asian Thought'.

[25] *W* 11: 26 [317]; *B* 3 Jan. 1888; *BGE* 56.

NOTE ON THE TEXT AND TRANSLATION

This translation is based on the text of the third edition published by C. G. Naumann (Leipzig, 1894), which is very similar to the current standard edition (*Kritische Gesamtausgabe*), edited by Giorgio Colli and Mazzino Montinari (Berlin and New York, 1967 ff.) also available as *Kritische Studienausgabe*, 15 vols. (Munich, 1980). The newer edition omits some punctuation (quotation-marks mainly), has some initial capitals in lower case, and drops some italics. There are only eight points at which a word is different, and these are pointed out in the Explanatory Notes. For the notes I have consulted the supplementary volume on *Zarathustra* in the *Kritische Gesamtausgabe*, and various online concordances to Luther's translation of the Bible. In providing the relevant citations I have used the King James translation, modifying it in the light of Luther's version when necessary to preserve the allusion—and adding '(Luther)' after the quotation in such cases.

In view of Nietzsche's saying that *Zarathustra* is to be taken as music, I have tried above all to convey the musicality of the text (which was not a priority for Walter Kaufmann or R. J. Hollingdale, authors of the best English translations so far). This has meant faithfully reproducing its paragraph structure and—in most cases— its punctuation, as well as all repetitions of words, phrases, and sentences. (Nietzsche's sometimes idiosyncratic use of quotemarks has been changed to conform with standard English usage.) I have attempted to retain as far as possible the alliterations and assonances, and above all the rhythms and cadences of the original, often by choosing English words that are similarly accented or have the same number of syllables as the German. Nietzsche uses an unusual number of hyphenated compounds in *Zarathustra* ('moral-mice', 'beggar-virtue', 'light-scarecrow', and so forth), often for the sake of a tighter rhythmic effect. I have retained the hyphenation in most cases, though rarely where the compound contains a possessive form ('father's-pain', 'tyrant's-madness'), since this overstretches English usage.

Inversion occurs frequently in the Luther Bible ('Thorns and thistles shall the ground bring forth to thee'), and is correspondingly more common in *Zarathustra* than in other German texts of the period. I have reproduced these inversions wherever it sounds natural enough in English ('No stranger to me is this wanderer'), resulting in a text where inversion is, appropriately, somewhat more common than is usual in English.

The most common verb in *Zarathustra* is *wollen*, 'to want, to will', and one of the book's central ideas is that of 'will (to power)'. I have accordingly translated *wollen* as 'to will' where apt, and have often used instead of 'want to' the more elegant 'would', as in: 'I love him who would not have too many virtues.' Courage (*Mut*) is a key virtue for Zarathustra, and the word *Mut* also appears in a variety of compound terms that play significant roles: *Unmut* (ill-humour), *Schwermut* (melancholy), *Übermut* (exuberance), *Mutwillen* (wilfulness). It is unfortunately impossible to signal the recurrence of the root term in translation. The text contains hardly any technical philosophical vocabulary: 'Being' (*Sein*) and 'Becoming' (*Werden*) are two notable exceptions, which I have capitalized because of their importance in Nietzsche's thought in general.

One of the greatest challenges to the translator is Nietzsche's fondness for adjectival nouns, the occurrences of which are impossible to render uniformly into English. Some examples: *die Mitleidigen*—those who pity (2. 3); *ihr Tugendhaften*—you virtuous ones (2. 5); *Von den berühmten Weisen*—On the Famous Wise Men (2. 8); *ihr Weisesten*—you who are wisest (2. 12); *ihr Erhabenen*—you sublime ones (2. 13); *ihr Gegenwärtigen*—you men of the present (2. 14); *ihr Reinen*—you pure ones (2. 15).

If Nietzsche had been writing in English, he would no doubt have used 'man' to mean 'the human being'. But there is an important distinction in his work between his enduring concern with the human being and humanity (*Mensch*) and his less frequent concern with men (*Männer*) as opposed to women. (In *Zarathustra* discussions of the human being outnumber discussions of men by a ratio of around ten to one.) Since some feminists have objected to Nietzsche's gender bias on the basis of translations that have him writing about 'men' when he is actually writing about *Menschen*, I have tried to carry the human/male (*Mensch/Mann*) distinction into English wherever possible. But where this would make for awkward English, I have settled for 'man' rather than 'human being'.

Since *Zarathustra* is a work of philosophy as well as a literary text,

I have tried to adhere to the principle of translating the same German term by the same term in English as much as possible. For the following terms, however, I have had to use more than one English word (with the more common listed first):

böse—evil, wicked;
Erkenntnis—understanding, knowledge;
erraten—to divine, guess;
fremd—alien, foreign, strange;
Geist—spirit, mind;
der freie Geist—the free mind (except in 2. 8, which is about spirit);
Gerechtigkeit—righteousness (*die Gerechten* in Luther's Bible are 'the righteous'), justice;
Glaube—belief, faith;
Gleichnis—allegory, parable;
göttlich—godlike, divine;
heilig—holy, sacred;
Herr—lord, master;
Heuchelei—hypocrisy, dissembling;
Not—need, distress;
Rede—speech, discourse;
Scham—modesty, shame, bashfulness;
schonen—to spare, take good care of;
schwer—heavy, weighty, difficult, hard;
Schwermut—heavy heart/spirits (except in the chapter title 'The Song of Melancholy');
Sinn—sense, meaning;
Tiere—beasts, animals (for Zarathustra's own animals, his eagle and serpent);
Traurigkeit—mournfulness, sadness;
Trübsal—sorrow, affliction;
Weg—way, path;
Zufall—chance (event), accident, coincidence.

For ease of reference, I have numbered the chapter headings in the book's four parts (paragraph numbers within chapters are Nietzsche's own).

The first English translation of *Zarathustra* (London, 1896) was done by Alexander Tille, a German scholar who had moved to Scotland, where he became a lecturer in German at the University of Glasgow. This translation, which had suffered from his not being a native English speaker, was thoroughly revised by Thomas Common, an independent scholar from Glasgow, and published in a new edition in 1905. It is perhaps fitting that a century later this new translation should be by another native of Glasgow.

I should like to thank for their kind advice Keith Ansell-Pearson, Manfred Henningsen, Martha Husain, Geir Sigurdsson, Franz-Martin Wimmer, and especially Laurence Lampert. My gratitude also to Jeff New for his careful checking of the typescript, to Judith Luna for her encouragement and judicious comments on the Introduction, and to James McRae for assistance with the Index.

SELECT BIBLIOGRAPHY

Biography

Bergmann, Peter, *Nietzsche, 'the last antipolitical German'* (Bloomington, Ind.: Indiana University Press, 1987).

Cate, Curtis, *Friedrich Nietzsche* (London: Hutchinson, 2002).

Gilman, Sander L. (ed.), *Conversations with Nietzsche*, trans. David Parent (New York: Oxford University Press, 1987).

Hayman, Ronald, *Nietzsche: A Critical Life* (London: Weidenfeld & Nicolson, 1980).

Krell, David Farrell, and Donald L. Bates, *The Good European: Nietzsche's Work Sites in Word and Image* (Chicago and London: University of Chicago Press, 1997).

Safranski, Rüdiger, *Nietzsche: A Philosophical Biography*, trans. Shelley Frisch (New York and London: W. W. Norton, 2002).

Critical Studies

Brobjer, Thomas H., *Nietzsche's Knowledge of Philosophy* (Urbana, Ill.: University of Illinois Press, 2005).

Deleuze, Gilles, *Nietzsche and Philosophy*, trans. Hugh Tomlinson (New York: Columbia University Press, 1983).

Gooding-Williams, Robert, *Zarathustra's Dionysian Modernism* (Stanford, Calif.: Stanford University Press, 2001).

Higgins, Kathleen Marie, *Nietzsche's Zarathustra* (Philadelphia: Temple University Press, 1987).

Hollinrake, Roger, *Nietzsche, Wagner, and the Philosophy of Pessimism* (London and Boston: Allen & Unwin, 1982).

Klossowski, Pierre, *Nietzsche and the Vicious Circle*, trans. Daniel W. Smith (Chicago and London: University of Chicago Press, 1997).

Lampert, Laurence, *Nietzsche's Task: An Interpretation of 'Beyond Good and Evil'* (New Haven and London: Yale University Press, 2001).

—— *Nietzsche's Teaching: An Interpretation of 'Thus Spoke Zarathustra'* (New Haven and London: Yale University Press, 1986).

Magnus, Bernd, *Nietzsche's Existential Imperative* (Bloomington, Ind.: Indiana University Press, 1978).

—— and Kathleen M. Higgins, *The Cambridge Companion to Nietzsche* (Cambridge and New York: Cambridge University Press, 1996).

Nishitani, Keiji, *The Self-Overcoming of Nihilism*, trans. Graham Parkes with Setsuko Aihara (Albany, NY: SUNY Press, 1990).

Parkes, Graham, *Composing the Soul: Reaches of Nietzsche's Psychology* (Chicago and London: University of Chicago Press, 1994).

—— (ed.), *Nietzsche and Asian Thought* (Chicago and London: University of Chicago Press, 1991).

Rosen, Stanley, *The Mask of Enlightenment: Nietzsche's Zarathustra* (Cambridge and New York: Cambridge University Press, 1995).

Shapiro, Gary, *Alcyone: Nietzsche on Gifts, Noise, and Women* (Albany, NY: SUNY Press, 1991).

Whitlock, Greg, *Returning to Sils-Maria: A Commentary to Nietzsche's 'Also sprach Zarathustra'* (New York: Peter Lang, 1990).

Further Reading in Oxford World's Classics

Aristotle, *The Nicomachean Ethics*, trans. Sir David Ross, revised J. R. Ackrill and J. O. Urmson.

The Dharmasutras, trans. Patrick Olivelle.

Goethe, J. W. von, *Elective Affinities*, trans. David Constantine.

—— *Faust: Part One* and *Faust: Part Two*, trans. David Luke.

Herodotus, *The Histories*, trans. Robin Waterfield, ed. Carolyn Dewald.

Hesiod, *Theogony and Works and Days*, trans. M. L. West.

Homer, *The Odyssey*, trans. Walter Shewring, ed. G. S. Kirk.

—— *The Iliad*, trans. Robert Fitzgerald, ed. G. S. Kirk.

Nietzsche, Friedrich, *Beyond Good and Evil*, trans. and ed. Marion Faber, with an introduction by Robert C. Holub.

—— *The Birth of Tragedy*, trans. and ed. Douglas Smith.

—— *On the Genealogy of Morals*, trans. and ed. Douglas Smith.

—— *Twilight of the Idols*, trans. and ed. Duncan Large.

Plato, *Republic*, trans. and ed. Robin Waterfield.

—— *Symposium*, trans. and ed. Robin Waterfield.

A CHRONOLOGY OF
FRIEDRICH NIETZSCHE

1844   Friedrich Wilhelm Nietzsche born in Röcken (Saxony) on 15 October, son of Karl Ludwig and Franziska Nietzsche. His father and both grandfathers are Protestant clergymen.

1846   Birth of sister Elisabeth.

1849   Birth of brother Joseph; death of father.

1850   Death of brother; family moves to Naumburg.

1858–64 Attends renowned boys' boarding-school Pforta, where he excels in classics. Begins to suffer from migraine attacks which will plague him for the rest of his career.

1864   Enters Bonn University to study theology and classical philology.

1865   Follows classics professor Ritschl to Leipzig University, where he drops theology and continues with studies in classical philology. Discovers Schopenhauer's philosophy and becomes a passionate admirer.

1867   Begins publishing career with essay on Theognis; continues publishing philological articles and book reviews till 1873.

1867–8 Military service in Naumburg, until invalided out after a riding accident.

1868   Back in Leipzig, meets Richard Wagner for the first time and quickly becomes a devotee. Increasing disaffection with philology: plans to escape to Paris to study chemistry.

1869   On Ritschl's recommendation, appointed Extraordinary Professor of Classical Philology at Basle University. Awarded doctorate without examination; renounces Prussian citizenship. Begins a series of idyllic visits to the Wagners at Tribschen, on Lake Lucerne. Develops admiration for Jacob Burckhardt, his new colleague in Basle.

1870   Promoted to full professor. Participates in Franco-Prussian War as volunteer medical orderly, but contracts dysentery and diphtheria at the front within a fortnight.

1871   Granted semester's sick leave from Basle and works intensively on *The Birth of Tragedy*. Germany unified; founding of the Reich.

1872   Publishes *The Birth of Tragedy out of the Spirit of Music*, which earns him the condemnation of professional colleagues. Lectures 'On the Future of our Educational Institutions'; attends laying of foundation stone for Bayreuth Festival Theatre.

1873   Publishes first *Untimely Meditation: David Strauss the Confessor and the Writer*.

1874   Publishes second and third *Untimely Meditations: On the Use and Disadvantage of History for Life* and *Schopenhauer as Educator*. Relationship with Wagner begins to sour.

1875   Meets musician Heinrich Köselitz (Peter Gast), who idolizes him.

1876   Publishes fourth and last *Untimely Meditation: Richard Wagner in Bayreuth*. Attends first Bayreuth Festival but leaves early and subsequently breaks with Wagner. Further illness; granted full year's sick leave from the university.

1877   French translation of *Richard Wagner in Bayreuth* published, the only translation to appear during his mentally active lifetime.

1878   Publishes *Human, All Too Human: A Book for Free Spirits*, which confirms the break with Wagner.

1879   Publishes supplement to *Human, All Too Human, Assorted Opinions and Maxims*. Finally retires from teaching on a pension; first visits the Engadine, summering in St Moritz.

1880   Publishes *The Wanderer and His Shadow*. First stays in Venice and Genoa.

1881   Publishes *Daybreak: Thoughts on the Prejudices of Morality*. First stay in Sils-Maria.

1882   Publishes *The Gay Science*. Infatuation with Lou Andreas-Salomé, who spurns his marriage proposals.

1883   Publishes *Thus Spoke Zarathustra: A Book for Everyone and Nobody*, Parts I and II (separately). Death of Wagner. Spends the summer in Sils and the winter in Nice, his pattern for the next five years. Increasingly consumed by writing.

1884   Publishes *Thus Spoke Zarathustra*, Part III.

1885   *Thus Spoke Zarathustra*, Part IV printed but circulated to only a handful of friends. Begins in earnest to amass notes for *The Will to Power*.

1886   Publishes *Beyond Good and Evil: Prelude to a Philosophy of the*

Future. Change of publisher results in new expanded editions of *The Birth of Tragedy* and *Human, All Too Human* (now with a second volume comprising the *Assorted Opinions and Maxims* and *The Wanderer and His Shadow*).

1887   Publishes *On the Genealogy of Morals: A Polemic*. New expanded editions of *Daybreak* and *The Gay Science*.

1888   Begins to receive public recognition: Georg Brandes lectures on his work in Copenhagen. Discovers Turin, where he writes *The Wagner Case: A Musician's Problem*. Abandons *The Will to Power*, then completes in quick succession: *Twilight of the Idols, or How to Philosophize with a Hammer* (first published 1889), *The Antichrist: Curse on Christianity* (f.p. 1895), *Ecce Homo, or How One Becomes What One Is* (f.p. 1908), *Nietzsche contra Wagner: Documents of a Psychologist* (f.p. 1895), and *Dionysus Dithyrambs* (f.p. 1892).

1889   Suffers mental breakdown in Turin (3 January) and is eventually committed to asylum in Jena. *Twilight of the Idols* published 24 January, the first of his new books to appear after his collapse.

1890   Discharged into the care of his mother in Naumburg.

1894   Elisabeth founds Nietzsche Archive in Naumburg (moving it to Weimar two years later).

1897   Mother dies; Elisabeth moves her brother to Weimar.

1900   Friedrich Nietzsche dies in Weimar on 25 August.

THUS SPOKE
ZARATHUSTRA

CONTENTS

SECOND PART

THIRD PART

FIRST PART

ZARATHUSTRA'S PROLOGUE

I

When Zarathustra was thirty years old, he abandoned his home and the lake of his home and went into the mountains. Here he enjoyed his spirit and his solitude and for ten years did not tire of them.* At last, however, there was a change in his heart—and so one morning with the dawn of morning he rose, stepped out before the sun, and spoke to it thus:

'Greetings, Great Star! What would your happiness be, were it not for those whom you illumine!*

'For ten years you have come up here to my cave: you would have grown weary of your light and of this course, without me, my eagle, and my serpent.

'But we were waiting for you every morning, took from you your overflow and also blessed you for it.

'Behold! I am overburdened with my wisdom: like the bee that has gathered too much honey, I need hands outstretched to receive it.*

'I should like to bestow and distribute, until the wise among human beings once again become glad of their folly and the poor once again of their riches.

'For that I must descend into the depths: just as you do in the evening when you go down behind the sea and still bring light to the underworld, you overrich star!*

'I must, like you, *go under*, as human beings call it, to whom I would go down.

'So bless me then, you tranquil eye, who can look without envy even upon all-too-great happiness!

'Bless the cup that wants to overflow, that the water may flow from it golden and carry everywhere the reflection of your delight!

'Behold! This cup wants to become empty again, and Zarathustra wants to become human again.'*

—Thus began Zarathustra's going-under.

*   *   *

2

Zarathustra climbed down the mountain alone and no one encountered him. But when he came into the forest, there suddenly stood before him an old man who had left his holy hut in order to search in the forest for roots. And thus spoke the old man to Zarathustra:

'No stranger to me is this wanderer: many years ago he passed by here before. Zarathustra he was called; but now he has transformed himself.

'Then you were carrying your ashes to the mountains: would you today carry your fire into the valleys? Do you not fear the arsonist's punishment?

'Yes, I recognize Zarathustra. Clear is his eye, and around his mouth no trace of disgust. Does he not walk like a dancer?

'Zarathustra is transformed, Zarathustra has become a child, Zarathustra is an awakened one: what do you want now among sleepers?*

'You lived in your solitude as if in the sea, and the sea bore you up. Alas, you want to climb onto land? Alas, you want to drag your body yourself again?'

Zarathustra answered: 'I love human beings.'

'But why', said the holy man, 'did I go into the forest and the desert? Was it not because I loved human beings all too much?

'Now I love God: human beings I love not. The human being is for me too incomplete an affair. Love of human beings would be the death of me.'

Zarathustra answered: 'What did I say of love! I bring human beings a present.'

'Give them nothing,' said the holy man. 'Rather take something from them and carry it for them: that will do them the greatest good—as long as it does you good!

'And if you would give to them, then give them nothing more than alms, and let them beg even for that!'

'No,' answered Zarathustra, 'I give no alms. For that I am not poor enough.'

The holy man laughed at Zarathustra and spoke to him thus: 'Then see to it that they accept your treasures! They are suspicious of solitaries, and do not believe that we come in order to bestow.

'Too lonely for them is the sound of our footsteps in the lanes. And when in their beds at night they hear a man going by long before the sun has risen, they surely ask themselves: Where is that thief going?

'Do not go to human beings but stay in the forest! Go rather even to the beasts! Why would you not be, like me—a bear among the bears, a bird among the birds?'

'And what does the holy man do in the forest?' asked Zarathustra.

The holy man answered: 'I make up songs and sing them, and as I make up songs, I laugh and weep and growl: thus do I praise God.

'With singing, weeping, laughing, and growling I praise the God who is my God. But what do you bring us as a present?'

When Zarathustra heard these words he saluted the holy man and said: 'What could I have to give to you! But let me go quickly, that I might take nothing from you!'—And thus they parted from each other, the old man and the younger, laughing, just like two boys laughing.

But when Zarathustra was alone again, he spoke thus to his heart:* 'Could this be possible! This old holy man in his forest has heard nothing of this yet, that *God* is *dead*!'—

*   *   *

3

When Zarathustra came to the nearest town, which lay on the edge of the forest, he found there a crowd of people gathered in the market-square, for it had been announced that a rope-dancer* would be appearing. And Zarathustra spoke to the people thus:

'*I teach to you the Overhuman*. The human is something that shall be overcome. What have you done to overcome it?

'All beings so far have created something beyond themselves: and you want to be the ebb of this great tide, and even go back to the beasts rather than overcome the human?

'What is the ape for the human being? A laughing-stock or a painful cause for shame. And the human shall be just that for the Overhuman: a laughing-stock or a painful cause for shame.

'You have made your way from worm to human, and much in you is still worm. Once you were apes, and even now the human being is still more of an ape than any ape is.*

'Whoever is the wisest among you is still no more than a discord and hybrid between plant and spectre. But do I bid you become spectres or plants?

'Behold, I teach to you the Overhuman!

'The Overhuman is the sense of the earth. May your will say: *Let the Overhuman be the sense of the earth!*

'I beseech you, my brothers, *stay true to the earth* and do not believe those who talk of over-earthly hopes! They are poison-mixers, whether they know it or not.

'They are despisers of life, moribund and poisoned themselves, of whom the earth is weary: so let them pass on!

'Once sacrilege against God was the greatest sacrilege, but God died, and thereby the sacrilegious died too. Sacrilege against the earth is now the most terrible thing, and to revere the entrails of the unfathomable more than a sense of the earth!

'Once the soul looked despisingly upon the body, and at that time this despising was the highest thing: she wanted the body to be lean, ghastly, and starved. Thus she thought to slip away from the body and the earth.

'Oh this soul was herself still lean, ghastly, and starved: and cruelty was the lust of this soul!

'But you too, my brothers, tell me: what does your body proclaim about your soul? Is your soul not poverty and filth and wretched contentment?

'Verily, a polluted stream is the human. One must be a veritable sea to absorb such a polluted stream without becoming unclean.

'Behold, I teach to you the Overhuman: it is this sea, in this can your great despising submerge itself.

'What is the greatest you could experience? It is the hour of the great despising. The hour in which even your happiness disgusts you and likewise your reason and your virtue.

'The hour when you say: "What good is my happiness! It is poverty and filth and wretched contentment. But my happiness should justify existence itself!"

'The hour when you say: "What good is my reason! Does it crave knowing as the lion craves its food? It is poverty and filth and wretched contentment."

'The hour when you say: "What good is my virtue! It has yet to set me raging. How tired I am of my good and my evil! All that is poverty and filth and wretched contentment!"

'The hour when you say: "What good is my righteousness! I do not see that I am a blaze of hot coals. But one who is righteous is a blaze of hot coals!"

'The hour when you say: "What good is my pitying! Is not pity the Cross upon which he who loves humankind is nailed? But my pitying is no crucifixion."

'Have you ever spoken thus? Have you ever cried thus? Ah, that I might already have heard you cry thus!

'Not your sin—your frugality rails against Heaven, the very avarice in your sin rails against Heaven!

'Where then is the lightning* to lick you with its tongue? Where is the madness with which you must be inoculated?

'Behold, I teach to you the Overhuman: it is this lightning, it is this madness!'—

When Zarathustra had spoken thus, someone from among the people shouted: 'We've heard enough about the rope-dancer: now let us see him too!' And all the people laughed at Zarathustra. But the rope-dancer, thinking the words concerned him, began his performance.

*   *   *

4

Zarathustra, however, looked at the people and was amazed. Then he spoke thus:

'The human is a rope, fastened between beast and Overhuman—a rope over an abyss.

'A dangerous across, a dangerous on-the-way, a dangerous looking back, a dangerous shuddering and standing still.

'What is great in the human is that it is a bridge and not a goal: what can be loved in the human is that it is a *going-over* and a *going-under*.

'I love those who do not know how to live except by going under, for they are those who go over and across.

'I love the great despisers, for they are the great reverers and arrows of yearning for the other shore.

'I love those who do not first seek behind the stars for a reason to go under and be sacrifices, but who sacrifice themselves to the earth, that the earth may one day belong to the Overhuman.

'I love him who lives in order to understand, and who wants to understand so that one day the Overhuman may live. And thus he wills his going-under.

'I love him who works and invents, that he may build a house for the Overhuman and prepare earth and animal and plant for its sake: for thus he wills his going-under.

'I love him who loves his virtue: for virtue is the will to go under and an arrow of yearning.

'I love him who holds back not one drop of spirit for himself, but wants to be wholly the spirit of his virtue: thus he strides as spirit across the bridge.

'I love him who makes of his virtue his addiction and his undoing: thus he wills for his virtue's sake to live on and to live no more.

'I love him who would not have too many virtues. One virtue is more virtue than two, because it has more knots for one's undoing to latch on to.

'I love him whose soul squanders itself, who wants no thanks and does not give back again: for he always bestows and would not preserve himself.*

'I love him who is ashamed when the dice fall in his favour, and who then asks: Have I been playing falsely then?—for he wills his own perishing.

'I love him who casts golden words before his deeds and always keeps even more than he promises: for he wills his going-under.

'I love him who justifies those to come in the future and redeems those gone in the past: for he wants to perish by those in the present.

'I love him who chastens his God because he loves his God:* for the wrath of his God must be his perishing.

'I love him whose soul is deep even in being wounded, and who can perish from the smallest experience: thus he goes gladly over the bridge.

'I love him whose soul is overfull, so that he forgets himself,* and all things are in him: thus all things become his going-under.

'I love him who has a free spirit and a free heart: then his head is simply the entrails of his heart,* yet his heart drives him to his going-under.

'I love all those who are as heavy drops, falling singly from the dark cloud that hangs over the human: they herald the coming of the lightning, and as heralds they also perish.

'Behold, I am a herald of the lightning and a heavy drop from the cloud: but this lightning is called *Overhuman*.'—

* * *

5

When Zarathustra had spoken these words, he looked at the people again and was silent. 'There they stand,' he said to his heart, 'there they laugh: they do not understand me, I am not the mouth for these ears.

'Must one first smash their ears before they learn to hear with their eyes?* Must one rumble like kettledrums and preachers of repentance? Or do they only believe a stammerer?

'They have something of which they are proud. But what do they call that which makes them proud? Culture, they call it: it distinguishes them from goatherds.

'Therefore they dislike hearing the word "despising" said of them. So now I will speak to their pride.

'So I will speak to them of what is most despicable: and that is *the last human*.'

And thus spoke Zarathustra to the people:

'The time has now come for the human to set a goal for itself. The time has now come for the human to plant the seed of its highest hope.

'Its soil is still rich enough for that. But this soil will some day become poor from cultivation, and no tall tree will be able to grow from it.

'Alas! The time will come when the human will no longer shoot the arrow of its yearning over beyond the human, and the string of its bow will have forgotten how to whir!

'I say to you: one must still have chaos within, in order to give birth to a dancing star. I say to you: you still have chaos within you.

'Alas! The time will come when the human will give birth to no more stars. Alas! There will come the time of the most despicable human, who is no longer able to despise itself.

'Behold! I show to you *the last human*.

' "What is love? What is creation? What is yearning? What is a star?"—thus asks the last human and then blinks.*

'For the earth has now become small, and upon it hops the last human, who makes everything small. Its race is as inexterminable as the ground-flea; the last human lives the longest.

' "We have contrived happiness"—say the last humans and they blink.

'They have left the regions where the living was hard, for one needs the warmth. One still loves one's neighbour and rubs up against him: for one needs the warmth.

'To fall ill and harbour mistrust is in their eyes sinful: one must proceed with care. A fool, whoever still stumbles over stones or humans!

'A little poison now and then: that makes for agreeable dreams. And a lot of poison at the end, for an agreeable dying.

'One continues to work, for work is entertainment. But one takes care lest the entertainment become a strain.

'One no longer becomes poor or rich: both are too burdensome. Who wants to rule any more? Who wants to obey? Both are too burdensome.

'No herdsman and one herd!* Everyone wants the same thing, everyone is the same: whoever feels differently goes voluntarily into the madhouse.

' "Formerly the entire world was mad"—say their finest and they blink.

'One is clever and knows all that has happened: so there is no end to their mockery. One still quarrels, but one soon makes up—else it is bad for the stomach.

'One has one's little pleasure for the day and one's little pleasure for the night: but one honours good health.

' "We have invented happiness"—say the last humans and they blink.—'

And here ended Zarathustra's first speech, which is also called 'the Prologue': for at this point the clamour and delight of the crowd interrupted him. 'Give us this last human, O Zarathustra'—so they cried—'Turn us into these last humans! Then you can have the Overhuman!' And the people all jubilated and clucked with their tongues. But Zarathustra became sad and said to his heart:

'They do not understand me: I am not the mouth for these ears.

'Too long have I lived in the mountains, and too much have I listened to streams and trees: now I talk to them as to goatherds.

'Unmoved is my soul and bright as the mountains in the morning. But they think I am cold and a mocker in fearful antics.

'And now they behold me and laugh: and even as they laugh, they still hate me. There is ice in their laughter.'

* * *

6

But then something happened that made every mouth mute and every eye stare. For in the meantime the rope-dancer had begun his work: he had emerged through a small door and was walking across the rope, which had been stretched between two towers and thus hung over the market-square and the people.* Just as he was halfway across, the small door opened again and a motley fellow, looking like a jester, jumped out and followed the first man with rapid steps. 'On you go, lame-foot,' he cried in a terrifying voice. 'On you go, you lazy beast, smuggler, paleface! Else I shall tickle you with my heel! What are you doing here between towers? You belong *in* the tower, and should be locked up; you are blocking the way for one who is better than you!'—And with each word he came closer and closer to him, and when he was only one step behind him the terrible thing happened that made every mouth mute and every eye stare:—he uttered a shriek like a Devil and jumped over the man who was in his way. But the latter, seeing his rival win like this, lost both his head and the rope: he jettisoned his pole and shot faster than it, like a whirlwind of arms and legs, down into the depths. The market-square and the people resembled the sea when a storm comes in: everything flew apart and around, and most of all at the place where the body was about to land.

Zarathustra however stood still, and the body fell right beside him, badly injured and broken, but not yet dead. After a while the shattered man regained consciousness and saw Zarathustra kneeling beside him. 'What are you doing here?' he said at last. 'I have long known that the Devil would trip me up. Now he is dragging me off to Hell: do you want to prevent him?'

'On my honour, friend,' answered Zarathustra, 'all you are speaking of does not exist: there is no Devil and no Hell. Your soul will be dead even sooner than your body: so fear nothing more!'

The man looked up mistrustfully. 'If you are speaking the truth,' he said, 'then I lose nothing when I lose my life. I am not much more than a beast that has been taught to dance by being dealt blows and meagre morsels.'

'Not so,' said Zarathustra. 'You have made danger your calling: there is nothing in that to despise. Now your calling has brought you down: therefore will I bury you with my own hands.'

When Zarathustra had said this, the dying man answered no further; but he motioned with his hand, as if he were feeling for Zarathustra's hand to thank him.

*   *   *

7

In the meantime evening came, and the market-square was shrouded in darkness: the people then dispersed, for even curiosity and horror become weary. But Zarathustra sat on the ground beside the dead man and was immersed in his thoughts: thus he forgot the time. But at last it became night, and a cold wind blew upon the lonely one. Then Zarathustra arose and said to his heart:

'Verily, a fine catch of fish* has Zarathustra brought in today! No human did he catch, but rather a mere corpse.

'Strange indeed is human existence and still without meaning: a jester can become its fatality.

'I want to teach humans the meaning of their Being: that is the Overhuman, the lightning from the dark cloud of the human.

'But still am I distant from them, and my sense does not speak to their senses. A mean am I still for humans, between a fool and a corpse.

'Dark is the night, dark are the paths of Zarathustra. Come, you cold and stiff companion! I shall carry you to where I can bury you with my own hands.'

*   *   *

8

When Zarathustra had said this to his heart, he loaded the corpse onto his back and set out on his way. And he had not yet gone a hundred paces before a man sneaked up to him and whispered in his ear—and behold! the one addressing him was the jester from the tower. 'Go away from this town, O Zarathustra,' he said. 'Too many people here hate you. You are hated by the good and the righteous and they call you their enemy and despiser; you are hated by the believers of right belief, and they call you a danger to the multitude. It was lucky for you that they laughed at you: and verily, you were talking just like a jester. It was lucky for you that you made company with the dead dog; by abasing yourself like that, you saved your own skin for today. But now go forth from this town—or tomorrow I shall jump over you, a living man over a dead one.' And when he had said this, the man disappeared; but Zarathustra walked on farther through the dark lanes.

At the gate of the town he was met by the gravediggers: they shone their torch in his face, recognized Zarathustra, and mocked him mightily. 'Zarathustra is carrying the dead dog away: how nice that Zarathustra has become a gravedigger! For our hands are too clean for this particular roast. Does Zarathustra want to rob the Devil of his mouthful? On you go then!* And good luck with your meal! If only the Devil were not a better thief than Zarathustra!—he will steal them both, he will eat them both!' And they laughed among themselves and all put their heads together.

Zarathustra said not a word in reply and went on his way. After walking for two hours, past forests and swamps, he had heard too much hungry howling of wolves and began to feel hungry himself. So he stopped at an isolated house where a light was burning.

'Now hunger waylays me,' said Zarathustra, 'like a robber. In forests and swamps my hunger waylays me and in the deep of night.

'Marvellous moods my hunger has. Often it comes to me only after mealtimes, and today it did not come the whole day: where can it have been?'

And with that Zarathustra knocked on the door of the house. An old man appeared; he was carrying a light and asked: 'Who comes to me here and to my wretched sleep?'

'A living man and a dead one,' said Zarathustra. 'Give me

something to eat and drink, which I forgot about today. He who feeds the hungry refreshes his own soul: thus does wisdom speak.'

The old man went away, but came back immediately and offered Zarathustra bread and wine. 'This is a wicked part of the world for the hungry,' he said; 'and that's why I live here. Beast and human come to me, the hermit. But bid your companion eat and drink too, he is wearier than you.' Zarathustra answered: 'My companion is dead: it will be difficult for me to persuade him.' 'That's nothing to me,' said the old man grumpily. 'Whoever knocks on my door also has to take what I offer him. Eat and then fare you well!'—

Thereupon Zarathustra walked for another two hours, trusting his path and the light of the stars: for he was used to walking at night and loved looking into the face of all that sleeps. But when the morning dawned Zarathustra found himself in a deep forest, and he could no longer see any path. So he laid the dead man in a hollow tree at his head—for he wanted to protect him from the wolves—and laid himself down on the mossy ground. And soon he fell asleep, weary in body, but with his soul unmoved.

*   *   *

9

Long did Zarathustra sleep, and not only the dawn passed over his countenance but also the forenoon. At last, however, his eyes opened: amazed, Zarathustra looked into the forest and the stillness; amazed, he looked into himself. He then quickly rose, like a seafarer who all at once sees land,* and rejoiced: for he saw a new truth. And then he talked thus to his heart:

'A light has dawned for me: companions I need and living ones— not dead companions and corpses that I carry with me wherever I will.

'But living companions I need, who follow me because they want to follow themselves—and to wherever I will.

'A light has dawned for me: let Zarathustra not talk to the people, but to companions! Zarathustra shall not become shepherd and sheepdog to a herd!*

'To lure many away from the herd—for that have I come. The people and herd shall be angry with me: Zarathustra wants to be called a robber by the herdsmen.

'Herdsmen, I say, but they call themselves the good and the right-eous. Herdsmen, I say: but they call themselves believers of right belief.

'Behold the good and the righteous! Whom do they hate the most? The one who breaks their tablets of values,* the breaker, the lawbreaker:—yet that is the creator.

'Behold the believers of all beliefs! Whom do they hate the most? The one who breaks their tablets of values, the breaker, the lawbreaker:—yet that is the creator.

'Companions the creator seeks and not corpses, nor herds or believers either. Fellow creators the creator seeks, those who inscribe new values on new tablets.

'Companions the creator seeks, and fellow harvesters: for all that is with him stands ripe for the harvest. But the hundred sickles are lacking: so he plucks ears of corn* and is sorely vexed.

'Companions the creator seeks, and such as know how to whet their sickles. Destroyers they will be called and despisers of good and evil. But harvesters are they and celebrants too.

'Fellow creators Zarathustra seeks, fellow harvesters and cele-brants Zarathustra seeks: what can he create with herds and herds-men and corpses!

'And you, my first companion, fare you well! Securely I buried you in your hollow tree, securely I hid you from the wolves.

'But now I part from you: the time has come. Between dawn of morning and dawn of morning a new truth has come to me.

'No herdsman shall I be, nor digger of graves. With the people I will not talk even one more time; for the last time I have spoken to a dead man.

'With the creators, the harvesters, the celebrants will I make com-pany: the rainbow will I show them and all the stairways to the Overhuman.

'To the solitaries shall I sing my song and to the dualitaries; and whoever yet has ears for the unheard-of, his heart will I make heavy with my happiness.

'To my goal will I go, I walk my walk; over those who hesitate and are dilatory I shall leap away. Thus may my going be their going-under!'

*　　*　　*

10

This Zarathustra had spoken to his heart as the sun stood at midday: then he looked inquiringly into the heights—for he heard above him the sharp cry of a bird. And behold! An eagle was sweeping in wide circles through the air, and on him hung a serpent,* not like prey, but like a friend: for she kept herself coiled like a ring around his neck.

'It is my animals!' said Zarathustra, and was glad in his heart.

'The proudest animal under the sun and the cleverest animal under the sun—they have come out on reconnaissance.

'They want to know whether Zarathustra is still alive. Verily, am I still alive?

'More dangerous I found it among human beings than among beasts; dangerous ways does Zarathustra walk. May my animals lead me!'

When Zarathustra had said this, he recalled the words of the holy man in the forest, then sighed and spoke thus to his heart:

'That I might be more clever! That I might be clever from the ground up, like my serpent!

'But that is to ask the impossible: so I ask my pride that it always go along with my cleverness!

'And if my cleverness should one day leave me—ah, how she loves to fly away—may my pride then fly with my folly!'—

—Thus began Zarathustra's going-under.

*   *   *

THE SPEECHES OF ZARATHUSTRA

1. On the Three Transformations

Three transformations of the spirit I name for you: how the spirit becomes a camel,* and the camel a lion, and the lion at last a child.

There is much that is heavy for the spirit, for the strong, weight-bearing spirit in which reverence dwells: the heavy and the hardest are what its strength desires.

What is heavy? Thus asks the weight-bearing spirit, and thus it kneels down, like the camel, and would be well laden.

What is heaviest, you heroes? Thus asks the weight-bearing spirit. That I may take it upon me and become well pleased with my strength.

Is it not this: lowering oneself, in order to hurt one's haughtiness? Letting one's folly shine forth, in order to mock one's wisdom?

Or is it this: separating from our cause when it celebrates victory? Climbing high mountains in order to tempt the tempter?*

Or is it this: feeding on the acorns and grass of understanding and for the sake of truth suffering hunger of the soul?

Or is it this: being sick and sending the comforters home, and making friends with deaf people who never hear what it is you want?

Or is it this: stepping into filthy waters, as long as they are the waters of truth, and not repelling cold frogs or hot toads?

Or is it this: loving those who despise us, and offering the spectre our hand when it wants to frighten us?

All these heaviest things the weight-bearing spirit takes upon itself: like the camel that presses on well laden into the desert, thus does the spirit press on into its desert.

But in the loneliest desert the second transformation occurs: the spirit here becomes a lion; it will seize freedom for itself and become lord in its own desert.

Its ultimate lord it seeks out here: his enemy it will become and enemy of his ultimate god; it will wrestle for victory with the great dragon.*

What is the great dragon that the spirit no longer likes to call Lord and God? 'Thou shalt' is the name of the great dragon. But the spirit of the lion says 'I will.'

'Thou shalt' lies in its way, sparkling with gold, a scaly beast,* and on every scale there glistens, golden, 'Thou shalt!'

Values thousands of years old glisten on these scales, and thus speaks the mightiest of all dragons: 'All value in things—that glistens on me.'

'All value has already been created, and all created value—that is me. Verily, there shall be no more "I will"!' Thus speaks the dragon.

My brothers, why is the lion needed in the spirit? Why does the beast of burden, which renounces and is reverent, not suffice?

To create new values—that even the lion cannot yet do: but to create for itself freedom for new creation—that is within the power of the lion.

To create freedom for oneself and a sacred Nay even to duty: for that, my brothers, the lion is needed.

To seize the right to new values—that is the most terrible seizure for a weight-bearing and reverent spirit. Verily, a predation it is to such a spirit and a matter for a predatory beast.

Once it loved, as most sacred for it, 'Thou shalt': now it must find delusion and caprice even in the most sacred, that it might seize its freedom from its love: for this predation the lion is needed.

But say, my brothers, what can the child yet do that even the lion could not do? Why must the predatory lion yet become a child?

Innocence the child is* and forgetting, a beginning anew, a play, a self-propelling wheel, a first movement, a sacred Yea-saying.

Yes, for the play of creating, my brothers, a sacred Yea-saying is needed: the spirit now wills *its own* will, the one who had lost the world attains *its own* world.*

Three transformations of the spirit have I named for you: how the spirit became a camel, and the camel a lion, and the lion at last a child.—

Thus spoke Zarathustra. And at that time he was staying in the town that is called: The Motley Cow.*

*   *   *

2. On the Professorial Chairs of Virtue

A wise man* was praised to Zarathustra for knowing how to talk well about sleep and about virtue: it was said that he was greatly revered and rewarded for this, and that all the young men were sitting before his professorial chair. Zarathustra went to him, and sat with all the young men before his chair. And thus spoke the wise man:

'Honour and shame in the face of sleep! That is the first thing! And avoid all those who sleep badly and stay awake at night!

'Even the thief feels shame in the face of sleep: he always steals softly through the night. But shameless is the night-watchman; shamelessly he bears his horn.

'It is no simple art to sleep: it is necessary after all to stay awake the whole day before.

'Ten times a day must you overcome yourself: that makes for a fine weariness and is opium for the soul.

'Ten times must you reconcile yourself with yourself again; for overcoming is bitterness, and the unreconciled sleep badly.

'Ten truths a day must you discover: else you will still be seeking truth at night, and your soul will stay hungry.

'Ten times a day must you laugh and be cheerful: else your stomach will disturb you during the night, that father of sorrow.

'There are few who know this: but one must possess all the virtues in order to sleep well. Shall I bear false witness? Shall I commit adultery?

'Shall I covet my neighbour's maidservant?* All that would not sit well with sound sleep.

'And even if one has all the virtues, there is one more thing to know how to do: to send even the virtues to sleep at the proper time.

'That they might not quarrel among themselves, the good little females! And over you, you unfortunate man!

'Peace with God and one's neighbour: thus does sound sleep will it. And peace even with one's neighbour's Devil! Else he will be haunting you at night.

'Honour authority and obedience, and even crooked authority!* Thus does sound sleep will it. How can I help it if power likes to walk on crooked legs?

'For me the best shepherd will always be he who leads his sheep to the greenest pasture:* this sits well with the soundest sleep.

'I do not want much honour, nor great treasures: that inflames the spleen. But one sleeps badly without a good name and a modest treasure.

'The company of a few is more welcome to me than evil company: but they must come and go at the right time. This sits well with the soundest sleep.

'Most pleasing to me are the poor in spirit, for they promote sleep. Blessèd are they,* especially when one always concedes that they are right.

'Thus runs the course of the day for the virtuous. And when night comes, I am careful not to summon sleep! He will not be summoned, sound sleep, he who is lord of the virtues!

'Instead I think what I have done and thought that day. Ruminating I ask myself, patient as a cow: So what were your ten overcomings?

'And what were the ten reconciliations and the ten truths and the ten laughters with which my heart enjoyed itself?

'Weighing such considerations and rocking in the cradle of forty thoughts, I am suddenly overwhelmed by sleep, the unsummoned, lord of the virtues.

'Sleep taps on my eyes: then they grow heavy. Sleep touches my mouth: then it stays open.

'Verily, on soft soles it comes to me, that dearest of thieves, and steals my thoughts away: stupid I stand there like this professorial chair.

'But not for long do I stand like this: I am already lying down.'—

When Zarathustra heard the wise man speak thus, he laughed in his heart: for a light had thereby dawned upon him. And he spoke thus to his heart:

'What a fool this wise man is with his forty thoughts: and yet I believe he is quite expert in sleeping.

'Fortunate is he who dwells in the vicinity of this wise man! Such sleep is infectious, and can infect one even through a thick wall.

'There is even magic in his professorial chair. And not in vain have the young men sat before the preacher of virtue.

'His wisdom is: to stay awake in order to sleep soundly. And verily, if there were no sense to life, and I had to choose nonsense, this would be for me too the most choiceworthy nonsense.

'Now I clearly understand what people were once seeking above all when they sought teachers of virtue. Sound sleep for themselves and opiate virtues to go with it!

'For all these much-lauded wise men with their professorial chairs, wisdom was sleep without dreams; they knew no better sense for life.

'And even today there are still some who are like this preacher of virtue, and not always as honest: but their time is up. And not much longer will they stand: they are already lying down.

'Blessèd are these sleepyheads, for they shall soon drop off.'—

Thus spoke Zarathustra.

*   *   *

3. On Believers in a World Behind

At one time Zarathustra too cast his delusion beyond the human, like all believers in a world behind. The work of a suffering and tortured God the world seemed to me then.

A dream the world seemed to me then, and the fable of a God; coloured smoke before the eyes of one divinely discontented.

Good and evil and pleasure and pain and I and Thou—coloured smoke they seemed to me before creative eyes. To look away from himself was what the creator wanted—so he created the world.

Drunken pleasure it is for the sufferer to look away from his suffering and lose himself. Drunken pleasure and loss of oneself the world once seemed to me.

This world, eternally imperfect, image of an eternal contradiction and imperfect image—a drunken pleasure for its imperfect creator:—thus the world once seemed to me.

Thus I too once cast my delusion beyond the human, like all believers in a world behind. Beyond the human in truth?

Ah, brothers, this God that I created was humans'-work and -madness, just like all Gods!

Human he was, and just a meagre piece of human and 'I'. From my own ashes and blaze it came to me, this spectre, and verily! Not from the Beyond did it come to me!

What happened, my brothers? I overcame myself as a sufferer; I carried my own ashes to the mountain; a brighter flame I made for myself. And behold! The spectre then *fled* from me!

Suffering it would be for me now, and torture for one who has convalesced, to believe in such spectres: suffering it would be for me now, and an abasement. Thus do I talk to believers in a world behind.

Suffering it was and incapacity—that is what created all worlds behind; and that brief madness of happiness which only the greatest sufferer experiences.

Weariness that wants to attain the ultimate in a single leap, in a leap of death, a poor and ignorant weariness that does not even want to will any more: that is what created all Gods and worlds behind.

Believe me now, my brothers! The body it was that despaired of the body—that groped with the fingers of deluded spirit for the ultimate walls.

Believe me now, my brothers! The body it was that despaired of the earth—that heard the Belly of Being talk to it.

And then it wanted to break through those ultimate walls with its head, and not only with its head—over to that 'other world'.

But the 'other world' is well concealed from humans, that de-humaned unhuman world that is a heavenly nothing; and the Belly of Being does not speak to humans at all, except as a human.

Verily, hard to demonstrate is all Being and hard to induce to speak. Tell me, brothers, is not the most peculiar of all things still the best demonstrated?

Yes, this I and the I's contradiction and confusion still speak most honestly of its Being, this creating, willing, valuing I, that is the measure and value of things.

And this most honest Being, the I—it talks of the body, and it still wants the body, even when it poetizes and raves and flutters with broken wings.*

Ever more honestly it learns to talk, the I: and the more it learns the more it finds words and honours for body and earth.

A new pride my I taught me, which I now teach to human beings: no longer to bury one's head in the sand of heavenly things, but to carry it freely, an earthen head* that creates a sense for the earth!

A new will do I teach to human beings: to will this path that human beings have walked blindly, and to call it good and no longer slink away from it, like the sick and the moribund!

The sick and moribund it was who despised body and earth and invented the heavenly realm and the redemptive drops of blood:* but even these sweet and dismal poisons they took from body and earth!

From their misery they wanted to escape, and the stars were too far for them. Then they sighed: 'Would that there were heavenly ways by which to slink off into another state of Being and happiness!'— then they invented their ruses and potions of blood!

From their bodies and this earth they imagined themselves transported, these ingrates. Yet to what did they owe the spasms and rapture of their transports? To their bodies and to this earth.

Gentle is Zarathustra with the sick. Verily, he does not rage against their kinds of comfort and ingratitude. May they become convalescents and overcomers and create for themselves a higher body!

Nor is Zarathustra angry with the convalescent when he eyes his delusion tenderly and at midnight sneaks around the grave of his God: but even his tears still suggest to me sickness and a sick body.

There have always been many sick people among those who poetize and long for God; furiously they hate the one who understands, and that youngest among the virtues which is called: honesty.

Backwards they always look toward dark ages: then indeed were delusion and faith another matter; the delirium of reason was God-similarity, and doubt was a sin.

All too well I know those who are God-similar: they want to be believed in, and that doubt should be a sin. All too well I also know what they themselves believe in most.

Verily, not in worlds behind and redemptive drops of blood: but the body is what they too believe in most, and their own body is their thing-in-itself.*

But a sickly thing it is to them, and gladly would they get out of their own skins. Therefore they listen to the preachers of death and themselves preach about worlds behind.

Listen rather, my brothers, to the voice of the healthy body: a more honest and purer voice is this.

More honestly and purely does the healthy body talk, being complete and four-square:* and it talks of the sense of the earth.

Thus spoke Zarathustra.

*　*　*

4. On the Despisers of the Body

To the despisers of the body will I say my word. Not that I would have them learn and teach differently, but simply say farewell to their own bodies—and thus become mute.

'Body am I and soul'—thus talks the child. And why should one not talk like children?

But the awakened one, the one who knows, says: Body am I through and through, and nothing besides; and soul is merely a word for something about the body.

The body is a great reason, a manifold with one sense, a war and a peace, a herd and a herdsman.

A tool of the body is your small reason too, my brother, which you call 'spirit', a small tool and toy of your great reason.

'I' you say, and are proud of this word. But the greater thing—in which you do not want to believe—is your body and its great reason: it does not say I, but does I.

What the senses feel, what the spirit knows, that never has its end in itself. But senses and spirit would like to persuade you that they are the end of all things: that is how vain they are.

Tools and toys are senses and spirit: behind them there yet lies the Self.* The Self seeks with the eyes of the senses too, it listens with the ears of the spirit too.

Always the Self listens and seeks: it compares, compels, conquers, destroys. It rules and is also the I's ruler.

Behind your thoughts and feelings, my brother, stands a mighty commander, an unknown wise man—his name is Self. In your body he dwells, he is your body.

There is more reason in your body than in your finest wisdom. And who knows to what end your body needs precisely your finest wisdom?

Your Self laughs at your I and its proud leapings. 'What are these leapings and soarings of thought to me?' it says to itself. 'A detour to my purpose. I am the leading-reins of the I and the prompter of its conceptions.'

The Self says to the I: 'Feel pain here!' And then it suffers and thinks about how it might suffer no more—and this is what it is *meant* to think.

The Self says to the I: 'Feel pleasure here!' Then it is happy and thinks about how it might be happy again—and this is what it is *meant* to think.

To the despisers of the body will I say a word. That they despise, that makes for respecting. What is it that created respecting and despising and value and willing?

The creating Self created for itself respecting and despising, it created pleasure and woe. The creating body created spirit for itself as a hand of its will.

Even in your folly and despising, you despisers of the body, you are serving your Self. I say to you: your Self itself wants to die and turns away from life.

No longer can it do what it wants the most—to create beyond itself. That is what it wants the most, that is its entire fervour.

But it has now become too late for that—so your Self wants to go under, you despisers of the body.

Your Self wants to go under, and therefore you became despisers of the body! For you are no longer able to create beyond yourselves.

And therefore you are now angry with life and the earth. An unconscious envy lurks in the squinting glance of your despising.

I do not walk your way, you despisers of the body! You are for me no bridges to the Overhuman! —

Thus spoke Zarathustra.

* * *

5. On Enjoying and Suffering the Passions

My brother, if you have a virtue, and it is your virtue, then you have her in common with no one else.

Of course, you want to call her by name and caress her; you want to pull at her ear and amuse yourself with her.

And behold! Now you have her name in common with the people, and have yourself become one of the people and the herd with your virtue!

You do better if you say: 'Inexpressible and nameless is that which is torment and delight to my soul and is even the hunger of my entrails too.'

May your virtue be too lofty for the familiarity of names: and if you must talk about her, be not ashamed to stammer about her.

So speak and stammer: 'This is *my* good, this I love; thus it pleases me fully, thus alone do *I* want the good.

'I do not will it as the law of a God, I do not will it as a human statute and need: let it not be a signpost to over-earths and paradises.

'It is an earthly virtue that I love: there is little cleverness in it, and least of all the reason of everyone.

'But this bird has built its nest with me: therefore I love and cherish it—and now it sits here upon its golden eggs.'

Thus shall you stammer in praise of your virtue.

At one time you had passions and called them evil. But now you are left with only your virtues: these have grown from out of your passions.

You set your highest goal in the heart of these passions: then they became your virtues and sources of joy.

And whether you were from the tribe of the violent-tempered or of the lustful or the fanatical believers or the seekers of vengeance:

In the end all your passions turned into virtues and all your devils into angels.

At one time you had wild dogs in your cellar: but in the end they transformed themselves into birds and delightful singers.

From your poisons you brewed your own balsam: you milked the cow of your sorrow—now you drink the sweet milk of her udder.

And nothing evil grows out of you any more, except for the evil that grows out of the conflict among your virtues.

My brother, if you are fortunate you will have one virtue and no more: thus you go more easily across the bridge.

It is a distinction to have many virtues, but a hard lot indeed; and many a one went into the desert and killed himself because he was weary of being a battle and battlefield of virtues.

My brother, are war and battle evil? But necessary is this evil, necessary are envy and mistrust and calumny among your virtues.

Behold, how each one of your virtues is covetous of the highest place: she wants your whole spirit, that it might be *her* herald; she wants your whole strength in wrath, hatred, and love.

Each virtue is jealous of every other, and a terrible thing is jealousy. Virtues too can perish through their jealousy.

Whoever is ringed about by the flames of jealousy will at last, like the scorpion, turn the poisonous sting against himself.

Ah, my brother, have you never seen a virtue slander herself and stab herself?

The human is something that must be overcome: and therefore shall you love your virtues—for by them will you finally perish.—

Thus spoke Zarathustra.

* * *

6. On the Pale Criminal

You would not kill, you judges and sacrificers, until the beast has nodded? Behold, the pale criminal has nodded: from out of his eye there speaks the great despising.

'My I is something that is to be overcome: my I is for me the great despising of the human': thus it speaks from out of this eye.

That he pronounced judgement on himself was his greatest moment: let the sublime man not relapse to what is lower in him!

There is no redemption for one who suffers from himself so much, unless it be a quick death.

Your killing, you judges, shall be compassion and not revenge. And as you kill, see to it that you yourselves justify life!

It is not enough that you are reconciled with the one you kill. May your sorrow be love for the Overhuman: thus may you justify your own living on!

'Enemy' shall you say, but not 'evil-doer'; 'sick man' shall you say, but not 'knave'; 'fool' shall you say, but not 'sinner'.

And you, scarlet judge, if you were to say out loud all you have already done in your thoughts, everyone would cry out: 'Away with this filth and poison-worm!'

But the thought is one thing, the deed is another, and another yet is the image of the deed. The wheel of grounds* does not roll between them.

An image made this pale man pale. Equal to his deed was he when he did it: but its image he could not endure after it was done.

He now saw himself always as doer of a single deed. Madness I call this: the exception now became for him the essence.

The chalk-line bewitches the hen; the line he followed bewitched his meagre reason—madness *after* the deed I call this.

Hear me, you judges! There is yet another kind of madness: and this is *before* the deed. Ah, you have not crawled deep enough into this soul!

Thus speaks the scarlet judge: 'But why did this criminal murder? He wanted to rob.' But I say to you all: his soul wanted blood, not loot; he was thirsting for the joy of the knife!

But his meagre reason was unable to grasp this madness and it won him over. 'What is the point of blood!' it said; 'Do you not at least want to steal something too? Or to take revenge?'

And he listened to his meagre reason: like lead did its speech lie upon him—and so he robbed when he murdered. He wanted not to be ashamed of his madness.

And now again the lead of his guilt lies upon him, and again his meagre reason is so stiff, so lamed, so heavy.

If only he could shake his head, his burden would roll off: but who can shake this head?

What is this man? A heap of sicknesses that reach out through the spirit into the world: there they want to catch their prey.

What is this man? A ball of wild snakes that are seldom at peace with each other—so they go forth singly and seek prey in the world.

Behold this poor body! What it suffered and desired, this poor soul interpreted for itself—and interpreted it as murderous pleasure and greed for the joy of the knife.

Whoever now becomes sick is overcome by the evil that is evil now: he wants to hurt with that which hurts him. But there have been other times and another evil and good.

Once doubting was evil and the will to self. At that time the sick became heretics and witches: as heretics and witches they suffered and wanted to inflict suffering.

But this will not enter your ears: it would harm your good men, you tell me. But what do your good men matter to me!

Much about your good men disgusts me, and verily it is not their evil. How I wish they had a madness through which they might perish, just like this pale criminal!

Verily, I wish their madness were called truth or loyalty or justice: but they have their virtue in order to live long, and in wretched contentment.

I am a railing by the torrent: grasp me, whosoever can! Your crutch, however, I am not.—

Thus spoke Zarathustra.

* * *

7. On Reading and Writing

Of all that is written, I love only that which one writes with one's own blood. Write with blood,* and you will discover that blood is spirit.

It is not at all easy to understand the blood of another: I hate those readers who are idlers.

Whoever knows the reader will do nothing more for the reader. Another century of readers—and the spirit itself will stink.*

That everyone may learn to read will in the long run corrupt not only writing but also thinking.

Once the spirit was God, then it became human, and now it is even becoming the mob.

Whoever writes in blood and aphorisms does not want to be read, but rather to be learned by heart.

In the mountains the shortest way is from summit to summit;* but for that you must have long legs. Aphorisms should be summits: and those to whom they are addressed should be tall and lofty.

The air thin and pure, danger near, and the spirit filled with a joyful wickedness: these things go well together.

I want to have goblins around me, for I am courageous. Courage that frightens spectres away creates goblins for itself—courage wants to laugh.

I no longer feel as you people do: this cloud that I see beneath me, hanging dark and heavy, about which I laugh—just this is your thunder-cloud.

You look upward when you desire uplifting. And I look downward because I am uplifted.

Who among you can laugh and be uplifted at the same time?

Whoever climbs the highest mountains laughs about all tragic plays and tragic wakes.

Courageous, untroubled, mocking, violent— thus does Wisdom want us: she is a woman and always loves only a warrior.

You say to me: 'Life is hard to bear.' But wherefore would you have in the morning your pride and in the evening your resignation?

Life is hard to bear: but do not pretend to be so sensitive! We are all of us pretty sturdy asses and she-asses.

What do we have in common with the rosebud, which trembles because a drop of dew lies on its body?

It is true: we love life, not because we are used to living, but because we are used to loving.

There is always a bit of madness in loving. But there is also always a bit of reason in madness.

And even to me, as one who is fond of life, it seems that butterflies and soap-bubbles, and whatever is like them among humans, know the most about happiness.

To see these light, foolish, delicate, moving little souls fluttering around—that seduces Zarathustra to tears and songs.

I should only believe in a God who knew how to dance.

And when I saw my Devil I found him serious, thorough, deep, and solemn: it was the Spirit of Heaviness*—through him do all things fall.

Not with wrath but with laughter does one kill. Come, let us kill the Spirit of Heaviness!

I have learned how to walk: since then I let myself run. I have learned how to fly: since then I will not be pushed before moving from my place.

Now I am light, now I am flying, now I see myself beneath myself, now a God dances through me.

Thus spoke Zarathustra.

*   *   *

8. On the Tree on the Mountainside

Zarathustra's eye had seen that a young man was avoiding him. And as he was walking alone one evening in the mountains that surrounded the town called 'The Motley Cow', behold: on his walk he came across this young man sitting leaning against a tree and looking wearily down into the valley. Zarathustra gripped the tree by which the young man was sitting and spoke thus:

'If I wanted to shake this tree here with my hands, I should not be able to.

'But the wind, which we do not see, tortures and bends it wherever it will. It is by invisible hands that we are bent and tortured the worst.'

Then the young man got up in confusion and said: 'I hear Zarathustra and I was just now thinking of him.' Zarathustra replied:

'Why does that frighten you?—But it is the same with the human as with the tree.

'The more it aspires to the height and light, the more strongly its roots strive earthward, downward, into the dark, the depths—into evil.'

'Yes into evil!' cried the young man. 'How is it possible that you uncovered my soul?'

Zarathustra smiled and spoke: 'Some souls one will never uncover, unless one first of all invents them.'

'Yes into evil!' cried the young man once more.

'You have spoken the truth, Zarathustra. I no longer trust myself since aspiring to the heights, and no one else trusts me—but how does this happen?

'I transform myself too fast: my today refutes my yesterday. I often skip over steps when I climb— no step forgives me that.

'When I get to the top I always find myself alone. No one talks to me, and the frost of solitude makes me shiver. What do I want then in the heights?

'My despising and my yearning increase together; the higher I climb, the more I despise him who climbs. What does he want then in the heights?

'How ashamed I am of my climbing and stumbling! How I mock

at my violent panting! How I hate the one who can fly! How weary I am in the heights!'

Here the young man fell silent. And Zarathustra contemplated the tree by which they were standing, and spoke thus:

'This tree stands alone here in the mountains; it has grown tall beyond human and beast.*

'And if it wanted to talk, it would have no one who could understand it: so tall has it grown.

'Now it is waiting and waiting—yet what is it waiting for? It dwells too near the seat of the clouds: is it perhaps waiting for the first lightning?'*

When Zarathustra said this, the young man cried with violent gestures: 'Yes, Zarathustra, you speak the truth. I desired my own going-under when I aspired to the heights, and you are the lightning for which I was waiting! Behold, what am I now that you have appeared among us? It is *envy* of you that has destroyed me!'—Thus the young man spoke, and wept bitterly. But Zarathustra put his arm around him and led him away.

And after they had walked together for a while, Zarathustra began to speak thus:

'It tears at my heart. Better than your words tell it, your eye tells me your entire peril.

'You are not yet free, you are still *seeking* freedom. Overly tired your seeking has made you, and over-wakeful.

'You aspire to the free heights, your soul thirsts for stars. But your wicked drives, too, thirst for freedom.

'Your wild dogs want their freedom; they bark with delight in their cellar* when your spirit strives to break open all prisons.

'To me you are still a prisoner who is plotting his freedom: ah, in such prisoners the soul becomes clever, but also deceitful and base.

'The liberated in spirit must yet purify himself. Much prison and mustiness is in him yet: his eye must yet become pure.

'Yes, I know your peril. But by my love and hope I beseech you: do not throw your love and hope away!

'Noble you feel yourself still, and even those who are aggrieved at you and give you the evil eye still feel you are noble. Know that a noble man stands in everyone's way.

'Even for the good a noble man stands in the way: and even if they call him a good man, they want thereby to push him aside.

'The noble man wants to create what is new and a new virtue. The good man wants what is old, and that the old be preserved.

'But this is not the danger of the noble man, that he might become a good man, but that he might become insolent, scornful, an annihilator.

'Ah, I have known noble men who lost their highest hope. And then they slandered all high hopes.

'Then they lived insolently in little pleasures, and beyond the day they hardly cast any goals.

' "Spirit is also lust"—this is what they said. Then the wings of their spirit broke: now it crawls around and besmirches what it gnaws.

'Once they thought to become heroes: now they are lechers. Grief and horror is the hero for them now.

'But by my love and hope I beseech you: do not throw the hero in your soul away! Hold sacred your highest hope!'—

Thus spoke Zarathustra.

* * *

9. On the Preachers of Death

There are preachers of death: and the earth is full of those to whom rejection of life must be preached.

Full is the earth of the superfluous; corrupted is life by the all too many. Let one use 'eternal life' to lure them away from this life!

'Yellow ones': this is the name for the preachers of death, or 'black ones'.* But I want to show them to you in yet other colours.

These are the terrible ones who carry within them the beast of prey, and have no other choice than lust or self-laceration. And even their lust is still self-laceration.

They have not even become human yet, these terrible ones: let them preach rejection of life and themselves pass away!

These are the consumptives of the soul: hardly are they born before they begin to die and to long for teachings of weariness and renunciation.

They want very much to be dead, and we should applaud their

wish! Let us guard against waking these corpses and damaging these living coffins!

They come across an invalid or an old man or a corpse;* and straightway they say, 'Life is refuted!'

But only they are refuted and their eye, which sees only one face of existence.

Shrouded in thick depression and eager for the small accidents that bring death: thus do they wait and grind their teeth together.

Or else again: they grasp after sweetmeats and mock their childishness in this; they cling to their straw of a life and mock their still clinging to a straw.

Their wisdom says: 'A fool is he who stays alive, but such fools are we! And this is just what is most foolish about life!'—

'Life is only suffering'—thus say others and do not lie: so see to it that *you* cease living! So see to it that the life that is only suffering ceases!

And let the teaching of your virtue resound thus: 'Thou shalt kill thyself! Thou shalt steal thyself away!'—

'Lust is a sin'—thus say some of those that preach death—'Let us step aside and beget no children!'

'Giving birth is laborious'—say others—'Why go on giving birth? One gives birth only to unfortunates!' And they too are preachers of death.

'Pity is needed'—thus say yet others. 'Please take what I have! Please take what I am! Life will then bind me that much less!'

If they were to pity from the ground up, they would spoil life for their neighbours. To be evil—that would be their proper goodness.

But they want to escape from life: what is it to them that with their chains and presents they bind others even tighter!—

And even you for whom life is furious labour and distraction: are you not very weary of life? Are you not very ripe for the preaching of death?

All of you for whom furious labour is dear and what is fast, and new, and strange—you tolerate yourselves poorly, your industry is flight and the will to forget yourselves.

If you believed in life more, you would throw yourselves away less on the moment. But for waiting you lack sufficient capacity—and even for laziness!

Everywhere the voices of those who preach death resound: and the earth is full of those to whom death must be preached.

Or else 'eternal life': it is the same to me—as long as they pass on to it quickly!

Thus spoke Zarathustra.

*   *   *

10. On War and Warrior-Peoples

By our best enemies we do not want to be spared, nor by those whom we love from the ground up. So let me now tell you the truth!

My brothers in warfare! I love you from the ground up; I am and have been of your kind. And I am also your best enemy. So let me now tell you the truth!

I know about the hatred and envy in your hearts. You are not great enough not to know hatred and envy. So be great enough then not to be ashamed of them!

And if you cannot be saints of understanding, then at least be for me its warriors. For they are the companions and precursors of such sainthood.

I see many soldiers: I should like to see many warriors! 'Uni-form' one calls what they wear: may what they hide with it not be uni-form too!

You shall be such for me that your eye is always seeking an enemy—*your* enemy. And with some of you there is hate at first sight.

You shall seek your enemy, you shall wage your war—and for your own thoughts!* And should your thought be defeated, your honesty shall still proclaim its triumph in that!

You shall love peace as a means to new wars. And the short peace more than the long.

For you I do not counsel work, but rather battle. For you I do not counsel peace, but rather victory. May your work be a battle, may your peace be a victory!

One can be silent and sit still only when one has arrow and bow: else one chatters and quarrels. May your peace be a victory!

You say it is the good cause that hallows even war? I say to you: it is the good war that hallows every cause.

War and courage have accomplished more great things than love of one's neighbour. Not your pitying but your bravery has so far saved the unfortunate.

What is good? you ask. To be brave is good. Let the little maidens say: 'To be good is to be pretty as well as touching.'

They call you heartless: but your hearts are true, and I love the modesty of your heartiness. You are modest about your flood, and others are modest about their ebb.

You are ugly? Well then, my brothers! Put the sublime around you, the mantle of the ugly!

And when your souls become great, they become exuberant, and in your sublimity there is wickedness. I know you well.

In wickedness is the meeting of the exuberant man with the weakling. But they misunderstand each other. I know you well.

You may only have enemies that are to be hated, but not enemies to be despised. You must be proud of your enemy: then the successes of your enemy are also your successes.

Rebellion—that is nobility in the slave. May your nobility be obedience! May your very commanding be an obeying!

To a good warrior, 'Thou shalt' sounds more pleasing than 'I will'. And all that is dear to you, you should first let yourselves be commanded to do.

May your love of life be love of your highest hope: and may your highest hope be the highest thought of life!

But your highest thought you shall receive as a command from me—and it is this: the human is something that is to be overcome.

So live your lives of obedience and of war! What use is living long! What warrior wants to be spared!

I do not spare you; I love you from the ground up, my brothers in war!—

Thus spoke Zarathustra.

*   *   *

11. On the New Idol

In some places there are still peoples and herds left, but not with us, my brothers: here there are states.

The state? What is that? Well then! Now open your ears for me, for now I say to you my word about the death of peoples.

State is the name for the coldest of all cold monsters. Coldly it tells lies; and this lie crawls out of its mouth: 'I, the state, am the people.'

That is a lie! Creators it was who created peoples and hung a faith and a love over them: thus they served the cause of life.

Annihilators are they who set up snares for the many and call them a state: they hang a sword and a hundred desires over them all.

Where a people still exists, it does not understand the state and hates it as an evil eye and a sin against customs and rights.

This sign I give to you: every people speaks its own tongue of good and evil: this the neighbour does not understand. It has invented its own language of customs and rights.

But the state lies in all the tongues of good and evil; and whatever it talks about, it lies—and whatever it has, it has stolen.

Everything about it is false; it bites with stolen teeth, and it snarls. Even its very entrails are false.

Confusion of the language of good and evil: this sign I give you as a sign of the state. Verily, the will to death is what this sign signifies! Verily, it beckons to the preachers of death!

Far too many are born: for the superfluous was the state invented!

Just see how it entices them, the far too many! How it devours them and chews them and chews them up again!

'On earth there is nothing greater than I: the ordering finger of God* am I'—thus bellows the great brute. And it is not only the long-eared and short-sighted that sink to their knees!

Ah, even to you, you great souls, it whispers its dismal lies! Ah, it divines the richer hearts that like to squander themselves!

Yes, it even divines you, you vanquishers of the old God! You have grown weary from the battle, and now your weariness still serves the new idol!

Heroes and worthies it would like to set up around itself, the new idol! How it likes to sun itself in the sunshine of good consciences—the coldest of brutes!

All things it will give *you*, if *you* worship it,* the new idol: thus it buys itself the lustre of your virtue and the glance of your proud eyes.

It wants to use you as bait for the far too many! Yes, a hellish artifice has been here devised, a horse of death, clattering in the trappings of godlike honours!

Yes, a dying for many has been here devised that glorifies itself as life: verily, a religious service of the heart for all preachers of death!

State I call it where all are poison-drinkers, the good and the base: state, where all can lose themselves, the good and the base: state, where the slow suicide of all—is called 'life'.

Just look at these superfluous creatures! They steal for themselves the works of inventors and the treasures of the wise: culture they call their theft—and everything turns for them to sickness and misfortune!

Just look at these superfluous creatures! Sick are they always; they vomit up their gall and call it a newspaper. They devour each other and cannot even digest themselves.

Just look at these superfluous creatures! Riches they acquire, and thereby become poorer. Power is what they want, and especially the crowbar of power, much money—these impotent creatures!

Look at them clamber, these nimblest of apes! They clamber over each other and thus drag themselves into the mud and the depths.

They all want to get to the throne: this is their madness—as if happiness were sitting on the throne! Often it is mud that sits on the throne—and often the throne also sits on mud.

Madmen they all seem to me, and clambering apes and over-ardent. Foul their idol smells to me, the coldest of brutes: foul they smell to me altogether, these idolaters.

My brothers, do you now want to suffocate in the fumes of their maws and desires! Rather shatter the windows and leap into the open air!

Get out of the way of the awful stench! Get away from the idolatry of the superfluous!

Get out of the way of the awful stench! Get away from the steam of these human sacrifices!

Free for great souls the earth still stands even now. Vacant still are many seats for the lonesome and the twosome,* around which there wafts the fragrance of silent seas.

Free still for great souls a free life stands. Verily, whoever possesses little is that much less possessed: praised be a moderate poverty!

There where the state ceases, only there does the human being begin who is not superfluous: there the song of the one who is necessary begins, the unique and irreplaceable melody.

There where the state *ceases*—cast your glance over there, my brothers! Do you not see it, the rainbow and the bridges of the Over-human?—

Thus spoke Zarathustra

*　*　*

12. On the Flies of the Market-Place

Flee, my friend, into your solitude! I see you deafened by the noise of great men and stung all over by the barbs of small ones.

Forest and rock know how to keep with you a dignified silence. Be again like the tree that you love, broad-branched: quietly listening it leans out over the sea.

Where solitude ceases, there begins the market-place; and where the market-place begins, there also begins the noise of the great play-actors* and the buzzing of poisonous flies.

In this world even the finest things amount to nothing without someone to make a show of them: great men the people call these showmen.

Little do the people comprehend what is great, which is: the creative. But they do have a sense for all showmen and play-actors of great matters.

Around inventors of new values the world revolves—invisibly it revolves. Yet around play-actors the people and fame revolve: that is 'the way of the world'.

Spirit the play-actor has, yet little conscience of the spirit. He always believes in that whereby he most strongly makes others believe—makes believe in *himself!*

Tomorrow he has a new belief and the day after tomorrow a newer one. Quick senses he has, like the people, and changeable weather.

To bowl over—that he calls: to demonstrate. To drive frantic—

that he calls: to convince. And blood counts for him as the best of all grounds.

A truth that slips only into refined ears he calls a lie and nothing. Verily, he believes only in Gods that make a great noise in the world!

Filled with solemn jesters is the market-place—and the people boast about their great men! These are their lords of the hour.

But the hour presses them: and so they press you. And from you too they want a Yea or Nay. Alas, you want to set down your chair between For and Against?

On account of these unconditional and obtrusive ones be without jealousy, you lover of truth! Never yet has truth hung on the arm of someone unconditional.

On account of these precipitous ones go back into your security: only in the market-place is one assailed by 'Yea?' or 'Nay?'.

Slow is experience for all deep wells: long must they wait before they know just *what* has fallen into their depths.

Far from the market-place and fame happens all that is great: far from the market-place and fame have the inventors of new values always lived.

Flee, my friend, into your solitude: I see you stung all over by poisonous flies. Flee to where raw and bracing air blows!

Flee into your solitude! You have lived too close to the petty and the wretched. Flee from their invisible revenge! Toward you they are nothing but revenge.

No longer raise your arm against them! Innumerable are they, and it is not your lot to be a swatter of flies.

Innumerable are these petty and wretched creatures; and for the collapse of many a proud structure raindrops and weeds have been sufficient.

You are no stone, but you have already become hollow from many drops. You will yet break and burst apart from many drops.

I see you wearied by poisonous flies;* I see you bloodily scratched in a hundred places: and your pride does not even want to be wrathful.

Blood they would like from you in all innocence, blood is what their bloodless souls desire—and therefore they sting in all innocence.

But, you who are deep, you suffer too deeply even from small wounds; and before you could even heal yourself, the same poison-worm was crawling over your hand.

Too proud are you to kill these sweet-toothed creatures. But beware lest it become your undoing to bear all their poisonous injustice!

They buzz around you with their praising too: importunity is their praising. They want the nearness of your skin and your blood.

They flatter you as they would a God or Devil; they whimper before you as before a God or Devil. What of it! Flatterers are they and whimperers, and nothing more.

They often present themselves as charming too. But that has always been the cleverness of cowards. Yes, cowards are clever!

They think of you much with their narrow souls—suspicious are you always for them! All that is thought of much becomes suspicious.

They punish you for all your virtues. They forgive you from the ground up only—for your mistakes.

Because you are gentle and of righteous disposition, you say: 'Innocent are they in their petty existence.' But their narrow souls think: 'Blameworthy is all great existence.'

Even when you are gentle toward them, they still feel despised by you; and they repay your beneficence with concealed maleficence.

Your wordless pride always goes against their taste; they rejoice if for once you are modest enough to be vain.

That which we recognize in someone else, we also inflame in that person. So beware of the petty!

Before you they feel petty, and their baseness glows and smoulders against you in invisible revenge.

Have you not noticed how often they became mute when you approached them, and how their strength went from them like smoke from a dying fire?

Yes, my friend, you are the bad conscience for your neighbours: for they are unworthy of you. Thus they hate you now and would dearly like to suck your blood.

Your neighbours will always be poisonous flies; that which is great in you—that itself must make them more poisonous and ever more fly-like.

Flee, my friend, into your solitude and to where raw and bracing air blows. It is not your lot to be a swatter of flies.—

Thus spoke Zarathustra.

* * *

13. On Chastity

I love the forest. In the cities it is bad to live: there are too many there that are in heat.

Is it not better to fall into the hands of a murderer than into the dreams of a woman in heat?

And just look at these men here: their eye says it—they know of nothing better on earth than to lie with a woman.

Mud is at the bottom of their souls; and woe, if their mud still has any spirit!

Would that you were perfect at least as beasts!* But to the beast belongs innocence.

Do I counsel you to deaden your senses? I counsel you to innocence of the senses.

Do I counsel you to chastity? Chastity is in some people a virtue, but in many almost a vice.

These latter abstain certainly: but the bitch sensuality looks enviously out of everything they do.

Even into the heights of their virtue and the coldness of the spirit this beast with its discord follows them.

And how nicely the bitch sensuality knows how to beg for a piece of spirit when a piece of flesh is denied her!

You love tragedies and everything that breaks the heart? But I am mistrustful of your bitch.

Your eyes are too cruel for me and you look lustfully at sufferers. Has your lust not merely disguised itself and called itself pity?

And this parable, too, I give to you: not a few who wanted to drive out their Devil have themselves entered into swine.*

Those for whom chastity is difficult should be counselled against it, that it might not become their path to Hell—that is, to mud and heat of the soul.*

Do I speak of filthy things? That is for me not the worst thing.

Not when the truth is filthy, but when it is shallow, is the one who understands reluctant to step into its waters.

Verily, there are those who are chaste from the ground up: they are gentler of heart, and laugh more readily and richly than you.

They even laugh about chastity and ask: 'What is chastity!

'Is chastity not folly? But this folly came to us and not we to it.

'We offered this guest shelter and our hearts: now it lives with us—may it stay as long as it wants!'

Thus spoke Zarathustra.

* * *

14. On the Friend

'One person is always too many around me'—thus thinks the solitary. 'Always one times one—that yields in the long run two!'

I and Me* are always too zealous in conversation: how could it be endured if there were no friend?

For the solitary the friend is always the third one: the third one is the cork that prevents the conversation of the two from sinking into the depths.

Ah, there are too many depths for all solitaries. Therefore they long so much for a friend and for his height.

Our belief in others betrays wherein we should like to believe in ourselves. Our yearning for a friend is our betrayer.

And often one wants with love simply to get over one's envy.* And one often attacks and makes enemies in order to conceal that one is open to attack.

'At least be my enemy!'—thus speaks true reverence, which does not dare to ask for friendship.

If one would have a friend, one must also want to wage war for him: and in order to wage war, one must *be able* to be an enemy.

One should honour even the enemy in one's friend.* Can you step up close to your friend without going over to him?

In one's friend one should have one's best enemy. You should be closest to him in your heart when you strive against him.

You want to wear no clothes in front of your friend? It should be your friend's honour that you present yourself to him as you are? But for that he wishes the Devil would take you!

Whoever makes no secret of himself incenses others: you have that much reason to fear nakedness! Yes, if you were Gods, then you could be ashamed of your clothes!

You cannot adorn yourself well enough for your friend: for you shall be to him an arrow and a yearning for the Overhuman.

Have you ever seen your friend asleep—so that you could see how he looks? What is then the face of your friend? It is your own face, in a rough and imperfect mirror.

Have you ever seen your friend asleep? Were you not shocked that your friend looks like that? Oh, my friend, the human is something that must be overcome.

In guessing and keeping silent the friend shall be a master: you must not want to see everything. Your dream shall betray to you what your friend does while awake.

May your compassion be a divining: that you might first know whether your friend wants compassion. Perhaps he loves in you the unbroken eye and the glance of eternity.

May compassion for the friend conceal itself under a hard shell; you shall lose a tooth biting on it. Thus will it have its subtlety and sweetness.

Are you pure air and solitude and bread and medicine for your friend? Many a one is unable to loosen his own chains* and yet is a redeemer for his friend.

Are you a slave? Then you cannot be a friend. Are you a tyrant? Then you cannot have friends.*

For far too long woman has harboured a slave and a tyrant within. Therefore woman is not yet capable of friendship: she knows only love.

A woman's love contains injustice and blindness toward all that she does not love. And even a woman's enlightened love still contains sudden attack and lightning and night along with the light.

Woman is still not capable of friendship: women are still cats, and birds too. Or, in the best case, cows.

Woman is still not capable of friendship. But tell me, you men, who among you is capable of friendship?

Oh your poverty, you men, and your meanness of soul! As much as you give to the friend I want to give even to my enemy, nor do I want thereby to have become poorer.

There is comradeship: now let there be friendship!

Thus spoke Zarathustra.

*   *   *

15. On the Thousand Goals and One*

Many lands has Zarathustra seen and many peoples: thus he discovered the good and evil of many peoples. No greater power has
Zarathustra found on earth than good and evil.

No people could live without first evaluating; but if it would maintain itself, it may not evaluate as its neighbour evaluates.*

Much that this people deemed good was for another a source of
scorn and shame: thus have I found it. Many things I found called
evil here, and there adorned with purple honours.

Never did one neighbour understand the other: ever was his soul
amazed at his neighbour's delusion and wickedness.

A tablet of things held to be good hangs over every people.
Behold, it is the tablet of its overcomings; behold, it is the voice of its
will to power.

Praiseworthy is what counts for a people as heavy and hard; what
is indispensable and hard is called good; and whatever liberates from
the highest need, what is rare, and hardest—that it glorifies as holy.

Whatever allows it to rule and conquer and shine, to the horror
and envy of its neighbour: that counts as the lofty, the first, the
measure, the meaning of all things.

Verily, my brother, once you have recognized a people's need and
land and sky and neighbour, you can surely guess the law of its
overcomings, and why it climbs on this ladder up to its own hope.

'Always shall you be the first and excel over others:* your jealous
soul shall love no one, unless it be the friend'—this made the soul of
the Greek tremble: with that he went his way to greatness.

'To tell the truth and to handle the bow and arrow well'*—this
seemed both dear and hard to that people from whom my name
comes—the name that is for me both dear and hard.

'To honour father and mother* and follow their will to the roots of
the soul': this tablet of overcoming another people hung over itself
and became powerful and eternal thereby.

'To practise loyalty and for the sake of loyalty to risk honour and
blood even for evil and dangerous causes': teaching itself thus
another people* conquered itself, and conquering itself thus it
became pregnant and heavy with great hopes.

Verily, human beings have given themselves all their good and evil.

Verily, they did not take it, they did not find it, nor did it come down to them as a voice from Heaven.

The human being first put values into things, in order to preserve itself—it created a meaning for things, a human's meaning! Therefore it calls itself 'human'—that is: the evaluator.

Evaluating is creating: hear this, you creators! Evaluating is itself the treasure and jewel of all valued things.

Through evaluating alone is there value: and without evaluating the kernel of existence would be hollow. Hear this, you creators!

Change of values—that means change of creators. Whoever must be a creator always annihilates.

Creators were at first peoples and only later individuals; verily, the individual is itself just the most recent creation.

Peoples once hung a tablet of the good over themselves. Love that wants to rule, and love that wants to obey, these together created for themselves such tablets.

Pleasure in the herd is older than pleasure in the I: and as long as the good conscience is called herd, only the bad conscience says: I.

Verily, the cunning I, the loveless, which wants its own benefit in the benefit of the many: that is not the origin of the herd* but its going-under.

It has always been lovers, and creators, that created good and evil. The fire of love glows in the names of all virtues as well as the fire of wrath.

Many lands has Zarathustra seen and many peoples: no greater power has Zarathustra found on earth than the works of the lovers: 'good' and 'evil' is their name.

Verily, a monster is the power of this praising and blaming. Tell me, who will subdue it for me, brothers? Tell me, who will throw the shackles over the thousand necks of this beast?*

A thousand goals have there been so far, for there have been a thousand peoples. Only the shackles for the thousand necks are still lacking: there is lacking the one goal. Humanity still has no goal.

But say to me now, my brothers: if humanity still lacks a goal, does it not also still lack—itself?—

Thus spoke Zarathustra.

* * *

16. On Love of One's Neighbour

You crowd around the neighbour and have beautiful words for it. But I say to you: Your love of the neighbour is your bad love of yourselves.*

You flee to the neighbour from yourselves and would like to make a virtue of it: but I see through your 'selflessness'.

The Thou is older than the I; the Thou has been pronounced holy, but not yet the I: so the human being crowds toward the neighbour.

Do I counsel love of the neighbour? Rather, I counsel flight from the nearest and love of the farthest!*

Higher than love of the nearest is love of the farthest and what is to come; higher yet than love of the human is for me love of causes and spectres.

This spectre that runs ahead of you, my brother, is more beautiful than you: why do you not give him your flesh and your bones? But you are afraid and run to your neighbour.

You cannot endure being with yourselves and do not love yourselves enough: now you want to seduce the neighbour into love and to gild yourselves with his error.

I would that you could not endure being with any kind of neighbour and their neighbours; then you would have to create out of yourselves your friend and his overflowing heart.

You invite a witness in when you want to speak well of yourselves; and when you have seduced him to think well of you, you also think well of yourselves.

It is not only he who talks contrary to what he knows who lies, but even more so he who talks contrary to what he does not know. And so you talk of yourselves in dealings with others and lie to yourselves and the neighbour.

Thus speaks the fool: 'Association with one's fellows corrupts the character, especially when one has none.'*

One man runs to the neighbour because he seeks himself, and the other because he would like to lose himself. Your bad love of yourselves makes solitude a prison for you.

It is those farther away who pay for your love of the neighbour; and as soon as five of you are together, a sixth always has to die.

I do not love your festivals either: too many play-actors I found there, and even the audience often behaved like play-actors.

Not the neighbour do I teach to you, but the friend. May the friend be to you a festival of the earth and a premonition of the Overhuman.

I teach to you the friend and his overfull heart. But one must know how to be a sponge if one would be loved by hearts that are overfull.

I teach to you the friend, in whom the world stands complete, a vessel of goodness—the creating friend, who always has a complete world to bestow.

And as the world rolled apart for him, so it rolls back together in rings, as the becoming of good through evil, as the becoming of purposes from chance.

May the future and the farthest be the cause of your today: in your friend shall you love the Overhuman as your own cause.

My brothers, to love of the neighbour I counsel you not: I counsel you to love of the farthest.

Thus spoke Zarathustra.

*   *   *

17. On the Way of the Creator

Do you want, my brother, to go into isolation? Do you want to seek the way to yourself? Then pause a while longer and listen to me.

'He who seeks will himself easily become lost. All isolation is guilt': thus speaks the herd. And you have long belonged to the herd.

The voice of the herd will still resound in you too. And if you will say, 'I no longer have one conscience with you,' it will be a lament and an agony.

Behold, this agony was itself born from the one conscience: and the final glimmer of this conscience still glows upon your misery.

But you want to go the way of your misery, which is the way to yourself? Then show me your right and your strength for that!

Are you a new strength and a new right? A first movement? A self-propelling wheel? Can you compel the very stars to revolve around you?

Ah, there is so much lusting for the heights! There is so much convulsion of the ambitious! Show me that you are not one of the lustful and ambitious!

Ah, there are so many great thoughts that do no more than a bellows: they just inflate and make emptier.

Free, you call yourself? Your ruling thought would I hear then, and not that you have escaped from a yoke.

Are you such as has the *right* to escape from a yoke? There are some who threw off their last shred of worth when they threw off their servitude.

Free from what? What is that to Zarathustra! Brightly shall your eye announce to me: free *for what?*

Can you give yourself your own evil and your own good, and hang your will over yourself as a law? Can you be your own judge and avenger of your law?

Terrible it is to be alone with the judge and avenger of one's own law. Thus is a star thrown out into desolate space and into the icy breath of being alone.

Today you still suffer from the many, you singular one: today you still have your courage whole and your hopes.

But one day solitude will make you weary, one day your pride will buckle and your courage gnash its teeth. One day you will cry, 'I am alone!'

One day you will see what is lofty in you no longer and what is base all too-closely; even what is sublime in you will frighten you like a spectre. One day you will cry: 'Everything is false!'

There are feelings that want to kill the solitary; if they do not succeed, well, then they themselves must die! But are you capable of being a murderer?

Do you, my brother, already know the word 'despising'? And the anguish of your righteousness in being righteous toward those who despise you?

You compel many to relearn about you: that they will hold against you. You came close to them and yet passed them by: that they will never forgive you.

You pass over and beyond them: but the higher you climb, the smaller you appear to the eye of envy. But most hated of all is the one who can fly.

'How could you want to be just toward me!'—you must say—'I myself choose your injustice as my allotted portion.'

Injustice and filth they throw at the solitary: but, my brother, if you want to be a star, you must shine no less brightly for them on that account!

And beware of the good and the righteous! They like to crucify those who invent their own virtue for themselves—they hate the solitary.

Beware also of the holy unity! For it, all that is not unitary is unholy; it also likes to play with fire—especially at the stake.

And beware also of the attacks of your love! Too quickly does the solitary extend his hand to anyone he meets.

To some people you may give not your hand, but only a slap with a paw: and I would that your paw might also have claws.

But the worst enemy you can encounter will always be yourself; you lie in wait for yourself in caves and forests.

You solitary, you are going the way to yourself! And your way leads past yourself, and past your Seven Devils!

A heretic will you be to yourself, and a witch and soothsayer and fool and doubter and unholy man and scoundrel.

You must want to consume yourself in your own flame:* how could you want to become new unless you have first become ashes!

You solitary, you are going the way of the creator: a God you would create for yourself out of your Seven Devils!

You solitary, you are going the way of the lover: yourself do you love, and therefore you despise yourself, as only lovers can despise.

The lover wants to create, because he despises! What does he know of love who has not had to despise precisely what he loved!

With your love go into your isolation, and with your creating, my brother: and only later will righteousness limp along after you.

With my tears go into your isolation, my brother. I love him who wants to create beyond himself and thereby perishes.—

Thus spoke Zarathustra.

*   *   *

18. On Old and Young Little Women

'Why do you slink so shyly through the twilight, Zarathustra? And what are you hiding so carefully under your cloak?*

'Is it a treasure that has been given to you? Or a child that has been born to you? Or are you now yourself going the ways of thieves, you friend of evil-doers?'—

'Verily, my brother!' said Zarathustra, 'It is a treasure that has been given to me: a little truth it is that I am carrying.

'But it is unruly like a young child; and if I do not hold its mouth shut, it will cry over-loudly.

'Today as I was going my way alone, at the hour when the sun is sinking, I encountered a little old woman who talked thus to my soul:*

' "Much has Zarathustra spoken to us women too, yet he has never spoken to us about woman."

'And I replied to her: "About woman one should talk only to men."

' "Talk to me too about woman," she said; "I am old enough to forget it straight away."

'And so I did the little old woman's bidding and spoke to her thus:

'Everything about woman is a riddle, and everything about woman has a single solution: that is, pregnancy.

'The man is for the woman a means: the end is always the child. But what is the woman for the man?

'Two things a genuine man wants: danger and play. Therefore he wants woman, as the most dangerous plaything.

'A man should be brought up for war, and a woman for the recuperation of the warrior: all else is folly.

'All too-sweet fruits—these the warrior does not like. Therefore he likes woman: still bitter is even the sweetest woman.

'A woman understands children better than a man does, but a man is more childlike than a woman is.

'In a genuine man a child is hidden: it wants to play. Well, ladies, now find me the child in the man!

'Let woman be a plaything, pure and fine, like a precious stone, illumined by the virtues of a world that is not yet here.

'Let the light of a star shine in your love! Let your hope be: "May I give birth to the Overhuman!"

'In your love let there be bravery! With your love you shall go after the one that fills you with fear!

'In your love let there be your honour! Otherwise a woman understands little about honour. But let this be your honour: always to love more than you are loved, and never to be second.

'Let man fear woman when she loves: for then she makes every sacrifice, and every other thing to her is worthless.

'Let man fear woman when she hates: for a man is in the ground of his soul only wicked, while a woman there is base.

'Whom does woman hate the most?—Thus spoke the iron to the magnet: "I hate you the most because you attract, but are not strong enough to pull me to you."

'The happiness of a man is: I will. The happiness of a woman is: he wills.

' "Behold, just now the world became perfect!"*—thus thinks any woman who obeys out of total love.

'And a woman must obey and find a depth for her surface. Surface is woman's disposition, a stormily moving skin over shallow waters.

'But a man's disposition is deep, its torrent rushes through subterranean caves: a woman senses its strength, but does not comprehend it.—

'Then the little old woman replied to me: "Many charming things has Zarathustra said, and especially for those who are young enough for them.

' "It is strange, Zarathustra does not know women well, and yet he is right about them! Is this because with woman no thing is impossible?*

' "So now take as thanks a little truth! I am certainly old enough for it!

' "Wrap it up and hold its mouth shut: or else it will cry overloudly, this little truth."

' "Give me, old woman, your little truth!" I said. And thus spoke the little old woman:

' "You are going to women? Then don't forget the whip!" '—*

Thus spoke Zarathustra.

* *
* *

19. On the Bite of the Adder

One day Zarathustra had fallen asleep under a fig-tree, for it was hot, and had laid his arms over his face. Then came an adder and bit him in the neck, so that Zarathustra cried out in pain.* When he had taken his arm from his face he looked at the snake: it recognized Zarathustra's eyes, writhed awkwardly, and wanted to get away. 'Oh no,' said Zarathustra. 'You have not yet accepted my thanks! You woke me at the right time: my way is still long.' 'Your way will be short,' said the adder sadly. 'My poison is deadly.' Zarathustra smiled. 'When did a dragon ever die from the poison of a snake?'—he said. 'But take your poison back! You are not rich enough to bestow it on me.' Then the adder fell about his neck again and licked his wound.

When Zarathustra told this one day to his disciples, they asked: 'And what, O Zarathustra, is the moral of your story?' Zarathustra answered them thus:

'The annihilator of morals they call me, the good and the righteous: my story is immoral.

'But if you have an enemy, do not repay his evil with good: for that would put him to shame. But rather prove that he has done something good for you.

'And rather be angry than put to shame! And if someone curses you, it does not please me that you then want to bless. Rather join in a little with the cursing!*

'And should a great wrong be done to you, then quickly commit five little ones in return! Horrible to behold is the one who is alone oppressed by being wronged.

'Did you know this already? A wrong shared is a half right. And he should take upon himself being wronged who is able to bear it!

'A little revenge is more humane than no revenge at all. And if the punishment be not also a right and an honour for the transgressor, then I do not like your punishing either.

'More noble it is to declare oneself wrong than to insist that one is right, especially when one is in the right. Only one must be rich enough for it.

'I do not like your cold justice; and from the eye of your judges there gazes always the executioner and his cold steel.

'Tell me, where is the justice to be found that is love with seeing eyes?

'Then devise for me the love that bears not only all punishment but also all guilt!

'Then devise for me the justice that acquits everyone except the one who judges!

'Do you want to hear this too? With one who would be just from the ground up, even a lie becomes a case of philanthropy.

'But how could I want to be just from the ground up! How can I give to each his own! Let this suffice me: I give to each my own.

'Finally, my brothers, beware of doing wrong to any solitaries! How could a solitary forget! How could he requite!

'Like a deep well is the solitary. Easy it is to throw a stone in; but if it sink to the bottom, tell me, who will want to fetch it out again?

'Beware of offending the solitary! But if you have done so, then you had better kill him too!'*

Thus spoke Zarathustra.

*   *   *

20. On Children and Marriage

I have a question for you alone, my brother: I cast this question like a sounding-lead into your soul, that I may know how deep it is.

You are young and wish for a child and marriage. But I ask you now: are you a human being with the *right* to wish for a child?

Are you the victor, the self-compeller, commander of the senses, master of your virtues? Thus I ask you.

Or is it the beast and dire need that speak out of your wish? Or isolation? Or discord with yourself?

I would that your victory and your freedom might yearn for a child. Living monuments shall you build to your victory and your liberation.

Over and beyond yourself shall you build. But first you must be built yourself, four-square in body and soul.

Not only onward shall you propagate yourself, but upward! May the garden of marriage help you to do so!

A higher body shall you create, a first movement, a self-propelling wheel—a creator shall you create.

Marriage: thus I call the will of two to create the one that is more than those who created it. Reverence for each other I call marriage, as for the willers of such a will.

Let this be the sense and the truth of your marriage. But that which the many too many call marriage, these superfluous creatures—ah, what do I call that?

Ah, such poverty of soul in a couple! Ah, such filth of soul in a couple! Ah, such wretched contentment in a couple!

Marriage they call all this; and they say that their marriages are made in Heaven.

Well I like it not, this Heaven of the superfluous! No, I like them not, these animals entangled in a heavenly net!

May the God also stay far from me who limps up to bless what he did not join together!*

Do not laugh at such marriages! What child would not have reason to weep over his parents?

Worthy this man seemed to me and ripe for the sense of the earth: but when I saw his wife, the earth seemed to me a house for the nonsensical.

Yes, I would that the earth might tremble in convulsions when a holy man and a goose mate with each other.

This man set out like a hero after truths but ended up catching a little dressed-up lie. His marriage he calls it.

That man was reserved in his behaviour and chose selectively. But all at once he spoiled his company once and for all: his marriage he calls it.

That man sought a maid with the virtues of an angel. But all at once he became the maid of a woman, and now he needs to become an angel beyond that.

Cautious have I found all buyers now, and all of them have cunning eyes. But even the most cunning still buys his wife in a poke.

Many brief follies—that is what you call love. And your marriage puts an end to many brief follies, as one long stupidity.

Your love of woman and woman's love of man: ah, would that it were sympathizing with suffering and disguised Gods! But for the most part two animals find each other out.

But even your finest love is only a rapturous allegory and painful heat. A torch it is, that shall light your way to higher paths.

Over and beyond yourselves shall you love some day! So first *learn* to love! And for that you have had to drink the bitter cup of your love.

Bitterness is in the cup of even the finest love: thus it arouses yearning for the Overhuman, thus it arouses thirst in you, the creator!

Thirst for the creator, an arrow and yearning for the Overhuman: speak, my brother, is this your will to marriage?

Holy I call such a will and such marriage.—

Thus spoke Zarathustra.

*   *   *

21. On Free Death

Many die too late, and some die too early. The teaching sounds strange: 'Die at the right time!'

Die at the right time: thus teaches Zarathustra.

Of course, if one never lives at the right time, how could one ever die at the right time? Would that such a one had never been born!— Thus I counsel the superfluous.

But even the superfluous still make a great thing of their dying, and even the hollowest nut still wants to be cracked.

Everyone considers dying important, but death is as yet no festival. Human beings have not yet learned how to consecrate the most beautiful festivals.*

The consummating death I show to you, that becomes for the living a spur and a promise.

Whoever consummates his life dies his own death, victoriously, surrounded by hopers and promisers.

Thus should one learn to die; and there should be no festival where one dying this way does not consecrate oaths of the living!

To die thus is best; but second-best is: to die fighting and to squander a great soul.*

But just as hateful to the fighter as to the victor is your grinning death, which slinks up like a thief—and yet comes as Lord.*

My death I praise to you, the free death, which comes to me because *I* will it.

And when shall I will it?—Whoever has a goal and an heir wants death at the right time for his goal and heir.

And from reverence for his goal and heir he will hang no more withered wreaths in the sanctuary of life.

Verily, I do not want to be like the rope-makers: they drag out their threads at length and so are themselves always walking backwards.

Many a one grows too old even for his truths and victories; a toothless mouth no longer has the right to every truth.

And each one that wants fame must betimes take leave of honour and practise the difficult art of—going at the right time.

One must cease letting oneself be eaten when one tastes best: this is known by those who want to be loved for long.

Sour apples there are, of course, whose lot wills that they wait until the last day of autumn: and they become ripe, yellow, and shrivelled all at once.

In some the heart ages first and in others the spirit. And some are old in their youth: but those who are young late stay young long.

For many a one life turns out badly: a poison-worm eats at his heart. Let him see to it that his dying turns out that much better.

Many a one never becomes sweet, but turns rotten already in the summer. Cowardice is what keeps him on the branch.

Many too many live and hang on their branches far too long. Would that a storm might come to shake all this worm-eaten rot from the tree!

Would that there might come preachers of *quick* death! Those would be for me the right storms and shakers of trees of life! But I hear only slow death preached and patience with everything 'earthly'.

Ah, you preach patience with the earthly? It is the earthly that has too much patience with you, you scandal-mongers!

Verily, too early did that Hebrew die whom the preachers of slow death honour: and for many since then it has been a catastrophe that he died too early.

He still knew only tears and the heavy heart of the Hebrew, together with hatred on the part of the good and the righteous—the Hebrew Jesus:* then he was overcome by a yearning for death.

If only he had remained in the wilderness and far from the good and the righteous! Perhaps he would have learned to live and learned to love the earth—and to laugh as well!

Believe me, my brothers! He died too early; he himself would have retracted his teaching if he had reached my age! Noble enough was he to retract!

But he had not yet matured. Immature is the youth's love and immature his hatred of humans and earth too. Still bound and heavy are his disposition and the wings of his spirit.

But in the man there is more of the child than in the youth, and less heaviness of heart: he has a better understanding of death and life.

Free for death and free in death, a sacred Nay-sayer when it is no longer time for Yea: thus is his understanding of death and life.

That your dying be no blasphemy against humans and earth, my friends: that is what I ask from the honey of your souls.

In your dying shall your spirit and your virtue still glow, like a sunset around the earth: or else your dying will have turned out badly.

Thus would I myself die, that you friends might love the earth more for my sake; and into earth will I turn again, that I might rest in her who bore me.

Verily, Zarathustra had a goal, he threw his ball: now you friends are heirs of my goal, to you I throw the golden ball.

More than anything I like to see you, my friends, throwing the golden ball! And so I linger a little longer on earth: forgive me for that!

Thus spoke Zarathustra.

*   *   *

22. On the Bestowing Virtue

I

When Zarathustra had taken leave of the town to which his heart had become attached and whose name is 'The Motley Cow', many who called themselves his disciples followed him and gave him escort. Thus they came to a crossroads: there Zarathustra told them that he wanted to walk alone from then on, for he was a friend of walking alone. His disciples handed him in farewell a staff, on the golden haft of which a serpent was coiled around the sun.* Zarathustra was delighted with the staff and leaned upon it; then he spoke thus to his disciples.

'Tell me now: how did gold assume the highest value? Because it is uncommon and of no use and luminous and mild in its lustre; it always bestows itself.

'Only as an allegory of the highest virtue did gold assume the highest value. Gold-like shines the glance of the one who bestows. The gleam of gold makes peace between moon and sun.

'Uncommon is the highest virtue and of no use, luminous it is and mild in its lustre: a bestowing virtue is the highest virtue.

'Verily, I divine you well, my disciples: you are striving, as I am, for the bestowing virtue. What would you have in common with cats and wolves?*

'This is your thirst, to become sacrifices and bestowals yourselves: and therefore you thirst to pile up all riches in your souls.

'Insatiably your soul strives for treasures and jewels, because your virtue is insatiable in wanting to bestow.

'You compel all things toward you and into you, that they may flow back out of your wells as gifts of your love.

'Verily, a predator of all values must such a bestowing love become; but whole and holy do I call such selfishness.

'Another selfishness there is that is all-too-poor, and starving, and which always wants to steal; a selfishness of the sick, a sick selfishness.

'With the eye of the thief it looks at everything that shines; with the greed of hunger it measures him who has plenty to eat; and it is always skulking around the table of those who bestow.

'Sickness speaks from such desire, and invisible degeneration; of the sickly body does the thieving greed of this selfishness speak.

'Tell me, my brothers: what do we consider bad and worst of all? Is it not *degeneration?*—And degeneration is what we always suspect when the bestowing soul is lacking.

'Upward leads our way, from genus across to over-genus. But a horror to us is the degenerating sense that says: "All is for me."

'Upward flies our sense: thus it is an allegory of our body, an allegory of elevation. Allegories of such elevations are the names of the virtues.

'Thus the body goes through history, becoming and fighting. And the spirit—what is that to the body? The herald, comrade, and echo of its conflicts and victories.

'Allegories are all names of good and evil: they do not express, they merely hint. A fool is he who wants knowledge of them!

'Pay heed now, my brothers, to every hour where your spirit wants to speak in allegories: there lies the origin of your virtue.

'Elevated is your body then and resurrected; with its rapture it delights the spirit, so that it becomes creator and evaluator and lover and benefactor of all things.

'When your hearts surge broad and full like a river, a blessing and danger to those who dwell nearby: there lies the origin of your virtue.

'When you are elevated above praise and blame, and your will would command all things, as the will of a lover: there lies the origin of your virtue.

'When you despise what is pleasant and the soft bed, and cannot bed down far enough away from the soft-hearted: there lies the origin of your virtue.

'When you are willers of one will, and this turning of all need is for you called necessity:* there lies the origin of your virtue.

'Verily, this is a new good and evil! Verily, a new and deeper rushing and the voice of a new source!

'Power it is, this new virtue; a ruling thought it is, and around it a clever soul: a golden sun, and around it the serpent of knowledge.'

*   *   *

2

Here Zarathustra fell silent for a while and looked with love upon his disciples. Then he continued to talk thus:—and his voice was transformed.

'Stay true to the earth for me, my brothers, with the power of your virtue! May your bestowing love and your understanding serve the sense of the earth! Thus I bid and beseech you.

'Do not let it fly away from the earthly and beat its wings against eternal walls! Ah, there has always been so much flown-away virtue!

'Lead, as I do, the flown-away virtue back to the earth—yes, back to body and life: that it may give the earth its sense, a human sense!

'In a hundred ways up to now has spirit as well as virtue flown away and made mistakes. Ah, in our bodies all this delusion and mistaking still dwell: body and will it has become there.

'In a hundred ways up to now has spirit as well as virtue experimented and gone astray. Yes, the human has been an experiment. Ah, much ignorance and error has become body in us!

'Not only the reason of millennia—but also their madness breaks out in us. Dangerous it is to be an heir.

'Still we fight step for step with the giant Chance, and over the whole of humanity there has reigned so far only nonsense, no sense.

'May your spirit and your virtue serve the sense of the earth, my brothers: and may the value of all things be posited anew by you! For that you shall be fighters! For that you shall be creators!

'Through knowing, the body purifies itself; experimenting with knowing, it elevates itself; for the one who understands, all drives sanctify themselves; for the one who is elevated, the soul becomes joyful.

'Physician, heal thyself:* thus will you heal your patient too. May this be his best remedy, that he might see with his own eyes one who makes himself whole.

'A thousand paths there are that have never yet been trodden; a thousand healths and hidden islands of life. Unexhausted and undiscovered are the human and human earth even now.

'Wake up and listen, you who are lonely! From out of the future come winds with stealthy beatings of wings; and for delicate ears there come glad tidings.

'You lonely ones of today, who withdraw to the side, you shall one day be a people: out of you, who have chosen yourselves, shall a chosen people grow:*—and out of them the Overhuman.

'Verily, a site of convalescence shall the earth yet become! And already a new fragrance wafts about it, bringing health—and a new hope!'

*   *   *

3

When Zarathustra had said these words, he was silent like one who has not said his last word; for a long time he weighed his staff doubtfully in his hand. At last he spoke thus:—and his voice was transformed.

'Alone I go now, my disciples! You too must go away now, and alone.* Thus I will it.

'Verily, I counsel you: go away from me and guard yourselves against Zarathustra! And better still: be ashamed of him! Perhaps he has deceived you.

'The man of understanding must be able not only to love his enemies, but also to hate his friends.

'One repays a teacher poorly if one always remains only a student. And why would you not pluck at my wreath?

'You revere me; but what if your reverence should some day collapse? Be careful lest a statue fall and kill you!*

'You say you believe in Zarathustra? But what does Zarathustra matter? You are my believers: but what do any believers matter?

'You had not yet sought yourselves: then you found me. Thus do all believers: that is why all belief is worth so little.

'Now I bid you lose me and find yourselves; and only when you have all denied me will I return to you.*

'Verily, with different eyes, my brothers, shall I then seek my lost ones; with a different love shall I then love you.

'And once more you shall have become my friends and children of one hope: then will I be with you for the third time, that I may celebrate the Great Midday with you.

'And this is the Great Midday, when the human stands in the middle of its path between beast and Overhuman and celebrates its way to evening as its highest hope: for it is the way to a new morning.

'Then will the one who goes under bless himself, that he may be one who goes over; and the sun of his understanding will stand at midday for him.

' *"Dead are all Gods:"** now we want the Overhuman to live"—may this be at the Great Midday our ultimate will!'—

Thus spoke Zarathustra.

*   *   *

SECOND PART

'—and only when you have all denied me will I return to you. Verily, with different eyes, my brothers, shall I then seek my lost ones; with a different love shall I then love you.'*

(*Zarathustra*, 'On the Bestowing Virtue')

1. The Child With the Mirror

Thereupon Zarathustra went back into the mountains again and to the solitude of his cave and withdrew from human beings: waiting like a sower who has cast forth his seed.* But his soul became full of impatience and desire for those whom he loved: for he still had a great deal to give them. This indeed is what is hardest: out of love to close the open hand and to preserve one's modesty as a bestower.

Thus months and years passed by for the lonely one; but his wisdom grew and caused him pain with its fullness.

One morning, however, he awoke well before dawn of morning, lay on his pallet for a long time in thought, and spoke at last to his heart:

'Why was I so frightened in my dream that I awoke? Did a child not come to me carrying a mirror?

' "O Zarathustra"—the child said to me—"Look at yourself in the mirror!"

'But when I looked in the mirror I cried out, and my heart was shaken: for it was not myself that I saw there, but a Devil's grimace and mocking laughter.

'Verily, all too well do I understand the dream's omen and admonition: my *teaching* is in danger, and weeds would be called wheat!*

'My enemies have grown powerful and have distorted the image of my teaching, such that my dearest ones must be ashamed of the gifts I have given them.

'My friends are lost to me; the hour has come for me to seek my lost ones!'—

With these words Zarathustra sprang up, but not like one who is anxious and gasps for air, but rather like a seer and singer who is overtaken by the spirit. Amazed, his eagle and his serpent looked upon him: for like dawn of morning an imminent happiness lay upon his countenance.

'What has happened to me, my animals?'—said Zarathustra. 'Am I not transformed! Did blissfulness not just come to me like a storm-wind?

'Foolish is my happiness and foolish things it will say: it is still too young—so have patience with it!

'Wounded am I by my happiness: all sufferers shall be my physicians!

'To my friends I now may go down again and also to my enemies! Zarathustra may speak again and bestow and do what is dearest for those dear to him!

'My impatient love overflows in torrents, downwards, toward rising and setting.* Out of silent mountains and thunderstorms of pain my soul rushes into the valleys.

'Too long have I yearned and looked into the distance. Too long have I belonged to solitude: thus I have unlearned being silent.

'Mouth have I become through and through, and the roaring of a stream out of towering cliffs: down into the valleys will I plunge my speech.

'And may the river of my love plunge through impassable places! How should a river not at last find its way to the sea!*

'Indeed a lake is within me, solitary and self-contained; but the river of my love draws it off—down to the sea!

'New ways I walk now, a new talk comes to me: weary have I grown, like all creators, of the old tongues. No longer does my spirit want to wander on worn-out soles.

'Too slowly runs all talking for me:—into your chariot I leap, storm! And even you would I whip on with my wickedness!

'Like a cry and jubilation will I voyage over distant seas, till I find the Isles of the Blest* where my friends are dwelling:—

'And my enemies among them! How I now love anyone to whom I may simply talk! Even my enemies belong to my blissfulness.

'And whenever I want to mount my wildest steed, it is always my spear that helps me up the best: it is the ever-ready servant of my foot:—

'The spear that I hurl against my enemies! How I now thank my enemies that I may finally hurl it!

'Too great has been the tension of my cloud: between peals of lightning-laughter I want to cast hail-showers into the depths.

'Mightily will my breast then heave, mightily will it blow its storm over the mountains: thus it will attain relief.

'Verily, like a storm my happiness comes and my freedom! But my enemies shall think that *the Evil One* is raging over their heads.*

'Yes, you too will be terrified, my friends, by my Wild Wisdom; and perhaps you will flee from her along with my enemies.

'Ah, if only I knew how to lure you back with shepherds' flutes! Ah, if only my lioness Wisdom could learn to roar tenderly! And much have we already learned together!

'My Wild Wisdom became pregnant on lonely mountains; on roughest rocks she bore her young, her youngest.

'Now she runs foolishly through the harsh desert, and seeks and seeks for a soft greensward—my old Wild Wisdom!

'On the soft greensward of your hearts, my friends!—on your love she would like to bed down her dearest!'

Thus spoke Zarathustra.

* * *

2. Upon the Isles of the Blest*

The figs are falling from the trees, they are good and sweet; and as they fall, their red skins burst. A north wind am I to all ripe figs.*

And thus, like figs, these teachings fall to you, my friends: now drink their juice and their sweet flesh! Autumn is all around and clear sky and afternoon.

Behold, what fullness is about us! And from out of such overflow it is beautiful to look out upon distant seas.

Once one said 'God' when one looked upon distant seas; but now I have taught you to say: Overhuman.

God is a supposition; but I would that your supposing might not reach farther than your creative will.

Could you *create* a God?—Then do not speak to me of any Gods! But you could surely create the Overhuman.

Perhaps not you yourselves, my brothers! But into fathers and forefathers of the Overhuman you could re-create yourselves: and may this be your finest creating!—

God is a supposition: but I would that your supposing might be limited by what is thinkable.

Could you then *think* a God?—But let will to truth mean this to you: that everything be transformed into what is humanly thinkable, humanly visible, humanly feelable! Your own senses you shall think through to the end!

And what you have called world, that shall be created only by you: your reason, your image, your will, your love it shall itself become! And verily, for your own blissfulness, you who understand!

And how could you want to endure life without this hope, you who understand? Neither into the incomprehensible nor the irrational could you have been born.

But that I might reveal my heart to you completely, dear friends: *if* there were Gods, how could I stand not to be a God! *Therefore* there are no Gods.

Well did I draw that conclusion; but now it draws me.—

God is a supposition: but who could drink down all the anguish of this supposition without dying? Shall the creator be deprived of his belief and the eagle of his soaring into eagle-distances?

God is a thought that makes all that is straight crooked and all that stands twist and turn. What? Time should be gone and all impermanence a mere lie?

To think this is a whirlwind and dizziness for human bones, and a vomiting for the stomach too: verily, the turning sickness I call it, to suppose such a thing.

Evil I call it and hostile to the human: all this teaching about the One and Plenum and Unmoved and Complete and Permanent!

All permanence—that is mere allegory!* And the poets lie too much.—

But of time and becoming shall the finest allegories tell: a praising shall they be and a justification of all impermanence!

Creating—that is the great redemption from suffering, and life's becoming lighter. But that the creator may be, that itself requires suffering and much transformation.

Yes, much bitter dying must there be in your lives, you creators! Thus are you advocates and justifiers of all impermanence.

For the creator to be himself the child that is newly born, he must also want to be the birth-giver and the pain of the birth-giver.

Verily, through a hundred souls I have gone my way and through a hundred cradles and pangs of birth. Many a leave have I taken already: I know the heart-rending final hours.*

But thus does my creating will, my fate, will it. Or, to say it more honestly: precisely such a fate—does my will will.

All that is sentient suffers through me and is in prisons: but my willing always comes to me as my liberator and joy-bringer.

Willing liberates: that is the true teaching of will and freedom—thus does Zarathustra teach it to you.

Willing-no-more and valuing-no-more and creating-no-more! Ah, that such great weariness might remain ever far from me!

In understanding, too, I feel only my will's joy in begetting and becoming; and if there be innocence in my understanding, that is because the will to beget is in it.

Away from God and Gods this will has lured me: what would there be to create if Gods—existed!

But to the human being it drives me again and again, my fervent creating-will; thus is the hammer driven to the stone.

Ah, you humans, in the stone there sleeps an image, the image of my images! Ah, that it must sleep in the hardest, ugliest stone!

Now my hammer rages fiercely against the prison. Fragments fly from the stone: what is that to me?

I want to perfect it: for a shadow came to me—of all things the stillest and lightest once came to me!

The beauty of the Overhuman came to me as a shadow. Ah, my brothers! What are the Gods to me now!—

Thus spoke Zarathustra.

*   *   *

3. On Those Who Pity

My friends, mocking talk has reached the ears of your friend: 'Just look at Zarathustra! Does he not wander among us as if among beasts?'

But it is better to talk thus: 'One who understands wanders among humans *as* among beasts.'

But for one who understands, the human being itself is: the beast that has red cheeks.*

How did this happen? Is it not because it has too often had to be ashamed?

Oh my friends! Thus speaks one who understands: Shame, shame, shame—that is the history of the human!

And therefore the noble bids himself not to shame others: he bids himself have shame before all that suffers.

Verily, I do not like them, the merciful, who are blessèd in their pitying:* too lacking are they in shame.

If I must have pity, then I do not want to be called such; and if I do have pity, then rather from a distance.

Gladly do I even cover my head and flee, before I can be recognized: and thus I bid you do too, my friends!

May my fate always lead non-sufferers, like you, across my path, and those with whom I *may* have hope and repast and honey in common!

Verily, I may have done this and that for sufferers: but better things it seemed I always did when I learned to enjoy myself better.

Ever since there have been human beings, they have enjoyed themselves too little: that alone, my brothers, is our original sin!

And if we learn to enjoy ourselves better, so do we best unlearn our hurting of others and our planning hurts for them.

Therefore I wash my hand if it has helped a sufferer; therefore I wipe my soul clean too.

Having seen the sufferer suffer, I was ashamed on account of his shame; and when I helped him, then I sorely injured his pride.

Acts of great kindness do not make people grateful, but rather vengeful; and if the small favour is not forgotten, it turns into a gnawing worm.*

'Be reserved in accepting! Confer distinction when you accept!'— thus I counsel those who have nothing to bestow.

But I myself am a bestower: I bestow gladly, as a friend to friends. But let strangers and the poor pluck the fruit from my tree themselves: that will make them less ashamed.

Beggars, however, should be abolished altogether! Verily, it is annoying to give to them and annoying not to give to them.

And likewise sinners and bad consciences! Believe me, my friends: pangs of conscience give people fangs.

But the worst of all are petty thoughts. Verily, better even to have done something wicked than to have thought something petty!

Of course you say: 'Pleasure in petty wickedness saves us from many a great evil deed.' But here one should not want to save.

Like a boil is the evil deed: it itches and irritates and then breaks out—it talks honestly.

'Behold, I am sickness'—thus talks the evil deed; that is its honesty.

But the petty thought is like a fungus: it crawls and cringes and wants to be nowhere—until the whole body is rotten and withered with little fungi.

But to him who is possessed by the Devil, this word I say in his ear: 'Better to bring your Devil up to be big! For you, too, there is still a way to greatness!'—

Ah, my brothers! One knows a little too much about everyone! And many a one becomes transparent to us, yet for that reason we still cannot get through him.

It is hard to live with human beings because being silent is so hard.

And not toward him who is repugnant to us are we most unfair, but toward him who means nothing to us.

But if you have a friend who is suffering, then be for his suffering a resting-place, yet as it were a hard bed, a camp-bed: thus will you serve him best.

And if a friend should do you wrong, then say: 'I forgive you what you did to me; but that you did it to *yourself*—how could I forgive that!'

Thus does all great love talk: it overcomes even forgiveness and pitying.

One should hold on to one's heart; for if one lets it go, how soon one then loses one's head!

Ah, where in the world has there been more foolishness than among those who pity? And what in the world has caused more suffering than the foolishness of those who pity?*

Woe to all lovers who do not still have a height that is above their pitying!

Thus spoke the Devil to me once: 'God too has his Hell: it is his love for human beings.'

And lately I heard him say this word too: 'God is dead; it is of his pity for human beings that God has died.'—

Be warned then against pitying: *from there* will a heavy cloud yet come to human beings! Verily, I understand weather-signs well!

But mark this word too: All great love is still above all its pitying: for it still wants to—*create* what is loved!

'Myself I sacrifice to my love, *and my neighbour like me**—thus goes the talk of all creators.

All creators, however, are hard.—

Thus spoke Zarathustra.

*   *   *

4. On the Priests

And one time Zarathustra made a sign to his disciples and spoke these words to them:

'Here are some priests: and although they are my enemies, pass them by quietly and with a sleeping sword!

'Among them too are heroes; many of them suffered too much— so they want to make others suffer.

'Evil enemies are they: nothing is more vengeful than their humility. And whoever attacks them will easily besmirch himself.

'Yet my blood is related to theirs; and I would know that my blood is honoured even in theirs.'—

And when they had passed by, Zarathustra was assailed by pain; and he had not long wrestled with his pain when he began to talk thus:

'I am sorry for these priests. They also go against my taste; but that is the least of my troubles since I have been among human beings.

'But I suffer and have suffered with them: prisoners are they to me and marked men. The one they call Redeemer has cast them into bondage:—

'Into bondage of false values and delusive words! Ah, that someone might yet redeem them from their redeemer!*

'They once thought that they had landed on an islet, when the sea was tossing them about; but behold, it was a sleeping monster!

'False values and delusive words: these are the worst monsters for mortals—long does catastrophe sleep and wait within them.

'But at last it comes and awakens and engulfs and devours whatever has built huts on it.

'Oh just look at these huts that these priests built for themselves! Churches they call their sweet-smelling caves.

'Oh what falsified light, what musty air! Here the soul to its heights may—not fly up!

'Rather thus does their faith command: "Up the steps on your knees, ye sinners!"*

'Verily, I would rather see one who is shameless than the contorted eyes of their shame and devotion!

'Who made for themselves such caves and penitence-steps? Was it not such as wanted to conceal themselves and were ashamed before the clear sky?

'And only when the clear sky again looks through broken ceilings, and down onto grass and red poppies on broken walls—will I turn my heart again to the abodes of this God.

'They have called God whatever contradicted and hurt them: and verily, there was much of the heroic in their adoration!

'And they knew no other way to love their God than by nailing the human being to the Cross!

'As corpses they meant to live, in black they decked out their corpse; in their speeches, too, I still smell the foul aroma of death-chambers.

'And whoever lives near to them lives near black ponds, from which the ominous toad sings its song with sweet profundity.

'Better songs they would have to sing to make me believe in their Redeemer: more redeemed would his disciples have to appear!

'Naked should I like to see them: for beauty alone should preach penitence. But whom could this masquerading misery ever persuade!

'Verily, their redeemers did not themselves come from freedom and from freedom's seventh Heaven! Verily, they themselves have never walked upon the carpets of understanding!

'Of gaps the spirit of these redeemers consisted; but into every gap they put their *delusion*, their stop-gap, which they called God.

'In their pitying their spirit had drowned, and whenever they swelled and overswelled with pitying, there always swam to the surface a prodigious folly.

'Zealously and with much shouting they drove their herd over their bridge: as if to the future there were but one bridge! Verily, these herdsmen themselves still belonged among the sheep!

'Little minds and capacious souls these shepherds had: but, my brothers, what little domains have even the most capacious souls been up to now!

'Blood-signs they wrote on the way that they walked, and their folly taught that one proves the truth with blood.

'But blood is the worst witness of truth; blood poisons the purest teaching, turning it into hearts' delusion and hate.

'And if one goes through the fire for one's teaching—what does that prove! It is more, verily, if one's own teaching comes out of one's own blaze!

'Sultry heart and cold head: where these come together there arises the roaring wind, the "Redeemer".

'Greater men have there been, verily, and higher born than those whom the people call redeemers, those roaring winds that carry one away!

'And from still greater men than all redeemers have been must you, my brothers, be redeemed, if you would find the way to freedom!

'Never yet has there been an Overhuman. Naked have I seen both, the greatest and the smallest human:—

'All-too-similar are they to each other still. Verily, even the greatest did I find—all-too-human!'—

Thus spoke Zarathustra.

*   *   *

5. On the Virtuous

One needs thunder and heavenly fireworks to address slack and sleepy senses.

But the voice of beauty talks softly: it slips into only the most awakened souls.

Gently my shield* trembled and laughed to me today; that is beauty's sacred laughter and trembling.

At you, you virtuous men, my beauty laughed today. And thus its voice came to me: 'They want moreover—to be paid!'

You want moreover to be paid, you virtuous ones! You want rewards for virtue and Heavens for earths and the eternal for your today?

And now you are angry with me for teaching that there is no reward- and pay-master? And verily, I do not even teach that virtue is its own reward.

Ah, this is my sorrow: they have lied reward and punishment into the ground of things—and now even into the ground of your souls, you virtuous ones!

But like the snout of the boar shall my words tear open the ground of your souls; ploughshare I want you to call me.

All the secrets of your ground shall come to light; and when you lie churned and broken up in the sun, your falsehood will also be separated from your truth.

For this is your truth: you are too *cleanly* for the filth of the words revenge, punishment, reward, retribution.

You love your virtue as the mother her child; but whoever heard of a mother's wanting to be paid for her loving?

It is your dearest self, your virtue. The thirst of the ring is in you: to reach itself once again, that is what every ring strives and turns for.

And like a dying star is every work of your virtue: its light is always still under way and wandering—and when will it ever be under way no longer?

Thus is the light of your virtue still under way, even when the work has been done. Though it may now be forgotten and dead, its beam of light still lives and wanders.

That your virtue may be your Self and not something foreign, a skin, a covering: that is the truth from the ground of your souls, you virtuous ones!—

But there are surely those for whom virtue is a spasm under the whip: and you have listened too much to their cries!

And others there are who call it virtue when their vices grow lazy; and if their hatred and their jealousy should stretch their limbs to rest, their 'righteousness' then wakes up and rubs its sleepy eyes.

And others there are who are drawn downward: their Devils drag them. But the farther they sink down, the more brightly glows their eye and the desire for their God.

Ah, their outcry too has reached your ears, you virtuous men: 'What I am *not*, that, that to me is God and virtue!'

And others there are who go along heavy and creaking, like carts that carry rocks downhill: they talk much of dignity and virtue— their brakes are what they call virtue!

And others there are who are like regular clocks that have been wound up; they go tick-tock and want that tick-tock to be called— their virtue.

Verily, with these I have my pleasure: when I find such clocks I shall wind them up with my mockery; and then they shall purr for me!

And others are proud of their handful of justice and for its sake commit outrages against all things, such that the world is drowned in their injustice.

Ah, how awful the word 'virtue' sounds from their mouths! And when they say: 'I am just', it always sounds like: 'I am just avenged!'*

With their virtue they want to claw out the eyes of their enemies; and they exalt themselves only in order to abase others.*

And then again there are such as sit in their swamp and talk thus from out of the rushes: 'Virtue—that is to sit quietly in one's swamp.

'We bite nobody and keep out of the way of him who wants to bite; and in all things we hold the opinion that is given us.'

And then again there are such as love gestures and think that virtue is a kind of gesture.

Their knees are always worshipping, and their hands are glorifications of virtue, but their hearts know nothing of it.

And then again there are such as consider it virtue to say, 'Virtue is necessary'; but basically they believe only that police are necessary.

And many a one who cannot see what is lofty in the human calls it virtue that he sees its baseness all-too-closely: thus he calls his evil eye virtue.

And some want to be edified and raised up, and call that virtue; while others want to be bowled over—and call that virtue too.

And in this way almost all believe that they have a share in virtue; and at the very least everyone wants to be an expert on 'good' and 'evil'.

But not for this has Zarathustra come, to say to all these liars and fools: 'What do *you* know about virtue! What *could* you know about virtue!'—

But rather so that you, my friends, might grow weary of the old words that you learned from the fools and liars:

Grow weary of the words 'reward', 'retribution', 'punishment', 'revenge in righteousness'—

Grow weary of saying: 'What makes an action good is that it is unselfish.'

Ah, my friends! That *your* Self be in the action, as the mother is in the child: let that be *your* word about virtue!

Verily, I have indeed taken from you a hundred words and your virtue's favourite playthings; and now you are angry with me, as children are angry.

They were playing by the sea—then came a wave and snatched their plaything into the deep: now they are crying.

But the same wave shall bring them new playthings and shower new colourful seashells before them!

Thus will they be consoled; and like them shall you too, my friends, have your consolations—and new colourful seashells!—

Thus spoke Zarathustra.

* * *

6. On the Rabble

Life is a fount of pleasure; but where the rabble drinks too, there all wells are poisoned.

Of all that is cleanly I am fond; but I do not like to see the grinning maws and the thirst of the unclean.

They cast their eye down into the well: now their repulsive smiling shines up at me from the well.

The holy water they have poisoned with their lechery; and when they called their filthy dreams pleasure, they even poisoned words too.

Reluctant the flame becomes when they put their moist hearts to the fire; the spirit itself seethes and smokes wherever the rabble approaches the fire.

Sweetish and overly soft does the fruit turn in their hands: wind-brittle and top-withered does their glance make the fruit-tree.

And many a one who turned away from life only turned away from the rabble: he did not want to share the well and flame and fruit with the rabble.

And many a one who went into the desert and suffered thirst with beasts of prey only wanted not to sit around the cistern with filthy camel-drivers.

And many a one who came like an annihilator and like a hailstorm to all orchards only wanted to put his foot in the jaws of the rabble and thereby to stop up its throat.

And this is not the mouthful on which I choked the worst, to know that for life itself enmity is needed and dying and torture-crosses:—

But once I asked, and almost choked on my question: what? is the rabble, too, *needed* for life?

Are poisoned wells needed and stinking fires and dirt-soiled dreams and maggots in the bread of life?

Not my hatred but my disgust gnawed hungrily at my life! Ah, I often grew weary of the spirit when I found that even the rabble was spirited.

And I turned my back on the rulers when I saw what they now call ruling: haggling and bargaining for power—with the rabble!

Among peoples of foreign tongues I dwelled, with closed ears:* that their haggling tongues might remain foreign to me and their bargaining for power.

And holding my nose, I wandered disgruntled through all of yesterday and today: verily, all of yesterday and today smells foully of the writing rabble!

Like a cripple who has gone deaf and blind and dumb: thus have I lived for long, that I might not live with the power- and writing- and pleasure-rabble.

Laboriously my spirit climbed up steps, and cautiously; alms of pleasure were its refreshment; on a staff did life creep along for the blind man.

Yet what happened to me? How did I redeem myself from disgust? Who rejuvenated my eye? How did I fly to heights where no more rabble sits at the well?

Did my disgust itself create wings for me and water-divining powers? Verily, into the highest heights I had to fly, that I might find again the fount of pleasure!

And find it I did, my brothers! Here in the heights the fount of pleasure wells up for me! And there is a life at which no rabble drinks too!

Almost too violently you stream for me, spring of pleasure! And often you empty the cup again, through wanting so much to fill it!

And still must I learn to approach you more moderately: all too violently does my heart still stream toward you:—

My heart, upon which my summer burns, short, hot, heavy-hearted, over-blissful: how my summer-heart craves your coolness!

Gone the hesitant sorrow of my spring! Passed on the wickedness of my snowflakes in June!* Summer have I become entirely and summer-midday!

A summer in the highest heights, with cold springs and blissful stillness: oh come, my friends, that the stillness might become even more blissful!

For these are *our* heights and our home: too high and boldly we live here for all unclean creatures and their thirst.

Just cast your clear eyes into the fount of my pleasure, you friends! How could that make it turbid! It shall laugh back to you with *its* own clarity.

In the tree called Future we build our nests; eagles shall bring to us lonely ones victuals in their beaks!

Verily, no victuals that the unclean might share with us! They would think that they were eating fire and would burn their mouths!

Verily, no homes do we hold ready here for the unclean! To their bodies our happiness would be an ice-cave, and to their spirits too!

And like strong winds we would live above them, neighbours to eagles, neighbours to snow, neighbours to the sun:* thus do strong winds always live.

And like a wind I would blow them asunder one day and with my spirit take their spirit's breath away: thus my future wills it.

Verily, a strong wind is Zarathustra to all low-lying lands; and this counsel does he give to his enemies and to all that spits and spews: 'Beware of spitting *into* the wind!'

Thus spoke Zarathustra.

*   *   *

7. On the Tarantulas

Look, there is the tarantula's hole! Do you want to see her in person? Here is her web: touch it so that it trembles.

Now she comes willingly: Welcome, tarantula! Your triangle and omen sits black upon your back; and I know too what sits within your soul.

Revenge sits within your soul: wherever you bite, there grow black scabs; with revenge your poison makes the soul whirl round!

Thus I talk to you in a parable, you who make people's souls whirl round, you preachers of *equality!* Tarantulas you are to me, and hidden vengeance-seekers!

But now I want to bring your hiding-places to light: therefore I laugh in your visages my laughter of the heights.

Therefore I rake your webs, that your rage might bring you out of your holes of lies, and your revenge jump out from behind your word 'justice'.

For *that humanity might be redeemed from revenge*: that is for me the bridge to the highest hope and a rainbow after lasting storms.

But of course the tarantulas want it otherwise. 'This precisely is what justice is for us, that the world be filled with the storms of our revenge'—thus they talk among themselves.

'Revenge we will practise and defamation of all who are not the same as us'—thus the tarantula-hearts vow to themselves.

'And "will to equality"—just that shall henceforth be the name for virtue; and against all that has power we will raise our outcry!'

You preachers of equality, the tyrants' madness of impotence cries out of you thus for 'equality': your most secret tyrants' desires disguise themselves thus in words of virtue!

Soured arrogance, repressed envy, perhaps the arrogance and envy of your fathers: they burst forth from you as flames and the madness of revenge.

What the father kept silent, that comes in the son to be spoken; and often I found the son to be the father's unveiled secret.

Enthusiasts they resemble: yet it is not the heart that inspires them—but rather revenge. And if they become refined and cold, it is not the spirit, but rather envy, that makes them refined and cold.

Their jealousy even leads them onto thinkers' paths; and this is the real mark of their jealousy—they always go too far: so that their weariness at last has to lie down to sleep, even on snow.

From each of their complaints sounds revenge, in their every eulogy is an infliction of pain; and to be judges seems to them the highest bliss.

Thus, however, I counsel you, my friends: Mistrust all in whom the drive to punish is powerful!

They are folk of poor breed and stock; out of their faces leer the executioner and the bloodhound.

Mistrust all those who talk much about their justice! Verily, it is not only honey that their souls are lacking.

And when they call themselves 'the good and the righteous', do not forget that nothing is lacking to make them Pharisees—except power!

My friends, I do not want to be confused and confounded with others.

There are some who preach my teaching of life: and at the same time they are preachers of equality, and tarantulas.

That they talk in favour of life even though they sit in their holes, these poison-spiders, turned away from life: this means they want thereby to cause pain.

They want to cause pain in those who now have power: for among these is the preaching of death still most at home.

Were it otherwise, the tarantulas would then teach otherwise: and they themselves were formerly the best world-slanderers and heretic-burners.

With these preachers of equality I will not be confused and con- founded. For thus does justice talk *to me*: 'Human beings are not equal.'

And they shall not become so either! For what would my love for the Overhuman be if I spoke otherwise?

On a thousand bridges and footpaths they shall throng toward the future, and more and more shall war and inequality be set amongst them: thus does my great love make me talk!

Devisers of images and spectres they shall become in their enmities, and with their images and spectres they shall yet fight the highest fight against themselves!

Good and evil, and rich and poor, and high and lowly, and all the names of values: weapons they shall be and clashing signs that life must itself overcome itself again and again!

Into the heights life wants to build itself with pillars and steps, this life itself: into far distances it will gaze, and out toward blissful sights of beauty—*therefore* it needs the heights!

And because it needs the heights it needs steps and opposition among steps and climbers! To climb is what life wills, and in climbing to overcome itself.

And now please look, my friends! Here, where the tarantula's hole is, the ruins of an ancient temple rise upward—look now for me with enlightened eyes!

Verily, whoever once towered up his thoughts in stone here knew about the secret of all life as much as the wisest!

That struggle and inequality are present even in beauty, and war for power and over-power: this he teaches us here in the clearest allegory.

How divinely vaults and arches break through each other here, as if in a wrestling-ring: how they strive against each other with light and shadow, these divine strivers—

Assured and beautiful as these, let us be enemies too, my friends! Divinely we want to strive *against* each other!—

Alas! The tarantula just bit me, my old enemy! Divinely assured and beautiful, she bit me on the finger!

'Punishment must there be and justice'—thus she thinks: 'not in vain shall he sing songs here in honour of enmity!'

Yes, she has just avenged herself! And alas! now she will make my soul too whirl round with revenge!

But so that I do *not* whirl round, my friends, tie me fast to this column here! Rather would I even be a stylite than a whirlpool of vengeance!*

Verily, no turning whirlwind is Zarathustra; and if he is a dancer, then never a tarantella-dancer!—

Thus spoke Zarathustra.

* * *

8. On the Famous Wise Men

The people you have served and the people's superstitions, all you famous wise men!—and *not* the truth! And for just that reason they paid you reverence.

And for that reason too they tolerated your unbelief, because it was for the people a joke and detour. Thus the master indulges his slaves and even takes delight in their exuberance.

But the one who is hateful to the people as a wolf is to dogs: that is the free spirit, enemy of fetters, the non-worshipper, the dweller in forests.

To hound him out of his lair—that has always been for the people 'the sense for what is right': and against him they still always set their sharpest-toothed dogs.

'For the truth is already here: for after all, the people is here! Woe, woe to those who seek!'—thus has it echoed through the ages.

You wanted to justify your people in their revering: that you called 'will to truth', you famous wise men!

And your hearts always said to themselves: 'From the people I have come: from there came to me also the voice of God.'*

Stubborn and clever, like the ass, you have always been the people's advocates.

And many a powerful man who wanted to fare well with the people harnessed in front of his steeds—a little ass, a famous wise man.

And now I would like for you, famous wise men, at long last to throw off the lion's skin altogether!

The skin of the beast of prey, brightly mottled, and the matted locks of the explorer, the seeker, the conqueror!

Ah, for me to believe in your 'truthfulness' you would first have to break your reverential will.

Truthful—thus I call the one who goes into Godless deserts and has broken his reverential heart.

In the yellow sands and burned by the sun he will squint thirstily at the islands rich in springs, where living beings repose beneath dark trees.

But his thirst does not persuade him to become like those comfortable creatures: for where there are oases, there are also images of idols.

Ravenous, violent, solitary, Godless: thus does the lion-will want itself.

Free from the happiness of vassals, redeemed from Gods and adorations, fearless and fearsome, great and solitary: such is the will of him who is truthful.

It is always in deserts that the truthful have dwelt, the free spirits, as the desert's masters; but it is in cities that the well-nourished, famous wise men dwell—the draught animals.

For they always draw, as asses—the *people's* cart!

Not that I am angry with them for that: but servants they remain for me, in harness, however brightly their golden harnesses may shine.

And often were they good servants and praiseworthy. For thus speaks virtue: 'If you have to serve, then seek the one to whom your service is of most use!

'The spirit and virtue of your master shall thrive through your being his servant: then you yourself will thrive with his spirit and his virtue!'

And verily, you famous wise men, you servants of the people! You yourselves have thrived with the people's spirit and virtue—and the people through you! To your own honour I say this!

But you are still of the people even with your virtues, a people with weakened eyes—a people that does not know what *spirit* is!

Spirit is the life that itself cuts into life: through its own torment it increases its own knowledge—did you already know that?

And the spirit's happiness is this: to be anointed and consecrated through tears as a sacrificial animal—did you already know that?

And the blindness of the blind man and his seeking and tapping shall yet bear witness to the power of the sun into which he gazed*— did you already know that?

And with mountains shall the one who understands learn *to build!* A small thing it is for the spirit to move mountains*—did you already know that?

You know only the spirit's sparks: you do not see the anvil that it is, nor the ferocity of its hammer!

Verily, you do not know the spirit's pride! But even less could you bear the spirit's modesty, should it ever want to talk!

And never yet could you cast your spirit into a pit of snow: you are not hot enough for that! Hence you know not the raptures of its coldness either.

But in all things you behave too familiarly with the spirit; and you have often made of wisdom a poorhouse and hospital for wretched poets.

You are no eagles: hence you have not experienced the happiness in terror that the spirit enjoys. And whoever is not a bird should not settle over abysses.

To me you are lukewarm:* whereas all deep understanding streams cold. Ice-cold are the innermost springs of the spirit: refreshment for hot hands and doers.

Honourable you stand there stiffly and with straight backs, you famous wise men!—not driven by any strong wind and will.

Have you never seen a sail going across the sea, rounded and swollen and trembling from the violence of the wind?

Like a sail, trembling from the violence of the spirit, my wisdom goes across the sea—my Wild Wisdom!

But you servants of the people, you famous wise men—how *could* you go with me!—

Thus spoke Zarathustra.

* * *

9. The Night-Song*

Night it is: now all springing fountains talk more loudly. And my soul too is a springing fountain.

Night it is: now all songs of lovers at last awaken. And my soul too is the song of a lover.

Something unstilled, unstillable is within me, that wants to become loud. A desire for love is within me, that itself talks in the language of love.

Light am I: ah, would that I were night! But this is my solitude, that I am girded round with light.

Ah, would that I were dark and night-like! How I would suckle at the breasts of light!

And you yourselves would I yet bless, you little twinkling stars and fireflies up above!—and be blissful from your light-bestowals.

But I live in my very own light, I drink back the flames that break out from within me.

I know none of the happiness of him who takes; and often have I dreamed that stealing must be more blessèd than taking.*

This is my poverty, that my hand never rests from bestowing; this is my envy, that I see expectant eyes and illumined nights of yearning.

Oh the wretchedness of all who bestow! Oh the eclipse of my sun! Oh the desire for desiring! Oh the ravenous hunger in satiety!

They take from me: but do I yet touch their souls? A chasm there is between giving and taking; and the smallest chasm is the last to be bridged.

A hunger grows from my beauty: I should like to cause pain to those I illumine, should like to rob those upon whom I have bestowed—thus I hunger after wickedness.

Withdrawing the hand when another hand reaches out for it; hesitating like the waterfall, which hesitates even in plunging—thus do I hunger after wickedness.

Such revenge my fullness devises; such spite now wells up from my solitude.

My joy in bestowing died away through bestowing, my virtue grew weary of itself in its overflow!

He who always bestows is in danger of losing his sense of shame; he who always distributes has hands and heart calloused from sheer distributing.

My eye no longer brims over at the shame of those who beg; my hand has grown too hard for the trembling of hands that are filled.

Where has the tear gone from my eye and the soft down from my heart? Oh the solitude of all who bestow! Oh the reticence of all who shine forth!

Many suns circle in barren space: to all that is dark they speak with their light—to me they are silent.

Oh this is the enmity of light toward that which shines: mercilessly it pursues its courses.

Unjust in its inmost heart toward that which shines; cold toward suns—thus wanders every sun.

Like a storm the suns fly along their courses, that is their wandering. Their inexorable will they follow, that is their coldness.

Oh, it is only you, dark ones, and night-like, who create warmth from that which shines! Oh, it is only you who drink milk and comfort from the udders of light!

Ah, ice is around me, my hand is burned on what is icy! Ah, thirst is within me, and it languishes after your thirst!

Night it is: ah, that I must be light! And thirst for the night-like! And solitude!

Night it is: now like a spring my desire flows forth from me—I am desirous of speech.

Night it is: now all springing fountains talk more loudly. And my soul too is a springing fountain.

Night it is: now all songs of lovers at last awaken. And my soul too is the song of a lover.—

Thus sang Zarathustra.

*   *   *

10. The Dance-Song

One evening Zarathustra was walking with his disciples through the forest; and as he was looking for a spring, behold, he came upon a green meadow surrounded by tranquil trees and bushes: and upon it young maidens were dancing with each other. As soon as the maidens recognized Zarathustra they stopped their dance; but Zarathustra approached them with a friendly gesture and spoke these words:

'Do not stop your dance, you charming maidens! No spoilsport has come to you with evil eye, no enemy of maidens.

'God's advocate am I before the Devil: but he is the Spirit of Heaviness. How should I, you light-footed girls, be enemy to godlike dances? Or to maidens' feet with well-turned ankles?

'Indeed I am a forest and a night of dark trees: but whoever does not fear my darkness will find rose-bowers too beneath my cypresses.

'And the little God one will find as well, who is to maidens the dearest one: beside the spring he lies, still, with his eyes closed.*

'Verily, in broad daylight he has fallen asleep, the lazybones! Has he perhaps been chasing too many butterflies?

'Do not be angry, beautiful dancers, if I chasten the little God somewhat! He will surely cry out and weep—but he is laughable even in his weeping!

'And with tear-filled eye he shall ask you for a dance; and I myself will sing a song for his dance:

'A dance- and mocking-song on the Spirit of Heaviness, my supreme and most powerful Devil, of whom they say he is "Lord of the world".'—*

And this is the song that Zarathustra sang* as Cupid and the maidens danced together.

Into your eye I looked of late, O Life! And into the unfathomable I seemed then to be sinking.

But you pulled me out with a golden fishing-rod; mockingly you laughed when I called you unfathomable.

'So runs the talk of all fishes,' you said; 'What *they* do not fathom is unfathomable.

'But changeable am I only and wild and in all things a woman, and not a virtuous one:

'Even though you men call me "the Profound" or "the Loyal", "the Eternal", "the Mysterious".

'But you men always confer on us your own virtues—ah, you virtuous ones!'

Thus she laughed, the Incredible; but I never believe her and her laughter when she speaks wickedly of herself.

And when I was talking between two pairs of eyes* with my Wild Wisdom, she said to me angrily: 'You will, you desire, you love, for that reason alone you *laud* Life!'

I had almost answered wickedly and told the Angry One the truth; and one cannot answer more wickedly than by 'telling the truth' to one's Wisdom.

Thus it stands, then, among us three. From the ground up I love only Life—and verily, most of all when I hate her!

But that I am fond of Wisdom and often too fond: that is because she reminds me so much of Life!

She has her eye, her laughter, and even her little golden fishing-rod: how can I help it if they two look so alike?

And when Life asked me once: 'Who is that then, this Wisdom?'—then I said eagerly: 'Ah yes now! Wisdom!

'One thirsts after her and is never sated, one looks through veils, one grabs through nets.

'Is she beautiful? How should I know! But the oldest of carps are still lured by her bait.

'Changeable she is and stubborn; I have often seen her bite her lip and drag her comb against the grain of her hair.

'Perhaps she is wicked and false, and a female in every way; but when she speaks ill of herself, precisely then is she most seductive.'

When I said this to Life, she laughed maliciously and closed her eyes. 'But of whom are you talking?' she said. 'Perhaps of me?

'And even if you were right—should one say *that* to my face! But please speak now of your Wisdom too!'

Ah, and then you opened your eye again, O beloved Life! And into the unfathomable I seemed to be sinking again.—

Thus sang Zarathustra. But when the dance was over and the maidens had gone away, he became sad.

'The sun has long since gone down,' he said at last. 'The meadow is damp, and a coolness comes from the forests.

'Something unknown is about me and is looking thoughtfully. What! You are still living, Zarathustra?

'Why? What for? Whereby? Where to? Where? How? Is it not folly to go on living?—

'Ah, my friends, it is the evening that questions thus from within me. Forgive me my sadness!

'Evening has come: forgive me that it has become evening!'

Thus spoke Zarathustra.

* * *

11. The Grave-Song

'Out there lies the Isle of the Graves, all silent; there also are the graves of my youth. Thither will I carry an evergreen wreath of life.'

Resolving thus in my heart, I voyaged over the sea.—

O you visions and apparitions* of my youth! O all you glances of love, you divine moments! How quickly you died away! I remember you today as my deceased.

From you, my dear deceased ones, there comes such a sweet scent, one that loosens the heart and tears. Verily, it agitates and loosens the heart of the lonely seafarer.

To this day am I the richest and most enviable man—I, the loneliest! For I *had* you once, and you still have me: tell me, to whom have there fallen, as to me, such rose-apples from the tree?

To this day am I the heir and rich earth of your love, flowering in memory of you with colourful wild-growing virtues, O most beloved!

Ah, we were made for staying close to each other, you strange and gentle wonders; and not as timid birds did you come to me and my desire—but as trusting creatures to one who trusts!

Yes, made for loyalty, like me, and for tenderest eternities: but now must I call you after your disloyalty, you divine glances and moments: no other name have I learned as yet.

Verily, too soon did you die, you fleeting creatures. Yet you fled not from me, nor I from you: innocent are we mutually in our disloyalty.

To kill *me* off you were strangled, you songbirds of my hopes! Yes, at you, my most beloved, did wickedness always shoot its arrows—to hit my heart!

And they hit! For you were always the dearest to my heart, my possessions and my being possessed: *therefore* you had to die so young and all-too-early!

At my most vulnerable possession the arrow was shot: that was you, whose skin is like down and even more like the smile that dies away at a glance!

But this word will I say to my enemies: What is all murder of humans compared with what you have done to me!

A more evil thing you have done to me than any murder is; something irretrievable you have taken from me—thus I now talk to you, my enemies!

For you murdered the visions and dearest wonders of my youth! My playfellows you took from me, those blessèd spirits! In their memory I lay down this wreath and this curse.

This curse upon you, my enemies! For you cut short what was eternal for me, as a tone breaks off in coldest night! Scarcely as a glinting of divine eyes it came to me—as a moment!

Thus in a fair hour my purity once spoke: 'Divine shall all beings be to me.'*

Then you assailed me with filthy spectres; ah, whither has that fair hour now fled!

'All days shall be holy to me'—thus the wisdom of my youth once talked: verily, the talk of a joyful wisdom!

But then you enemies stole from me my nights and sold them to sleepless torment: ah, whither has that joyful wisdom now fled?

Once I craved favourable omens from birds:* then you led a monster of an owl across my path, a repulsive one. Ah, whither has my tender desire now fled?

All disgust I once vowed to renounce: then you transformed those near and nearest to me into pus-filled boils. Ah, whither has my noblest vow now fled?

As a blind man I once walked blessèd paths: then you flung filth in the blind man's way: and now his old blind-man's footpath disgusts him.*

And when I did what was hardest and celebrated the victory of my overcomings: then you made those who loved me scream that I was hurting them the most.*

Verily, that was always your doing: you spoiled for me my finest honey and the industry of my finest bees.

To my charity you have always dispatched the most impudent beggars; around my sympathy you have always crowded the incurably shameless. Thus did you wound my virtue in its faith.

And if I then laid down what was most sacred to me as a sacrifice, straightway your 'piousness' would add its fatter gifts beside: so that in the fumes of your fat what was most sacred to me would suffocate.

And once I wanted to dance as I had never danced before: away beyond all Heavens I wanted to dance. But then you won over my dearest singer.

And now he struck up a hideous muted tune; ah, he trumpeted like a dismal horn in my ears!

Murderous singer, instrument of wickedness, most innocent! There I stood ready for the finest dance: then you murdered with your tones my finest ecstasy!

Only in the dance can I tell the allegory of the highest things— and now my highest allegory has remained unspoken in my limbs!

Unspoken and unredeemed has my highest hope remained! And all the visions and consolations of my youth have died!

How could I bear it?* How did I make use of and overcome such wounds? How did my soul rise again from these graves?

Yes, something invulnerable, unburiable, is within me, something that explodes rock: that is *my will*. Silently it strides and unchanging through the years.

It wants to walk its way on my feet, my ancient will; hard-hearted is its temper and invulnerable.

Invulnerable am I only in the heel.* To this day you live and stay self-same, most patient one! To this day you continue to break through all graves!

In you there also lives on what is unredeemed from my youth; and as life and youth you sit here hopeful upon yellow grave-ruins.

Yes, you are still for me the demolisher of every grave: hail to thee, my will! And only where there are graves are there resurrections.—*

Thus sang Zarathustra.—

*　　*　　*

12. On Self-overcoming

'Will to truth' you call it, you who are wisest, that which drives you and puts you in heat?

Will to the thinkability of all beings: thus *I* call your will!

All beings you want first to *make* thinkable: for you doubt with healthy suspicion whether they really are thinkable.

But they shall fit and bend themselves to you! Thus your will wills it. Smooth shall they become and subject to the spirit, as its mirror and reflected image.

That is your entire will, you who are wisest, as a will to power; and even when you talk of good and evil and of valuations.

You still want to create the world before which you can kneel: that is your ultimate hope and intoxication.

The unwise, of course, the people—they are like a river on which a bark drifts along: and in the bark, solemn and disguised, sit the valuations.

Your will and your values you have placed on the river of Becoming; what the people believe to be good and evil betrays to me an ancient will to power.

You it was, you who are wisest, who put such guests in this bark and gave them grandeur and proud names—you and your imperious will!

Now the river carries your bark farther: it *must* carry it. Little does it matter if the broken wave foams and angrily opposes the keel!

Not the river is your danger and the end of your good and evil, you who are wisest, but that will itself, the will to power—the unexhausted procreative life-will.

But that you may understand my word about good and evil: to that end will I say to you my word about Life and the way of all the living.*

The living did I pursue; I followed the greatest and the smallest paths, that I might understand its way.

With a hundredfold mirror I caught its look when its mouth was closed, that its eye might speak to me. And its eye did speak to me.

But wherever I found the living, there too I heard the speech about obedience. All that is living is something that obeys.

And this is the second thing: whoever cannot obey himself will be commanded. That is the way of the living.

But this is the third thing that I heard: that commanding is harder than obeying. And not only because the commander bears the burden of all who obey, and this burden can easily crush him:—

An experiment and a risk appeared to me in all commanding; and always when it commands, the living puts its own self at risk.

Yes, even when it commands itself, there too it must make amends for its commanding. For its own law it must become judge and avenger and sacrificial victim.

But how does this happen! thus I asked myself. What persuades the living so that it obeys and commands, and in commanding still practises obedience?

Now hear my word, you who are wisest! Test in earnest whether I have crept into the very heart of Life, and into the very roots of her heart!

Where I found the living, there I found will to power; and even in the will of one who serves I found a will to be master.

That the weaker should serve the stronger, of this it is persuaded by its will, which would be master over what is weaker still: this pleasure alone it does not gladly forgo.

And just as the smaller yields to what is greater, that it might have pleasure and power over the smallest: so does even the greatest yield, and risks for the sake of power—life itself.

That is the yielding of the greatest, that it is risk and danger, and a dice-playing for death.

And wherever there is sacrifice and service and loving glances: there too is the will to be master. By secret paths the weaker slinks into the fortress and into the very heart of the more powerful—and there steals power.

And this secret did Life herself tell to me.* 'Behold,' she said, 'I am *that which must always overcome itself*.

'Indeed, you call it will to procreate or drive for a purpose, for what is higher, farther, more manifold: but all this is one and one secret.

'I would rather go under than renounce this one thing: and verily, where there is going-under and falling of leaves, behold, there life sacrifices itself—for power!

'That I must be struggle and Becoming and purpose and conflict of purposes: ah, whoever guesses my will also guesses along what *crooked* ways it has to walk!

'Whatever I create and however much I love it—soon I must oppose both it and my love: thus my will wills it.

'And even you, who understand, are only a path and footstep of my will: verily, my will to power even walks on the feet of your will to truth!

'He surely missed the mark who shot at the truth with the words "will to existence": this will—does not exist!

'For what does not exist cannot will; yet what already exists, how could that then will to exist!

'Only, where Life is, there too is will: though not will to life, but— thus I teach you—will to power!

'Much is valued by the living more highly than life itself; but out of this very valuing there speaks—will to power!'—

Thus did Life once teach me: and with this, you who are wisest, I go on to solve the riddle of your hearts.*

Verily, I say to you: good and evil that are not transitory—there is no such thing! From out of themselves they must overcome themselves again and again.

With your values and words of good and evil you exercise force, you valuators: and this is your hidden love and the radiance, trembling, and overflowing of your souls.*

But a stronger force grows out of your values and a new overcoming, on which egg and eggshell shatter.

And whoever must be a creator* in good and evil: verily, he must first be an annihilator and shatter values.

Thus does the highest evil belong to the highest good: but this latter is the creative.—

Let us at least *talk* of this, you who are wisest, grim though it may be. Remaining silent is grimmer; all truths that are kept silent become toxic.

And so let everything shatter that *can* shatter on our truths! There is many a house still to build!—

Thus spoke Zarathustra.

* * *

13. On Those Who Are Sublime

Still is the bottom of my sea: who would guess that it harbours such sportive monsters!

Unshakeable are my depths: but they sparkle with swimming riddles and laughter.

A sublime one I saw today, extremely solemn, a penitent of the spirit: oh how my soul laughed at his ugliness!

With puffed-up chest and like those who hold their breath in: thus he stood there, the sublime one, in silence:

Decked out with ugly truths, spoils from his hunt, and rich in torn garments; many thorns hung on him too—yet I saw no rose there.

Laughter he still has not learned, nor beauty. Gloomily this hunter came back from the forest of understanding.

From battle with wild beasts he has returned home: but from out of his seriousness there still peers a wild beast—one not overcome!

Like a tiger about to spring he stands there still; but I do not like these tensed-up souls, and hostile is my taste toward all these withdrawn creatures.

And you say to me, friends, there is no disputing over taste and tasting? But all of life is a dispute over taste and tasting!*

Taste: that is weight and at the same time scales and weigher; and woe to anything living that would live without disputes over weight and scales and weighers!

And should he become weary of his sublimity, this sublime man, only then would his beauty emerge—and only then would I taste him and find him tasty.

And only when he turns away from himself will he leap over his own shadow—and verily! into *his own* sunlight.

All-too-long he sat in the shade, and the penitent of the spirit's cheeks grew pale; he has almost starved to death on his expectations.

Despising still lingers in his eye; and disgust plays around his mouth. He does indeed rest now, but his rest has not yet lain down in the sun.

The bull he should emulate; and his happiness should smell of earth and not of despising the earth.

As a white bull I should like to see him, snorting and bellowing as he pulls the plough: and his bellowing should be in praise of all that is earthly!

Dark is his countenance still; his hand's shadow plays upon it. Shadowed still is the sense of his eye.

His deed itself still shadows him: the hand darkens the doer. His deed is something he has still not overcome.

Much as I love in him the neck of the bull, I now would see the eye of the angel too.

His hero's will too he must yet unlearn: let him be elevated and not merely sublime:—the aether itself should elevate him, as the will-less one!

He has subdued monsters, he has solved riddles: but he should also redeem his own monsters and riddles, and transform them into heavenly children.

As yet his understanding has not learned how to smile and be without jealousy; as yet his streaming passion has not become quite still in beauty.

Verily, not in satiety shall his desire fall silent and disappear, but in beauty! Gracefulness belongs to the generosity of the great-hearted.

With his arm laid over his head: thus should the hero rest, thus should he overcome his resting too.

But precisely for the hero is the *beautiful* of all things the most difficult. Unwinnable is the beautiful by any violent will.

A little more, a little less: just that is in this case much, that is here the most.

To stand with relaxed muscles and unharnessed will: that is the most difficult thing for you all, you sublime ones!

When power becomes gracious and descends into the visible: beauty I call such a descent.

And from nobody do I want just such beauty as much as from you, you powerful one: may your goodness be your ultimate self-overpowering.*

Of all evil I deem you capable: for that reason I want from you the good.

Verily, I have often laughed at the weaklings who think themselves good merely because they have lame paws!

For the virtue of the pillar shall you strive: more beautiful it becomes and more slender, but within harder and more weight-bearing, the farther it ascends.

Yes, you sublime one, one day you shall yet become beautiful and hold up the mirror to your own beauty.

Then will your soul shudder with godlike desires,* and there will be adoration even in your vanity!

For this is the secret of the soul: only when the hero has abandoned her is she approached, in a dream, by—the over-hero.—*

Thus spoke Zarathustra.

* * *

14. On the Land of Culture*

Too far did I fly into the future: a horror overwhelmed me.

And when I looked around, behold! time was my only contemporary.

I then flew back again, toward home—and ever more swiftly: and so I came to you, you men of the present, and to the land of culture.

For the first time I brought with me an eye for you, and a healthy desire: verily, with yearning in my heart I came.

But what happened to me? Anxious as I was—I simply had to laugh! Never had my eye seen anything so colourfully sprinkled!*

I laughed and laughed, while my foot was still trembling and my heart as well: 'This must be the home of all the world's paint-pots!' I said.

Daubed with fifty blotches on face and limbs: thus you sat there to my amazement, you men of the present!

And with fifty mirrors around you, that flattered and repeated your display of colours!

Verily, you could wear no better masks, you men of the present, than your own faces! Who could ever—*recognize* you!

Inscribed all over with signs of the past, and these signs themselves overpainted with new signs: thus have you concealed yourselves well from all sign-readers!

And even for an examiner of kidneys, who would ever believe that you had any! You seem to be baked with colours and glued scraps of paper.

All ages and peoples peek out colourfully through your veils; all customs and beliefs speak out colourfully from your gestures.

If one could remove your veils and wraps and colours and gestures, there would be just enough left over to frighten away the birds.

Verily, I myself am the frightened bird that once saw you naked and without colours; and I flew away when the skeleton beckoned to me lovingly.

Rather would I be a day-labourer in the underworld* and among the shades of times past!—Even the denizens of the underworld are plumper and fuller than you!

This, yes this, is bitterness to my bowels, that I can endure you neither naked nor clothed, you men of the present!

All that is unfamiliar about the future, and whatever has made fugitive birds shudder, is truly more familiar and more comfortable than your 'actuality'.

For thus you speak: 'Actual are we entirely, and without belief or superstition': thus you thump your chests—ah, even though you have none!

Indeed, how should you be *capable* of belief, you colourfully sprinkled creatures!—you who are paintings of all that has ever been believed!

Walking refutations are you of belief itself, and a limb-breaking of all thought. *Unworthy of belief*: thus *I* call you, you actual men!

All ages gossip against each other in your spirits; and even the dreams and gossip of all ages were much more real than your waking life is!

Unfruitful are you: *therefore* you lack all belief. But whoever had to create, he always also had prophetic dreams and astral signs—and believed in belief!—

Half-open gates are you, at which gravediggers wait. And this is *your* actuality: 'Everything is worthy of perishing.'*

Ah, how you stand before me, you unfruitful men, how lean in the ribs! And many a one among you has already seen this himself.

And he said: 'Did a God secretly purloin something from me there, as I slept? Verily, enough to make for himself a little female!*

'Amazing is the poorness of my ribs!' Thus has many a man of the present already spoken.

Indeed you are laughable to me, you men of the present! And especially when you wonder at yourselves!

And woe to me if I were not able to laugh at your wonderment, and had to drink down all that is repulsive in your bowls!

But I want to make lighter of you now, since I have a *heavy* burden to bear; and what is it to me if beetles and winged worms alight on my load!

Verily, it shall not on that account feel heavier! And not from you, you men of the present, shall the great weariness come over me.—

Ah, where shall I climb to now with my yearning! From all mountains I look out for father- and mother-lands.

But a homeland I found nowhere: unsettled am I in all settlements and a departure at all gates.

Alien to me and a mockery are the men of the present, to whom my heart recently drove me; and I have been driven out from all father- and mother-lands.*

So now I still love only my *children's land*, undiscovered, in the farthest sea: for that land I bid my sails search and search.

In my children I want to make up for being the child of my fathers, and in all the future—for *this* present!

Thus spoke Zarathustra.

* * *

15. On Immaculate Perception*

When the moon rose yesterday, he looked as if he wanted to give birth to a sun: so large and pregnant did he lie on the horizon.

But a liar was he with his pregnancy; and I would still rather believe in the man in the moon than in the woman.

Indeed he is not much of a man either, this timid night-reveller. Verily, with a bad conscience he passes over the roofs.

For he is lecherous and jealous, the monk in the moon, lusting after the earth and after all the joys of lovers.

No, I like him not, this tomcat on the roofs! Repugnant I find all those who slink around half-closed windows!

Pious and silent he passes over carpets of stars:—but I do not like soft-stepping men's feet on which not even a spur jingles.

The step of everything honest speaks out; but the cat steals its way across the ground. Behold, cat-like the moon approaches, and dishonestly.—

This parable I give to you sentimental hypocrites, to you, the 'pure perceivers'! You are what *I* call—lechers!

You too love the earth and the earthly: I have divined you well!— but there is shame in your love and bad conscience—you resemble the moon!

Your spirit has been persuaded to despise what is earthly, but not your entrails: and *they* are what is strongest in you!

And now your spirit is ashamed of doing the will of your entrails, and to avoid its own shame it sneaks along by-ways and lying-ways.

'This would be for me the highest thing'—thus your lying spirit talks to itself—'To look upon life without desire and not like a dog with its tongue hanging out:

'To be happy in looking, with a will that has died, without the grasping or greed of selfishness—the whole body cold and ashen, but with drunken moon-eyes!

'This would be for me the dearest thing'—thus the seduced one seduces himself—'To love the earth as the moon loves her, and to touch her beauty with the eye alone.

'And let this be for me the *immaculate* perception of all things: that I want nothing from things, except that I may lie there before them like a mirror with a hundred eyes.'—

Oh, you sentimental hypocrites, you lechers! You lack innocence in your desire, so now you slander desiring itself!

Verily, not as creators, procreators, or enjoyers of becoming do you love the earth!

Where is there innocence? Where there is the will to procreate. And whoever wants to create beyond himself, he has for me the purest will.

Where is there beauty? Wherever I *must will* with all my will; where I want to love and go under, that an image might not remain mere image.

Loving and going-under: that has rhymed for eternities.* Will to love: that means being willing to die too. Thus I talk to you cowards!

But now your emasculated leering wants to be called 'contemplation'! And that which lets itself be touched by cowardly eyes shall be baptized 'beautiful'! Oh, you befoulers of noble names!

But this shall be your curse, you immaculate ones, you pure perceivers: that you shall never give birth, even though you lie large and pregnant on the horizon!

Verily, you fill your mouths with noble words; and we are to believe that your hearts are overflowing, you habitual liars?*

But *my* words are tiny, despised, crooked words: gladly I pick up whatever at your mealtimes falls under the table.*

Yet even with such words can I—tell hypocrites the truth! Yes, my fishbones, seashells, and thorny leaves shall—tickle hypocrites' noses!

Bad air always surrounds you and your mealtimes; for your lecherous thoughts, your lies and little secrets, are there in the air!

So dare for once to believe yourselves—yourselves and your entrails! Whoever does not believe himself, always lies.

With the mask of a God you have decorated yourselves, you 'pure ones': into the mask of a God your repulsive ringworm has crawled.*

Verily, you are deceivers, you 'contemplatives'! Even Zarathustra was at one time fooled by your godlike skins; he never guessed that they were crammed with coils of snakes.

The soul of a God I once fancied I saw at play in your play, you pure perceivers! No better art I once fancied there was than your arts!

Snake excrement and horrid stench were hidden from me by the distance, and that a lizard's cunning was creeping here lecherously.

But then I came *close* to you: the day came to me—and it now comes to you—when the moon's love affair came to an end!

But look now! Caught in the act and pale he stands there—before dawn of morning!

For she comes already, and glowing—*her* love for the earth is coming! Innocence and creator-desire is all solar love!

But look now, as she rises impatiently over the sea! Do you not feel the thirst and the hot breath of her love?

At the sea she wants to suck and drink its depths up to her heights: now the desire of the sea rises with its thousand breasts.

It *wants* to be kissed and sucked by the sun's thirst; it *wants* to become air and height and a footpath of light and itself light!

Verily, like the sun I love life and all deep seas.

And this is what perception is for *me*: all depths shall rise up—to my heights!—

Thus spoke Zarathustra.

*   *   *

16. On the Scholars

As I lay sleeping, a sheep ate at the ivy-wreath on my brow—ate and said: 'Zarathustra is no longer a scholar.'

Said that and strutted abruptly off and proudly. A child told me about it.

I like to lie here where the children play, beside the ruined wall, among thistles and red poppies.

A scholar am I still to the children and also to the thistles and red poppies. Innocent are they, even in their wickedness.

But to the sheep I am a scholar no longer: thus my fate wills it— blessèd be my fate!

For this is the truth: I have moved out of the house of the scholars, and I even slammed the door behind me.

Too long did my soul sit hungry at their table; I am not, as they are, trained to pursue understanding as a kind of nut-cracking.

Freedom I love and the air over fresh earth; rather would I sleep on ox-hides than on their honours and respectabilities.

I am too hot and burned by my own thoughts: often it almost takes my breath away. Then must I go out into the open and away from all dusty rooms.

But they sit coolly in the cool shade: they want in all things to be mere spectators and are wary of sitting where the sun burns down upon the steps.

Like those who stand in the street and gape at the people passing by, they too wait and gape at thoughts that others have thought.

If one grasps them with one's hands they give off a cloud of dust like sacks of flour, involuntarily: but who would guess that their dust comes from corn and from the yellow delight of summer fields?

When they pose as wise, I am chilled by their little proverbs and truths: their wisdom often smells as if it came from the swamp; and verily, I have even heard a frog croaking in it!

Skilful are they, with clever fingers: what does *my* simplicity want with their multiplicity! All kinds of threading and knotting and weaving their fingers understand: thus they work at the stockings of the spirit!*

Fine clockworks are they: one must only take care to wind them up properly! Then they tell the hour without fail and make a modest noise besides.

Like mills they work and like pounders: one has only to throw them some seed-corn!—they surely know how to grind corn small and make white dust out of it.

They keep a sharp eye on each other and are not at all trustful. Inventive in petty craftiness, they wait for those whose knowing walks on lame feet—like spiders they wait.

I have seen them always carefully preparing their poisons; and they always put on gloves of glass beforehand.

They also know how to play with loaded dice; and I have found them playing so eagerly that they were sweating.

We are alien to each other, and their virtues go even more against my taste than their falsehoods and loaded dice.

And when I lived among them, I lived above them. Over that they became angry at me.

They want to hear nothing of it when someone passes over their heads; and so they set up wood and earth and rubbish between me and their heads.

Thus they muffled the sound of my steps: and so far I have been most poorly heard by the most scholarly ears.

All human faults and weaknesses they set up between themselves and me:—'false floors' they call that in their houses.

But notwithstanding I pass with my thoughts *over* their heads; and even if I wanted to walk on my own mistakes, I would still be above them and over their heads.

For human beings are *not* equal: thus speaks justice. And what I want, *they* would have no right to want!

Thus spoke Zarathustra.

*　＊　＊

17. On the Poets

'Now that I know the body better'—said Zarathustra to one of his disciples—'the spirit is to me only *quasi* spirit; and all "permanence"—that is also only an allegory.'

'I heard you say that once before,' answered the disciple; 'and at that time you added: "But the poets lie too much." Why then did you say that the poets lie too much?'

'Why?' said Zarathustra. 'You ask me why? I do not belong to those whom one may ask about their Why.

'Is my experience then of yesterday? It is long ago that I experienced the grounds for my opinions.

'Would I not have to be a vat of memory if I wanted to carry my grounds around with me too?

'It is already too much for me to hold my opinions myself; and many a bird still flies away.

'And now and then I also find a stray creature inside my dovecote,* one that is strange to me and trembles when I lay my hand upon it.

'So what did Zarathustra once say to you? That the poets lie too much?—But Zarathustra too is a poet.

'Now do you believe that he was telling the truth here? Why do you believe that?'

The disciple answered: 'I believe in Zarathustra.' But Zarathustra shook his head and smiled.

'Belief does not make me blessèd,' he said, 'least of all belief in me.*

'But given that someone said in all seriousness that the poets lie too much: well he is right—*we* do lie too much.

'We also know too little and are poor learners: so we are obliged to lie.

'And who among us poets has not adulterated his wine? Many a poisonous hodge-podge has been produced in our cellars; many an indescribable thing has been done there.

'And because we know so little, the poor in spirit are pleasing to our hearts, especially when they are young females!

'And we are even desirous of those things that the old females tell each other in the evenings. We ourselves call that the Eternal Feminine* in us.

'And as if there were a special secret access to knowing that is *blocked* for those who learn things, so do we believe in the people and its "wisdom".

'But this all poets believe: that whoever lies in the grass or on lonely slopes and pricks up his ears will discover somewhat of the things that are between Heaven and earth.

'And if tender emotions should come to them, the poets always think that Nature herself is in love with them:

'And that she creeps up to their ears in order to tell them secrets and amorous flattering-speeches: of this they boast and brag before all mortals!

'Ah, there are so many things between Heaven and earth of which only the poets have let themselves dream!*

'And especially *above* Heaven: for all Gods are poets' allegories, poets' deceptions!

'Verily, we are drawn ever upward—but simply to the realm of the clouds: upon these we place our motley manikins and call them Gods and Overhumans:—

'For they are just light enough for these cloud-chairs! —all these Gods and Overhumans.

'Ah, how weary I am of all this inadequacy that shall at all costs be an event! Ah, how weary I am of the poets!'

When Zarathustra spoke thus, his disciple was angry with him, but kept silent. And Zarathustra too kept silent; and his eye had turned inward, as if looking into far distances. At last he sighed and drew a breath.

'I am of today and former times,' he said then. 'But there is something in me that is of tomorrow and the day after tomorrow and times to come.

'I have grown weary of the poets, the old ones and the new ones: superficial are they all to me, and shallow seas.

'They have never taken their thought deep enough: therefore their feeling never sank down to the grounds.

'A little lust and a little boredom: that has so far been their best reflection.

'So much spectre's-breath and -flitting has all their harp-jangling been to me; what have they ever known of the fervour of tones!—

'Nor are they cleanly enough for me: they all muddy their waters, that they might appear deep.

'And they like thereby to pose as reconcilers: but mediators and mixers they remain for me, and half-and-halfers and unclean too!—

'Ah, I cast my net into their seas and wanted to catch fine fish; but I always pulled up the head of some old God or other.

'Thus the sea gave to him who was hungry a stone.* And they themselves may well have come from the sea.

'To be sure, one does find pearls in them: and they themselves are all the more like hard crustaceans. And instead of a soul I often found within them salty slime.

'They learned from the sea its vanity too: is the sea not the peacock of peacocks?

'Even before the ugliest of all buffaloes it unfurls its tail, and it never wearies of its lace-fan of silver and silk.

'Defiantly the buffalo looks on, in its soul close to the sand, closer still to the thicket, but closest of all to the swamp.

'What are beauty and sea and peacock-finery to him! This allegory I tell to the poets.

'Verily, their spirit itself is the peacock of peacocks and a sea of vanity!

'Spectators the poet's spirit wants, even if they be only buffaloes!—

'But I have grown weary of this spirit, and I see the day coming when it will grow weary of itself.

'Transformed have I seen the poets already and their look turned back on themselves.

'Penitents of the spirit have I seen coming: they grew out of the poets.'—

Thus spoke Zarathustra.

* * *

18. On Great Events

There is an island in the sea—not far from Zarathustra's Isles of the Blest—on which a fire-mountain* steadily smokes. The people say of it, and especially the old women among the people say, that it is placed like a block of stone in front of the gate to the underworld, but that through the fire-mountain itself a narrow path descends that leads to this gate to the underworld.

Around the time, then, that Zarathustra was dwelling in the Isles of the Blest, it happened that a ship dropped anchor by the island on which the smoking mountain stands; and its crew went ashore in order to shoot rabbits. But toward the hour of midday, when the captain and his men were together again, they suddenly saw a man approaching through the air, and a voice said distinctly: 'It is time! It is high time!' But as the figure came its closest to them—for it flew past quickly like a shadow in the direction of the fire-mountain—they realized to their great consternation that it was Zarathustra. For they had all seen him before, except the captain himself, and they loved him as the people love: that is, with love and awe mixed in equal proportions.

'Look up there!' said the old helmsman. 'There goes Zarathustra on his way to Hell!'—*

Around the same time that these sailors landed on the fire-island, the rumour was going around that Zarathustra had disappeared; and when his friends were questioned, they said that he had embarked on a ship at night without saying where he was travelling to.

Thus disquiet arose among them; but three days later the sailors' story added to this disquiet—and now all the people were saying that the Devil had taken Zarathustra away. His disciples of course laughed at such talk, and one of them even said: 'Sooner would I believe that Zarathustra has taken the Devil away.' But in the ground of their souls they were all of them filled with concern and yearning; therefore great was their joy when on the fifth day Zarathustra appeared among them.

And this is the story of Zarathustra's conversation with the fire-hound:

'The earth', he said, 'has a skin; and this skin has diseases.* One of these diseases is called, for example, "humanity".

'And another one of these diseases is called "fire-hound": about *him* human beings have told themselves many lies and had many lies told to them.

'To fathom this mystery I voyaged across the sea: and I saw the truth naked, verily! barefoot up to the neck.

'Concerning the fire-hound I am now well informed, and likewise with all the outflow- and overthrow-devils of whom not only little old women are afraid.

' "Out with you, fire-hound, out from your depths!" I cried. "And confess how deep these depths really are! Where does it come from, what you are snorting up here?

' "You drink copiously from the sea:* that your salty eloquence betrays! Truly, for a hound of the depths you take your nourishment too much from the surface!

' "At best I regard you as the ventriloquist of the earth: and whenever I heard overthrow- and outflow-devils speak, I found them to be like you: salty, mendacious, and superficial.

' "You all know how to roar and darken the air with ashes! You are the best braggarts and have learned ad nauseam the art of bringing mud to a boil.

' "Wherever you are, there must always be mud close by,* and much that is spongy, cavernous, and constricted: and that wants to attain freedom.

' " 'Freedom' is what you all most like to bellow: but I have unlearned my belief in 'great events' whenever they are surrounded by so much bellowing and smoke.

' "And believe me, friend Hellishnoise! The greatest events—those are not our loudest but our stillest hours.

' "Not around the inventors of new noise, but around the inventors of new values does the world revolve; *inaudibly* it revolves.

' "And admit it now! Little had ever happened by the time your noise and smoke dissipated. What does it matter if a town was mummified and a statue lies in the mud!

' "And this further word I say to the overthrowers of statues. That is indeed the greatest folly, to cast salt into the sea and statues into the mud.

' "In the mud of your despising the statue lay: but that is precisely its law, that from despising both life and living beauty grow for it again!

' "With more godlike features it now rises again, and seductive through suffering: and verily! it will thank you yet for having overthrown it, you overthrowers!

' "But this counsel I give to kings and churches and all that is weak from age and in virtue—do let yourselves be overthrown! That you may come to life again, and to you may come—virtue!"—

'Thus I talked before the fire-hound: but then he interrupted sullenly and asked: "Church? What is that then?"

' "The Church?" I answered. "That is a kind of state, and indeed the most mendacious kind. But keep quiet, hypocritical hound! For surely you know your own kind best!

' "Like yourself the state is a hypocritical hound; like you it likes to speak with smoke and bellowing—so as to make believe, like you, that it speaks from the belly of things.

' "For it wants to be by all means the most important beast on earth, the state; and people even believe it."—

'When I had said that, the fire-hound acted like one insane with envy. "What?" it yelled, "The most important beast on earth? And people even believe it?" And so much steam and so many hideous voices came out of his maw that I thought he would suffocate from wrath and envy.*

'At last he became calmer, and his puffing abated. But as soon as he was quiet, I said laughing:

' "You are angry, fire-hound: so I am right about you!

' "And that I may continue in the right, now hear about another fire-hound, one that really speaks from the heart of the earth.

' "Gold he exhales and golden rain: thus his heart wills it. What are ashes and smoke and boiling mud to one such as him!

' "Laughter flutters forth from him like colourful clouds; ill-disposed is he toward your gurgling and spewing and intestinal rumblings!

' "This gold, however, and this laughter—these he takes from the heart of the earth: for you should at least know this—*the heart of the earth is of gold.*"*

'When the fire-hound heard this, he could no longer stand listening to me. Ashamed, he drew in his tail, said "Bow-Wow!" in a tiny little voice, and crawled down into his cave.'—

Thus recounted Zarathustra. But his disciples were barely listening, so great was their desire to tell him about the sailors, the rabbits, and the flying man.

'What am I to think of that!' said Zarathustra. 'Am I then a spectre?

'But it will have been my shadow. You have surely heard something of the Wanderer and his Shadow?

'But this much is certain: I must keep him on a shorter leash—else he will yet ruin my reputation.'

And once more Zarathustra shook his head and was amazed. 'What am I to think of that!' he said once more.

'Why did the spectre cry: "It is time! It is high time!"
'*For what* is it then—high time?'—

Thus spoke Zarathustra.

*　　*　　*

19. The Soothsayer

'—and I saw a great mournfulness come over humankind. The best
became weary of their works.

'A teaching went forth, and a belief along with it: "All is empty, all
is the same, all has been!"*

'And from all hills it echoed again: "All is empty, all is the same,
all has been!"

'We have indeed harvested: but why did all our fruits turn rotten
and brown? What fell down to us here last night from the evil moon?

'In vain was all our work; our wine has turned to poison; an evil
eye has scorched our fields and hearts yellow.

'Dry have we all become; and should fire fall on us, we are scattered
like ashes:—and even fire itself we have made weary.

'All our wells have dried up, and even the sea has retreated. All
ground wants to tear open, but the depths do not want to devour!

' "Ah, where is there yet a sea in which we can drown": thus
resounds our lament—echoing over shallow swamps.

'Verily, we have even become too weary to die; now are we still
awake and live on—in burial chambers!'—

Thus Zarathustra heard a soothsayer speak; and the prophecy
touched his heart and transformed him. Sadly he wandered around
and wearily; and he became like those of whom the soothsayer had
spoken.

'Verily,' he said to his disciples, 'just a little while and this long
twilight will be upon us. Ah, how am I to preserve my light through
that!

'Let it not be extinguished by this mournfulness! For farther
worlds shall it be a light, and for the farthest nights!'

Thus troubled in his heart, Zarathustra wandered about; and for
three days he took neither drink nor food, had no rest, and lost his

speech. At last it happened that he fell into a deep sleep. But his disciples sat around him in long night-watches, and they waited with concern to see whether he would awaken and talk again and convalesce from his affliction.

And this is the speech that Zarathustra gave when he awoke; his voice, however, came to his disciples as if from a great distance:

'Now listen to the dream that I dreamt, my friends, and help me divine its meaning!

'A riddle it is to me still, this dream; its meaning is hidden within it and imprisoned and does not yet soar above it with liberated wings.

'All life I had renounced, thus did I dream. A night- and grave-watchman I had become, in the lonely mountain-castle of death.

'Up there I guarded his coffins: the musty vaults stood filled with such signs of his victory. From within glass coffins life that had been overcome looked out at me.

'I breathed in the smell of dust-filled eternities: sultry and dust-filled my soul lay there. And who could ever have aired his soul in such a place!

'Brightness of midnight was ever around me; solitude cowered beside her; and, as a third, the rasping stillness of death, the worst of my female companions.

'Keys I was carrying, the rustiest of all keys; and I knew how to open the most creaking of all gates with them.

'Like a malicious croaking the sound reverberated through long passageways when the wings of the gate were moved: fiendish was the cry of this bird, since it wanted not to be wakened.

'But still more frightening and heart-constricting was it when silence fell again and all around was quiet, and I sat alone in that menacing silence.

'Thus time passed at a crawl for me, if there still was any time: what do I know of it! But at last something happened that awakened me.

'Three times blows struck the gate like thunder-claps, and three times the vaults echoed and howled in response: then I went to the gate.

' "Alpa!" I cried. "Who carries his ashes up the mountain? Alpa! Alpa! Who carries his ashes up the mountain?"*

'And I turned the key and pulled on the gate with all my might. But it refused to open even a finger's width:

'Then a roaring wind tore its wings asunder: whistling, shrilling, and piercing, it cast before me a black coffin:

'And amidst the roaring and whistling and shrilling the coffin burst open and spewed forth a thousand peals of laughter.

'And from a thousand masks of children, angels, owls, fools, and child-sized butterflies it laughed and jeered and roared at me.

'I was sorely afraid: it threw me down. And I screamed with horror, as I have never screamed before.

'But my own screams awoke me—and I came to myself again.'—

Thus Zarathustra recounted his dream and then fell silent: for he did not yet know the dream's interpretation. But the disciple he loved the most sprang up, grasped Zarathustra's hand, and said:

'Your life itself interprets this dream for us, O Zarathustra!

'Are you not yourself the wind with the shrill whistling that tears open the gates of the castles of death?

'Are you not yourself the coffin full of colourful wickednesses and angel-masks of life?

'Verily, like a thousand peals of child's laughter Zarathustra comes into all death-chambers, laughing at these night- and grave-watchmen, and whoever else might rattle such dismal keys.

'You will frighten and overthrow them with your laughter; fainting and reawakening will demonstrate your power over them.

'And even if the long twilight comes and the weariness of death, you will not go under and set in our Heaven, you advocate of life!

'New stars you have let us see and new glories of the night sky; verily, laughter itself have you stretched over us like a colourful pavilion.*

'Now child's-laughter will ever well up out of coffins; now a strong wind will ever come victoriously to all death-weariness: for this you are our guarantor and soothsayer!

'Verily, *of them you have dreamt*, your enemies: that was your heaviest dream!

'But just as you awoke from them and came to yourself, so shall they awake from themselves—and come to you!'—

Thus spoke the disciple; and all the others now crowded around Zarathustra and grasped him by the hands and wanted to persuade him to leave his bed and his mournfulness and to return to them. But Zarathustra sat upright on his pallet, and with a strange look.* Just like one who returns home from a long sojourn in strange lands, he looked at his disciples and examined their faces; yet he still did not recognize them. But when they lifted him up and set him on his feet, behold, then all at once his eye was transformed; he understood all that had happened, stroked his beard, and said in a firm voice:

'Well then! This has its time now; but see to it, my disciples, that we make for ourselves a good meal, and quickly! Thus I mean to atone for awful dreams!

'But the soothsayer shall eat and drink by my side: and verily, I still want to show him a sea in which he can drown!'

Thus spoke Zarathustra. But then he gazed long into the face of the disciple who had played dream-interpreter, and at the same time shook his head. —

*   *   *

20. On Redemption

As Zarathustra was going across the great bridge one day, the cripples and beggars surrounded him,* and a hunchback spoke to him thus:

'Behold, Zarathustra! Even the people are learning from you and coming to believe in your teaching: but in order for them to believe you completely, one thing more is needed—you must first persuade us cripples too! Now here you have a fine selection, and verily, an opportunity with more than one forelock! The blind you can cure and the lame make to walk again; and from him who has too much on his shoulders, you could well take a little away—that, I think, would be the right way to make the cripples believe in Zarathustra!'*

But Zarathustra replied thus to him who had spoken: 'If one takes the hump away from the hunchback, one thereby takes away his spirit—thus the people teach. And if one gives the blind man back his eyes, he will see too many grievous things on earth: such that he will curse the one who cured him. But he who makes the lame man walk does him the greatest harm: for no sooner can he walk than his vices run away with him—thus the people teach about cripples. And why should Zarathustra not also learn from the people, if the people learn from Zarathustra?

'But this is what matters least to me since I have been among human beings, that I see: "This one lacks an eye, that one an ear, and a third a leg, and there are others who have lost their tongue or nose or head."

'I see and have seen worse things, and many things so vile that I should not want to speak of them all nor remain silent about some: namely, human beings lacking in everything except one thing of which they have too much—human beings who are nothing more than a large eye, or a large mouth or a large belly or anything at all large—inverse cripples I call such beings.*

'And when I came out of my solitude and went across this bridge for the first time, I could not believe my eyes and had to look, and look again, before saying at last: "That is an ear! An ear as large as a human being!"* Then I looked more closely, and in fact under the ear there was something else moving, something pitifully small and meagre and puny. And in truth, the enormous ear was sitting on a thin little stalk—but the stalk was a human being! With the help of a magnifying glass one could even make out an envious little face, as well as a bloated little soul dangling from the stalk. The people told me, however, that the huge ear was not only a human being but a great human being, a genius. But I never did believe the people when they talked of great human beings—and I held to my belief that it was an inverse cripple, with too little of everything and too much of one thing.'

When Zarathustra had talked thus to the hunchback and to those whose mouthpiece and advocate he was, he turned to his disciples in profound discouragement and said:

'Verily, my friends, I walk among human beings as among fragments and severed limbs of human beings!

'This is to my eye the most terrible thing: that I find human beings in ruins and scattered as if over a battle- and slaughter-field.

'And when my eye flees from now to the past, it always finds the same thing: fragments and severed limbs and dreadful accidents—but no human beings!*

'The now and the formerly upon earth—ah! my friends—that is what *I* find most unbearable; and I should not be able to live if I were not also a seer of that which must come.

'A seer, a willer, a creator, a future himself and a bridge to the future—and alas, also as it were a cripple by this bridge: Zarathustra is all this.

'And you too have often asked yourselves: "Who is Zarathustra to us? What shall we call him?" And like me you gave yourselves questions in response.

'Is he a promiser? Or a fulfiller? A conqueror? Or an inheritor? An autumn? Or a ploughshare? A physician? Or one who has convalesced?

'Is he a poet? Or a truthful man? A liberator? Or a subduer? A good man? Or an evil one?

'I walk among human beings as among fragments of the future: that future which I envisage.

'And this is all my composing and striving,* that I compose into one and bring together what is fragment and riddle and cruel coincidence.

'And how could I bear to be human if the human being were not also a composer-poet and riddle-guesser and the redeemer of coincidence!

'To redeem that which has passed away and to re-create all "It was" into a "Thus I willed it!"—that alone should I call redemption!

'Will—that is the liberator and joy-bringer: that is what I taught you, my friends! And now learn this as well: the will itself is still a prisoner.

'Willing liberates: but what is it called that puts even the liberator in fetters?

' "It was": that is the will's gnashing of teeth and loneliest sorrow. Powerless with respect to what has been done—it is an angry spectator of all that is past.

'Backwards the will is unable to will; that it cannot break time and time's desire—that is the will's loneliest sorrow.

'Willing liberates: what does willing itself devise, that it might be free of its sorrow and mock at its dungeon?

'Alas, every prisoner becomes a fool! Foolish too the way the imprisoned will redeems itself.

'That time does not run backwards, this arouses the will's fury; "That which was"—that is the stone which it cannot roll away.*

'And so it rolls stones away in fury and ill-humour, and takes revenge on whatever does not, like itself, feel fury and ill-humour.

'Thus did the will, the liberator, take to hurting: and upon all that can suffer it takes revenge for its inability to go backwards.

'This, yes this alone, is what *revenge* itself is: the will's ill-will toward time and its "It was".

'Verily, a great folly dwells in our will; and it has become a curse for all that is human that this folly has acquired spirit!

'*The spirit of revenge*: that, my friends, has been up to now humanity's best reflection; and wherever there was suffering, there was always supposed to be punishment.

'For "punishment" is what revenge calls itself: with a hypocritical word it makes itself a good conscience.

'And because there is suffering in whatever wills, from its inability to will backwards—thus willing itself and all life were supposed to be—punishment!

'And then cloud upon cloud rolled across the spirit, until at last madness preached: "Everything passes away, therefore everything deserves to pass away!"*

' "And this is itself justice, that law of time that time must devour its children":* thus did madness preach.

' "Morally things are ordered according to justice and punishment. Oh where is there redemption from the flux of things and the punishment 'existence'?" Thus did madness preach.

' "Can there be redemption when there is eternal justice? Alas, the stone 'It was' cannot be rolled away: eternal must all punishments be, too!" Thus did madness preach.

' "No deed can be annihilated: so how could it be undone through punishment! This, this is what is eternal in the punishment 'existence': that existence itself must eternally be deed and guilt again!

' "Unless the will should at last redeem itself and willing should become not-willing—": but you know, my brothers, this fable-song of madness!

'I led you away from such fable-songs when I taught you: "The will is a creator."

'All "It was" is a fragment, a riddle, a cruel coincidence—until the creating will says to it: "But thus I willed it!"

'—Until the creating will says to it: "But thus do I will it! Thus shall I will it!"

'But has it ever spoken thus? And when will this happen? Has the will been unharnessed yet from its own folly?

'Has the will yet become its own redeemer and joy-bringer? Has it unlearned the spirit of revenge and all gnashing of teeth?

'And who has taught it reconciliation with time, and something higher than any reconciliation?

'Something higher than any reconciliation the will that is will to power must will—yet how shall this happen? Who has yet taught it to will backwards and want back* as well?'

—But at this point in his speech it happened that Zarathustra suddenly fell silent and looked like one who is terrified in the extreme. With a terrified eye he looked at his disciples; his eye pierced their thoughts and the motives behind their thoughts as if with arrows. But after a while he laughed again and said, pacified:

'It is hard to live with human beings, because keeping silent is so hard. Especially for one who is garrulous.'—

Thus spoke Zarathustra. But the hunchback had listened to the conversation and kept his face covered the while; and when he heard Zarathustra laugh, he looked up curiously and said slowly:

'But why does Zarathustra speak otherwise to us than to his disciples?'*

Zarathustra replied: 'What is so surprising in that! With hunch-backs one may well speak in a hunchbacked way!'

'Good,' said the hunchback. 'And with students one may well tell tales out of school.

'But why does Zarathustra speak otherwise to his students—than to himself?'—

*   *   *

21. On Human Cleverness

Not the height: the precipice is terrifying!

The precipice, where the glance plunges *downward* and the hand reaches *upward*. There the heart is made dizzy by its double will.

Ah, friends, can you perhaps guess what is my heart's double will?

This, this is *my* precipice and my danger, that my glance plunges into the height and my hand would like to hold on and support itself—by the depths!

To the human my will fastens itself, with fetters I bind myself to the human, because I am swept upward to the Overhuman: for that is where my other will aims.

And *for that* I live blindly among human beings, just as if I did not know them: that my hand might not wholly lose its belief in what is firm.

I do not know you humans: this darkness and consolation is often spread about me.

I sit at the gateway for every rogue and ask: Who wants to deceive me?

This is the first instance of my human cleverness, that I let myself be deceived so as not to be on guard against deceivers.

Ah, if I were on guard against the human, how could the human be an anchor for my ball! Too easily would I be swept upward and away!

This providence lies over my fate, that I must be without foresight.

And whoever does not want to die of thirst among humans must learn to drink out of all glasses; and whoever wants to stay clean among humans must know how to wash even with dirty water.

And thus I often spoke to myself in consolation: 'Well then! Come on, old heart!* A misfortune misled you: enjoy this as your—good fortune!'

But this is my other human cleverness: I am more considerate toward the *vain* than the proud.

Is not wounded vanity the mother of all tragedies? But wherever pride is wounded, there surely grows something even better than pride is.

In order for life be good to watch, its play must be well acted: but for that one needs good play-actors.

Good play-actors I found all vain people to be: they act and want people to like watching them—all their spirit is behind this will.

They direct themselves, they invent themselves; in their vicinity I love to watch life—this cures a heavy heart.

Therefore I am considerate toward the vain, for they are physicians to my heavy heart and keep me gripped by the human as by a play.

And then: who could fathom in the vain man the full depth of his modesty! I am kind to him and sympathetic because of his modesty.

From you he would learn belief in himself: he feeds on your glances; he eats praise out of your hands.

He even believes your lies when you lie well about him: for deep down his heart sighs: 'What am *I*!'

And if the true virtue is one that is not aware of itself: well, the vain man is not aware of his modesty!—

But this is my third human cleverness, that I do not let the sight of *evil* be spoiled for me by your fearfulness.

It is bliss for me to see the wonders hatched by a hot sun: tigers and palm-trees and rattlesnakes. Among humans, too, a hot sun hatches a fine brood and much that is worthy of wonder in those who are evil.

Indeed, just as your wisest ones did not seem so wise to me, so too I found human wickedness to be less than its reputation.

And I often asked myself, shaking my head: Why go on rattling, you rattlesnakes?

Verily, for evil, too, there is yet a future! And the hottest south is for the human being still undiscovered.

How much is now called grossest wickedness that is only twelve shoes wide and three months long!* But some day greater dragons will come into the world.

For, that the Overhuman might not lack his dragon, the Over-dragon that is worthy of him, much hot sun must yet burn upon damp primeval forest!

Your wild cats must first have become tigers, and your poisonous toads crocodiles: for the good hunter shall have good hunting!*

And verily, you good and righteous men! In you there is much that is laughable, and especially your fear of what has hitherto been called 'Devil'!

So foreign are your souls to what is great, that the Overhuman would *terrify* you with his goodness!

And you who are wise and knowledgeable, you would flee from the burning sun of that wisdom in which the Overhuman pleasurably bathes his nakedness!

You highest humans that my eye has encountered! This is my doubt concerning you, and my secret laughter: I suspect that you would call my Overhuman—Devil!

Ah, I have grown weary of these highest and best men: from their 'height' I longed to go upward, onward, away to the Overhuman!

A horror overcame me when I saw these best men naked: then I grew wings on which to soar into distant futures.*

Into farther futures, more southerly souths, than any artist has dreamed of: to a realm where Gods are ashamed of all clothes!

But *you* I want to see disguised, you neighbours and fellow humans, and well decked out, and vain, and dignified, as 'the good and the righteous'—

And disguised would I myself sit among you—that I might *fail to recognize* you and me: this then is my final human cleverness.—

Thus spoke Zarathustra.

*   *   *

22. The Stillest Hour*

What has happened to me, my friends? You see me troubled, driven forth, unwillingly obedient, ready to go away—ah, to go away from *you!*

Yes, once again must Zarathustra go back to his solitude: but this time the bear goes unhappily back to his cave!

What happened to me? Who ordered this?—Ah, my angry mistress wills it thus, she has spoken to me: have I ever told you her name?

Yesterday towards evening there spoke to me *my Stillest Hour*: that is the name of my terrible mistress.

And thus it happened—for I must tell you everything, that your hearts might not harden against me for departing so suddenly!

Do you know the terror of him who falls asleep?—

He is terrified down to his toes, because the ground gives way and the dream begins.

This I tell you in a parable. Yesterday, at the stillest hour, the ground gave way: the dream began.

The hand moved forward, the clock of my life drew breath*— never have I heard such stillness around me: so that my heart was terrified.

Then it spoke to me without voice: '*You know it, Zarathustra?*'—

And I screamed in terror at this whispering, and the blood drained from my face: but I remained silent.

Then it spoke to me once again without voice: 'You know it, Zarathustra, but you do not say it!'—

And at last I answered like one defiant: 'Yes, I know it, but I will not say it!'

Then it spoke to me again without voice: 'You *will* not, Zarathustra? Can this be true? Do not hide yourself in your defiance!'—

And I wept and trembled like a child and said: 'Ah, I did want to, but how can I! Excuse me just from this! It is beyond my strength!'

Then it spoke to me again without voice: 'What do you matter, Zarathustra! Speak your word and break!'—

And I answered: 'Ah, is it *my* word? Who am *I*? I wait for one more worthy; I am not even worth being broken by it.'

Then it spoke to me again without voice: 'What do you matter? You are not yet humble enough for me. Humility has the toughest hide.'—

And I answered: 'What has the hide of my humility not already endured! I dwell at the foot of my heights: how high are my summits? No one has yet told me. But my valleys I know well.'

Then it spoke to me again without voice: 'Oh Zarathustra, whoever has to move mountains also moves valleys and lowlands.'—*

And I answered: 'My words have yet to move a mountain, and what I talked of did not reach human beings. I did indeed go to human beings, but I have not yet arrived among them.'

Then it spoke to me again without voice: 'What do you know of *that*! The dew falls upon the grass when the night is most silent.'—*

And I answered: 'They mocked me when I found my own way and went it; and in truth my feet trembled at that time.

'And thus they spoke to me: "You have unlearned the way, and now you are unlearning how to walk!"'

Then it spoke to me again without voice: 'What does their mockery matter! You are one who has unlearned obeying: now shall you command!

'Do you not know who is most needed by all? The one who commands great things.

'To accomplish great things is difficult: but more difficult is to command great things.

'That is what is most unpardonable in you: you have the power, and you do not want to rule.'—

And I answered: 'I lack the lion's voice for commanding.'*

Then it spoke to me again like a whispering: 'It is the stillest words that bring on the storm. Thoughts that come on doves' feet direct the world.*

'O Zarathustra, you shall go as a shadow of that which must come: thus will you command, and commanding lead the way.'—

And I answered: 'I am ashamed.'

Then it spoke to me again without voice: 'You must yet become a child and without shame.

'The pride of youth is still upon you, for you became young quite late: but whoever wants to become a child must yet overcome his youth.'—

And I pondered long, and trembled. But at last I said what I had said at first: 'I will not.'

Then laughter erupted around me. Alas, how this laughter tore at my entrails and slashed open my heart!

And it spoke to me for the last time: 'Oh Zarathustra, your fruits are ripe, but you are not ripe for your fruits!

'So you must go back to your solitude: for you are yet to become mellow.'—

And again there was laughter and fleeing: then it became still around me as if with a twofold stillness. But I lay on the ground, and the sweat poured from my limbs.

—Now you have heard all, and why I must go back to my solitude. Nothing have I kept back from you, my friends.

But this too you have heard from me, *who* is still the most reticent of all human beings—and wills to be so!

Ah, my friends! I might still have something more to say to you; I might still have something more to give to you!* Why do I not give it? Am I then miserly?—

But when Zarathustra had spoken these words, the force of his pain and the nearness of the parting from his friends overwhelmed him, such that he wept loudly; and no one knew how to console him. That night, however, he went away alone and left his friends.

*   *   *

THIRD PART

'You look upward when you desire uplifting. And I look downward because I am uplifted.

Who among you can laugh and be uplifted at the same time?

Whoever climbs the highest mountains laughs about all tragic plays and tragic wakes.'

(*Zarathustra*, 'On Reading and Writing')

1. The Wanderer

It was around midnight when Zarathustra made his way over the ridge of the island, that he might reach the other shore by early morning: for there he wanted to board a ship. On that shore there was a good roadstead at which foreign ships too liked to drop anchor; and these would take on board people who wanted to leave the Isles of the Blest and cross the sea. As Zarathustra was climbing the mountain, he thought on the way of the many lonely wanderings he had undertaken since his youth, and of how many mountains and ridges and summits he had already climbed.

'I am a wanderer and a mountain-climber,' he said to his heart. 'I do not love the plains, and it seems that I cannot sit still for long.

'And now whatever may come to me yet as fate and experience—a wandering will be in it and a climbing of mountains: in the end one experiences only oneself.*

'The time has flowed past when accidents could still befall me; and what *could* still fall to me now that would not already be my own!

'It simply comes back, it finally comes home to me—my own self, and what of myself has long been abroad and scattered among all things and accidents.

'And one more thing do I know: I stand now before my last summit and before that which has been saved up for me for the longest time. Ah, on my hardest way I must set out! Ah, I have begun my loneliest wandering!

'But whoever is of my kind does not avoid such an hour, the hour that says to him: "Only now are you going your way of greatness! Summit and abyss—they are now joined in one!

' "You are going your way of greatness: now what had hitherto been your ultimate danger has become your ultimate refuge!

' "You are going your way of greatness: this must now be your best courage, that there is no longer any way behind you!

' "You are going your way of greatness; here no one shall creep after you! Your own foot has effaced the way behind you, over which is written: Impossibility.

' "And if you now lack all ladders, you must learn how to climb on your own head: how else could you want to climb upward?

' "On your own head and away beyond your own heart! Now what was mildest in you must yet become what is hardest.

' "Whoever has constantly protected himself will at last become sickly from so much protection. Praised be what makes hard!* I do not praise the land where butter and honey—flow!*

' "One must learn to *look away* from oneself in order to see *much*: this hardness is necessary for every climber of mountains.

' "But whoever tries with an importunate eye to understand, how should he see more than the foregrounds of all things!

' "But you, O Zarathustra, wanted to see the grounds of all things and their backgrounds: so you must now climb over yourself— onward, upward, until you have even your stars *beneath* you!

' "Yes! To look down upon myself and even upon my stars: that alone would I call my *summit*; that is still left for me as my *ultimate* summit!" '—

Thus spoke Zarathustra to himself as he climbed, consoling his heart with hard sayings: for he was sore at heart as never before. And when he came to the top of the mountain-ridge, behold, there lay the other sea spread out before him; and he stood still and was silent for a long time. And the night was cold at this height, and clear and bright with stars.

I recognize my lot, he said at last in sorrow. Well then! I am prepared. My ultimate solitude has just begun.

Ah, this black and sorrowful sea beneath me! Ah, this pregnant night-like moroseness! Ah, fate and sea! To you must I now climb *down!*

Before my highest mountain I stand and before my longest wandering: therefore I must first descend deeper than I have ever done before:

—deeper into pain than I have ever descended, even into its blackest flood! Thus my fate wills it. Well then! I am prepared.

Where do the highest mountains come from? I once asked. Then I learned that they come from out of the sea.*

The evidence is inscribed in their stone and in the walls of their summits. It is from the deepest that the highest must come to its height.—

Thus spoke Zarathustra on the peak of the mountain, where it was cold; but when he drew near to the sea and stood at last alone beneath the cliffs, he had grown weary on the way and fuller of yearning than ever before.

Everything is still asleep now, he said. Even the sea is asleep. Drunk with sleep and strangely its eye regards me.

But its breath is warm; that I feel. And I also feel that it is dreaming. In its dreams it writhes upon hard pillows.

Hark! Hark! How it groans from evil memories! Or from evil expectations?

Ah, I am sad along with you, you dark monster, and even angry at myself for your sake.

Alas, that my hand has insufficient strength! Verily, I would dearly like to redeem you from your evil dreams!—

And as Zarathustra spoke thus, he laughed at himself with bitterness and a heavy heart. What, Zarathustra! he said. Would you even sing consolation to the sea?

Ah, you loving fool, Zarathustra, over-blissful in your trusting! But thus have you always been: you have always approached trustingly all that is terrible.

You have always wanted to caress every monster. A puff of warm breath, a soft tuft on the paw—and at once you were ready to love and to lure it.

For *love* is the danger of the loneliest, love of anything *if only it is alive!* Laughable, verily, are my folly and my modesty in love!

Thus spoke Zarathustra and laughed at himself a second time: but then he thought of the friends he had left behind—and as if he had wronged them with his thoughts, he was angry at what he had thought. And it soon happened that the laugher wept:—from wrath and yearning Zarathustra wept bitterly.*

*   *   *

2. On the Vision and Riddle

I

When the rumour spread among the sailors that Zarathustra was on board—for another man had embarked with him at the same time who came from the Isles of the Blest—there arose great curiosity and anticipation. But Zarathustra remained silent for two days and was cold and deaf with sadness, such that he responded to neither looks nor questions. Then on the evening of the second day he opened his ears again, though he still remained silent: for there was much that was strange and dangerous to be heard on this ship, which came from far away and would sail even farther. But Zarathustra was a friend to all those who journey far and do not like to live without danger. And behold! At last through his listening his own tongue was loosened, and the ice of his heart broke up:—and so he began to talk thus:

To you, bold searchers, tempters, experimenters,* and whoever has embarked with cunning sails upon terrifying seas—

to you, who are drunk with riddles, glad of twilight, whose souls are lured with flutes to every confounding chasm:

—for you do not want to grope along a thread with cowardly hand; and, where you can *guess*, you hate to *deduce*—

to you alone I recount the riddle that I *saw*—the vision of the loneliest.—

Gloomily I walked of late through a corpse-coloured twilight—gloomily and hard of heart, with lips pressed together. Not only one sun had gone down for me.

A path that climbed defiantly through boulders, malicious, desolate, not graced by weed or shrub: a mountain-path crunched beneath my foot's defiance.

Mutely striding over the mocking clatter of pebbles, trampling the stone that made it slide: thus my foot forced its way upward.

Upward:—in defiance of the spirit that drew it downward, drew it abyssward, the Spirit of Heaviness, my Devil and arch-enemy.

Upward:—although he sat on me, half dwarf, half mole;* lame; laming; dripping lead into my ear, lead-drop thoughts into my brain.

'O Zarathustra,' he whispered mockingly, syllable by syllable, 'you philosophers' stone!* You threw yourself up, but every upthrown stone must   fall!

'O Zarathustra, you philosophers' stone, you slingshot-stone, you star-pulverizer! You threw yourself so high—but every upthrown stone—must fall!

'Sentenced to yourself and to your own stoning: O Zarathustra, far indeed you threw the stone—but onto *you* will it come falling back!'

Then the dwarf fell silent, and that lasted long. But his silence oppressed me; and being two in such a way is truly more lonely than being one!

I climbed, I climbed, I dreamed, I thought—but everything oppressed me. Like a sick man I was, whom his wicked torment makes weary, and who again is wakened from his sleep by a still more wicked dream.—

But there is in me something I call courage: this has up to now struck dead my every discouragement. This courage finally bade me stand still and speak: 'Dwarf! You! Or I!'—

For courage is the best of killers—courage that *attacks:* for in every attack is ringing play.*

The human being, however, is the most courageous beast: it has thereby overcome every other beast. With ringing play it has so far overcome every pain; although human pain is the deepest pain.

Courage also strikes dead the dizziness one feels at the abyss: and where would the human being not stand at the abyss! Is seeing not itself—seeing the abyss?

Courage is the best of killers: courage strikes even pitying dead. But pitying is the deepest abyss: as deeply as the human being sees into life, so deeply does it also see into suffering.

But courage is the best of killers, courage that attacks: it even strikes death dead, for it says: 'Was *that* life? Well then! One more time!'*

But in such a saying there is much ringing play. He that hath ears, let him hear.—*

*   *   *

2

'Stop, dwarf!' I said. 'I, or you! But I am the stronger of us two—for you do not know my abyss-deep thought! *That*—you would not be able to bear!'

Then something happened that made me lighter: for the dwarf jumped down from my shoulder, out of curiosity! And he squatted down on a rock in front of me. But there was a gateway right where we had stopped.

'Behold this gateway, dwarf!' I continued. 'It has two faces. Two ways come together here: nobody has ever taken them to the end.

'This long lane back here: it goes on for an eternity. And that long lane out there—that is another eternity.

'They contradict themselves, these ways; they confront one another head on, and here, at this gateway, is where they come together. The name of the gateway is inscribed above it: "Moment."

'But whoever should walk farther on one of them—on and on, farther and farther: do you believe, dwarf, that these ways contradict themselves eternally?'—

'All that is straight lies,' murmured the dwarf contemptuously. 'All truth is crooked; time itself is a circle.'

'You Spirit of Heaviness!' I said angrily. 'Do not make it too light and easy for yourself! Or I shall leave you squatting where you squat, Lamefoot—and I carried you *up!*

'Behold', I said, 'this moment! From this gateway Moment a long eternal lane runs *backward:* behind us lies an eternity.

'Must not whatever among all things *can* walk have walked this lane already? Must not whatever among all things *can* happen have happened, and been done, and passed by already?

'And if everything has already been, what do you think, dwarf, of this moment? Must this gateway too not already—have been?

'And are not all things knotted together so tightly that this moment draws after it *all* things that are to come? *Thus*— —itself as well?

'For whatever among all things *can* walk: in this long lane *out*, too—it *must* walk once more!—

'And this slow-moving spider, crawling in the moonlight, and this moonlight itself, and I and you in the gateway, whispering together, whispering of eternal things—must we not all have been here before?

'—and must come again and walk in that other lane, out there, before us, in this long and dreadful lane—must we not eternally come back again?—'

Thus was I talking, and ever more softly: for I was afraid of my own thoughts and the motives behind them. Then, suddenly, I heard a dog *howling* nearby.

Had I ever heard a dog howl like that? My thoughts ran back. Yes! When I was a child, in the most distant childhood:

—at that time I heard a dog howl like that. And saw him too, bristling, with his head stretched up, trembling, in stillest midnight, when even dogs believe in ghosts:

—so that I was moved to compassion. For just then the full moon was passing, silent as death, over the house: just then it stood still, a rounded glow—still upon the flat roof, as if upon alien property:—

that was why the dog was terrified: for dogs believe in thieves and ghosts. And when again I heard that howling, I was moved to compassion once again.

Where had the dwarf gone now? And the gateway? And the spider? And all the whispering? Had I been dreaming? Had I woken up? Between wild cliffs I stood all at once, alone, desolate, in the most desolate moonlight.

But a man was lying there! And there! the dog, jumping about, bristling, whimpering. Now it saw me coming—then it howled again, then it *cried*:—had I ever heard a dog cry for help like that?

And verily, what I then saw, I have never seen the like. A young shepherd I saw, writhing, choking, convulsing, his face distorted, and a heavy black snake hanging out of his mouth.

Have I ever seen so much disgust and pallid horror on one face? Had he perhaps been asleep? Then the snake crawled into his throat—and bit itself fast there.

My hand tugged at the snake and tugged:—in vain! it could not tug the snake out of his throat. Then it cried out of me: 'Bite off! Bite off!

'Bite the head off! Bite it off!'—thus it cried out of me, my horror, my hate, my disgust, my compassion, all my good and bad cried out of me with a single cry.—

You bold men around me! You searchers, tempters, experimenters, and whoever among you has embarked with cunning sails upon unexplored seas! You who are glad for riddles!

Now guess for me the riddle that I saw then; now interpret for me the vision of the loneliest!

For it was a vision and a premonition:—*what* did I see then in the parable? And *who* is it that must yet come some day?

Who is the shepherd into whose throat the snake thus crawled? *Who* is the man into whose throat all that is heaviest and blackest will crawl?

—But the shepherd bit, as my cry had counselled him; he bit with a good bite! Far away he spat out the head of the snake—and then sprang up.

No longer shepherd, no longer human—one transformed, illumined, who *laughed!* Never yet on earth had a human being laughed as *he* laughed!

Oh, my brothers, I heard a laughter that was no human laughter—and now a thirst gnaws at me, a yearning, that will never be stilled.

My yearning for this laughter gnaws at me: oh how can I bear to go on living! And how could I bear to die right now!—*

Thus spoke Zarathustra.

*   *   *

3. On Blissfulness Against One's Will

With such riddles and bitterness in his heart Zarathustra voyaged across the sea. But when he was four days' journey away from the Isles of the Blest and his friends, he had overcome all his pain: victorious and with a firm foothold he stood once again upon his fate. And then Zarathustra spoke thus to his jubilant conscience:

Alone am I again and want to be so, alone with clear sky and open sea;* and again afternoon is about me.

It was afternoon when I found my friends for the first time, and afternoon the second time too:—at the hour when all light becomes more still.

For whatever of happiness is still under way between Heaven and earth, that now seeks shelter in a lightened soul: it is *from happiness* that all light has now become more still.

O afternoon of my life! Once *my* happiness too climbed down to the valley, that it might seek shelter: there it found these open and hospitable souls.

O afternoon of my life! What have I not given up, that I might have one thing: this living plantation of my thoughts and this morning light of my highest hope!

Companions the creator once sought and children of *his* own hope: and behold, it turned out that he could not find them, except he first create them himself.

Thus I am in the middle of my work, going to my children and returning from them: for the sake of his children Zarathustra must perfect himself.

For from the ground up one loves only one's child and work; and where there is great love of oneself, it is the true sign of pregnancy: thus have I found it.

My children are still becoming green for me in their first spring, standing close together and shaken in common by the winds, the trees of my garden and my finest soil.

And verily! where such trees stand together, there *are* isles of the blest!

But one day I want to dig them up and place each one on its own: that it might learn solitude and defiance and caution.

Gnarled and crooked and with pliable hardness shall it then stand there by the sea, a living lighthouse of invincible life.

There where the storms rush down to the sea, and the mountain's elephant-trunk drinks, each one shall have its day- and night-watches, for *its* own testing and recognition.

It shall be recognized and tested to see whether it is of my kind and descent—whether it is master of a long will, reticent even when it speaks, and yielding in such a way that in giving it *takes*:—

—that it might one day become my companion and a fellow creator and celebrant with Zarathustra—such a one as inscribes my will upon my tablets: for the greater perfection of all things.

And for its sake and for those like it I must perfect *myself*: for that I now evade my happiness and offer myself to all unhappiness—for *my* ultimate testing and recognition.

And verily, it was time for me to go; and the wanderer's shadow and the longest while and the stillest hour—all talked to me saying: 'It is high time!'

The wind blew through my keyhole and said to me 'Come!' My door flew open cunningly and said to me 'Go!'

But I lay there chained to love of my children: it was desire that set this snare for me, desire for love, that I might fall prey to my children and lose myself in them.

To desire—this now means to me: to have lost myself. *I have you, my children!* In this having, all shall be security and nothing desire.

But the sun of my love lay brooding upon me, and Zarathustra was cooking in his own juice—then shadows and doubts flew over and beyond me.

For frost and winter I was already yearning: 'Oh that frost and winter might make me crack and crunch again!' I sighed:—then icy mists arose from within me.

My past broke open its graves, and many a pain that had been buried alive awakened: they had merely been sleeping, concealed in burial shrouds.

Thus everything called out to me in signs: 'It is time!' But I—did not hear: until at last my abyss stirred itself and my thought bit me.

Ah, you abyss-deep thought, who are *my* thought! When shall I find the strength to hear you burrowing and no longer tremble?*

Up into my throat my heart pounds when I hear you burrowing! Your silence will yet throttle me, you who are abyss-deeply silent!

Never yet have I dared to summon you *up:* it was quite enough that I—bore you with me! As yet I have not been strong enough for the ultimate lion's-exuberance and -wilfulness.

Your heaviness has always been terrifying enough for me: but one day I shall yet find the strength and the lion's voice to summon you up!

Once I have overcome myself in that, then will I overcome myself in something even greater; and a *victory* shall be the seal of my perfection!—

Meanwhile I am drifting still on uncertain seas; chance flatters me, with its smooth tongue; forward and backward I look—and still I see no end.*

The hour of my final struggle has not yet come to me—or is it coming to me now? Verily, with insidious beauty sea and life surround and look at me!

O afternoon of my life! O happiness before evening! O haven on high seas! O peace in the uncertain! How I mistrust you all!

Verily, mistrustful am I of your insidious beauty! I resemble the lover who mistrusts the all-too-velvety smile.

Just as he pushes away his most beloved, still tender in his hardness, out of jealousy—so I push away this blissful hour.

Away with you, you blissful hour! With you there came to me a blissfulness against my will! Willing to suffer my deepest pain I stand here:—you have come at the wrong time!

Away with you, you blissful hour! Rather take shelter there—with my children! Hurry! and bless them yet before evening with *my* happiness!

Now evening approaches: the sun is sinking. There it goes—my happiness!—

Thus spoke Zarathustra. And he waited for his unhappiness the entire night: but he waited in vain. The night remained clear and still, and happiness itself came closer and closer to him. Toward morning, however, Zarathustra laughed to his heart and said mockingly: 'Happiness is pursuing me. That comes from my not pursuing women. Happiness, however, is a woman.'

* * *

4. Before the Sunrise

O Heaven above me, so pure! so deep! You light-abyss! Beholding you I shudder with godlike desires.

Into your height I cast myself—that is *my* depth! In your pureness I hide myself—that is *my* innocence!

The God is veiled by his beauty: thus you conceal your stars. You do not talk: *thus* you proclaim to me your wisdom.

Mute over the roaring sea you have risen for me today, your love and your bashfulness speak a revelation to my roaring soul.

That you came to me beautifully, veiled in your beauty, that you speak to me mutely, revealed in your wisdom:

Oh how should I not divine all that is bashful in your soul! *Before* the sun you came to me, the loneliest one.

We are friends from the very beginning: we have grief and gray dawn and ground in common; the sun as well we have in common.

We do not talk to each other, because we know too many things: we are mutually silent; we smile our knowing to one another.

Are you not the light to my fire? Have you not the sister-soul to my insight?

Together we learned all things; together we learned to climb above ourselves to ourselves and to smile cloudlessly:—

—to smile down cloudlessly from luminous eyes and from far-off distances, while beneath us constraint and purpose and guilt steam like rain.

And when I wandered alone, *for what* did my soul hunger during nights and on wrong paths? And when I climbed mountains, *whom* did I always seek, if not you, on mountains?

And all my wandering and mountain-climbing: that was mere necessity and a help in my helplessness:—*to fly* is alone what my entire will wants, to fly far into *you!*

And whom have I hated more than drifting clouds and everything that stains you? And even my own hatred I hated, because it too stained you!

At drifting clouds I am aggrieved, these slinking, predatory cats: they take from you and me what we have in common—the enormous and unbounded Yea- and Amen-saying.*

At these mediators and mixers we are aggrieved, the drifting clouds: these half-and-halfers that have never learned to bless, nor from the ground up to curse.

Rather would I sit in a barrel beneath a closed Heaven, rather sit in the abyss without a Heaven, than see you, Heaven of light, be stained by drifting clouds!

And often I longed to tie them fast with jagged golden lightning-wires, so that like the thunder I could beat a tattoo on their kettle-bellies:—

—a furious kettle-drummer because they rob me of your Yea! and Amen! you Heaven above me, so pure! so bright! You light-abyss!—because they rob you of *my* Yea! and Amen!

For I would sooner have even noise and thunder and weather-curses than this suspicious, dubious cat-like stillness; and also among human beings I hate the most all pussyfooters and half-and-halfers and doubting, hesitating, drifting clouds.

And 'whoever cannot bless shall *learn* to curse!'—this bright clear teaching fell to me from a bright clear Heaven, this star still stands even on black nights in my Heaven.

But I am a blesser and a Yea-sayer, if only you are around me, so pure! so bright! You light-abyss!—into all abysses I carry my blessing Yea-saying.

A blesser I have become and a Yea-sayer: and for that I struggled long and was a wrestler, that I might one day wrest my hands free for blessing.

But this is my blessing: to stand over each and every thing as its own Heaven, as its round roof, its azure bell and eternal security:* and blessèd is he who blesses thus!

For all things are baptized at the fount of eternity and beyond good and evil; but good and evil are themselves mere intervening shadows and dampening sorrows and drifting clouds.

Verily, a blessing it is and no blasphemy when I teach: 'Over all things stands the Heaven Accident, the Heaven Innocence, the Heaven Contingency, the Heaven Exuberance.'

'Lord Contingency'*—that is the oldest nobility in the world, which I restored to all things when I redeemed them from their bondage under Purpose.

This freedom and Heaven-serenity I placed like an azure bell over all things, when I taught that over them and through them no 'eternal will'—wills.

This exuberance and this folly I put in place of that will, when I taught: 'In all things is one thing impossible—rationality!'

A *little* reason, to be sure, a seed of wisdom scattered from star to star—this pinch of leaven is mixed into all things: for the sake of folly is wisdom mixed into all things!*

A little wisdom is no doubt possible; but this blessèd certainty I found in all things: that they would rather—*dance* on the feet of chance.

O Heaven above me, so pure! so high! That is what your pureness means to me, that there is no eternal reason-spider and -spider-web:—

—that for me you are a dance-floor for Godlike accidents, that for me you are a Gods' table for Godlike dice and dice-throwers!—

But are you blushing? Did I speak something unspeakable? Did I blaspheme when I wanted to bless you?

Or is it bashfulness at our being together that has made you blush?—Do you bid me leave and be silent because now—the *day* comes?

The world is deep—and deeper than ever the day has thought. Not everything may be put into words before the day. But the day comes: so let us now part!

O Heaven above me, so bashful! so glowing! O you my happiness before the sunrise! The day comes: so let us now part!—

Thus spoke Zarathustra.

*   *   *

5. On the Virtue That Makes Smaller

I

When Zarathustra was on dry land again, he did not go straight back to his mountains and his cave, but rather pursued many ways and questions and investigated this and that, so that he said jokingly of himself: 'Behold a river that takes many meanderings to flow back to its source!' For he wanted to experience what had happened to *humanity* in the meantime: whether it had become greater or smaller. And one time he saw a row of new houses, and he was amazed and said:

'What is the meaning of these houses? Verily, no great soul has put them up in its own likeness!

'Could some silly child have taken them out of his toy-box? If only another child would put them back into his box now!

'And these rooms and chambers: can *men* go in and out of them? They look to me to be made for silken dolls, or for compulsive nibblers who perhaps also let themselves be nibbled.'

And Zarathustra stood still and thought awhile. At last he said sadly: '*Everything* has become smaller!

'Everywhere I see lower gates: whoever is of *my* kind can still just manage to get through but—must stoop to do so!

'Oh when shall I come back home again, where I no longer have to stoop—no longer have to stoop *before those who are small!*—And Zarathustra sighed and gazed into the distance.

On that same day, however, he delivered his speech on the virtue that makes smaller.

* * *

2

I walk among this people and keep my eyes open: they do not forgive me for not being envious of their virtues.

They snap at me because I say to them: For small people small virtues are needed— and because it is hard for me to accept that small people are *needed!*

Here I am still like the rooster in a foreign barnyard, who is snapped at even by the hens; and yet I am not unkind to these hens on that account.

I am polite to them, as toward every small irritation; to be prickly toward what is small strikes me as wisdom for hedgehogs.

They all talk about me when they sit around the fire in the evening—they talk about me, but no one thinks—of me!

This is the new stillness I have learned: their noise about me spreads a cloak over my thoughts.

They noise among themselves: 'What does this gloomy cloud want with us? Let us make sure it does not bring a plague upon us!'

And recently a woman pulled back her child when it wanted to come to me: 'Take the children away!'* she cried. 'Such eyes scorch children's souls.'

They cough when I speak: they believe that coughing is an objection to strong winds—they guess nothing of the roaring of my happiness!

'We have no time yet for Zarathustra'—thus they object; but what does a time matter that 'has no time' for Zarathustra?

And even if they should praise me: how could I go to sleep on *their* praise? Their lauding is for me a girdle of thorns: it scratches me even as I put it from me.

And this too I learned among them: the one who praises makes as if he were giving back, though in truth he wants to be given more!

Ask my foot whether it likes their tunes of lauding and luring!

Verily, to such a beat and tick-tock it likes neither to dance nor to stand still.

To small virtue they would like to lure and laud me; to the tick-tock of small happiness they would like to persuade my foot.

I walk among this people and keep my eyes open: they have become *smaller* and are becoming smaller still:—*but this comes from their doctrine of happiness and virtue*.

For they are modest in virtue too—because they want contentment. But with contentment only a modest virtue is compatible.

To be sure, even they learn in their own way how to stride and stride forward: I call it their *hobbling*. They thereby become an obstacle for anyone in a hurry.

And many among them go forward while looking back, with stiffened necks: those I enjoy running up against.

Foot and eyes should not lie, nor expose each other's lies. But there is much lying among the small people.

Some of them can will, but most are merely willed. Some of them are genuine, but most are bad play-actors.

There are play-actors without knowing it among them and play-actors against their will—genuine souls are always rare, especially genuine play-actors.

There is little manfulness here: therefore their women are becoming mannish. For only one who is man enough will—*redeem the woman* in the woman.

And this dissembling I found to be worst among them: that even those who command dissemble the virtues of those who serve.

'I serve, you serve, we serve'—thus prays even the dissembling of the rulers here—and woe, if the first lord is *only* the first servant!*

Ah, even into their dissembling my eye's curiosity flew astray; and well I divined all their fly's happiness and their buzzing around sun-warmed window-panes.

So much kindness, so much weakness I see. So much righteousness and pitying, so much weakness.

Round, righteous, and kind they are to each other, just as grains of sand are round, righteous, and kind to other grains of sand.

Modestly to embrace a small happiness—that they call 'submission'! and at the same time they are already squinting modestly after a new small happiness.

At bottom they naively want one thing most of all: that nobody should hurt them. And so they forestall everyone by doing them good.

This however is *cowardice*: even though it be called 'virtue.'

And if they should once speak roughly, these small people, *I* hear in it only their hoarseness—for any draught will make them hoarse.

Clever they are: their virtues have clever fingers. But they are lacking fists: their fingers know not how to fold themselves into fists.

Virtue for them is whatever makes one modest and tame: with that they have made the wolf into a dog and the human being itself into the human's best domestic animal.

'We have set down our chair in the *middle*'—that is what their smirking says to me—'And equally far from dying swordsmen and contented sows.'

This, however, is—*mediocrity*: even though it be called moderation.—

* * *

3

I walk among this people and let many a word fall: but they know neither how to take nor how to retain.

They are amazed that I have not come there to revile venery and vice; and verily, I have not come to warn against pickpockets either!

They are amazed that I am not prepared to make their cleverness wittier and sharper-pointed: as if they did not already have enough clever boys whose voices grate on me like slate pencils!

And when I call out: 'A curse on all the cowardly Devils within you, who like to whimper and clasp their hands and worship'; they then call out: 'Zarathustra is godless.'

And especially their teachers of submission call this out—but in just their ears I love to shout: 'Yes! I *am* Zarathustra, the Godless!'

These teachers of submission! To wherever it is small and sick and scabby they crawl, like lice; and only my disgust prevents me from cracking them.

Well then! This is my prayer for *their* ears: I am Zarathustra, the Godless, who now says, 'who is more godless than I, that I might enjoy his instruction?'

I am Zarathustra, the Godless: where shall I find my equal? And all those are my equals who give themselves their own will and rid themselves of all submission.

I am Zarathustra, the Godless: I still cook up every chance event in *my* pot. And only when it is quite cooked do I bid it welcome, as *my* food.

And verily, many a chance event came to me imperiously: but even more imperiously did my *will* speak back to it—then it went down imploringly on its knees—

—imploring that it might find shelter and heart with me, and urging me flatteringly: 'But see, O Zarathustra, how only a friend comes to a friend!'—

Yet why am I talking, when no one has *my* ears! And so I want to call it out to all the winds:

You are becoming ever smaller, you small people! You are crumbling away, you who are contented! I shall yet see you perish—

—from your many small virtues, from your many small abstentions, from your many small submissions!

Far too tender, far too yielding: thus is your earth and soil! But for a tree to become *great*, it wants to strike hard roots around hard rocks!

Even what you abstain from weaves at the web of all human future; even your nothingness is a spiderweb and a spider that lives on the future's blood.

And when you take, it is like stealing, you of small virtue; but even among rogues *honour* says: 'One should only steal where one cannot plunder.'

'It will be given'—that is also a teaching of submission. But I say to you, you contented ones: *It will be taken* and will be taken from you more and more!

Ah, that you would put from you all *half* willing and be as resolute for lethargy as for action!

Ah, that you would understand my *word*: 'Do whatever you will— but first be such as are *able to will!*'

'Do love your neighbour as yourselves—but first be for me such as *love themselves*—

'—who love with great love, who love with great despising!' Thus speaks Zarathustra, the Godless.—

Yet why am I talking, when no one has *my* ears! Here it is still an hour too early for me.

My own precursor am I among this people, my own cockcrow through all dark lanes.

But *their* hour will come! And mine will come too! By the hour they become smaller, poorer, more barren—poor weeds! poor earth-soil!

And *soon* they shall stand there for me like parched grass and steppe, and verily! weary of themselves—and thirsting, rather than for water, for *fire*!*

O blessèd hour of lightning! O mystery before midday!—Raging fires will I yet make of them one day and heralds with tongues of flame:—*

—they shall yet proclaim one day with tongues of flame: It is coming, it is near, *the Great Midday!*

Thus spoke Zarathustra.

* * *

6. Upon the Mount of Olives*

Winter, a wicked guest, sits at home with me; blue are my hands from his friendship's handshake.

I honour him, this wicked guest, but I gladly let him sit alone. Gladly I run away from him; and, if one runs *well*, one can outrun him!

With warm feet and warm thoughts I run to where the wind is still—to the sun-filled corner of my Mount of Olives.

There I laugh at my stern guest and yet think well of him, for keeping the flies away at home and silencing many a small noise.

For he cannot bear it when a mosquito wants to sing, far less two; he even makes the lanes lonely, so that at night the moonlight is afraid there.

He is a hard guest—but I honour him; nor do I pray, as the weaklings do, to the pot-bellied fire-idol.*

Rather a little chattering of teeth than a worshipping of idols!— thus my kind wills it. And I am especially aggrieved at all fire-idols that are in heat, musty and steaming.

Whomever I love, I love more in winter than in summer; I mock my enemies better and more heartily, now that winter is sitting at home with me.

Heartily in truth, and even when I *crawl* into bed—there my bundled-up happiness continues to laugh wilfully; and my dream of lies laughs too.

I—a crawler? Never in my life have I crawled before the powerful; and if ever I lied, I lied out of love. Therefore I am glad even in my winter-bed.

A meagre bed warms me more than an opulent one, for I am jealous of my poverty. And in winter it is most loyal to me.

I begin every day with a bit of wickedness, in that I mock the winter with a cold bath: this makes my severe house-guest grumble.

I also like to tickle him with a small wax candle: so that at last he releases the Heavens to me from an ash-gray dawning.

For I am especially wicked in the morning: at the early hour when the bucket clatters at the well and the horses whinny warmly through grayish lanes:—

Impatiently I wait there, till at last the luminous Heaven arises, the snow-bearded winter-Heaven, that white-haired old man—

—the winter-Heaven, most silent, who often even conceals his sun!

Was it from him that I learned the long and luminous silence? Or did he learn it from me? Or did each of us devise it on his own?

The origin of all good things is thousandfold—all good and wilful things spring into existence from sheer joy: how should they always do that—just one time only!

A good and wilful thing is the long silence too, and to look out like the winter-Heaven from a luminous round-eyed countenance—

—like him to conceal one's sun and one's unshakeable solar will: verily, this art and this winter-wilfulness I have learned *well*.

It is my favourite wickedness and art that my silence has learned not to betray itself through silence.

Rattling both words and dice I can outwit the solemn warders: past all these severe inspectors shall my will and purpose slip by.

That no one might see down into my ground and ultimate will— for that I devised my long and luminous silence.

Thus I found many a clever one: he veiled his countenance and muddied his waters, that no one might see through him to his depths.

But precisely to him came the cleverer mistrusters and nut-crackers: and precisely from him did they fish out his best-concealed fish!

But those who are clear, and upright, and transparent—they are for me the cleverest of the silent: for their ground is so *deep* that even the clearest water does not—betray them.—

You snow-bearded silent winter-Heaven, round-eyed and white-haired above me! O you heavenly allegory of my soul and its wilfulness!

And *must* I not conceal myself, like one who has swallowed gold—so that they do not slit open my soul?

Must I not walk on stilts, so that they *overlook* my long legs—all these enviers and sufferers that are around me?

These smoke-filled, overheated, worn-out, withered, distempered souls—how *could* their envy endure my happiness!

So I show them only the ice and the winter on my summits—and *not* that my mountain yet winds around itself all girdles of the sun!

They hear only the whistling of my winter storms, and *not* that I also sail over warm seas, like yearning, heavy, torrid south winds.

They even have pity on my accidents and coincidences—but *my* word says: 'Suffer coincidence to come unto me: innocent it is, like a little child!'*

How *could* they endure my happiness, unless I wrapped coincidences and winter-deprivations and polar-bear caps and snow-Heaven cloaks around my happiness!

—unless I had mercy on their very *pity*: the pity of these enviers and sufferers!

—unless I myself sighed before them and chattered with cold, and patiently *allowed* myself to be wrapped in their pity!

This is the wise wilfulness and good will of my soul: that it *does not conceal* its winter and its frosty storms; nor does it even conceal its chilblains.

One person's solitude is the fleeing of an invalid; another's solitude is a fleeing *from* the invalids.

Let them *hear* me chattering and sighing from the winter's cold, all these poor and squinting knaves around me! With such sighing and chattering I still flee from their overheated rooms.

Let them sympathize and sigh with me about my chilblains: 'On the ice of his understanding he will yet *freeze* to death!'—thus they wail.

In the meantime I run with warm feet to and fro upon my Mount of Olives: in the sun-filled corner of my Mount of Olives I sing and mock all pitying.—

Thus sang Zarathustra

*   *   *

7. On Passing By

Thus, walking slowly through many peoples and many kinds of towns, Zarathustra returned by such detours to his mountains and his cave. And behold, he thereby came unexpectedly to the gate of the *great city*: and here a frothing fool with hands outspread leaped before him and barred his way. But this was the same fool that the people called 'Zarathustra's ape': for he had gathered something of the phrasing and cadences of Zarathustra's speech and also liked to borrow from the treasure of his wisdom. And the fool spoke thus to Zarathustra:

'O Zarathustra, here is the great city: here you have nothing to seek and everything to lose.

'Why would you want to wade through this mire? Have pity on your feet!* Rather spit upon the city gate and—turn back!

'Here is Hell for solitaries' thoughts: here great thoughts are boiled alive and then cooked down small.

'Here all great feelings decay: here only tiny skin-and-bone feelings are allowed to rattle!

'Do you not already smell the slaughterhouses and soup-kitchens of the spirit? Does this city not steam with the fumes of slaughtered spirit?

'Do you not see souls hanging there like limp and filthy rags?— And they even make newspapers from these rags!

'Do you not hear how the spirit has here been reduced to a play on words? It vomits forth repulsive verbal swill!—And they even make newspapers from this verbal swill.

'They hurry each other along and yet know not—where to? They heat each other up and yet know not—for what? They tinkle with their cans, they jingle with their gold.

'They are cold and so seek warmth in spirituous liquors; they are overheated and so seek coolness in frozen spirits; they are all ailing and addicted to public opinions.

'All venery and vice is at home here; but there are also virtuous people here, and much in the way of skilful institutional virtue:—

'Much skilful virtue with writing-fingers and behinds hardened by sitting and waiting, blessed with little stars on the chest and well-stuffed rumpless daughters.

'There is also much piety here and much devout spittle-licking, flattery-dripping before the God of armies.*

' "From on high" the stars and the gracious spittle trickle down;* toward on high each and every starless bosom yearns.

'The moon has its own court, and the court has its mooncalves: but to all that comes from the court the beggar-folk and all skilful beggar-virtue pray.

' "I serve, you serve, we serve"—thus all skilful virtue prays to the prince on high: that the well-earned star may at last be pinned on the narrow bosom!

'But the moon still revolves around all that is earthly: so even the prince revolves around the most earthly thing of all—but that is the gold of the shopkeepers.

'The God of armies is no God of gold bars; the prince may reflect, but the shopkeeper—directs!

'By all that is bright and strong and good in you, O Zarathustra! Spit upon this city of shopkeepers and turn back!

'Here all blood flows putrid and tepid and spumy through all veins: spit upon the great city, which is the great cesspool where all the scum pools together!

'Spit upon the city of flattened souls and narrow breasts, of sharpened eyes and sticky fingers—

'—upon the city of the importunate, those who are shameless, the scrawlers and bawlers, overheatedly ambitious:

'—where everything putrid and of ill repute, lusting and dusking, overrated and ulcerated and conspiratorial festers together:—

'—spit upon the great city and turn back!'— —

But here Zarathustra interrupted the frothing fool and held his mouth shut.

'Have done at last!' cried Zarathustra. 'Your speech and manner have long since disgusted me!

'Why did you live for so long in the swamp that you yourself had to become a frog and a toad?

'Does a putrid and spumy swamp-blood not now flow through your own veins, that you have learned to croak and blaspheme thus?

'Why did you not go into the forest? Or plough the earth? Is the sea not full of grass-green islands?

'I despise your despising; and if you have warned me—why have you not warned yourself?

'Out of love alone shall my despising and my bird of omen fly up: but not out of the swamp!—

'They call you my ape, you frothing fool: but I call you my grunting swine—with your grunting you spoil for me my praise of folly.

'What was it, then, that made you begin grunting? That no one has *flattered* you enough:—therefore you sat yourself down in this filth, that you might have grounds for much grunting—

'—that you might have grounds for much *revenge!* For revenge, you vain fool, is what all your frothing is: I have divined you well!

'But your fool's words harm *me*, even when you are right! And if Zarathustra's words *were* even a hundred times right, by my words *you* would always—*do* wrong!'

Thus spoke Zarathustra; and he looked at the great city, sighed, and was long silent. At last he spoke thus:

I too am disgusted by this great city and not only by this fool. Here as there, there is nothing to be made better, nothing to be made worse.

Woe unto this great city!*—And would that I might already see the pillar of fire in which it will be consumed!*

For such pillars of fire must precede the Great Midday. Yet this has its own time and its own fate.—

This teaching, however, I give to you, fool, in parting: Where one can no longer love, there one should—*pass by*!—

Thus spoke Zarathustra and passed by the fool and the great city.

*   *   *

8. On Apostates

I

Ah, does everything already lie wilted and gray that but recently stood green and colourful on this meadow? And how much honey of hope have I carried from here to my beehives!

These young hearts have already all become old—and not even old! only weary, common, comfortable:—they call it 'we have become pious again'.

Just recently I saw them in early morning striding out on courageous feet: but the feet of their understanding became weary, and now they are even slandering their morning-courage!

Verily, several of them once raised their legs like dancers, and the laughter in my wisdom beckoned to them:—then they thought better of it. Just now I saw some of them bent over—crawling toward the Cross.*

Around light and freedom they fluttered once like mosquitoes and young poets. A little older, a little colder: and already they are mystifiers and mutterers and hearthside-squatters.

Did their hearts perhaps grow despondent because solitude had swallowed me like a whale?* Did their ears perhaps hearken yearningly *in vain* for me and my trumpet- and herald-calls?

—Ah, there are always only a few of them whose hearts have lasting courage and exuberance; and in those the spirit, too, remains patient. The rest, however, are *cowardly*.

The rest: those are always the great majority, the commonplace, the superfluous, the many too many—they are all of them cowardly!—

Whoever is of my kind will find that the experiences of my kind too will cross his path: such that his first companions will have to be corpses and jesters.

His second companions, however—they will call themselves his *believers*: a lively swarm, much love, much folly, much beardless veneration.

To these believers whoever is of my kind among men should not bind his heart; whoever knows the cursory-cowardly kind of humanity should not believe in these springtimes and colourful meadows!

If they *could do* otherwise, then they would also *will* otherwise. Half-and-halfers spoil everything whole. That leaves become withered—what is there to mourn there!

Let them fly and fall, O Zarathustra, and do not mourn! Better yet blow with rustling winds among them—

blow among these leaves, O Zarathustra: so that all that is *withered* might run from you all the faster!—

*   *   *

2

'We have become pious again'—thus these apostates profess; and many among them are even too cowardly to profess thus.

Those I look in the eye—to their faces I say and to the blushing of their cheeks: You are such as are *praying* again!

But it is a disgrace to pray! Not for everyone, but for you and me and whoever else has his conscience in his head. For *you* it is a disgrace to pray!

You know it well: your cowardly Devil within, who would gladly like to clasp his hands and lay his hands in his lap and be more comfortable:—this cowardly Devil urges you, 'there *is* a God!'

Thereby, however, you belong to the kind that shuns the light, who cannot rest where there is light; now you must daily bury your head deeper in night and mist!

And verily, you have chosen the hour well: for just now the birds of night are again flying out. The hour has come for all light-shunning folk, the evening- and leisure-hour, when there is no— 'leisure'.

I hear and smell it: their hour for the hunt and procession has come; not indeed for a wild hunt,* but for a tame and lame and snooping soft-treading and soft-praying hunt—

—for a hunt after soulful moral-mice: all the mousetraps of the heart have been set again! And wherever I lift a curtain, a little moth comes tumbling out.

Was it perhaps sitting there together with another little night-moth? For everywhere I smell little hidden-away communities; and wherever there are closets, there are new devotees inside and the fumes of devotees.

They spend long evenings sitting together and saying: 'Let us become as little children again* and say, "Dear God"!'—their mouths and stomachs ruined by pious confectioners.

Or they spend long evenings watching a cunning lurking cross-spider* that preaches cleverness to the spiders themselves and teaches thus: 'Under crosses there is good spinning!'

Or they sit the whole day with fishing-rods beside swamps and think themselves *deep* in doing so; but whoever fishes where there are no fish I do not even call superficial!

Or they learn to play the harp in pious-pleasing style from a composer of songs, who would dearly like to harp his way into young females' hearts—for he has grown weary of the old females and their hymns of praise.

Or they learn to shudder from a learned half-madman, who waits in darkened rooms for the spirits to come to him*—and the spirit then deserts him!

Or they listen to an old roving bumbling and grumbling piper, who learned the mournfulness of tones from mournful winds; now he whistles after the wind and preaches mournfulness in mournful tones.

And some of them have even become night-watchmen: now they know how to blow horns and walk around at night waking up old affairs that had long since gone to sleep.

Five sayings about old affairs I heard last night by the garden wall: they came from just such old and troubled dried up night-watchmen.

'For a father he doesn't take good enough care of his children: human fathers do far better!'—

'He's too old! He doesn't take care of his children at all any more'—thus answered the other night-watchman.

'But does he *have* any children? No one can prove it, if he doesn't prove it himself! For a long time I've wanted him to prove it thoroughly for once.'

'Prove it? As if *he* had ever proved anything! Proof is hard for him; he thinks it's so important that we should *believe* him.'

'Yes! yes! Belief makes him saved, belief in him.* That's so much the way with old people. It's that way for us too!'—

—Thus the two old night-watchmen and light-scarecrows spoke to each other, and thereupon tooted mournfully into their horns: thus it happened last night by the garden wall.

But my heart writhed with laughter and wanted to break and did not know where to go and sank into my midriff.

Verily, this will yet be the death of me, that I choke with laughter when I see asses drunk and hear night-watchmen thus doubting God.

For is it not *long* past the time for all such doubts? Who may yet awaken such old and sleeping light-shunning affairs!

For with the old Gods things came to an end long ago:—and verily, they had a good and joyful Gods' end!

Theirs was no mere 'twilight' death*—that is a lie! Rather: one day they—*laughed* themselves to death!

This happened when the most godless words issued from a God himself—the words: 'There is one God! Thou shalt have no other God before me!'—*

—an old wrath-beard of a God, most jealous, forgot himself thus:—

And thereupon all the Gods laughed and rocked on their chairs and shouted: 'Is just this not Godliness, that there are Gods, but no God?'

He that hath ears, let him hear.—

Thus talked Zarathustra in the town that he loved and which is called 'The Motley Cow'. For from here he had to walk only two more days in order to come again to his cave and to his animals; and his soul rejoiced constantly at the nearness of his return home.—

*   *   *

9. The Return Home

O Solitude! You are my *home*, Solitude! Too long have I lived wild in wild and foreign lands for me not to come home to you in tears!

Now just threaten me with your finger, as mothers threaten, now smile to me, as mothers smile, now just say: 'And who was that, who once stormed away from me like a storm-wind?—

'—who cried in parting: Too long have I sat with Solitude, and so unlearned being silent! *That*—you have surely learned now?

'O Zarathustra, I know all: and that among the many you were *lonelier*, you singular one, than ever you were with me!

'Loneliness is one thing, solitude is another: *that*—you have learned now! And that among human beings you will always be wild and strange:

'—wild and strange even when they love you: for they want *to be treated gently* by everything!

'But here you are at home with yourself in your own house; here you can talk freely about everything and shake out all grounds, for nothing here is ashamed of oblique, obdurate feelings.

'Here all things come caressingly to your discourse and flatter you: for they want to ride on your back. On every allegory you ride here to every truth.

'Directly and sincerely you may talk here to all things: and verily, like praise it rings in their ears that someone should—talk frankly with all things!

'Another thing, however, is being lonely. For, do you remember, O Zarathustra? When at that time your bird called high above you, as you stood in the forest, indecisive, where to? unknowing, close to a corpse:—

'—when you said: May my animals lead me! More dangerous I found it among human beings than among beasts.—*That* was loneliness!

'And do you remember, O Zarathustra? When you sat on your island, a fount of wine among empty buckets, giving and giving away, pouring and pouring out among the thirsty:

'—till at last you sat alone and thirsty among drunkards and lamented every night, "Is receiving not more blessèd than giving? And stealing more blessèd still than receiving?"*—*That* was loneliness!

'And do you remember, O Zarathustra? When your Stillest Hour came and drove you away from yourself, when she spoke in a wicked whisper: "Speak and break!"—

'—when she made you repent of all your waiting and being silent, and discouraged your humble courage: *That* was loneliness!'—

O Solitude! You are my home, Solitude! How blissfully and tenderly your voice talks to me!

We do not question each other, we do not complain to each other, we go openly with each other through open doors.

With you it is open and clear; and even the hours here run by on lighter feet. For in the dark time weighs more heavily than in the light.

Here the words and word-shrines of all Being spring open for me: all Being wants to become word here, all Becoming wants to learn from me here how to talk.

Down there, however—there all talking is in vain! There forgetting and passing by are the best wisdom: *that*—I have now learned!

Whoever wanted to grasp everything about human beings would have to grapple with everything. But for that my hands are too clean.

I do not even like to breathe in their breath; ah, that I lived for so long amidst their noise and foul breath!

Oh blissful stillness about me! Oh purest odours about me! Oh how this stillness draws purest breaths from a deep breast! Oh how it listens, this blissful stillness!

But down there—there it is all mere talk, and everything goes unheard. One might ring out one's wisdom with bells: the shopkeepers in the market-place will out-jingle it with pennies!

With them it is all mere talk, and no one can understand any more. Everything falls through, nothing falls into deep wells any more.

With them it is all mere talk, and nothing comes of it or reaches its end. Everything cackles, but who still wants to sit quietly on the nest and hatch the eggs?

With them it is all mere talk, and everything is talked to pieces. And whatever was yesterday still too hard for the time itself and its teeth: today it hangs, mangled by scraping and gnawing, out of the maws of the men of today.

With them it is all mere talk, and everything is betrayed. And what was once regarded as secret and a secrecy of profound souls, today belongs to the street-trumpeters and other such butterflies.

O humankind, you wondrous thing! You noise in dark lanes! Now you lie behind me once again:—my greatest danger lies behind me!

In caring and pitying my greatest danger has always lain;* and all humankind wants to be treated gently and pitied.

Withholding truths, with a fool's hand and a foolishly fond heart and rich in pity's little lies—thus have I always lived among human beings.

Disguised I have sat among them, prepared to misjudge *myself*, that I might endure *them*, and glad to urge myself, 'you fool, you do not know human beings!'

One forgets human beings when one lives among them: there is too much foreground in all humans—what is *there* for far-seeing, far-seeking eyes!

And when they misjudged me, I treated them gently for it, fool that I was, more than I did myself: accustomed to hardness against myself and often even taking revenge on myself for this gentle treatment.

Stung all over by poisonous flies and hollowed out, like a stone, by many drops of wickedness, thus I sat among them and said to myself still: 'Everything small is innocent of its smallness!'

Especially those who call themselves 'the good' I found to be the most poisonous flies: they sting in all innocence, they lie in all innocence; how *could* they be—righteous toward me!

Whoever lives among the good, pity teaches him to lie. Pity makes the air stifling for all free souls. For the stupidity of the good is unfathomable.

To conceal myself and my richness—*that* I learned down there: for I found everyone still poor in spirit. This was the lie of my pitying, that I knew about everyone,

—that I saw and smelled with everyone what was *enough* spirit for him and what was already *too much* spirit!

Their pedantic wise men: I called them wise, not pedantic—thus I learned to swallow my words. Their gravediggers: I called them explorers and testers—thus I learned to mix up my words.

The gravediggers dig up illnesses for themselves. Under old ruins lurk evil vapours. One should not stir up the morass. One should live upon mountains.

With blissful nostrils I again breathe mountain-freedom! Redeemed is my nose at last from the smell of all humankind!

Tickled by keen breezes, as if by sparkling wines, my soul *sneezes*—sneezes and jubilates to itself: *Gesundheit!*

Thus spoke Zarathustra.

*   *   *

10. On the Three Evils

I

In a dream, in the last dream of the morning, I stood today in the foothills—beyond the world, I held a scales and *weighed* the world.

Oh how dawn of morning came to me too soon: she glowed me awake, the jealous dawn! Jealous is she always of my morning-dream glowings.

Measurable for one who has time, weighable for a good weigher, flyable for strong wings, guessable for Godlike nut-crackers: thus did my dream find the world:—

My dream, a bold sailor, half ship, half hurricane, reticent as a butterfly, impatient as a falcon: yet what patience and time it had today for weighing the world!

Did my wisdom perhaps comfort it secretly, my laughing waking day-wisdom, who mocks all 'infinite worlds'? For she says: 'Where there is force, there *number* will become mistress: she has more force.'

How confidently my dream looked upon this finite world, not eager for the new, nor eager for the old, not fearfully, nor imploringly:—

—as if a full apple offered itself to my hand, a ripe golden apple, with a cool soft silken skin: thus did the world offer itself to me:—

—as if a tree waved to me, broad-branched, strong-willed, bent down like an arm-rest and even like a foot-rest for one weary of the way: thus did the world stand on my foothills:—*

—as if delicate hands were carrying a shrine toward me, a shrine open to the delight of bashful and adoring eyes: thus did the world offer itself to me today:—

—not riddle enough to scare away human love, not solution enough to put to sleep human wisdom: a humanly good thing was the world to me today, which is slandered as so evil!

How grateful I am to my morning-dream, that early today I thus weighed the world! As a humanly good thing it came to me, this dream and heart's consoler!

And that I might do the same during the day and learn and imitate from the dream what is best in it: I now want to put the three most evil things on the scales and weigh them humanly well.—

Whoever taught us to bless there, also taught us to curse: what are the three most cursed things in the world? These will I put on the scales.

Sensuality, the lust to rule, selfishness: these Three have so far been cursed the most and slandered and lied about the worst—these Three will I weigh humanly well.

Come now! Here are my foothills and there is the sea: *that* rolls toward me, shaggy, fawningly, the faithful old hundred-headed dog-monster that I love.

Come now! Here will I hold the scales over the rolling sea: and I also choose a witness to watch this—you, you solitary tree, strong-scented, broad-vaulted, that I love!—

By what bridge does the now go over to the sometime? Under what compulsion does the high compel itself down to the low? And what bids even the highest—grow up farther?—

Now the scales stand even and still: three weighty questions have I thrown in, three weighty answers the other pan holds.

* * *

2

Sensuality: for all hair-shirted body-despisers their thorn and stake, and cursed as 'world' by all believers in a world behind: for it mocks and makes fools of all teachers of confusion and delusion.*

Sensuality: for the rabble the slow fire over which they are roasted; for all worm-eaten wood, for all stinking rags the ever-ready rutting- and stewing-oven.

Sensuality: for free hearts innocent and free, the garden-happiness of the earth, all futures' exuberance of thanks to the now.

Sensuality: only for the wilted a sweetish poison, but for the lion-willed the great heart-strengthener, and the reverently preserved wine of wines.

Sensuality: the great allegory-happiness for higher happiness and highest hope. For to many a one is marriage promised and more than marriage—

—to many a one who is stranger to himself than man is to woman:

and who has fully grasped *how strange* to each other man and woman are!

Sensuality:—yet I want to have fences around my thoughts and also even around my words, lest swine and swooners break into my gardens!—*

Lust to rule: the scalding scourge of the hardest among the hard-hearted; the cruel torture that reserves itself for the very cruellest; the dismal flame of living pyres.

Lust to rule: the wicked gadfly inflicted upon the vainest peoples; the mocker of all uncertain virtue, who rides upon every steed and every pride.

Lust to rule: the earthquake that breaks and breaks open all that is rotten and hollow; the rolling growling punishing shatterer of whited sepulchres;* the lightning question-mark beside premature answers.

Lust to rule: in the face of whose look the human being crawls and cowers and slaves away and becomes lower than snake and swine— until the great despising at last cries out from it—

Lust to rule: the terrible teacher of the great despising who preaches in the face of cities and kingdoms, 'away with you!'—until it cries out of them themselves, 'away with *me*!'

Lust to rule: which is alluring even to the pure and lonely and climbs up into self-sufficient heights, glowing like a love that alluringly paints purple blissfulness on earthen-Heavens.

Lust to rule: but who would call it *lust* when what is high longs downward for power! Verily, there is nothing sick or lustful in such longing and condescension!

That the lonely heights might not remain eternally lonely and sufficient unto themselves; that the mountain might come down to the valley and the winds of the heights to the lowlands:—

Oh who could find the right baptism- and virtue-names for such a yearning! 'Bestowing virtue'—thus did Zarathustra once name the unnameable.

And at that time it happened also—and verily, it happened for the first time!—that his word hallowed *selfishness*, the wholesome, healthy selfishness that wells up from a powerful soul:—

—from a powerful soul, to which the lofty body belongs, one that is beautiful, victorious, restorative, around which each and every thing becomes a mirror:

—the supple and persuasive body, the dancer, whose allegory and epitome is the self-enjoying soul. Such bodies' and souls' self-enjoyment calls itself: 'virtue.'

With its words of good and bad such self-enjoyment screens itself as if with sacred groves; with the names of its happiness it banishes all that is despicable.

Away from itself it banishes all that is cowardly; it speaks: Bad— *that is* cowardly! Despicable it deems those who are always worrying, sighing, complaining, and whoever is concerned to glean even the smallest advantages.

It also despises all grief-burdened wisdom; for verily, there is also wisdom that blooms in the dark, a nightshade-wisdom, which is always sighing: 'All is vain!'

Timid mistrustfulness it regards as paltry, and anyone who would have oaths instead of looks and hands: also all wisdom that is all-too-mistrustful—for such is the way of cowardly souls.

More paltry still does it deem whoever is eager to please, who is like a dog that immediately lies on its back, and who is humble; for there is also wisdom that is humble and dog-like and pious and eager to please.

It regards as altogether hateful and disgusting whoever never wants to defend himself, who swallows down poisonous spittle and evil looks, who is all-too-tolerant, all-suffering, all-temperate: for that is the way of the servile.

Whether one be servile before Gods and Godlike kicks, or before humans and stupid humans' opinions: upon *all* that is servile it spits, this blessèd selfishness!

Bad: that is what it calls all that is dejected and niggardly-servile, unfree blinking eyes, oppressed hearts, and that falsely yielding kind that kisses with thick and cowardly lips.

And pseudo-wisdom:* that is what it calls all that servants and old men and the weary make jokes about; and especially all nasty, pseudo-clever, over-clever priests' folly!

The pseudo-wise, however, all the priests, the world-weary, and those whose souls are of the womanish and servile kind—oh what wicked tricks have they played for so long on selfishness!

And precisely this was considered virtue and called virtue: *that* one should play wicked tricks on selfishness! And 'selfless'—that is what those world-weary cowards and cross-spiders with good reason wished to be!

But for all these the day is now at hand, the transformation, the sword of judgement, *the Great Midday*: then shall much be revealed!*

And whoever pronounces the I wholesome and sacred and selfishness blessèd, verily, he will also say what he knows, as a soothsayer: '*See, it is coming, it is nigh, the Great Midday!*'

Thus spoke Zarathustra.

*   *   *

11. On the Spirit of Heaviness

I

My blunt mouth—is of the people: too coarsely and heartily I talk for silky rabbits. And even stranger do my words sound to all ink-fishes and quill-foxes.

My hand—is a fool's hand: woe to all tables and walls, and whatever still has room for fools' drawings, fools' scrawlings!

My foot—is a horse's foot; with it I trot and clip-clop over sticks and stones, crisscrossing all fields, with the Devil's pleasure in all swift galloping.

My stomach—is perhaps an eagle's stomach? For it likes lambs' meat best. But it is certainly a bird's stomach.

Nourished on innocent things and on little, ready and impatient to fly, to fly away—that is now my kind: how could there not be something of the bird's kind in it!

And especially my being enemy to the Spirit of Heaviness makes me of the bird's kind: and verily, deadly enemy, arch-enemy, primal enemy! Oh whither has my enmity not already flown and flown astray!

About that I could surely sing a song— —and *will* sing one: although I am alone in an empty house and must sing it to my own ears.

Other singers there are, to be sure, for whom only a full house loosens their throat, makes their hand loquacious, their eye expressive, their heart awake: — those I do not resemble.—

2

Whoever one day teaches humans to fly will have shifted all bound-ary-stones; all boundary-stones will themselves fly into the air before him, and the earth he will baptize anew—as 'the Light One'.

The ostrich runs faster than the fastest horse, but even he still thrusts his head heavily into heavy earth: thus does the human who cannot yet fly.

Heavy are both earth and life for him; and thus the Spirit of Heaviness *wills* it! But whoever wants to become light and like a bird, he must love himself:—thus *I* teach.

Not of course with the love of the sickly and the chronically ill: for in them even self-love stinks!

One must learn to love oneself—thus I teach—with a wholesome and healthy love: so that one can tolerate being with oneself and does not have to roam about.

Such roaming about baptizes itself 'love of the neighbour': with this word they have lied and dissembled the most, and especially those who were a heavy burden to all the world.

And verily, this is no commandment for today and tomorrow, to *learn* to love oneself. Rather, of all arts this is the most subtle, cunning, ultimate, and most patient.

For all that is one's own is well hidden from its owner; and of all treasure hoards it is one's own that is excavated last—thus the Spirit of Heaviness brings it about.

Almost from the cradle on they endow us with weighty words and values: 'good' and 'evil'—that is what this dowry is called. For the sake of these they forgive us for being alive.

And for that purpose they suffer the little children to come unto them, that one might forbid them in good time to love themselves: thus the Spirit of Heaviness brings it about.

And we—we faithfully bear what they endow us with, on sturdy shoulders and over rugged mountains! And should we sweat, they say to us: 'Yes, this life is a heavy burden!'

But only for itself is the human a heavy burden! This is because it carries on its shoulders too much that is alien. Like the camel it kneels down and lets itself be well laden.

Especially the strong, weight-bearing human in whom reverence dwells: too many *alien* weighty words and values it loads upon itself—so that life now seems like a desert!

And verily! Much that is one's *own* is a heavy burden too! And much that is within the human is like an oyster: namely, disgusting and slippery and hard to grasp—

—such that a noble shell with noble decoration must intercede. But this art too must one learn: to *have* a shell and handsome sheen and clever blindness!

But again much about the human is deceptive, in that many a shell is paltry and pathetic and too much shell. Much hidden goodness and strength is never divined; the most exquisite morsels often go untasted!

The ladies know this, the most exquisite ones: a little fatter, a little thinner—oh how much fate there is in so very little!

The human is hard to discover and its own self hardest of all; often the spirit lies about the soul. Thus the Spirit of Heaviness brings it about.

But he has discovered himself who can say: This is *my* good and evil; with that he has struck dumb the mole and dwarf who says: 'Good for all, evil for all.'

Verily, nor do I like those for whom each and every thing is good and this world is even the best.* Such as these I call the all-contented.

All-contentment, which knows how to taste everything: that is not the best taste! I respect the rebellious selective tongues and stomachs, that have learned to say 'I' and 'Yes' and 'No'.

But to chew and digest everything—that is truly the way of swine! Always to say Yea-haw—that only the ass has learned, and whoever is of his spirit!—

Dark yellow and warm red: thus *my* taste wills it—which mixes blood into all colours. But whoever whitewashes his house betrays to me a whitewashed soul.

Some of them in love with mummies, and others with spectres; and both alike hostile to all flesh and blood—oh how they both go against my taste! For I do love blood.

Nor do I want to reside and abide where everyone spits and spews: this is now *my* taste—I would much rather live among thieves and perjurers. No one carries gold in his mouth.

But even more repulsive do I find all lickspittles; and the most repulsive beast of a human that I found, I baptized parasite: it did not want to love yet wanted to live on love.

Wretched I call all those who have only one choice: to become evil beasts or else evil tamers of beasts: near such creatures I would never set up tabernacles.*

Wretched I call also those who must always *wait*—they go against my taste: all those tax-collectors and grocers and kings and other grounds- and shopkeepers.

Verily, I too learned how to wait, and from the ground up—but only how to wait for *myself*. And above all I learned how to stand and walk and run and jump and climb and dance.

But this is my teaching: whoever wants to learn to fly must first learn to stand and walk and run and climb and dance:—one cannot fly into flying!

With rope-ladders I learned to climb up to many a window, with nimble legs I clambered up tall masts: to sit atop tall masts of understanding seemed no small bliss to me—

—to flicker like small flames on tall masts: a small light, to be sure, and yet a great consolation for sea-driven sailors and castaways!

By many different paths and ways have I come to my truth; not on one ladder alone have I climbed to the heights from which my eye roams into my distances.

And only with reluctance did I ever ask the way—that always went against my taste! Rather I would question and try out the ways themselves.

A trying and questioning was all my going: and verily, one must also *learn* how to answer such questioning! But this is my taste:

—not good, not bad, but *my* taste, about which I am no longer secretive or ashamed.

'This—is just *my* way:—where is yours?' Thus I answered those who asked of me 'the way'. For *the* way—does not exist!

Thus spoke Zarathustra.

*   *   *

12. On Old and New Tablets*

1

Here I sit and wait, with old shattered tablets around me as well as new half-inscribed tablets.* When will my hour come?

—the hour of my going down, going-under: for one more time will I go to human beings.

For that I now wait: for first the signs must come to me, that it be *my* hour—namely, the laughing lion with the flock of doves.

Meanwhile I talk, as one who has time, to myself. No one recounts to me anything new: so I recount myself to myself.—

*   *   *

2

When I came to human beings I found them sitting on an old conceit: all of them believed they had long known what good and evil were for the human being.

An old and tired affair all talk of virtue seemed to them; and whoever wanted to sleep well would even speak of 'good' and 'evil' before going to sleep.

This somnolence I disturbed when I taught: what good and evil are, *that nobody knows*—unless it be the creator!

—But that is the one who creates humanity's goal and gives the earth its sense and its future: he alone *makes it that* anything is good or evil.

And I bade them overturn their old professorial chairs, and wherever this old conceit had sat; I bade them laugh at their great masters of virtue and saints and poets and world-redeemers.

At their gloomy wise men I bade them laugh, and whoever had sat as a black scarecrow, warning, on the Tree of Life.

On their great avenue of graves I sat down beside carrion and vultures—and I laughed at all their 'past' and its rotting and decaying glory.

Verily, like preachers of repentance and fools I raised a wrathful hue-and-cry over all their great and small—that their best is so

very small! That their most evil is so very small!—thus did I
laugh.

My wise yearning cried and laughed from out of me, born upon
mountains, a wild wisdom verily!—my great wing-beating yearning.

And often it tore me away and up and out and in the midst of
laughing: and then indeed I flew quivering, an arrow, through sun-
drunken rapture:

—out into far futures that no dream as yet had seen, into hotter
souths than artists had ever dreamed of: to where Gods in their
dances are ashamed of all clothes:—

—for I now speak in parables and like poets hobble and stutter:
and verily, I am ashamed that I must still be a poet!—

Where all Becoming seemed to me a Gods'-dancing and Gods'-
wilfulness, and the world released and unrestrained and fleeing back
to itself:—

—as an eternal fleeing- and reseeking-themselves of many Gods,
as the blissful self-contradicting, self-rehearing, self-rebelonging of
many Gods:—

Where all time seemed to me a blissful mockery of moments,
where necessity was freedom itself, blissfully playing with the thorn
of freedom:—

Where I also found my old Devil and arch-enemy again, the Spirit
of Heaviness and all that he created: compulsion, statute, need and
consequence and purpose and will and good and evil:—

For must there not exist that *over* which one dances and dances
away? Must there not exist, for the sake of the light and the lightest,
moles and heavy dwarves?—

* * *

3

It was there too that I gleaned the word 'Overhuman' from the way,
and that the human is something that must be overcome,

—that the human is a bridge and not a goal: counting itself blissful
on account of its midday and evening, as the way to new dawnings:

—the Zarathustra-Word of the Great Midday, and whatever else I
hung over the human, like a purple afterglow of evenings.

Verily, I also let them see new stars along with new nights; and over clouds and day and night I went on to spread laughter out like a colourful canopy.

I taught them all *my* composing and striving: to compose and carry into one whatever about the human is fragment and riddle and cruel coincidence—

—as poet, unriddler, and redeemer of coincidence I taught them to work creatively on the future, and creatively to redeem—all that *was*.

To redeem what is past in human beings, and to re-create all 'It was' until the will speaks: 'But thus I willed it! Thus shall I will it—'

—This I called redemption, and this alone I taught them to call redemption.— —

Now I await *my* redemption, that I might go to them for the last time.

For I want to go to human beings one more time: *down among* them will I go under, dying will I give them my richest gift!

From the sun I learned this, when it goes down, so over-rich: gold it scatters then over the sea out of inexhaustible richness—

—so that even the poorest fisherman rows with *golden* oars! For this I saw once and did not weary of my tears in watching.— —

Like the sun will Zarathustra too go down: now he sits here and waits, with old shattered tablets about him and new ones too—half-inscribed.

*   *   *

4

Behold, here is a new tablet: but where are my brothers who will carry it with me down to the valley and into hearts of flesh?—*

Thus my great love of the farthest demands it: *Do not spare your neighbour!* The human is something that must be overcome.

There are many different paths and ways of overcoming—look *you* to them! But only a jester thinks: 'The human can also be *overjumped.*'

Overcome yourself even in your neighbour: and a right that you can seize for yourself you should not let yourself be given!

What you do, no one can do back to you. Behold, there is no retribution.

Whoever cannot command himself, he shall obey. And many a one *can* command himself, but much is still lacking before he can obey himself too!

* * *

5

Thus the way of noble souls wills it: they want nothing *gratis*, and least of all life.*

Whoever is of the rabble wants to live gratis; we others, however, to whom life has given itself—we are always wondering *what* we can best give *in return!*

And verily, it is a distinguished speech that says: 'Whatever life promises *us*, that promise will *we* keep—to life!'

One shall not want to enjoy where one does not give enjoyment. And—one shall not *want* to enjoy!

For enjoyment and innocence are the most bashful things: they both want not to be sought. One shall *have* them—but one shall sooner *seek* both guilt and pain!—

* * *

6

O my brothers, whoever is a firstling is always sacrificed.* But just now are we firstlings.

We all are bleeding on secret sacrificial tables, we all are burning and roasting to the honour of old idol-statues.*

Our best is yet young: that excites old gums. Our flesh is tender, our fleece is only a lamb's fleece:—how could we fail to excite old idol-priests!

In us ourselves he dwells still, the old idol-priest, who roasts what is best in us for his own feast. Ah, my brothers, how could firstlings fail to be sacrifices!

But thus our kind wills it; and I love those who would not preserve themselves. Those who go under I love with my entire love: for they also go over.—

* * *

7

Being true—few are *capable* of that! And he who can, does not yet will it! Least capable of all, however, are the good.

Oh, these good men!—*Good men never tell the truth*; for the spirit, being good in such measure is a sickness.

They give in, these good men, they resign themselves, their heart repeats the words, their ground obeys: but he who obeys *does not listen to himself!*

All that the good call evil must come together, that one truth may be born: O my brothers, are you, too, wicked enough for *this* truth?

The daring risk, the long mistrust, the cruel Nay, sheer satiety, the cutting into the living—how seldom does *that* come together! But it is from such a seed that—truth is engendered!

Beside the wicked conscience has all *science** hitherto grown up! Shatter, shatter for me, you who understand, the old tablets!

*   *   *

8

When planks span the water, when bridges and railings soar over the river: verily, then no one is believed who then says: 'Everything is in flux.'*

But even the blockheads contradict him. 'What?' say the blockheads. 'You say everything is in flux? But there are planks and railings *over* the flux!'

'*Over* the flux everything is firm, all the values of things, the bridges, concepts, all "Good" and "Evil": all that is *firm!*'—

And when the hard winter comes, the flux-animal-tamer, then even the wittiest learn mistrust; and verily, it is not only blockheads who then say: 'Should everything not—*stand still?*'

'At its ground everything stands still'*—that is a real winter-doctrine, a fine thing for an unfruitful time, a fine consolation for hibernators and stay-at-homes.

'At its ground everything stands still'—but *against this* the thaw-wind preaches!

The thaw-wind, a bull that is no ploughing bull—a raging bull, a destroyer that with wrathful horns breaks the ice! Ice, however— — *breaks bridges!*

O my brothers, is everything *now* not *in flux?* Have not all railings and bridges fallen into the water? Who *could* still *cling* to 'Good' and 'Evil'?

'Woe to us! Hail to us! The thaw-wind blows!'—Proclaim thus for me, O my brothers, throughout all the streets!*

*   *   *

9

There is an old delusion that is called good and evil. Around sooth-sayers and astrologers has the wheel of this delusion turned up to now.

Once people *believed* in soothsayers and astrologers, and *therefore* they believed: 'All is fate: you shall, for you must!'

Then again people mistrusted all soothsayers and astrologers: and *therefore* they believed: 'All is freedom: you can, for you will!'

O my brothers, about stars and the future there has hitherto been only surmise, and not knowledge; and *therefore* about good and evil there has hitherto been only surmise, and not knowledge!

*   *   *

10

'Thou shalt not rob! Thou shalt not kill!'—such words were once called holy; before them one bent the knee and bowed the head and took off one's shoes.*

But I ask you now: Where have there ever been better robbers and killers in the world than these holy words have been?

Does all life not itself comprise—robbing and killing? And that such words were called holy, was *truth* itself not thereby—killed?

Or was it a preaching of death that called holy whatever contradicted and spoke against all life?—O my brothers, shatter, shatter for me the old tablets!

*   *   *

11

This is my pity for all that is past, that I can see: it has been abandoned—

—abandoned to the favour, the spirit, the madness of every generation that comes up, and which reinterprets all that has been as a bridge to itself!

A great despot could come, a shrewd fiend who would and could compel all that is past with his favour and disfavour: until it became a bridge to him and a portent and herald and cockcrow.

This, however, is the other danger and object of my pitying:— whoever is of the rabble, his memory goes back to his grandfather— but with the grandfather time stops.*

Thus all that is past is abandoned: for it could come to pass one day that the rabble would become master, and all of time be drowned in shallow waters.

Therefore, O my brothers, there is need of a *new nobility* that is the opponent of all rabble and everything despotic and writes anew on new tablets the word 'noble'.

For there is need of many nobles and many kinds of nobles, *that there may be nobility!* Or, as I once spoke in a parable: 'Just this is Godliness, that there are Gods, but no God!'

*   *   *

12

O my brothers, I dedicate and direct you to a new nobility: you shall become for me progenitors and cultivators and sowers of the future—

—verily, not to a nobility that you could buy like shopkeepers and with shopkeepers' gold: for of little value is anything that has its price.

Not whence you come shall henceforth constitute your honour, but whither you are going! Your will and your foot, which wills beyond you yourselves—may those constitute your new honour!

Verily, not that you have served some prince—what are princes worth now!—or that you have become a bulwark for that which stands, that it might stand more firmly!

Not that your lineage has become courtly in courts, and you have learned to stand, colourfully, like a flamingo, for long hours in shallow ponds.

For *being able* to stand is a merit in a courtier; and all courtiers believe that bliss after death consists in—*being allowed* to sit!—

Also not that a spirit they call holy led your ancestors to much-praised lands that *I* praise not: for where the worst of all trees grew, the Cross—about that land there is nothing to praise!—

—and verily, wherever this 'Holy Spirit' led its knights too, in such crusades there were always goats and geese and criss- and cross-patches *at the head!*—

O my brothers, not back shall your nobility look, but *ahead!* Refugees shall you be from all father- and forefather-lands!

Your *children's land* you shall love: may this love be your new nobility—the undiscovered land, in the farthest sea! For that I bid your sails search and search!

In your children you shall *make amends* for being children of your fathers:* *thus* shall you redeem all that is past! This new tablet I place over you!

* * *

13

'Wherefore live? All is vanity! Living—that is threshing straw; living—that is consuming oneself in fire and yet not becoming warm.'—

Such antiquarian chatter still counts as 'wisdom'; but though it is old and smells musty, *therefore* is it all the more honoured. Even mould ennobles.—

Children might talk thus: they are *afraid* of fire because it burned them! There is much childishness in the old books of wisdom.

And whoever 'threshes straw', how should he be allowed to malign threshing! Such fools should surely be muzzled!*

Such people seat themselves at the table and yet bring nothing to it, not even a healthy appetite: and then they blaspheme, 'All is vanity!'

But to eat and drink well, O my brothers, is truly no paltry art! Shatter, shatter for me the tablets of those who are never happy!

* * *

14

'Unto the pure, all things are pure'*—thus speaks the people. I, however, say to you: Unto swine, all things become swine!

Therefore the fanatics and head-hanging devotees, whose hearts hang down too, preach: 'The world itself is a filthy monster.'

For they are all unclean in spirit; but especially those who have neither rest nor repose unless they see the world *from behind*—those believers in a world behind!

To them I say to their faces, though it may not sound pleasant: The world is like the human being in having a backside—*that much* is true!

There is much filth in the world: *that much* is true! But this does not mean that the world itself is a filthy monster!

There is wisdom in this, that much in the world smells foul: disgust itself creates wings and source-divining powers!

In what is best there is still something disgusting; and the best is still something that must be overcome!—

O my brothers, there is much wisdom in this, that there is much filth in the world!—

*   *   *

15

These sayings I heard pious behind-world believers speak to their consciences, and verily, without guile or falsity—though there is nothing more false in the world, or more guileful:

'Just let the world be the world! Do not lift even a finger against it!'

'Let him who wants to, strangle people and stab them and strip them and flay them: do not lift even a finger against it! From this will they yet learn to renounce the world.'

'And your own reason—that shall you yourself throttle and strangle; for it is reason of this world—therefore will you yourself learn to renounce the world.'—

—Shatter, shatter for me, O my brothers, these old tablets of the pious! Unsay for me the sayings of the slanderers of the world!

*   *   *

16

'Whoever learns much will unlearn all violent desiring'—this is whispered today in all dark lanes.

'Wisdom makes weary; worthwhile is—nothing; thou shalt not desire!'—this new tablet I found hanging even in open markets.

Shatter for me, O my brothers, shatter for me this *new* tablet too! The world-weary hung it up and the preachers of death, and also the jailers: for behold, it too is a preaching of servitude!—

Because they learned badly and not what is best, and everything too early and everything too hastily; because they *ate* badly, that is why they have upset stomachs—

—for their spirit is an upset stomach: *that* is what counsels them to die! For verily, my brothers, the spirit *is* a stomach!

Life is a fount of pleasure: but in whomever the upset stomach talks, the father of sorrow, for him are all wells poisoned.

To understand: that is *pleasure* for the lion-willed! But whoever has become weary is himself merely 'willed', and is the sport of every wave.

And thus is it always with weak natures: they lose themselves on their own ways. And at last their weariness asks: 'Why did we ever take any ways! It is all the same!'

To *their* ears it sounds delightful when it is preached: 'Nothing is worth while! Ye shall not will!' But this is a preaching of servitude.

O my brothers, as a fresh roaring wind does Zarathustra come to all that are weary of the way; many noses he will yet make sneeze!

Even through walls my free breath blows, and into all prisons and imprisoned spirits!

Willing liberates: for willing is creating; thus I teach. And *only* for the sake of creating shall you learn!

And even learning shall you first *learn* from me, learning well!— He that hath ears, let him hear!

* * *

17

There stands the bark—over there it goes perhaps into the great Nothing.—But who wants to climb aboard this 'Perhaps'?

No one among you wants to climb aboard the bark of death! Why would you then be *world-weary!*

World-weary! And you have not even parted from the earth yet! I have always found you still lusting for the earth, still in love with your own earth-weariness!

Not for nothing does your lip hang down—for a little earthly wish sits upon it still! And in your eyes—does a tiny cloud of unforgotten earthly pleasure not float there?

There are on earth many good inventions, some useful, others pleasing: for their sake the earth is to be loved.

And so many kinds of things have been well invented there that it is like a woman's breasts: useful and at the same time pleasing.

But you who are world-weary! You who are earth-lazy! You shall be lashed with switches! With switch-lashes shall your legs be made sprightly again.

For: if you are not sick and decrepit wretches of whom the earth is weary, then you are cunning sloths or sweet-toothed hiding pleasure-cats. And if you will not *run* merrily again, then you shall—pass away!

For one who is incurable should not want to be a physician: thus Zarathustra teaches:—so you shall pass away!

But it takes more *courage* to make an end of it than to make a new verse: that is something all physicians and poets know.—

*   *   *

18

O my brothers, there are tablets created by weariness, and tablets, putrid ones, created by laziness: though they may speak similarly, they would be heard differently.—

Behold this languisher here! Only one step is he from his goal, but from weariness he has defiantly lain down here in the dust: this brave fellow!

From weariness he yawns at the way and the earth and the goal and himself: not one step farther will he go—this brave fellow!

Now the sun burns down upon him, and dogs lick at his sweat: but he lies there in his defiance and will rather languish—*

—languish one step away from his goal! Verily, you will yet have to drag him into his Heaven by the hair*—this hero!

Better yet, leave him lying where he has lain down, so that sleep may come to him, the consoler, with cooling plashing rain:

Leave him lying, until he awakes by himself—until he by himself disavows all weariness and whatever weariness taught through him!

Only, my brothers, shoo the dogs away from him, the lazy slinkers, and all the swarming vermin:—

—all the swarming vermin of 'the cultured', who on the sweat of every hero—feast themselves!—

*　*　*

19

I draw circles around myself and sacred boundaries; fewer and fewer climb with me upon ever higher mountains:—I build a mountain-range from ever more sacred mountains.—

But wheresoever you may climb with me, O my brothers: see to it that no *parasite* climbs with you!

Parasite: that is a worm, crawling, clinging, that wants to fatten itself on your sick and wounded recesses.

And *this* is its art, that it divines where climbing souls are growing weary: in your grief and discouragement, in your tender modesty, it builds its disgusting nest.

Where the strong are weak, and the noble all too mild—there it builds its disgusting nest: the parasite lives where the great have small wounded recesses.

Which is the highest kind of all beings and which the most paltry? The parasite is the most paltry kind; but whoever is of the highest kind will nourish the most parasites.

For the soul that has the longest ladder and so reaches down deepest: how should the most parasites not sit on that?—

—the most comprehensive soul, that can run and stray and roam the farthest within itself; the most necessary soul, that out of pleasure plunges itself into chance:—

—the being soul, that dives into Becoming; the having soul, that *wills* to enter willing and longing—

—that flees from itself and retrieves itself in the widest circle; the wisest soul, which folly exhorts most sweetly—

—the soul that loves itself the most, in which all things have their streaming and counter-streaming and ebb and flood:—oh how should *the highest soul* not have the worst parasites?

*   *   *

20

O my brothers, am I then cruel? But I say: to what is falling one should give a further push!

Everything of today—it is falling, falling into decay: who would want to keep it! But I—I *will* give it a further push!

Do you know the delight that rolls rocks into steep depths?— These humans of today: just look at them rolling into my depths!

A prelude am I to better players, O my brothers! An example! *Do* according to my example!*

And whomever you do not teach to fly, teach him for me—*to fall faster!*—

*   *   *

21

I love those who are brave: but it is not enough to be an old swords-man—one must also know how and whom to fight!

And there is often more bravery in restraining oneself and passing by: *so that* one might save oneself for a worthier enemy!

You shall have only enemies to be hated, but not enemies to be despised: you must be proud of your enemy; thus I taught once before.

For the worthier enemy, O my friends, shall you save yourselves: therefore you must pass many things by—

—especially many of the rabble, who yell in your ears about folk and peoples.

Keep your eyes clear of their For and Against! There is much right there, and much wrong: whoever looks on becomes angry.

Gawking in there, rushing in there—there these are one: therefore go away into the forest and let your swords sleep!

Go *your* ways! And let folk and peoples go theirs!—dark ways, verily, where not even one hope lightens the weather any more!

Let the shopkeeper rule there, where all that still glisters—is shopkeepers' gold! It is the time of kings no more: what today calls itself the people deserves no kings.

Just see how these peoples themselves now do the same as the shopkeepers: they glean even the smallest advantages from every piece of rubbish!

They lie in wait for each other, they lie to take something from each other—and they call that 'being good neighbours'. Oh blissful time far off, when a people would say to itself: 'Over other peoples will I—be *lord!*'

For, my brothers: the best shall rule, the best also *wills* to rule! And where the teaching is different, there—the best is *lacking*.

*   *   *

22

If *they*—had bread for nothing, woe! For what would *they* scream! What sustains them—is what truly entertains them; and it shall be hard for them!

Beasts of prey are they: in their 'working'—there is still preying, in their 'earning'—there is still outwitting! Therefore it shall be hard for them!

Better beasts of prey shall they thus become, more refined, cleverer, *more like humans*: for the human being is the best beast of prey.

The human being has already robbed all beasts of their virtues: which means that of all beasts it has been hardest for humans.

Only the birds are still above them. And if humans should learn to fly, woe! *To what heights*—would their pleasure in preying fly!

*   *   *

23

Thus will I have man and woman: the one adept in war, the other adept in birth, but both adept in dancing with head and legs.

And we should consider any day lost, on which we have not danced once! And we should call any truth false, that has not been accompanied by one burst of laughter!

*   *   *

24

Your marriage-ceremonies: see to it that they do not come to bad *conclusions!* You concluded too quickly: from that *follows*—marriage-breakings!

And rather marriage-breaking than marriage-bending, marriage-dissembling!—A female once told me: 'Admittedly I broke the marriage, but only after the marriage broke—me!'

A mismatched couple I always found to be the worst thirsters for revenge: they lay the blame on the whole world for their no longer being single.

That is why I want honest people to say to each other: 'We love each other: may we *see to it* that we hold each other dear! Or shall our promising be a missing?'

—'Give us a little time and a small marriage, so that we can see whether we are fit for a great marriage! It is a great thing always to be two!'

Thus I counsel all honest people; and what would my love for the Overhuman be and for all that shall come, if I were to counsel and speak otherwise!

To propagate yourselves not only onward, but *upward*—to that end, O my brothers, may the garden of marriage help you!

*   *   *

25

Whoever has become wise concerning ancient origins, behold, he will in the end seek out sources of the future and new origins.—

O my brothers, it will not be long before *new peoples* arise and new sources rush downward into new depths.

For the earthquake—that covers many wells with debris, and creates much languishing: but it also brings inner strengths and secrets up to the light.

The earthquake makes manifest new sources. In the earthquakes of ancient peoples new sources break open.

And whoever then cries: 'Behold here a well for many that are thirsty, one heart for many that are yearning, one will for many

instruments': around him a *people* will gather, that is: many experimenters.

Who can command, who must obey—*that is the experiment here!*
Ah, with what lengthy searching and guessing and failing and learning and experimenting anew!

Human society: this is an experiment, thus I teach—a lengthy
searching: but the search is for commanders!—

—an experiment, O my brothers! And *not* a 'contract'!* Shatter,
shatter for me such words of the soft-hearted and half-and-halfers!

*   *   *

26

O my brothers! With whom does the greatest danger of all human
future lie? Is it not with the good and the righteous?—

with those who speak and feel in their hearts: 'We already know
what is good and righteous, and we have it too; woe to those who are
still seeking here!'

And whatever harm the evil may do, the harm done by the good is
the most harmful harm!

And whatever harm even the world-slanderers may do, the harm
done by the good is the most harmful harm.

O my brothers, one man once saw into the hearts of the good and the
righteous, and said: 'They are Pharisees.'* But he was not understood.

The good and the righteous themselves could not understand
him: their spirit is imprisoned in their good conscience. The stupidity of the good is unfathomably clever.

But the truth of the matter is this: the good *must* be Pharisees—
they have no choice!

The good *must* crucify him who invents his own virtue! That *is* the
truth!

But the second one to discover their land, the land, heart, and soil
of the good and the righteous: that was he who then asked: 'Whom
do they hate the most?'

The *creator* is who they hate the most: he who breaks tablets and
old virtues, the breaker—they call him a law breaker.

For the good—they *cannot* create: they are always the beginning
of the end—

—they crucify him who writes new values on new tablets, they sacrifice the future *to themselves*—they crucify all human future!

The good—they have always been the beginning of the end.—

* * *

27

O my brothers, have you understood these words too? And what I once said about the 'last human'?— —

With whom does the greatest danger for all human future lie? Is it not with the good and the righteous?

Shatter, shatter for me the good and the righteous!—O my brothers, have you understood these words too?

* * *

28

You flee from me? You are terrified? You tremble at these words?

O my brothers, when I bade you shatter the good and the tablets of the good: only then did I ship the human being out onto its high seas.

And only now does there come to it the great terror, the great looking-about, the great sickness, the great disgust, the great seasickness.

False coasts and false securities the good have taught you; in the lies of the good you were born and bred. Everything has been lied about and twisted around down to its ground by the good.

But whoever discovered the land 'Human' also discovered the land 'Human Future'. Now you shall be seafarers for me, valiant ones, patient ones!

Walk upright for me betimes, O my brothers, learn to walk upright! The sea is stormy: many want to right themselves again with your help.

The sea is stormy: everything is in the sea. Well then! Come now! You old seamen's hearts!

What of fatherland! *Thither* will our helm go, where our *children's land* is! Out there, stormier than the sea, does our great yearning storm!—

* * *

29

'Why so hard?'—the kitchen-coal once said to the diamond. 'Are we not after all close relatives?'—

Why so soft? O my brothers, thus *I* ask you. Are you not after all—my brothers?

Why so soft, so pliant and yielding? Why is there so much denying, self-denying in your hearts? So little fate in your glances?

And if you will not be fates and unrelenting: how could you— conquer with me?

And if your hardness will not flash and cut and cut to shreds: how could you one day—create with me?

For creators are hard. And blessedness must it seem to you to press your hand upon millennia as upon wax—

—blessedness, to write upon the will of millennia as upon bronze—harder than bronze, nobler than bronze. Only the noblest is altogether hard.

This new tablet, O my brothers, I place over you: *Become hard!*—

*   *   *

30

O you, my Will! You turning of all need, *my own* necessity! Preserve me from all small victories!

You fatality of my soul, which I call fate! You in-me! Over-me! Preserve and save me for a single great fate!

And your ultimate greatness, my Will, save it for your ultimate test—that you be unrelenting *in* your victory! Ah, who has not suc- cumbed to his own victory!

Ah, whose eye would not darken in this drunken twilight! Ah, whose foot would not stumble and be unable in victory—to stand!—

—That I may one day be ready and ripe in the Great Midday: ready and ripe like glowing bronze, a lightning-pregnant cloud and swelling milk-udder:—

—ready for myself and for my most hidden Will: a bow lusting for its arrow, an arrow lusting for its star:—

—a star ready and ripe in its midday, glowing, penetrated, blissful with annihilating sun-arrows:—

—a sun itself and an unrelenting sun-will, ready for annihilation in victory!

O Will, turning of all need, you *my own* necessity! Save me for one great victory!— —

Thus spoke Zarathustra.

*   *   *

13. The Convalescent

1

One morning, not long after his return to the cave, Zarathustra sprang up from his pallet like a madman, screamed in a terrifying voice, and acted as if there were still someone lying on the pallet who would not get up. And so loudly did Zarathustra's voice resound that his animals came to him in fright, and from every cave and nook and cranny in the neighbourhood of Zarathustra's cave all the beasts slipped away—flying, fluttering, crawling, jumping, according to the kind of foot or wing that had been given them. But then Zarathustra spoke these words:

Get up, abyss-deep thought, out of my depths! I am your cock and morning-dawning, you sleepy worm:* up! up! My voice shall surely crow you awake!

Take off the fetters from your ears: listen! For I will hear you! Up! Up! Here is thunder enough that even graves will learn to listen!

And wipe away sleep and all that is stupid and blind from your eyes! Now hear me with your eyes as well: my voice is a healing potion even for those born blind.

And once you are awake you shall stay awake eternally. It is not *my* way to waken great-grandmothers from their sleep in order to bid them—sleep on!*

You are stirring, stretching, death-rattling? Up! Up! Do not death-rattle—you shall talk to me! Zarathustra, the Godless, summons you!

I, Zarathustra, the advocate of life, the advocate of suffering, the advocate of the circle*—you I summon, my most abyss-deep thought!

Hail to me! You are coming—I hear you! My abyss is *speaking*, my ultimate depth I have turned out into the light!

Hail to me! Come! Give me your hand——ha! let go! Haha!——Disgust, disgust, disgust!———woe is me!

*   *   *

2

But hardly had Zarathustra spoken these words when he collapsed like a dead man and lay for a long time like one dead. But when he came to himself again, he was pale and trembling and remained lying down, and for a long time he wanted neither food nor drink. Thus he remained for seven days; but his animals did not leave him by day or night, except when the eagle flew off to fetch nourishment. And whatever he collected from his plundering he laid on Zarathustra's pallet, so that Zarathustra eventually lay under a heap of yellow and red berries, grapes, rose-apples, fragrant herbs, and pine-cones. And at his feet two lambs were spread out, which the eagle had with difficulty stolen from their shepherds.

At last, after seven days, Zarathustra raised himself up on his pallet, took a rose-apple in his hand, smelled it, and found its fragrance delightful.* Then his animals believed that the time had come to talk with him.

'O Zarathustra,' they said, 'you have now lain like this for seven days, with heavy eyes: will you not at last stand on your feet again?

'Step out from your cave: the world awaits you like a garden. The wind is playing with heavy fragrances that would come to you; and all streams would like to follow you.

'All things are yearning for you, while you have stayed alone for seven days—do step out from your cave! All things would be your physicians!

'Has a new understanding come to you then, sour and heavy? Like yeast-soured dough you lay there, then your soul rose and swelled over all its brims.—'

'—O my animals,' replied Zarathustra, 'do chatter on thus and let me listen to you!* It is so refreshing to hear you chatter: where there is chatter, there the world lies for me like a garden.

'How lovely it is that there are words and tones: are words and tones not rainbows and seeming-bridges between what is eternally separated?

'To every soul belongs another world; for every soul every other soul is a world behind.

'Between just what is most similar does seeming deceive most beautifully: for the smallest cleft is the hardest to bridge.

'For me—how could there be an outside-me? There is no outside! But with all tones we forget that; how lovely it is that we forget!

'Are things not furnished with names and tones so that human beings might refresh themselves with things? It is a beautiful foolery, this speaking: with it human beings can dance over all things.

'How lovely is all this talking and all these lies of tones! With such tones our love dances on colourful rainbows.'—

—'O Zarathustra,' said his animals in reply, 'for those who think as we do all things are already dancing: they come and shake hands and laugh and flee—and come back again.

'Everything goes, everything comes back; eternally rolls the wheel of Being. Everything dies, everything blooms again, eternally runs the year of Being.

'Everything breaks, everything is joined anew; eternally is built the same house of Being. Everything separates, everything greets itself again; eternally true to itself remains the ring of Being.*

'In every now Being begins; around every here rolls the ball of there. The centre is everywhere.* Crooked is the path of eternity.'—

'Oh you pranksters and barrel-organs!' answered Zarathustra, and smiled once again. 'How well you know what had to be fulfilled in seven days:—

'—and how that monster crawled into my throat and choked me! But I bit its head off and spat it forth from me.

'And you—have you simply made a hurdy-gurdy song of it all?* But now I lie here, still weary from this biting and spitting out, still sick from my own redemption.

'*And you simply watched all this?* O my animals, are you, too, cruel? Did you simply want to watch my great pain, just as humans do? For the human being is the cruellest beast.

'At tragedies, bullfights, and crucifixions has it so far felt most contented on earth; and when it invented Hell for itself, behold, that was then its Heaven on earth.

'When the great human being screams—the small one comes running up, with his tongue hanging out lasciviously. Yet he calls this his "pitying".

'The small human being, and especially the poet—how eagerly he accuses life in words! Hear him, but do not fail to hear the pleasure that lies within all accusing!

'These accusers of life: life overcomes them with the bat of an eyelid. "You love me?" says the bold-faced woman. "Wait a little longer: I do not have time for you just yet."

'The human being is the cruellest beast toward itself; and in all that calls itself "sinner" and "cross-bearer" and "penitent", do not fail to hear the lust that lurks in this lamenting and accusing!

'And I myself—do I thereby want to become humanity's accuser? Ah, my animals, this alone have I learned so far, that for the human its most evil is necessary for its best—

'—that all that is evil is its best *strength* and the hardest stone for the highest creator; and that the human must become better *and* more evil:—

'Not to *this* stake was I bound, that I know that the human being is evil—rather I screamed, as no one has ever screamed:

' "Alas, that its most evil is so very small! Alas, that its best is so very small!"

'The great loathing for the human being—*that* is what choked me and had crawled into my throat; and what the soothsayer foretold: "All is the same, nothing is worthwhile, knowing chokes."

'A long twilight limped ahead of me, a death-weary, death-drunken mournfulness that was talking with a yawning mouth.

' "Eternally it recurs, the human being you are so weary of, the small human being"—thus yawned my mournfulness and dragged its feet and could not go to sleep.

'The humans' earth became for me a cave, its chest sank in, all that was alive became for me humans' decay and bones and mouldering past.

'My sighing sat upon all humans' graves and could no longer stand up again; my sighing and questioning croaked and choked and gnawed and carped by day and night:

'—"Ah, the human being recurs eternally! The small human being recurs eternally!"—

'Naked I once saw them both, the greatest and the smallest

human being: all-too-similar to each other—all-too-human, even the greatest!

'All-too-small the greatest!—That was my loathing for the human! And eternal recurrence even of the smallest!—That was my loathing for all existence!

'Ah, disgust! disgust! disgust!'——Thus spoke Zarathustra and sighed and shuddered, for he remembered his sickness. But then his animals did not let him talk any further.

'Speak no further, you convalescent!'—thus his animals answered him. 'But go out to where the world awaits you like a garden.

'Go out to the roses and the bees and the flocks of doves! But especially to the songbirds, that you may learn from them how to *sing!*

'For singing is for convalescents: the healthy man likes to talk. And even if the healthy man wants songs, he still wants other songs than the convalescent.'

—'Oh you buffoons and barrel-organs, do be quiet!'—answered Zarathustra, and smiled at his animals. 'How well you know what comfort I devised for myself in those seven days!

'That I should have to sing again—*that* is the comfort I devised for myself and *this* the convalescence: do you want to make a hurdy-gurdy song of it again?'

—'Speak no further,' his animals answered him once more. 'Better still, dear convalescent, first fashion yourself a lyre, a new lyre!

'For do you not see, O Zarathustra! For your new songs you will need new lyres.

'Sing and foam over, O Zarathustra. With new songs you must heal your soul: that you might bear your enormous fate, which has been no human's fate up to now!

'For your animals know well, O Zarathustra, who you are and must become: behold, *you are the teacher of eternal recurrence*—that is now *your* fate!

'That you must be the first to teach this teaching—how should this great fate not be your greatest danger and sickness too!

'Behold, we two know what you teach: that all things recur eternally and we ourselves with them, and that we have already been here an eternity of times, and all things with us.

'You teach that there is a Great Year of Becoming, a monster of a Great Year,* which must like an hour-glass turn itself over anew, again and again, that it may run down and run out ever anew:—

'—such that all these years are the same, in the greatest and smallest respects—such that we ourselves are in each Great Year the same as ourselves, in the greatest and smallest respects.

'And if you wanted to die now, O Zarathustra: behold, we also know how you would then speak to yourself:—but your animals beseech you not to die quite yet!

'You would speak, and without trembling, rather breathing a sigh of relief: for a great heaviness and sultriness would have been lifted from you, most patient of men!—

' "Now I die and fade away," you would say, "and in an instant I am nothing. Souls are as mortal as bodies are.

' "But the knot of causes in which I am entwined recurs—it will create me again! I myself belong to the causes of eternal recurrence.

' "I come again, with this sun, with this earth, with this eagle, with this serpent—*not* to a new life or a better life or a similar life:

' "—I come eternally again to this self-same life, in the greatest and smallest respects, so that again I teach the eternal recurrence of all things—

' "—so that again I speak the word of the Great Earth- and Humans-Midday, and again bring to human beings the tidings of the Overhuman.

' "I have spoken my word, I now shatter on my word: thus my eternal lot wills it—as a herald I now perish!"

'So the hour has come when the one who goes under blesses himself. Thus—*ends* Zarathustra's going-under.'— —

When the animals had spoken these words they were silent and waited for Zarathustra to say something to them: but Zarathustra did not hear that they were silent. Rather, he lay still with his eyes closed, like one who sleeps, though he was not asleep: for he was just then conversing with his soul. But the serpent and the eagle, on finding him thus silent, honoured the great stillness around him and discreetly stole away.

*　　*　　*

14. On the Great Yearning*

O my soul, I taught you to say 'Today' as well as 'Someday' and 'Formerly' and to dance your round-dance* over every here and there and yonder.

O my soul, I redeemed you from all little nooks, I swept dust, spiders, and twilight away from you.

O my soul, I washed small bashfulness and nook-virtue away from you and persuaded you to stand naked before the eyes of the sun.

With the storm that is called 'spirit' I blew over your billowing sea; every cloud I blew away, and I myself strangled the strangler that is called 'sin'.

O my soul, I gave you the right to say Nay like the storm, and to say Yea as the open Heavens say Yea: quiet as light you stand and now withstand all storms of negation.

O my soul, I gave you back the freedom over created and uncreated: and who knows, as you know, the delight of the future-to-be?

O my soul, I taught you the despising that does not make things wormeaten, the great, the loving despising that loves most where it despises most.

O my soul, I taught you to persuade so well that you persuade the grounds themselves over to you: like the sun that persuades even the sea up to its own height.

O my soul, I took from you all obeying, knee-bending and 'Lord'-saying; I myself gave you the name 'Turning of Need' and 'Fate'.

O my soul, I gave you new names and colourful playthings, I called you 'Fate' and 'Circumference of Circumferences' and 'Umbilical Cord of Time' and 'Azure Bell'.

O my soul, I gave your soil all wisdom to drink, all new wines as well as all immemorially old strong wines of wisdom.

O my soul, every sun I poured upon you and every night and every silence and every yearning—then you grew up for me just like a vine.

O my soul, over-rich and heavy you stand there now, a vine with swelling udders and close-crowded brown-turning grapes of gold:—

—crowded and pressed by your happiness, waiting out of overflow and still bashful about your waiting.

O my soul, now there is nowhere a soul that would be more loving and more comprehensive and encompassing! Where would future and past be closer together than in you?

O my soul, I have given you all, and all my hands have become empty for you—and now! Now you say to me, smiling and heavy of heart: 'Which of us should be thankful?—

'—should the giver not be thankful that the taker has taken? Is bestowing not a need? Is taking not—being merciful?'—

O my soul, I understand the smile of your heavy heart: your own over-richness now stretches out yearning hands!

Your fullness looks out over roaring seas and seeks and waits; the yearning of over-fullness looks out from the Heaven of your smiling eyes!

And verily, O my soul! Who could see your smiling and not dissolve into tears? The angels themselves dissolve into tears at the over-kindness of your smiling.

Your kindness it is and over-kindness that would not complain and weep: and yet your smiling, O my soul, longs for tears and your trembling mouth for sobbing.

'Is all weeping not a complaining? And all complaining not an accusing?' Thus you talk to yourself, and therefore, O my soul, you would smile rather than pour out your grief.

—pour out in torrential tears all your grief over your fullness and over all the keen urge of the vine for the vintner and vintner's knife!

But if you will not weep, not weep out your purple heaviness of heart, you will then have to *sing*, O my soul!—Behold, I myself am smiling, as I foretell such things to you:

—to sing, and with a roaring song, till all seas become quite still, that they may hearken to your yearning—

—till over quiet and yearning seas the bark floats, the golden wonder, around whose gold all good and bad and wonderful things now frolic:—*

—and many great and small beasts too, and all that has light and wonderful feet, with which to run along violet-blue pathways—

—over to the golden wonder, the free-willed bark, and to its master: that, however, is the vintner, who waits with his diamond vintner's knife—

—your great releaser, O my soul, the nameless— —for whom only future songs will find names! And verily, your breath is already fragrant with future songs—

—already you glow and dream, already you drink thirstily from all deep resounding comfort-wells, already your heavy heart reposes in the blissfulness of future songs!— —

O my soul, now have I given you all and even my ultimate, and all my hands have become empty for you:— *That I bade you sing*, behold, that was my ultimate!

That I bade you sing, speak now, speak: *which* of us should now— be thankful?—But better still: sing for me, sing, O my soul! And let me be thankful!—

Thus spoke Zarathustra.

*   *   *

15. The Other Dance-Song*

I

'Into your eye I looked of late, O Life: gold I saw in your night-eye glinting—my heart stood still from such delight:

'—a golden-hued boat I saw glinting on nocturnal waters: a sink-ing and drinking and ever-winking golden-hued rocking-boat!

'At both of my feet, quite raging to dance, you cast a long glance: a laughing and questioning and penetrating rocking-glance:

'Twice only you brandished your rattle with delicate hands— inspiring my feet with a strong urge to dance.—

'My heels started pulsing, my toes began listening for what you would propose: for the dancer has his ear—deep down in his toes!

'I leaped straight toward you: then you jumped back from my leaping; as toward me then the tongues of your flaming flying hair came sweeping!

'I leaped away from you, and from your wild serpents: there you stood now, half-turning, your eye smold'ring like incense.

'With crooked glances—you teach me crooked courses; on crooked courses my feet learn—ruses!

'I fear you when near, I love you afar; your fleeing attracts me, your seeking entraps me:—I suffer, but what would I not suffer gladly for you!

'Whose coldness inflames me, whose hatred seduces, whose fleeing is binding, whose mocking—just touches:

'—who would not hate you, you great female binder, entwiner, seducer, and seeker and finder! Who would not love you, you innocent, impatient, and swift-as-wind, child-eyed sinner!

'Where are you taking me, you paragon and playmate? And now you flee me again, you sweet wildcat and ingrate!

'I dance after you, following the faintest trace that lingers. Where are you? Give me your hand! Or one of your fingers!

'Here are caves and also thickets: we are treading unknown ground!—Stop! Stand still! Are those not owls and bats that are fluttering round?

'You screech-owl! You flying bat! Why all this aping? Where are we? From the dogs you have learned all this howling and yapping.

'You bare so delightfully your dainty white teeth again; your evil eyes dart at me through your matted curly mane.

'This is a dance over hedge and ditch clear: I am the hunter—will you be my hound or else my deer?

'Now you are right by me! So swiftly, you wicked leaper, you! Now I am up! and away!—Oh no! I have fallen myself as I tried to leap too!

'Look at me lying here, exuberant one, and pleading for mercy! Gladly would I go with you—on paths more worth traversing!

'—on the path of love through quiet colourful bushes! Or there along by the lake, where swim and dance goldfishes!

'Are you weary now? Over yonder are sheep and warm sunset hues: is it not sweet to sleep when shepherds play their tunes?

'Are you now so weary? I shall carry you, just let your arms sink! And if you are thirsty—I have something for you, but your mouth will not drink!—

'—Oh this accursèd nimble and agile serpent and slippery witch! Where have you gone? But here on my face I now feel from your hand two spots and red blotches that itch!

'I truly am weary of always being your sheepish shepherd's dream! You witch, if I have sung to you so far, now for me you shall— scream!

'You shall dance and also scream to my whip-crack's brisk tempo! I did not forget the whip, did I?—No!'—

* * *

2

Then Life answered me thus and in so doing stopped up her delicate ears:

'O Zarathustra! Please don't crack your whip so terribly! For well you know: noise murders thoughts*—and just now such tender thoughts are coming to me.

'We are a couple of true good-for-nothings and evil-for-nothings. Beyond good and evil we found our island and our own green meadow—we two alone! Therefore must we be good to each other!

'And even if we do not love each other from the ground up—must one then dislike the other just because one does not love from the ground up?

'And that I am fond of you and often too fond, that you know: and the grounds for that are that I am jealous of your Wisdom. Ah, that crazy old madwoman Wisdom!

'If your Wisdom should ever desert you, ah! then my love too would desert you just as swiftly.'—

Thereupon Life looked pensively behind her and about her and said softly: 'O Zarathustra, you are not true enough to me!

'You have long not loved me as much as you say you do; I know you are thinking that you want to leave me soon.

'There is an ancient heavy heavy booming-bell: at night its booming comes all the way up to your cave:—

'—and when you hear this bell at midnight strike the hour, between the strokes of one and twelve you think—

'—you think then, O Zarathustra, well I know, of how you want to leave me soon!'—

'Yes,' I answered hesitantly, 'but you also know that—' And I said something into her ear, right through her tangled yellow crazy locks of hair.

'You *know* that, O Zarathustra? No one knows that.— —'

And we looked at each other and gazed upon the soft green meadow, over which the cool evening was just then spreading, and wept with one another.—But just then Life was dearer to me than all my Wisdom had ever been.—

Thus spoke Zarathustra.

* * *

3

One!

O man! Take care!

Two!

What does Deep Midnight now declare?

Three!

'I sleep, I sleep—

Four!

'From deepest dream I rise for air:—

Five!

'The world is deep,

Six!

'Deeper than day had been aware.

Seven!

'Deep is its woe—

Eight!

'Joy—deeper still than misery:

Nine!

'Woe says: Now go!

Ten!

'Yet all joy wants Eternity—

Eleven!

'—wants deepest, deep Eternity!'

Twelve!

* * *

16. The Seven Seals*
(or: The Yea- and Amen-Song)

I

If I am a soothsayer and filled with that soothsaying spirit which wanders along a high ridge between two seas—

wanders between past and future as a heavy cloud—an enemy of sultry lowlands and of all that is weary and cannot die or live:

ready for lightning in the dark bosom and for the redemptive ray of light, pregnant with lightning-bolts that say Yea! laugh Yea!, for soothsaying rays of lightning:—

—but blessèd is the one who is pregnant thus! And verily, long must one hang as heavy weather on the mountains if one is some day to kindle the light of the future!—

Oh how should I not lust after Eternity and after the nuptial ring of all rings—the ring of recurrence!

Never yet have I found the woman from whom I wanted children, except for this woman whom I love: for I love you, O Eternity!*

For I love you, O Eternity!

* * *

2

If ever my wrath broke graves open, shifted boundary-stones, and rolled old shattered tablets* into sheerest depths:

If ever my scorn blew mouldy words away, and I came as a broom against cross-spiders and as a driving wind to old and damp burial chambers:

If ever I sat rejoicing where ancient Gods lie buried, blessing and loving the world beside the monuments of the old world-slanderers:—

—for I even love churches and Gods' graves, as long as the sky looks down with a pure eye through their dilapidated roofs; gladly I sit like grass and red poppies on dilapidated churches—

Oh how should I not lust after Eternity and after the nuptial ring of all rings—the ring of recurrence?

Never yet have I found the woman from whom I wanted children, except for this woman whom I love: for I love you, O Eternity!

For I love you, O Eternity!

*　*　*

3

If ever a breath came to me of that creative breath and heavenly necessity that compels even accidents to dance stellar round-dances:

If ever I laughed the laugh of that creative lightning which is followed grumblingly, but obediently, by the long thunder of the deed:

If ever I played dice with Gods at the Gods' table of the earth, so that the earth quaked and broke open and pushed up floods of fire:—

—for the earth is a Gods' table and trembles with creative new words and Gods' dice-throws:—

Oh how should I not lust after Eternity and after the nuptial ring of all rings—the ring of recurrence?

Never yet have I found the woman from whom I wanted children, except for this woman whom I love: for I love you, O Eternity!

For I love you, O Eternity!

*　*　*

4

If ever I drank full draughts from that foaming spice- and mixing-jug in which all things are well mixed:

If ever my hand poured the farthest to the nearest and fire to spirit and joy to pain and the wickedest to the kindest:

If I myself am a grain of that redemptive salt which ensures that all things in the mixing-jug are well mixed:—

—for there is a salt that binds good to evil; and even the most evil is good for spicing and for the ultimate foaming-over:—

Oh how should I not lust after Eternity and after the nuptial ring of all rings—the ring of recurrence?

Never yet have I found the woman from whom I wanted children, except for this woman whom I love: for I love you, O Eternity!

For I love you, O Eternity!

*   *   *

5

If I am fond of the sea and all that is of the sea's kind, and even fondest when it angrily contradicts me:

If that joy in searching is in me that drives my sails on to the undiscovered, if a seafarer's joy is in my joy:

If ever my rejoicing shouted: 'The coast has disappeared—now the last chain has fallen from me—

'—boundlessness roars all about me, far and away space and time sparkle,* well then! Come on, old heart!'—

Oh how should I not lust after Eternity and after the nuptial ring of all rings—the ring of recurrence?

Never yet have I found the woman from whom I wanted children, except for this woman whom I love: for I love you, O Eternity!

For I love you, O Eternity!

*   *   *

6

If my virtue is a dancer's virtue, and I have often leaped with both feet into golden-emerald rapture:

If my wickedness is a laughing wickedness, at home under rose-bowers and hedges of lilies:

—for in laughter is all evil compacted, but pronounced holy and free by its own blissfulness:—

And if this is my Alpha and Omega: that all that is heavy become light, all body become dancer, all spirit become bird—and verily that is my Alpha and Omega!—*

Oh how should I not lust after Eternity and after the nuptial ring of all rings—the ring of recurrence!

Never yet have I found the woman from whom I wanted children, except for this woman whom I love: for I love you, O Eternity!

For I love you, O Eternity!

* * *

7

If ever I spread tranquil Heavens over me and soared with my own wings into my own Heavens:

If I swam playfully in deep light-distances, and if to my freedom some bird-wisdom came:—

—but thus bird-wisdom speaks: 'See, there is no above, no below! Throw yourself around, and out, and back, you who are light! Sing! speak no more!

'—Are all words not made for those who are heavy? Do all words not lie for one who is light! Sing! speak no more!'—

Oh how should I not lust after Eternity and after the nuptial ring of all rings—the ring of recurrence?

Never yet have I found the woman from whom I wanted children, except for this woman whom I love: for I love you, O Eternity!

For I love you, O Eternity!

* * *

FOURTH AND LAST PART

Ah, where in the world has there been more foolishness than among those who pity? And what in the world has caused more suffering than the foolishness of those who pity?

Woe to all lovers who do not still have a height that is above their pitying!

Thus spoke the Devil to me once: 'God too has his Hell: it is his love for human beings.'

And lately I heard him say this word too: 'God is dead; it is of his pity for human beings that God has died.'—

(*Thus Spoke Zarathustra*, 'On Those Who Pity')

1. The Honey Sacrifice

—And again months and years flowed over Zarathustra's soul, and he did not heed them; but his hair turned white. One day, as he sat on a rock in front of his cave and quietly looked out—one looks out from there over the sea, and away over winding abysses—his animals walked thoughtfully around him and at last set themselves in front of him.

'O Zarathustra,' they said, 'are you perhaps looking out for your happiness?'—'What does happiness matter!' he answered. 'I have long ceased striving after happiness: I am striving after my work.'—'O Zarathustra,' said the animals again, 'you say that as one who has more than enough of the good. Are you not lying in a sky-blue lake of happiness?'—'You pranksters,' replied Zarathustra and laughed. 'How well you chose that image! But you know too that my happiness is heavy and not like a flowing wave of water: it presses me and will not leave me, and behaves like melted tar.'—

The animals again walked thoughtfully around him and then set themselves in front of him once more. 'O Zarathustra,' they said, 'is *that* why you yourself are becoming ever more sallow and darker, though your hair would appear white and flaxen? For behold, you are sitting in your own tar!'—'What are you saying now, my animals,' said Zarathustra laughing. 'Verily, I slandered when I spoke of tar. What is happening to me is what goes on in all fruits that are ripening. It is the *honey* in my veins that is making my blood thicker and also my soul more tranquil.'*—'So will it be, O Zarathustra,' answered the animals and pressed themselves against him. 'But will you not climb a high mountain today? The air is clear, and today one can see more of the world than ever.'— 'Yes, my animals,' he answered, 'you counsel well and after my own heart: I will indeed climb a high mountain today! But see to it that there is honey on hand there, yellow, white, fine, ice-cool golden comb-honey. For know that I want to offer the honey sacrifice up there!'—

But when Zarathustra was up on the heights he sent the animals home, who had led him there, and found that he was now alone:— then he laughed heartily, looked around, and spoke thus:

That I spoke of sacrifices and honey sacrifices was simply the cunning of my speech and, verily, a useful folly! Up here I may surely talk more freely than in front of solitaries' caves and solitaries' animals.

Sacrifice what! I squander what is given to me, I, a squanderer with a thousand hands: how could I call that—sacrificing!

And when I desired honey, I simply desired bait and sweet syrup and gum, at which even growling bears and wondrous surly wicked birds lick their lips:

—at the best bait, as is necessary for hunters and fishermen. For if the world is like a dark forest of beasts and a pleasure-garden for all wild hunters, then it seems to me rather and preferably an abyss-deep and rich sea,

—a sea full of colourful fishes and crabs that even Gods would desire, who would become fishers in it and throwers of nets: so rich is the world in wondrous things, both great and small!

Especially the humans' world, the humans' sea:—into *that* I now cast my golden fishing-rod and say: Open up, you humans' abyss!*

Open up and cast up to me your fishes and glistening crabs! With my best bait shall I lure today the most wondrous human-fishes!

—my happiness itself shall I cast out into all expanses and distances, between sunrise, midday, and sunset, to see whether many human-fishes will not learn to wriggle and tug at my happiness.

Until, biting on my sharp and well-hidden hooks, they must come up to *my* height, the most colourful abyss-groundlings to the most wicked among all human-fish catchers.

That is who I am from the ground up and the beginning: pulling, attracting, drawing out, bringing up, a drawer, raiser, and taskmaster of discipline, who once and not in vain urged himself: 'Become the one you are!'*

May humans thus now come *up* to me: for I still await the signs that it is time for my descent; for I myself am not yet going down, as I must, among human beings.

Therefore I wait here, cunning and mocking on high mountains, not impatient, nor patient, but rather as one who has unlearned even patience—because he no longer 'endureth'.*

For my fate is leaving me time: has it perhaps forgotten me? Or is it sitting behind a large rock in the shade and catching flies?

And verily, I am grateful to it, my eternal fate, for not rushing and pressing me but leaving me time for jesting and wicked tricks: so that today I have climbed this high mountain in order to fish.

Has a human being on high mountains ever caught fish? And even if it be folly, what I want and pursue up here: this is still better than becoming solemn down there from waiting, and green and sallow—

—a pompous wrath-snorter from waiting, a sacred howling-storm from the mountains, an impatient fellow who shouts down into the valleys: 'Listen, else I shall whip you with the scourge of God!'

Not that I would become angry at such ragers for that: as laughing-stocks they are good enough! They must surely be impatient, these great din-kettledrums that will find a voice today or never!

But I and my fate—we do not talk to Today, nor do we talk to Never: for talking we surely have patience and time and more than time. For one day he must come after all and may not pass by.

Who must come one day and may not pass by? Our great *hazar*, that is our great far-off humans' realm, the Zarathustra-realm of a thousand years*— —

How far-off might this 'far-off' be? What does that matter to me! But I am no less certain of it on that account—with both feet I stand securely on this ground,

—on an eternal ground, on hard primeval rock, on this highest hardest primeval mountain-range, to which all winds come as to a weather-divide, asking Where? and Whence? and Whither?

Here laugh, laugh, my bright and wholesome wickedness! From high mountains throw down your glittering scorn-laughter! With your glittering, bait for me the most beautiful human-fishes!

And whatever in all seas belongs to *me*, my in-and-for-me* in all things—fish *that* out for me, lead *that* up here to me: for that am I waiting, the wickedest of all fishermen.

On out, on out, my fishing-rod! On down, and in, bait of my happiness! Drip down your sweetest dew, my heart's honey! Bite, my fishing-rod, into the belly of all black sorrow!

On out, on out, my eye! Oh how many seas all about me, what

dawning human futures! And above me—what rose-red stillness! What unclouded silence!

*   *   *

2. The Cry of Need

On the next day Zarathustra again sat on the rock in front of his cave, while the animals roamed about the world outside in order to bring him back fresh food—as well as fresh honey: for Zarathustra had consumed and squandered the old honey down to the last drop. But as he sat there, with a stick in his hand, tracing the outline of his shadow on the ground, thinking—and, verily! not about himself and his shadow—he was suddenly terrified and gave a start: for he saw beside his own shadow another shadow. And as he looked about himself quickly and stood up, behold, there was the soothsayer standing beside him, the same one he had once given to eat and drink at his table, the proclaimer of the great weariness who taught: 'All is the same, nothing is worthwhile, world is without meaning, knowing chokes.' But his countenance had been transformed in the meantime; and when Zarathustra looked into his eyes he again felt terror in his own heart: so many ill tidings and ash-gray lightning-bolts were coursing across this face.

The soothsayer, who perceived what was happening in Zarathustra's soul, wiped his hand across his countenance as if he wanted to wipe it away; and Zarathustra did likewise. And when they had both silently composed and strengthened themselves in this way, they shook hands, as a sign that they wanted to recognize each other again.

'I bid you welcome,' said Zarathustra, 'you soothsayer of the great weariness; not for nothing shall you once have been my guest at table. Eat and drink with me today too, and forgive the fact that a contented old man sits at the table with you!'—'A contented old man?' replied the soothsayer, shaking his head. 'But whoever you may be or want to be, O Zarathustra, you have been it up here for the longest time—in a short time your boat shall sit on dry land no more!'—'Am I really sitting on dry land?' asked Zarathustra laughing.—'The waves around your mountain', answered the soothsayer, 'are rising higher and higher, the waves of great need and sorrow: soon they will lift up your boat and carry you away.'—Zarathustra was silent at this and was amazed.—'Do you still hear nothing?' continued the soothsayer. 'Is there not a rushing and roaring from out of the depths?' Zarathustra was silent again and listened: then he heard a long, long cry, which the abysses threw back and forth and carried farther, for none of them wanted to keep it: so evil was the sound.

'You proclaimer of ill tidings,' said Zarathustra at last. 'That is a cry of need and the cry of a human being, which may well come out of a black sea. But what does humans' need matter to me! My ultimate sin, that has been saved for me—perhaps you know what it is called?'

—'*Pity*!' answered the soothsayer from an overflowing heart, and raised both hands aloft.—'O Zarathustra, I come that I might seduce you to your ultimate sin!'—

And no sooner had these words been spoken than the cry resounded again, longer and more anxious than before, and also much nearer. 'Do you hear? Do you hear, O Zarathustra?' cried the soothsayer. 'The cry is meant for you, it is calling you. Come, come, come; it is time, it is high time!'—

Zarathustra thereupon fell silent, confused and shaken. At last he asked, like one who hesitates in himself: 'And who is it that is calling for me?'

'But surely you know,' answered the soothsayer vehemently. 'What are you hiding from yourself? *The superior human* is who is crying for you!'*

'The superior human?' cried Zarathustra, seized by horror. 'What does *that* want? What does *that* want? The superior human! What does that want here?'—and his skin became covered with sweat.

But the soothsayer did not respond to Zarathustra's anxiety, but listened and listened into the depths. And when it had been quiet down there for a long time, he turned his gaze back and saw Zarathustra standing there trembling.

'O Zarathustra,' he began in a mournful voice, 'you do not stand there like one whose happiness sets him spinning: you will have to dance in order not to collapse!

'But even if you wanted to dance for me and to leap all your side-ways-leaps, nobody shall be permitted to say to me: "Behold, here dances the last happy human being!"

'In vain would one come up to this height to seek *him* here: caves he would surely find* and hinter-caves, hiding-places for those who are hidden, rather than mine-shafts of happiness and treasure chambers and new gold-veins of happiness.

'Happiness—how could one ever find happiness among such recluses and solitaries! Must I yet seek the ultimate happiness on the Isles of the Blest and far away between forgotten seas?

'But all is the same, nothing is worthwhile, no seeking avails, nor are there Isles of the Blest any more!'— —

Thus sighed the soothsayer; but at his last sigh Zarathustra again became bright and assured, like one emerging from a deep ravine into the light. 'No! No! Three times no!' he cried in a strong voice, and stroked his beard.—'*That* I know better! There are still Isles of the Blest! Be quiet about *that*, you sighing set of mourning-pipes!

'Stop babbling about *that*, you rain-cloud in the forenoon! For do I not stand here, soaked by your sorrow and drenched like a dog?

'Now I shall shake myself and run away from you, that I might become dry again: there is no need to wonder at that! Do you think me discourteous? But this is *my* court.

'But as far as your superior human is concerned: well then! I shall seek him at once in that forest—*thence* came his cry. Perhaps an evil beast is pursuing him there.

'He is in *my* domain: here shall he not come to harm! And verily, there are many evil beasts about me!'—

With these words Zarathustra turned to go. Then the soothsayer spoke: 'O Zarathustra, you are a rogue!

'For well I know: you want to be rid of me! You would rather run into the forest and pursue evil beasts!

'But what does it avail? Come evening you will have me again in any case: in your own cave I shall be sitting, patient and heavy as a log—waiting for you!'

'So be it!' Zarathustra shouted back as he went away. 'And whatever is mine in my cave also belongs to you, my dear guest!

'And if you should yet find honey in there, well then! please lick it up, you growling bear, and sweeten your soul! For in the evening we should both be in good spirits,

'—in good spirits and glad that this day has come to an end! And you yourself shall dance to my songs as my dancing bear.

'You do not believe it? You are shaking your head? Well then! Come now, old bear! But I too—am a soothsayer.'

Thus spoke Zarathustra.

* * *

3. Conversation With the Kings

I

Zarathustra had not been on his way for even an hour in his mountains and forests when all at once he saw a strange procession.* On the very path that he wanted to go down, two kings were coming along, adorned with crowns and sashes of purple and colourful as flamingoes: they were driving before them a laden ass.* 'What do these kings want in my realm?' said Zarathustra in astonishment to his heart, and swiftly concealed himself behind a bush. But when the kings came abreast of him, he said, half aloud, like someone talking to himself: 'How strange! How strange! How does this go together? Two kings I see—and only one ass!'

Then the two kings came to a halt, smiled, looked toward the place from which the voice came, and then looked each other in the eye. 'One perhaps thinks that sort of thing among us, too,' said the king on the right. 'But one does not say it out loud.'

The king on the left, however, shrugged his shoulders and answered: 'That may well be a goatherd. Or a solitary who has lived too long among rocks and trees. For a complete lack of society spoils one's good manners.'

'Good manners?' rejoined the other king angrily and bitterly. 'Whom are we trying to avoid now? Is it not "good manners"? Our "polite society"?

'Rather live, verily, among solitaries and goatherds than with our gilded false over-rouged rabble—even though it call itself "polite society",

'—even though it call itself "nobility". But that is all false and rotten, the blood above all, thanks to ancient bad sicknesses and bad healing-artists.

'The finest and dearest to me even today is a healthy peasant, coarse, cunning, stubborn, enduring: that is today the noblest kind.

'The peasant is today the finest; and the peasant's kind should be master! It is the reign of the rabble—I no longer let myself be deceived. Rabble, however, means: mish-mash.

'Rabble mish-mash: everything therein is mixed up with everything else, saint and scoundrel and Junker and Jew and every kind of creature from Noah's Ark.

'Good manners! Everything with us is false and rotten. No one knows any more how to revere: it is precisely from *that* that we are running away. They are cloying importunate dogs; they gild palm-leaves.

'This disgust chokes me, that we kings have ourselves become false, covered over, and disguised by the old and yellowed pomp of our grandfathers, showpieces for the stupidest and the slyest, and whoever else today haggles over power.

'We *are* not the first—and yet must *appear* to be:* we have finally become tired and disgusted with all this deception.

'We have avoided the riff-raff, all these bawlers and scribbling blowflies, the stench of shopkeepers, the wriggling of the ambitious, the foul breath—pshaw, to live among the riff-raff,

'—pshaw, to count as the first among the rabble! Ah, disgust! disgust! disgust! What do we kings matter any more!'—

'Your old sickness is attacking you,' said the king on the left at this point. 'Disgust is attacking you, my poor brother. But of course you know that someone is listening to us.'

Immediately Zarathustra, who had opened his ears and eyes to these speeches, stood up from his hiding-place, stepped up to the kings, and began:

'He who is listening to you, and listening to you gladly, O kings, is called Zarathustra.

'I am Zarathustra, who once said: "What do kings matter any more!" Forgive me, but I was glad when you said to each other: "What do we kings matter?"

'But this is *my* realm and my dominion: what might you be seeking in my realm? Perhaps you *found* on your way what *I* am seeking: namely, the superior human.'

When the kings heard this they beat their breasts and said with a single voice: 'We are found out!

'With the sword of these words you have cut through the densest darkness of our hearts. You have discovered our need, for behold! We are on our way, that we might find the superior human—

'—the human who is superior to us: even though we are kings. To him we are leading this ass. For the supreme human shall also be on earth the supreme lord.

'There is no harsher misfortune in all human fate than when the powerful of the earth are not also first among men. Then everything becomes false and awry and monstrous.

'And when they are even last among men and more beasts than humans: then the rabble's stock rises higher and higher, and at last rabble-virtue even says: "Behold, I alone am virtue!" '—

'What did I just hear?' answered Zarathustra; 'what wisdom in kings! I am delighted, and, verily, I am already longing to make a rhyme upon it:—

'—even if it be a rhyme that is not for everyone's ears. I unlearned long ago any consideration for long ears. Well then! Come now!'

(But at this point it so happened that the ass, too, managed to speak; but it said clearly and with ill will, 'Yea-Ah'.)

> 'Once upon a time—the year One, I think—
> Thus spoke the Sibyl,* drunken without drink:
> "Woe, all goes awry, I know!
> Downfall! Downfall! Ne'er sank the world so low!
> Rome became a whore and a fine whorehouse too,*
> Rome's Caesars became beasts, and God himself—
> a Jew!" '

*　　*　　*

2

The kings drank in these rhymes of Zarathustra's; but the king on the right said: 'O Zarathustra, how well we did to go forth to see you!

'For your enemies showed us your image in their mirror: there you looked out with the grimace of a Devil and mocking laughter, so that we were afraid of you.

'But what could we do! Again and again you pierced us in the ears and heart with your sayings. Then at last we said: What does it matter how he looks!

'We must *hear* him, him who teaches: "You shall love peace as a means to new wars, and the short peace more than the long!"

'No one has ever spoken such warlike words: "What is good? To be brave is good. It is the good war that hallows every cause."

'O Zarathustra, at such words the blood of our fathers stirred in our bodies: it was like the speech of spring to old wine-casks.

'When the swords would whip around each other like red-flecked serpents, then did our fathers become well disposed toward life; the sun of peace seemed to them bland and lukewarm, and the long peace even shameful.*

'How they sighed, our fathers, when they saw lightning-shiny dried-out swords on the wall! Like those they thirsted for war. For a sword wants to drink blood and sparkles with desire.'— —

—As the kings thus eagerly talked and chattered about the happiness of their fathers, Zarathustra was overcome by no small desire to mock their eagerness: for these were evidently very peaceable kings that he saw before him, with aged and refined faces. But he restrained himself. 'Well then!' he said. 'Yonder leads the way, and there lies Zarathustra's cave; and this day shall have a long evening! But now a cry of need calls me urgently away from you.

'It honours my cave if kings will sit and wait in it: but, to be sure, you may have to wait a long time!

'But really! What does it matter! Where does one better learn today how to wait than in courts? And all the virtue now remaining to kings—is it not today called: *being capable* of waiting?'

Thus spoke Zarathustra.

* * *

4. The Leech

And Zarathustra walked thoughtfully farther and deeper, through forests and past marshy land; but, as happens to everyone who thinks about difficult things, he thereby stepped on someone unwittingly. And behold, all at once a cry of pain and two curses and twenty unpleasant insults splashed up into his face: so that in his fright he raised his staff and in addition struck the one stepped on. But he straightway regained his composure, and his heart laughed at the folly he had just committed.

'Forgive me,' he said to the one stepped on, who had angrily arisen and sat down. 'Forgive me and, above all, first listen to an allegory.

'Just as a wanderer who dreams of distant things unwittingly stumbles over a sleeping dog on a lonely road, a dog lying in the sun:

'—as both then start up and go at each other like deadly enemies, frightened to death the two of them: thus it happened with us.

'And yet! And yet—how little was lacking that they might have caressed each other, this dog and this lonely man! They are both after all—lonely!'

—'Whoever you may be,' said the one stepped on, still angry, 'you step too close to me with your allegory too, and not only with your foot!

'For behold, am I then a dog?'—and thereupon the sitting one stood up and drew his bare arm out of the swamp. For at first he had been lying stretched out on the ground, concealed and unrecognizable like those who lie in wait for swamp-game.

'But what are you doing?' cried Zarathustra in fright, for he saw a stream of blood flowing down the man's bare arm.—'What has happened to you? Were you bitten, you poor wretch, by some evil beast?'

The bleeding man laughed, still furious. 'What is it to you!' he said and was about to go on his way. 'Here I am at home and in my own realm. Let whoever would question me do so: but to a blockhead I shall hardly give an answer.'

'You are wrong,' said Zarathustra compassionately and held him fast. 'You are wrong: here you are not at home but in my realm, and here shall no one come to harm.

'You may call me whatever you will—I am the one I must be. I myself call myself Zarathustra.

'Well then! Yonder leads the way up to Zarathustra's cave: it is not far—will you not tend your wounds in my home?

'It has gone badly, you poor wretch, in this life of yours: first the beast bit you, and then—the human stepped on you!'— —

But when the one stepped on heard Zarathustra's name, he was transformed. 'What is happening to me!' he cried out. '*Who* concerns me any more in this life other than this one human being, namely Zarathustra, and that one beast which lives on blood, the leech?

'For the sake of the leech I lay here by this swamp like a fisherman, and my outstretched arm had already been bitten ten times when a still fairer leech came after my blood: Zarathustra himself!

'What good fortune! What a miracle! Praised be this day that lured me to this swamp! Praised be the best and most vital cupping-glass that is alive today; praised be the great conscience-leech, Zarathustra!'—

Thus spoke the one stepped on; and Zarathustra was pleased by his words and their refined and respectful manner. 'Who are you?' he asked and offered him his hand. 'Between us much remains to be cleared up and cheered up: but already, it seems to me, the day is becoming clear and bright.'

'I am *the conscientious in spirit*,' answered the one who had been asked. 'As for things of the spirit, no one easily takes them more strictly, narrowly, and severely than I do, except he from whom I learned this: Zarathustra himself.

'Rather know nothing than half-know many things! Rather be a fool on one's own account than a wise man in the opinion of others! I—get to the ground of things.

'—what does it matter whether it be great or small? Whether it be called swamp or Heaven? A handsbreadth of ground suffices for me: if only it really be ground and soil!

'—a handsbreadth of ground: on that one can stand. In the right science of conscience there is nothing great and nothing small.'

'Then perhaps you are the connoisseur of the leech?' asked Zarathustra. 'And you pursue the leech down to the ultimate grounds, you conscientious one?'

'O Zarathustra,' answered the one stepped on, 'that would be something immense: how could I undertake such a thing!

'But what I am a master and connoisseur of, that is the leech's *brain*:—that is *my* world!

'And it is indeed a world! But forgive me that here my pride speaks up, for I do not have my equal here. That is why I said, "Here I am at home".

'How long have I been pursuing this one thing, the brain of the leech, that the slippery truth might here no longer slip away from me! Here is *my* realm!

'—for this I have thrown away everything else; for this everything else has become the same for me; and close by my knowing lies my black unknowing.

'The conscience of my spirit wills it thus from me, that I might know one thing and otherwise know nothing: all half measures of the spirit disgust me, and everything vaporous, hovering, fanatical.

'Where my honesty ceases, I am blind and also want to be blind.* But where I want to know, I also want to be honest, which means severe, strict, narrow, cruel, unrelenting.

'Because *you*, O Zarathustra, once said: "Spirit is the life that itself cuts into life": that introduced and seduced me to your teaching. And verily, with my own blood I have increased my own knowing!'

—'As appearances teach,' rejoined Zarathustra; since the blood was still flowing down the bare arm of the conscientious one. For ten leeches had bitten into it.

'O you wondrous companion, how much this appearance teaches me, namely you yourself! And perhaps I had better not pour everything into your strict ears!

'Well then! Here we must part! Yet I would gladly find you again. Yonder leads the way up to my cave: tonight you shall be my dear guest there!

'I would also gladly make amends to your body for Zarathustra's stepping on you with his feet: I shall think about that. But now a cry of need calls me urgently away from you.'

Thus spoke Zarathustra.

*   *   *

5. The Sorcerer*

I

But as Zarathustra was going around a rock he saw, not far below him, on the same path, a man who was throwing his limbs about like a madman and eventually collapsed on the ground on his belly. 'Stop!' said Zarathustra then to his heart. 'This must surely be the superior human, from whom that awful cry of need came—I will see if I can be of help here.' But when he ran up to the place where the figure lay on the ground, he found a trembling old man with staring eyes; and however much Zarathustra tried to help him up and set him on his feet again, it was all in vain. Nor did the unfortunate man even seem to notice that there was someone beside him; rather, he kept looking about with pathetic gestures, like one abandoned and deserted by all the world. But at last, after much shivering, twitching, and self-contorting, he began to wail thus:*

> 'Who warms me, who loves me still?
> Give me hot hands!
> Give burning heart's coal-warmers!
> Stretched out here, shivering,
> Like one half dead, whose feet are gently warmed—
> Shaken, alas! by unknown winter fevers,
> Trembling from sharp and icy frost-arrows,
> Hunted by you, severe thought!
> Unnameable! Well veiled! Terrifying!
> You huntsman behind the clouds!
> Struck down by your lightning-bolt,
> You scornful eye that stares at me from the dark:
> —thus I lie, and
> Bend myself, twist myself, tortured
> By all the eternal torments,
> Well smitten
> By you, cruellest huntsman,
> You unknown presence—God!
>
> Strike deeper!
> Strike one more time!
> Now pierce, now break this heart!*
> What means this torture
> With tooth-blunted arrows?
> Why do you stare again,
> Not weary yet of human pain,
> With joyous-gloating Gods' lightning-eyes?
> You want not to kill,
> Just torture, torture?
> Why—torture *me*,
> You joyful-gloating unknown secret God?—
>
> Haha! You are stealing near?
> At such a midnight hour

What do you want? Speak!
You oppress me, press me—
Ha! already too close!
Away! Away!
You hear me breathing,
You overhear my heart,
Jealous divinity—
Of what are you so jealous?
Away! Away! Now why the ladder?
Will you *enter*,
Into my heart,
Clamber in, into my most secret
And my most hidden thoughts?
How shameless! Unknown hidden—thief!
What do you want by stealing,
What do you want by listening,
What do you want by torturing,
You torturer!
You—hangman-God!
Or else shall I, just like a dog,
Roll over for you?
So yielding, inspired beyond myself,
And—wag my love to you?

In vain! Pierce deeper,
Cruellest barb! No,
No dog—just your game am I,
Cruellest huntsman!
The proudest of your prisoners,
You robber behind the clouds!
Speak at last!
What do you want, lurking waylayer, from *me*?
All lightning-shrouded! Unknown presence! Speak,
What do you *want*, unknown secret—God?— —

What? A ransom?
How much do you want?
Demand a lot—thus says my pride!
And speak little—thus says my other pride!

Haha!
Me—you want? Me?
Me—whole? . . .

Haha!
And torture me, fool that you are,
You torture to death my pride?
Give me *love*—who warms me still?
Who loves me still?—give me hot hands,
Give burning heart's coal-warmers
Give me, the loneliest,
Whom ice, ah! sevenfold frozen ice
Teaches to languish for enemies,
For enemies themselves.
Give, yes give up,
Cruellest enemy,
To me—*yourself!*—

Now gone!
He himself has fled,
My last and sole companion,
My great enemy,
My unknown one,
My hangman-God!—

—No! Come back now,
With all your gruesome tortures!
To the last of all the lonely
Oh do come back!
All my torrents of tears now run
To you their course!
And the very last flame of my heart
To *you* blazes up!
Oh do come back,
My unknown secret God! My pain! My ultimate—
                              happiness!'

                    *   *   *

2

—But by this time Zarathustra could restrain himself no longer, and he took his staff and set to beating the wailer with all his strength. 'Stop it!' he screamed at him with furious laughter. 'Stop it, you play-actor!* You counterfeiter! You liar from the ground up! I recognize you well!

'I will warm your legs for you, you wicked sorcerer; and well I know how to make things *hot* for the likes of you!'

—'Leave off,' said the old man and sprang up from the ground. 'Beat me no more, O Zarathustra! I was doing that only as a game!

'Such things belong to my art: it was you that I wanted to try out when I rehearsed that trial for you! And verily, you have seen through me well!

'But you too—have given me no small part of yourself to try out: you are *hard*, wise Zarathustra! Hard you strike with your "truths", and your cudgel extracts from me—*this* truth!'

—'Do not flatter,' answered Zarathustra, still excited and frowning darkly, 'you play-actor from the ground up! You are false: why do you talk—of truth!

'You peacock of peacocks, you sea of vanity, *what* were you playing before me, you wicked sorcerer; in *whom* was I meant to believe when you were wailing in such a manner?'

'*The penitent of the spirit*,' said the old man. '*Him* was I playing: you yourself once invented this term—

'—the poet and sorcerer who eventually turns his spirit against himself, one transformed, who freezes to death from his wicked knowledge and conscience.

'And you may as well admit it: it took a long time, O Zarathustra, before you saw through my art and lie! You *believed* in my need when you held my head in both your hands—

'—I heard you wailing, "He has been loved too little, loved too little!" That I deceived you that much, over this my wickedness inwardly rejoiced.'

'You may have deceived more subtle ones than me,' said Zarathustra harshly. 'I am not on my guard against deceivers; I *must* be without caution: thus my lot wills it.

'But you—*must* deceive: that well do I know you! You must always be ambiguous, tri- quadri- and quintiguous! Even what you just now confessed was by far not true and not false enough for me!

'You wicked counterfeiter, how could you do otherwise! You would even put rouge on your illness if you showed yourself naked to your physician.

'Just as you put rouge on your lie when you said: "I was doing that *only* as a game!" It was also *serious*, for you *are* something of a penitent of the spirit!

'I divine you well: you became the enchanter of all, but for yourself you have no lies or cunning left—you yourself are disenchanted with yourself!

'You harvested disgust as your single truth. No word of yours is true any longer, except your mouth: that is, the disgust that still clings to your mouth.'— —

—'But who are you?' screamed the old sorcerer in a defiant voice. 'Who dares talk thus to *me*, the greatest man alive today?'—and green lightning shot from his eye toward Zarathustra. But immediately he was transformed and said mournfully:

'O Zarathustra, I am weary, and my arts fill me with disgust; I am not *great*, so why do I dissemble! But, as you well know—I was seeking greatness!

'I wanted to represent a great human being and I persuaded many: but this lie went beyond my strength. And now it shatters me.

'O Zarathustra, everything about me is a lie; but that I am being shattered—this shattering is *genuine!*'—

'It is to your honour,' said Zarathustra gloomily as he looked down to the side. 'It is to your honour that you sought greatness, but it betrays you too. You are not great.

'You wicked old sorcerer, *this* is what is best and most honest about you, and what I honour in you: that you grew weary of yourself and expressed it by saying, "I am not great".

'*For this* I honour you as a penitent of the spirit: and even if only for a passing breath, for this one moment you were—genuine.

'But speak: what are you seeking here in *my* forests and rocks? And when you laid yourself down in *my* way, what kind of trial were you wanting from me?—

'—to what were you tempting *me*?'—

Thus spoke Zarathustra, and his eyes sparkled. The old sorcerer was silent for a while, and then he said: 'Was I tempting you? I am only—seeking.

'O Zarathustra, I am seeking one who is genuine, upright, simple, univocal, a man of total honesty, a repository of wisdom, a saint of understanding, a great human being!

'For do you not know it, O Zarathustra? *I am seeking Zarathustra.*'

—And here a long silence arose between the two men; but Zarathustra sank deep into himself, such that he closed his eyes. But then, turning back to his interlocutor, he grasped the sorcerer's hand and said, full of courteousness and cunning:

'Well then! Yonder leads the way up, to where Zarathustra's cave lies. There you may seek whomever you may like to find.

'And ask my animals for advice, my eagle and my serpent: they shall help you seek. But my cave is large.

'I myself, to be sure—I have never yet seen a great human being. For what is great, the eye of the most refined men today is too coarse. It is the reign of the rabble.

'Many a one have I seen who stretched and inflated himself, so that the people screamed: "Look there, a great human being!" But what good are all bellows! In the end the wind comes out.

'In the end a frog that has blown itself up for too long bursts:* then the wind comes out. To prick a windbag in the belly, that I call a fine pastime. Hear that, you lads!

'This today belongs to the rabble: who *knows* any more what is great, and what is small! Who has ever had good luck seeking greatness! Only a fool: the fool is lucky.

'You are seeking great human beings, you wondrous fool? Who *taught* you that? Is today the time for that? Oh you wicked seeker, why—are you tempting me?'— —

Thus spoke Zarathustra, his heart consoled, and he continued laughing on his way.

* * *

6. Retired From Service

But not long after Zarathustra had freed himself from the sorcerer, he again saw someone sitting by the path he was taking, namely a tall man in black and with a haggard pale face: *this* man vexed him greatly. 'Woe,' he said to his heart, 'there sits disguised misery, looking like one of the priestly sort: what do *they* want in my realm?

'What! Hardly do I escape that sorcerer before I have another of those black magicians cross my path—

'—some witch-master with laying-on of hands, a dark miracle-worker by God's own grace, an anointed world-slanderer that the Devil may take!

'But the Devil is never in the place where he would be in place: he always comes too late, this accursed dwarf and clubfoot!'—

Thus cursed Zarathustra impatiently in his heart, and wondered how he might with averted gaze slip by the man in black. But behold, it happened otherwise. For at that very moment the sitting one had already espied him; and not unlike one whom unexpected good fortune has befallen, he sprang up and came toward Zarathustra.

'Whoever you may be, dear wanderer,' he said, 'help one who has lost his way, a seeker, an old man who may easily come to harm here!

'This world here is strange and remote to me, and I have heard wild beasts howling; and the one who could have afforded me protection is himself no more.

'I was seeking the last pious human, a holy man and solitary, who alone in his forest had as yet heard nothing of what today all the world knows.'

'*What* does all the world know today?' asked Zarathustra. 'Perhaps this, that the old God is no longer alive in whom all the world once believed?'

'As you say,' answered the old man in a troubled tone. 'And I served that old God up to his final hour.

'But now I am retired from service, without a master, and yet not free, nor cheerful at any time, unless it be in my memories.

'That is why I climbed into these mountains, that I might at last make a celebration for myself again, as is proper for an old pope and church-father: for know that I am the last pope!—a celebration of pious memories and religious services.

'But now he himself is dead, the most pious human, that holy man in the forest who constantly praised his God with singing and growling.

'Him I found not when I found his hut—but rather two wolves in there, that were howling over his death—for all the beasts loved him well. Then I ran away.

'Had I come thus into these forests and mountains in vain? Then my heart resolved that I should seek another, the most pious of all those who do not believe in God—that I should seek Zarathustra!'

Thus spoke the old man and gazed sharply at the one who was standing before him; but Zarathustra grasped the old pope by the hand and beheld it long with admiration.

'Behold, venerable one,' he then said, 'what a beautiful long hand! That is the hand of one who has always dispensed blessings. But now it holds fast the one you are seeking: me, Zarathustra.

'It is I, the godless Zarathustra, who likes to say: Who is more godless than I, that I might enjoy his instruction?'—

Thus spoke Zarathustra, and with his glances he pierced through the thoughts and after-thoughts of the old pope. At last the latter began:

'Whoever loved and possessed him the most has now also lost him the most—

'—behold, am I myself not the more godless of us two? But who could ever rejoice over that?'—

—'You served him up to the last,' said Zarathustra thoughtfully, after a profound silence. 'Do you know *how* he died? Is it true what they say, that pity choked him,

'—that he saw how *the human* hung on the Cross, and could not bear it; that love of the human became his Hell and at last his death?'— —

But the old pope did not answer, but looked aside shyly and with a pained and gloomy expression.

'Let him go,' said Zarathustra after long reflection, during which he continued to look the old man straight in the eye.

'Let him go; he is gone. And although it is to your honour that you only speak well of the deceased, you know as well as I do *who* he was, and that he walked wondrous ways.'

'Speaking in confidence, under our three eyes only,' said the old pope cheerfully (for he was blind in one eye), 'in things pertaining to God I am more enlightened than Zarathustra himself—and have the right to be so.

'My love served him for many long years; my will followed his entire will. But a good servant knows everything, even including things that his master hides from himself.

'He was a hidden God,* full of secrecy. Verily, he even came by a son in no other way than by subterfuge. At the portal of belief in him stands adultery.

'Whoever praises him as a God of love does not think highly enough of love itself. Did this God not want to be a judge as well? But the true lover loves beyond reward and retribution.

'When he was young, this God from the Orient, he was hard and vengeful and built himself a Hell for the delight of his favourites.

'But at last he became old and soft and mellow and pitying, more like a grandfather than a father, but most of all like a doddering old grandmother.

'Then he sat, shrivelled, in his stove-corner, fretting over his weak legs, world-weary, will-weary, and one day he suffocated on his all-too-great pity.'— —

'You old pope,' interjected Zarathustra at this point, 'did you observe *that* with your own eyes? It could indeed have happened that way: that way *and* otherwise too. When Gods die, they always die many kinds of death.

'But very well! This way or that, this way and that—he is gone! He offended the taste of my ears and eyes; worse I should not like to say of him.

'I love all that looks clearly and talks honestly. But he—you know well, you old priest, there was something of your kind in him, the priestly kind—he was ambiguous.

'He was also unclear. How angry he was at us, this wrath-snorter, because we understood him poorly! But why did he not speak more clearly?

'And if it was the fault of our ears, why did he give us ears that heard him so poorly? If there was mud in our ears, well then! who put that into them?

'Too much turned out badly for him, this potter,* who never completed his apprenticeship! But that he took revenge on his pots and creatures for turning out badly—that was a sin against *good taste*.

'Even in piousness there is good taste: *that* is what eventually said, "Away with *such* a God! Rather no God, rather make one's fate on one's own account, rather be a fool, rather be God oneself!" '

—'What is this I hear!' said the old pope at this point, pricking up his ears. 'O Zarathustra, you are more pious than you believe, with such lack of belief! Some God in you must have converted you to your godlessness.

'Is it not your piety itself that no longer lets you believe in a God?

And your over-great honesty will yet lead you away beyond good and evil too!

'For behold: what has been saved up for you? You have eyes and hands and mouth that are from all eternity predestined for blessing. One does not bless by hand alone.

'In your vicinity, even though you would be the most godless one, I sense a secret, sacred fragrance from long benedictions: it makes me feel well and ill together.

'Let me be your guest, O Zarathustra, for a single night! Nowhere on earth shall I feel better now than with you!'—

'Amen! So shall it be!' said Zarathustra in great amazement. 'Yonder leads the way up, to where Zarathustra's cave lies.

'Gladly, in truth, would I lead you there myself, venerable one, for I love all who are pious. But now a cry of need calls me urgently away from you.

'In my domain shall no one come to harm; my cave is a fine haven. And most of all I should like to set everyone who is mournful on firm land and firm legs again.

'But who could lift *your* heavy spirits from your shoulders? For that I am too weak. Long, verily, may we have to wait before someone awakens your God for you again.

'For this old God is no longer alive: he is thoroughly dead.'—

Thus spoke Zarathustra.

* * *

7. The Ugliest Man*

—And again Zarathustra's feet ran through mountains and forests, and his eyes searched and searched, but the one they wanted to see, the great sufferer and crier of need, was nowhere to be seen. But he rejoiced in his heart all throughout his way and was thankful. 'What good things', he said, 'has this day given me, in recompense for having begun so badly! What strange interlocutors I have found!

'On their words will I now chew a long time, as on fine kernels; small shall my teeth grind and crush them, until they flow like milk into my soul!'—

But as the path again curved around a rock, all at once the land-scape changed, and Zarathustra entered upon a realm of death. Here black and red cliffs rose up abruptly: no grass, no trees, no birdsong. For it was a valley that all beasts avoided, even the beasts of prey; only a species of ugly, thick, green snake, when it grew old, would come here to die. Therefore the shepherds called this valley 'Serpents' Death'.*

But Zarathustra sank into a black reminiscence, for it seemed to him that he had stood in this valley once before. And much that was heavy descended upon his mind, so that he walked slowly and ever more slowly and at last stood still. But then he saw, when he opened his eyes, something sitting by the path, in the form of a human being yet hardly like a human being, something inexpressible. And at one blow Zarathustra was overcome by great shame for having laid eyes on such a thing: blushing all the way to his white hair, he averted his gaze and lifted his foot in order to leave this dreadful place. But then the dead wasteland became loud: for from the ground there welled up a gurgling and rattling, just as water at night gurgles and rattles in stopped-up water pipes; and at last it became a human's voice and human's speech:—which sounded thus:

'Zarathustra! Zarathustra! Guess my riddle! Speak, speak! What is *revenge on the witness?*

'I lure you back, here is slippery ice! See to it, see to it that your pride does not break its legs here!

'You think yourself wise, proud Zarathustra! So guess the riddle then, you cracker of hard nuts—the riddle that I am! Speak then: who am *I?*'

—But when Zarathustra had heard these words—what do you suppose then happened to his soul? *He was assailed by pity*; and all at once he sank down, like an oak-tree that has long resisted many woodcutters—heavily, suddenly, to the terror even of those who wanted to fell it. But then he quickly stood up from the ground again, and his countenance hardened.

'I recognize you well,' he said in a voice of brass. '*You are the murderer of God!* Let me go.

'You *could not endure* him who saw *you*—who saw you all the time and through and through, you ugliest man! You took revenge on this witness!'*

Thus spoke Zarathustra and made to depart; but the inexpressible creature grasped at the hem of his garment and began anew to gurgle and to grope for words. 'Stay!' he said at last—

—'Stay! Do not pass by! I have guessed what axe it was that struck you to the ground. Hail to you, O Zarathustra, that you are standing again!

'You divined, I know it well, how he feels who killed him—the murderer of God. Stay! Sit down with me, it is not in vain.

'To whom did I want to go, if not to you? Stay, sit down! But do not look at me! Honour thus—my ugliness!

'They persecute me: now *you* are my last refuge. *Not* with their hate, *not* with their henchmen—oh, such persecution would I mock and be proud and happy!

'Has not all that has been successfully pursued up to now been pursued by the well-persecuted? And whoever persecutes well easily learns how to *follow*:—for he is already—behind! But it is their *pity*—

'—their pity is what I am fleeing from and seeking refuge with you. O Zarathustra, protect me, you my last refuge, the only one who divined me:

'—you divined how he feels who killed *him*. Stay! And if you will go, you impatient one, do not go the way that I came. *That* way is bad.

'Are you angry with me because I have already talked and gibbered for too long? Because I am already giving you advice? But know that I am he, the ugliest man,

'—who also has the largest, heaviest feet. Where *I* have gone, the way is bad. I tread all ways to death and to ruin.

'But that you passed me by, keeping silent; that you blushed, I saw it well: by that I recognized you as Zarathustra.

'Anyone else would have thrown me his alms, his pitying, with glance and speech. But for that—I am not beggar enough, that you have divined—

'—for that am I too *rich*, rich in what is great, in what is fearsome, in what is most ugly, in what is most inexpressible! Your shame, O Zarathustra, did me *honour!*

'With difficulty I escaped from the throng of the pitying,—that I might find the only one today who teaches, "Pitying is importunate":—you, O Zarathustra!

'—be it pitying on the part of a God, or of human beings: pitying goes against modesty. And not wanting to help can be more noble than the virtue that jumps in.

'But *that* is what counts today as virtue itself for all little people, pitying: they have no reverence for great misfortune, for great ugliness, for great foundering.

'Over all of them I look away, just as a dog looks away over the backs of teeming flocks of sheep. They are little well-wooled well-willed gray people.

'Just as a heron looks despisingly away over shallow ponds, with its head tucked back: so I look away over the swarm of little gray waves and wills and souls.

'For too long they have been given rights, these little people: *thus* were they also in the end given power—so now they teach: "Good is only what little people call good."

'And "truth" is today now what the preacher said, who himself came from among them, that wondrous holy man and spokesman for the little people, who testified of himself: "I—am the truth."*

'This immodest man has now long been making the cockscomb of the little people rise—he who taught no small error when he taught: "I—am the truth."

'Was an immodest man ever answered more politely?—But you, O Zarathustra, passed him by and said: "No! No! Three times No!"

'You warned against his error, you were the first to warn against pitying—not everyone, nor nobody, but yourself and your kind.

'You are ashamed of the shame of the great sufferer; and verily, when you say "from pitying there comes a great cloud, beware, you humans!"

'—when you teach "all creators are hard, all great love is above its pitying": O Zarathustra, how well versed in weather-signs you seem to me!

'But you yourself—warn yourself against *your* pitying too! For many are on their way to you, many who are suffering, doubting, despairing, drowning, freezing—

'I warn you against me too. You guessed my best, worst riddle, me myself and what I did. I know the axe that fells you.

'But he—*had to* die: he saw with eyes that saw *everything*—he saw the depths and grounds of the human, all its veiled disgrace and ugliness.

'His pitying knew no shame: he crawled into my filthiest corner. This most inquisitive, over-importunate, over-pitying creature had to die.

'He saw *me* always: on such a witness I wanted to take revenge—or else not live myself.

'The God who saw everything, *even the human*: this God had to die! The human cannot *endure* that such a witness should live.'

Thus spoke the ugliest man. But Zarathustra rose and readied himself to go: for he was chilled to his very marrow.

'You inexpressible creature, he said, 'You warned me against your way. As thanks for that I praise mine to you. Behold, up yonder lies Zarathustra's cave.

'My cave is large and deep and has many corners; there the most hidden creature can find a place to hide. And just nearby are hundreds of nooks and creep-holes for crawling, fluttering, and jumping beasts.

'You outcast, who cast yourself out, you do not want to live among humans and humans' pity? Well then, do as I do! Thus will you learn from me too: only the one who does, learns.*

'And first and foremost speak with my animals! The proudest and the cleverest animal—they should be the right advisors for us both!'— —

Thus spoke Zarathustra and went on his way, still more thoughtfully and slowly than before: for there was much that he was asking himself and did not readily know how to answer.

'How poor is the human after all!' he thought in his heart. 'How ugly, how wheezing, how full of hidden shame!

'I am told that the human being loves itself: ah, how great must this self-love be! How much despising it has against it!

'This creature, too, loved himself, even as he despised himself—a great lover is he for me and a great despiser.

'No one have I found up to now who despised himself more profoundly: even *that* is height. Woe, was *he* perhaps the superior human whose cry I heard?

'I love the great despisers. But the human is something that must be overcome.'— —

* * *

8. The Voluntary Beggar

When Zarathustra had left the ugliest man, he found himself freezing and feeling alone: for much that was cold and lonely had run through his senses, so that as a result his limbs too were becoming colder. But as he climbed higher and higher, up, then down, now past green meadows, but also across rocky places where no doubt an impatient stream had once made its bed: then all at once he began to feel warmer again and more tender.

'What has happened to me?' he asked himself. 'Something warm and lively refreshes me, which must be somewhere nearby.

'Already I feel less alone; unknown companions and brothers surround me, their warm breath touching my soul.'

But when he peered about him, searching for the consolers of his solitude: behold, they were cows standing all together on a hillock, whose nearness and smell had warmed his heart.* But these cows seemed to be listening eagerly to someone speaking, and were paying no attention to the one who was approaching. But when Zarathustra was quite close to them he distinctly heard a human voice issuing from the midst of the cows; and they had apparently all turned their heads toward the speaker.

Thereupon Zarathustra jumped up to them eagerly and pushed the beasts aside, for he feared that someone had sustained an injury here that would hardly be healed by the sympathy of cows. But in this he was mistaken; for behold, there was a man sitting on the ground who seemed to be urging the cows not to be afraid of him, a peaceable man and sermonizer on the mount,* from whose eyes goodness itself was preaching. 'What do you seek here?' cried Zarathustra in consternation.

'What do I seek here?' he answered. 'The same as you are seeking, you disturber of the peace! Namely, happiness on earth.

'To that end I want to learn from these cows. For, I want you to know, I have already been urging them for half a morning, and they were just about to instruct me. So why then do you disturb them?

'Except we be converted and become as cows, we shall not enter into the Kingdom of Heaven.* For there is one thing we should learn from them: chewing the cud.

'And verily, if a man shall gain the whole world and not learn this

one thing, chewing the cud: what is he profited!* He would not be rid
of his misery

'—his great misery: but today it is called *disgust*. Who today does
not have his heart, mouth, and eyes filled with disgust? You too! You
too! But just look at these cows!'—

Thus spoke the sermonizer on the mount and then turned his
gaze toward Zarathustra—for up to now it had rested lovingly on the
cows: but then it was transformed. 'Who is this I am speaking with?'
he cried in fright, and sprang up from the ground.

'This is the man without disgust, this is Zarathustra himself, who
has overcome the great disgust; this is the eye, this is the mouth, this
the heart of Zarathustra himself.'

And as he spoke thus, he kissed the hands of the one to whom he
was talking, his eyes overflowing with tears, and altogether behaved
like one to whom a costly gift and jewel falls unexpectedly from
Heaven. And the cows beheld all this and were amazed.

'Do not speak of me, you wondrous man! Dear fellow!' said
Zarathustra, restraining his tenderness. 'First speak to me about
yourself! Are you not the voluntary beggar who one day threw away
great riches—

'—who was ashamed of his riches and the rich, and fled to the
poorest, that he might pour out his heart and plenty to them? But
they received him not.'*

'But they received me not,' said the voluntary beggar. 'You know
that already. And so I went in the end to the beasts and to these
cows.'

'And so you learned', Zarathustra interrupted the speaker, 'that it
is harder to give rightly than to receive rightly, and that to bestow
well is *an art* and the ultimate most subtle master-art of goodness.'

'Especially nowadays,' answered the voluntary beggar: 'today
when all that is base has become insurgent and coy and in its own
way haughty: namely, in the mob's way.

'For the hour has come, well you know, for the great, bad, long,
slow mob- and slave-insurrection: it grows and grows!

'Those who are base are now indignant at all beneficence and
small donations; and let the over-rich be on their guard!

'Whoever today, like big-bellied bottles, lets drops fall out of
all-too-narrow necks:—people today are happy to break the necks of
such bottles.

'Lascivious greed, bilious envy, aggrieved vengefulness, mob-pride: all that flew in my face. It is no longer true that the poor are blessèd. But the Kingdom of Heaven is with the cows.'

'And why not with the rich?' asked Zarathustra temptingly, warding off the cows who were trustingly nuzzling their peaceable friend.

'Why do you tempt me?' answered the latter. 'You yourself know it even better than I. What was it after all that drove me to the poorest, O Zarathustra? Was it not disgust with the richest among us?

'—with the convicts of riches, who glean advantage from every piece of rubbish, with cold eyes and lewd thoughts; with this rabble which stinks to high Heaven,

'—with this gilded counterfeit mob, whose fathers were pick-pockets or carrion-birds or rag-pickers, with females compliant, lascivious, forgetful:—for they are all of them not far from being whores—

'Mob above, mob below! What are "poor" and "rich" today still! I have unlearned this distinction—I fled from it all, farther, ever farther, until I came to these cows.'

Thus spoke the peaceable man, and himself panted and sweated with his words: such that the cows were again amazed. But Zarathustra kept looking him in the face with a smile, as he was talking so harshly, and then he silently shook his head.

'You do yourself violence, you sermonizer on the mount, when you use such harsh words. For such harshness neither your mouth nor your eye was made.

'Nor even, it seems to me, your very stomach: for *it* opposes all this raging and hating and foaming over. Your stomach wants milder things: you are no butcher.

'You seem to me rather a man of plants and roots. Perhaps you crush grains. But you are certainly averse to pleasures of flesh and rather love honey.'

'You have divined me well,' replied the voluntary beggar, his heart relieved. 'I do love honey, and I also crush grains, for I was seeking what tastes delightful and makes one's breath pure:

'—also what takes time, a day's and mouth's work for gentle idlers and lazybones.

'Of course these cows have taken it farthest: they invented for themselves chewing the cud and lying in the sun. They also abstain from all heavy thoughts, which distend the heart.'

—'Well then!' said Zarathustra: 'you should also see *my* animals, my eagle and my serpent—their like is not to be found on earth today.

'Behold, yonder leads the way to my cave: be its guest tonight. And talk with my animals of the happiness of animals—

'—until I myself come home. For now a cry of need calls me urgently away from you. You will also find fresh honey up there, ice-cool golden comb-honey: eat of it!*

'But now straightway take leave of your cows, you wondrous man! dear fellow! hard though it may be for you. For they are your warmest friends and instructors!'—

'—With the exception of one, who is even dearer to me,' answered the voluntary beggar. 'You yourself are good and even better than a cow, O Zarathustra!'

'Away, away with you! you awful flatterer!' cried Zarathustra wickedly. 'Why do you spoil me with such praise and honey-flattery?'

'Away, away from me!' he cried once again, and swung his staff at the affectionate beggar. But the latter ran swiftly away.

*   *   *

9. The Shadow

But hardly had the voluntary beggar run off and Zarathustra was alone again, when he heard behind him a new voice: this one called, 'Stop! Zarathustra! Wait a minute! It is me, O Zarathustra, I, your shadow!' But Zarathustra did not wait, for he was overwhelmed by sudden irritation at such crowds and throngs in his mountains. 'Where has my solitude gone?' he said.

'It is truly becoming too much to bear: this mountain-range is teeming; my realm is no longer of *this* world;* I now need new mountains.

'My shadow calls me? What does my shadow matter! Let him run after me! I—shall run away from him.'

Thus spoke Zarathustra to his heart and ran off. But the one behind him followed after him, so that there were soon three runners one behind the other: namely, the voluntary beggar in front, then

Zarathustra, and thirdly and in the rear his shadow. They did not run like this for long, for Zarathustra soon became aware of his folly and with a single shrug shook all irritation and satiety from him.

'What!' he said. 'Have not the most laughable things always happened among us old solitaries and holy men?

'Verily, my folly has grown tall in the mountains! Now I hear six old fools' legs clattering along behind each other!

'But can Zarathustra be afraid of a shadow? It seems to me in any case that he has longer legs than I.'

Thus spoke Zarathustra, laughing with his eyes and entrails, then stood still and turned quickly around—and behold, he almost thereby threw his pursuer and shadow to the ground: so hard on his heels was the latter following him, and so weak was he too. For when he examined him with his eyes, he was frightened as by a sudden ghost: so thin, swarthy, hollow, and time-worn did this pursuer look.

'Who are you?' asked Zarathustra fiercely. 'What are you doing here? And why do you call yourself my shadow? I do not like you.'

'Forgive me', answered the shadow, 'for its being me. And if you do not like me, well then, O Zarathustra! I must then praise you and your good taste.

'A wanderer am I, who has already followed on your heels a long way: always under way, but without a goal, also without a home: such that I am really not far from being the eternal Wandering Jew, except that I am not eternal, nor am I a Jew.

'What? Must I be under way for evermore? Whirled by every wind, unsteady, driven onward? O earth, you have become too round for me!

'On every surface I have already sat, and like weary dust I have gone to sleep on mirrors and window-panes. Everything takes from me; nothing gives; I become thin—I am almost like a shadow.

'But after you, O Zarathustra, have I flown and followed for the longest time, and even when I hid from you, I was still your best shadow. Wherever you even sat, I sat too.

'With you I haunted the farthest, coldest worlds, like a spectre that voluntarily runs over winter-roofs and snow.

'With you I strove to enter everything forbidden, the worst, and farthest: and if there is anything of virtue in me, it is that I have feared no prohibition.*

'With you I shattered whatever my heart had revered; all boundary-stones and images I overthrew; I pursued the most dangerous wishes—verily, beyond every kind of crime have I gone at some time.

'With you I unlearned my belief in words and values and great names. When the Devil sheds his skin, does his name not fall away too? For that, too, is a skin. The Devil himself is perhaps—skin.

' "Nothing is true, everything is permitted":* thus I spoke to myself. Into the coldest waters I plunged, with head and heart. Ah, how often I therefore stood there naked as a red crab!

'Ah, where has all my goodness gone, and all shame and all belief in those who are good! Ah, where is that mendacious innocence that I once possessed, the innocence of the good and their noble lies!

'Too often, verily, did I follow hard on the heels of the truth: then it kicked me in the face. Sometimes I thought I was lying, and behold! only then did I hit—the truth.

'Too much has become clear to me: now nothing matters to me any more. Nothing lives any longer that I love—so how should I still love myself?

' "To live as it pleases me, or not to live at all": thus I will it; thus does even the most holy man will it. But woe! how can anything still—please *me*?

'Do *I*—still have a goal? A haven for which *my* sails are heading?

'A good wind? Ah, only one who knows *whither* he is sailing knows which wind is good and his fair wind.

'What was left for me? A heart weary and bold; an unsteady will; fluttering wings; a broken backbone.

'This searching for *my* home: O Zarathustra, well you know, this searching was *my* affliction: it consumes me.

' "Where is—*my* home?" That is what I ask and search and have searched for, and have not found. Oh eternal everywhere, oh eternal nowhere, oh eternal—in vain!'

Thus spoke the shadow, and Zarathustra's face grew longer at its words. 'You are my shadow!' he said at last, mournfully.

'Your danger is no small one, you free spirit and wanderer! You have had a wretched day: see to it that you do not have a still more wretched evening!

'To such restless creatures as you, even a prison will at last seem bliss. Have you ever seen imprisoned criminals sleeping? They sleep peacefully, enjoying their new security.*

'Beware that some narrow belief, a harsh, severe illusion, does not catch you in the end! For you are now seduced and tempted by anything that is narrow and firm.

'You have lost your goal: woe, how will you laugh off and get over this loss? Thereby—have you also lost your way!

'You poor rambler, daydreamer, you weary butterfly! Would you have a resting-place and homestead this evening? Then go up to my cave!

'Yonder leads the way to my cave. And now will I run quickly away from you. Already it is as if a shadow lay upon me.

'I will run alone, that it may become bright around me again. For that I must stay on my feet merrily and long. But this evening at my home there will be—dancing!'— —

Thus spoke Zarathustra.

*   *   *

10. At Midday

—And Zarathustra ran and ran and found no one else and was alone and found himself again and again and enjoyed and relished his solitude and thought of good things—for hours on end. But around the hour of midday, when the sun stood directly over Zarathustra's head, he was passing an old crooked and gnarled tree that had been embraced by the rich love of a grape-vine and was thus hidden from itself: and from this vine an abundance of yellow grapes hung down toward the wanderer. He then felt a desire to slake a slight thirst and to pluck for himself a grape; but even as he was reaching out his arm to do this, he felt a greater desire for something else: namely, to lie down beside the tree, around the hour of perfect midday, and to sleep.

This Zarathustra did; and no sooner was he lying on the ground, in the stillness and secrecy of the colourful grasses, than he forgot his slight thirst and fell asleep. For, as Zarathustra's saying goes: One thing is more necessary than another.* Only his eyes remained open: for they were not tired of seeing and admiring the tree and the love of the vine. But in falling asleep Zarathustra spoke thus to his heart:

'Still! Still! Did the world not just become perfect?* But what is happening to me?

'Just as a delicate breeze, unseen, dances upon an inlaid sea, lightly, feather-lightly: so—sleep dances upon me.

'My eyes he does not press closed; my soul he leaves awake. Light is he, verily! feather-light.

'He persuades me, I know not how? He touches me inwardly with flattering hand, he compels me. Yes, he compels me, that my soul might stretch herself out:—

'—how she becomes long and weary, my wondrous soul! Has the evening of a seventh day come to her precisely at midday?* Has she wandered blissfully among good and ripe things for too long?

'She stretches herself out long, long—longer! She lies still, my wondrous soul. Too much that is good she has tasted already, this golden mournfulness oppresses her, she curls up her lips.

'—Like a ship that has sailed into its stillest cove: now she leans up against the earth, weary from long voyages and uncertain seas. Is the earth not more loyal?

'Just as such a ship leans against the land, nestling:—then it is enough that a spider spin its thread out to her from the land. No stronger hawsers are needed then.

'Like such a weary ship in the stillest cove: thus I rest now close to the earth, loyal, trusting, waiting, bound to it by the softest threads.

'Happiness! Happiness! Would you perhaps sing, O my soul? You lie in the grass. But this is the secret solemn hour, when no shepherd blows his flute.

'Forbear! Hot midday sleeps upon the meadows. Do not sing! Still! The world is perfect.

'Do not sing, you grass-wings, O my soul! Do not even whisper! Just look—still! The old midday sleeps; he moves his mouth: is he not just now drinking a drop of happiness—

'—an old brown drop of golden happiness, golden wine? It flits away over him, his happiness laughs. Thus—laughs a God. Still!—

'—"Happily, how little is really sufficient for happiness!" Thus I spoke once and thought myself clever. But it was blasphemy: *that* have I learned now. Clever fools talk better.

'Precisely the least, the softest, lightest, a lizard's rustling, a breath, an instant, a moment's glance—*a little* makes for the *best* happiness. Still!

'—What happened to me: hearken! Did time just fly away? Am I not falling? Did I not fall—hearken! into the well of eternity?

'—What is happening to me? Still! I am stung—woe—in the heart? In the heart! O shatter, shatter, heart, after such happiness, after such a sting!

'—What? Did the world not just become perfect? Round and ripe? Oh the golden round hoop—whither does it fly? Do I run after it! Quick!

'Still——' (and here Zarathustra stretched himself and felt that he was sleeping).

'Up!' he said to himself, 'you sleeper! You midday-sleeper! Well then, come now, you old legs! It is time and over-time; many a good stretch of way is still left for you—

'Now you have slept your fill, but for how long? Half an eternity! Well then, come now, my old heart! For how long after such a sleep must you—wake your fill?'

(But then he fell asleep once again, and his soul contradicted him and resisted and lay down again)—'Leave me alone! Still! Did the world not just become perfect? Oh the golden round ball!'—

'Get up,' said Zarathustra, 'you little thief, you lazybones! What? Still stretching, yawning, sighing, falling down into deep wells?

'Who are you then! O my soul!' (and here he was startled because a ray of sunlight fell from the Heavens onto his face).

'O Heaven above me,' he said with a sigh and sat upright, 'are you looking at me? Are you listening to my wondrous soul?

'When will you drink this drop of dew that has fallen upon all earthly things—when will you drink this wondrous soul—

'—when, O well of eternity! you serene and ghastly midday-abyss! when will you drink my soul back into you?'

Thus spoke Zarathustra and rose from his resting-place by the tree as from a strange drunkenness: and behold, there stood the sun still directly above his head. But one could rightly infer from this that Zarathustra had not been asleep for long.

*   *   *

11. The Welcome

It was not until late afternoon that Zarathustra, after long searching and roaming about in vain, came home again to his cave. But when he came opposite it, not twenty paces away, something happened that he was least expecting just then: once again he heard the great *cry of need*. And, amazingly! this time it came from his own cave. But it was a long, multifarious, strange cry, and Zarathustra clearly discerned that it was composed of many voices: even though, when heard from a distance, it might sound like a cry from a single mouth.

Zarathustra then leaped toward his cave, and behold! what a scene awaited him after this overture! For there they were sitting together, all the people he had encountered during the day: the king on the right and the king on the left, the old sorcerer, the pope, the voluntary beggar, the shadow, the conscientious in spirit, the mournful sooth-sayer, and the ass. But the ugliest man had put on a crown and slung two purple sashes about him, for he was fond, like all who are ugly, of disguising and beautifying himself. And in the midst of this miser-able company stood Zarathustra's eagle, bristling and unsettled, for he was supposed to respond to too many things for which his pride had no response. And the clever serpent hung around his neck.

Zarathustra beheld all this with great amazement; but then he examined each one of his guests with genial curiosity, read their souls, and was amazed anew. In the meantime the assembled guests had risen from their seats and were waiting with reverence for Zarathustra to speak. But Zarathustra spoke thus:

'You despairers! You wondrous men! Was it then *your* cry of need that I heard? And now I also know where he is to be found for whom I searched in vain today: *the superior human—*

'—in my own cave he sits, the superior human! But why am I amazed! Have I myself not lured him to me with the honey-sacrifice and cunning call-notes of my happiness?

'Yet it seems to me that you are poor company for yourselves, for do you not make each other's hearts morose, you need-criers, when you sit together here? Someone else must come,

'—someone to make you laugh again, a good cheerful buffoon, a dancer and a wind and madcap, any kind of old fool: what do you think?

'Yet forgive me, you despairers, for talking before you in such small words, unworthy, verily, of such guests! But you cannot guess *what* makes my heart so wilful:

'—you yourselves do this, and the sight of you, forgive me! For anyone becomes courageous who observes someone despairing. To encourage someone in despair—everyone thinks himself strong enough for that.

'To me you have given this strength—a good gift, my worthy guests! A right-minded guests' gift. Well then, do not be angry now if I also offer you something of mine.

'This is my realm and my domain: but whatever is mine shall for this evening and this night be yours. My animals shall serve you: let my cave be your place of rest!

'By my hearth and home no one shall despair; in my preserve I protect everyone from his wild beasts. And that is the first thing I offer you: security!

'But the second thing is: my little finger. And once you have *that*, please take the whole hand, well then! and the heart with it! Be welcome here, be welcome, my dear guests!'

Thus spoke Zarathustra and laughed with love and wickedness. After this welcome his guests bowed once more and remained reverently silent. Then the king on the right responded to him in their name.

'By this, O Zarathustra, the way you proffered us your hand and welcome, do we recognize you as Zarathustra. You have humbled yourself before us, and almost caused pain to our reverence:—

'—but who would be able like you to humble himself with such pride? *That* in itself uplifts us, and is a tonic for our eyes and hearts.

'Just to see this alone would we gladly climb higher mountains than this one. For we have come as sightseers, wanting to see that which makes clouded eyes bright.

'And behold, all our need-crying is a thing of the past. Our senses and hearts now stand open and are delighted. Little is lacking: and our courage becomes quite wilful.

'There is nothing, O Zarathustra, that grows more delightfully on earth than a lofty, strong will: that is earth's fairest growth. An entire landscape is invigorated by one such tree.

'To the pine I compare whoever grows up high like you, O

Zarathustra: long, silent, hard, alone, of the finest most pliant wood, magnificent—

'—but reaching out at last with strong green branches for *his* domain, asking strong questions of winds and weather and whatever is at home in the heights,

'—answering more strongly, a commander, victorious: oh who would not climb high mountains in order to see such growths?

'At your tree here, O Zarathustra, even the gloomy one, the failure, refreshes himself; at the sight of you even the restless one becomes secure and heals his heart.

'And verily, toward your mountain and tree are many eyes today directed; a great yearning has arisen, and many a one has learned to ask: Who is Zarathustra?

'And those into whose ears you have ever dripped your song and your honey: all the hidden, the solitaries, the dualitaries, all at once spoke to their hearts:

' "Does Zarathustra still live? It is no longer worth while living, all is the same, all is in vain: or else—we must live with Zarathustra!"

' "Why does he not come, who has for so long announced himself?" thus do many ask. "Did solitude swallow him? Or else shall we perhaps come to him?"

'Now it comes to pass that solitude itself becomes ripe and breaks open, like a grave that breaks open and can no longer contain its dead. Everywhere one sees the resurrected.

'Now the waves are rising and rising around your mountain, O Zarathustra. And however high your height may be, many must come up to you; your boat shall not sit on dry land much longer.

'And that we despairers have now come to your cave and are already despairing no more: this is but an omen and sign that better men are on their way to you—

'—for this itself is on its way to you, the last remnant of God among humans: all those with the great yearning, the great disgust, the great satiety,

'—all who do not want to live, except they learn *to hope* again— except they learn from you, O Zarathustra, the *great* hope!'

Thus spoke the king on the right and grasped Zarathustra's hand in order to kiss it; but Zarathustra warded off his veneration and stepped back in fright, silently and suddenly, as if fleeing into far distances. But after a short while he was back with his guests again, looked at them with bright, enquiring eyes, and spoke:

'My dear guests, you superior humans, I would talk with you in clear, germane German. It was not for *you* that I was waiting here in these mountains.'

('Clear, germane German? God have mercy!' said the king on the left at this point, aside. 'It is obvious that he does not know our dear Germans, this wise man from the Orient!

'But what he means is, "coarse, solid German"*—well then! That is nowadays by no means in the worst taste!')

'You may all truly be superior humans,' Zarathustra continued: 'but for me—you are not high and strong enough.

'For me, that is: for what is inexorable in me and remains silent, but will not be silent for ever. And if you belong to me, then it is not as my right arm.

'For whoever himself stands on sick and frail legs, like you, wants above all, whether he knows it or conceals it from himself: that he might be *spared*.

'My arms and my legs, however, I do not spare; *I do not spare my warriors*: how could you then be fit for *my* warfare?

'With you I would spoil my every victory. And many a one among you would collapse at the mere sound of my loud drums.

'Nor are you beautiful and well-born enough for me. I need clear smooth mirrors for my teachings; on your surfaces even my own image is distorted.

'Your shoulders are weighed down by many a burden, many a memory; many a wicked dwarf crouches in your corners. And there is a mob hidden in you too.

'And even if you are important and of a superior kind: there is much in you that is crooked and misshapen. There is not a smith in the world who could hammer you straight and into proper form.

'You are mere bridges: may superior humans stride over and across you. You signify steps: so do not be angry with him who climbs over you and up to *his* height!

'From your seed may there one day grow a genuine son and con-summate heir, even for me: but that is far off. You are not yourselves those to whom my estate and name belong.

'It is not for you that I am waiting here in these mountains; it is not with you that I may go down for the last time. Only as signs have you come to me, that superior ones are on their way to me—

'—you are *not* those of the Great Yearning, of the Great Disgust, of the Great Satiety, nor that which you called the leftover remnants of God.

'—No! No! Three times No! It is for *others* that I am waiting here in these mountains, nor will I lift my foot from here without them,

'—for those who are superior, stronger, more victorious, better tempered, such as are built four-square in body and soul: *laughing lions* must come!

'Oh, my dear guests, you wondrous men—have you as yet heard nothing of my children? And that they are on their way to me here?

'Speak to me then of my gardens, of my Isles of the Blest, of my beautiful new kind—why do you not speak to me of those?

'This guests' gift I entreat from your love, that you speak to me of my children. For this I am rich, for this I became poor: what did I not give,

'—what would I not give, that I might have one thing: *these* children, *this* living plantation, *these* trees of life of my will and of my highest hope!'

Thus spoke Zarathustra, and suddenly paused in his speech: for his yearning overwhelmed him, and he closed his mouth and eyes as his heart was so moved. And all his guests were silent too, and stood still in dismay: only the old soothsayer made signs with his hands and gestures.

*　*　*

12. The Last Supper*

At this point the soothsayer interrupted Zarathustra's welcome and his guests' response: he rushed up like one who has no time to lose, grasped Zarathustra's hand, and cried: 'But Zarathustra!

'One thing is more necessary than another, you say so yourself: well then, one thing is now more necessary *for me* than everything else.

'A word at the right time: did you not invite me to a *meal*? And there are many here who have come a long way. Surely you would not feed us with speeches?

'Besides, all of you have been thinking too much of freezing, drowning, choking, and other conditions of bodily need: but no one has thought of *my* need, namely, starvation—'

(Thus spoke the soothsayer; and when Zarathustra's animals heard these words they ran off in fright. For they realized that whatever they had brought in during the day would not be sufficient to fill this one soothsayer alone.)

'And also dying of thirst,' continued the soothsayer. 'And although I hear water plashing here, like speeches of truth, that is copiously and unflaggingly: I—want *wine*!

'Not everyone is like Zarathustra a born water-drinker. Nor is water fit for those who are weary and wilting: *for us* wine is proper —*that* alone provides immediate convalescence and extempore health!'

On this occasion, since the soothsayer desired wine, it happened that the king on the left too, the silent one, spoke for once. 'As for wine,' he said, '*we* have taken care of that, I and my brother, the king on the right: we have wine enough—an entire ass's load. So nothing is lacking but bread.'

'Bread?' replied Zarathustra and laughed. 'Bread is one thing that solitaries do not have. But man does not live by bread alone,* but also by the flesh of good lambs, of which I have two:

'—*These* shall be slaughtered at once and prepared with spices and sage:* thus I love them. Nor is there a lack of roots and fruit, good enough for gourmets and epicures; nor of nuts and other riddles to be cracked.

'Thus shall we shortly have a fine meal. But whoever would eat with us must also lend a hand, including the kings. For with Zarathustra even a king may be a cook.'

This suggestion appealed to the hearts of all those present: only the voluntary beggar objected to meat and wine and spices.

'Just listen to this glutton Zarathustra!' he said in jest. 'Does one repair to caves and high mountains in order to have such meals?

'Now, to be sure, I understand what he once taught us: "Praised be a moderate poverty!" and why he wants to abolish beggars.'

'Be of good cheer,' Zarathustra answered him, 'just as I am.

Stay with your custom, you admirable man: crush your grains, drink your water, praise your cooking; as long as it makes you happy!

'I am a law only for my own; I am not a law for all. But whoever belongs with me must have strong bones, and light feet too,

'—eager for wars and festivals, no obscurantist, no dreamer, as ready for the hardest things as for his festival, healthy and hale.

'The best belongs to my own and to me; and if it is not given us, then we take it:—the best food, the clearest sky, the strongest thoughts, the most beautiful women!'—

Thus spoke Zarathustra; but the king on the right replied: 'Strange! Has one ever heard such clever things from the mouth of a wise man?

'And verily, that is the strangest thing about a wise man, if in addition to all that he is clever and not an ass.'

Thus spoke the king on the right and was amazed; but the ass responded to his speech with ill will, 'Yea-Ah'. But this was the beginning of that long meal that is called 'The Last Supper' in the history books. But in the course of it there was talk of nothing else than *the superior human*.

*   *   *

13. On the Superior Human*

I

When I came to human beings for the first time, I committed the solitary's folly, the great folly: I set up in the market.

And in speaking to everyone, I spoke to no one. But in the evening rope-dancers were my companions, and corpses too; and I myself almost a corpse.

But with the new morning there came to me a truth: then I learned to say, 'What does the market matter to me, and the mob and mob-noise and long mob-ears!'

You superior humans, learn from me this: In the market no one believes in superior humans. And if you want to speak there, very well! But the mob blinks: 'We are all equal.'

'You superior humans'—so the mob blinks—'There are no

superior humans, we are equal, the human is human; before God—
are we all equal!'

Before God!—But now this God has died. But before the mob we
would not be equal. You superior humans, go away from the market!

*   *   *

2

Before God!—But now this God has died! You superior humans,
this God was your greatest danger.

Only since he has lain in the grave have you again been resurrected. Only now does the Great Midday come; only now does the
superior human become—lord and master!

Have you understood this word, O my brothers? You are terrified:
do your hearts become dizzy? Does the abyss yawn before you here?
Does the hell-hound yelp at you here?

Well then! Come now, you superior humans! Only now does the
mountain of the human future go into labour.* God has died: now *we*
want—the Overhuman to live.

*   *   *

3

The most concerned minds today ask: 'How is the human to be
preserved?' But Zarathustra is the first and only one to ask: 'How is
the human to be *overcome?*'

I have the Overhuman at heart, *that* is my first and only concern—and *not* the human: not the nearest, not the poorest, not the
most suffering, not the best.—

O my brothers, what I can love in the human is that it is a going-
over and a going-under. And in you, too, there is much that makes
me love and hope.

That you have despised, you superior humans, that gives me hope.
For the great despisers are the great reverers.

That you have despaired, in that there is much to revere. For you
have not learned how to submit; you have not learned the little
clevernesses.

For today the little people have become lord and master: they all preach submission and acquiescence and cleverness and industry and considerateness and the long and-so-forth of the small virtues.

Whatever is of the female kind, whatever comes from the menial's kind and especially the mob mish-mash: *that* would now become lord of all human fate—oh disgust! disgust! disgust!

That is what asks and asks and never tires: 'How does the human preserve itself, best, longest, most comfortably?' With that—they are the lords of today.

Overcome for me these lords of today, O my brothers—these little people: *they* are the Overhuman's greatest danger!

Overcome for me, you superior humans, the little virtues, the little clevernesses, the grain-of-sand considerations, the ant-like irritations, the pitiful comforts, the 'happiness of the greatest number'—!*

And rather despair than submit. And, verily, I love you for not knowing how to live today, you superior humans! For thus do *you*—live best!

*   *   *

4

Do you have courage, O my brothers? Are you stout-hearted? *Not* courage before witnesses but solitaries' and eagles' courage, which not even a God witnesses any more?

Cold souls, mules, blind men, drunkards I do not call stout-hearted. Stout of heart is he who knows fear, but *conquers* fear, who sees the abyss, but with *pride*.

Whoever sees the abyss, but with an eagle's eyes, whoever with an eagle's talons *grasps* the abyss: he has courage.— —

*   *   *

5

'The human is evil'—thus spoke all the wisest to me in consolation. Ah, if only this were still true today! For evil is the human's best strength.

'The human being must become better and more evil'—thus *I* teach. What is most evil is necessary for the Overhuman's best.

It may have been good for that preacher of the little people that he suffered and bore man's sin.* But I take delight in great sin as my great *consolation.*—

But such words are not for long ears. Nor does every word belong in every mouth. These are subtle and remote things: sheep's hooves shall not grasp at them!

*   *   *

6

You superior humans, do you suppose that I am here to make good what you have spoiled?

Or that I want henceforth to give you sufferers more comfortable beds? Or to show to you who are restless, lost, and have climbed astray, new and easier uphill footpaths?

No! No! Three times No! More and more of your kind, and ever better ones, shall perish—for you shall have it worse and worse and ever harder. Thus alone—

—thus alone does the human grow into the height where lightning strikes and shatters it: high enough for lightning!

My mind and my yearning go out to the few, and what is long, and far: what could your small, copious, brief misery matter to me!

You do not yet suffer enough for me! For you suffer from yourselves, and have not yet suffered from *the human*. You would lie if you said otherwise! None of you suffers what *I* have suffered.— —

*   *   *

7

It is not enough for me that lightning no longer does harm. I do not want to conduct it away: it shall rather learn—to work for *me.*—

My wisdom has long been gathering like a cloud, becoming stiller and darker. Thus does every wisdom that shall one day give birth to *lightning.*—

For these humans of today I do not want to be a *light*, nor to be called a light. *Them*—I want to blind: lightning of my wisdom! Put their eyes out!

*   *   *

8

Will nothing beyond your capacities: there is a rank falseness in those who will beyond their capacities.

Especially when they will great things! For they arouse mistrust of great things, these subtle counterfeiters and play-actors:

—till in the end they are false before themselves, squint-eyed, whitened worm-rot, cloaked in strong words, in display-virtues, in glittering false deeds.

Be very careful here, you superior humans! For I count nothing more precious today or more rare than honesty.

Does this today not belong to the mob? But the mob does not know what is great, what is small, what is straight and honest: it is innocently crooked, and always lies.

*   *   *

9

Have a healthy mistrust today, you superior humans, you stout-hearted ones! You open-hearted ones! And keep your grounds a secret! For this today belongs to the mob.

Whatever the mob once learned to believe without grounds, who could by providing grounds—overthrow it?

And in the market one convinces through gestures.* But grounds make the mob mistrustful.

And if truth achieved victory for once, then ask yourselves with healthy mistrust: 'What mighty error has fought on its behalf?'

Beware also of the scholars! They hate you: for they are unfruitful! They have cold and dried-up eyes; before them every bird lies defeathered.

Such men boast that they do not lie: but inability to lie is far from being love of the truth. Beware now!

Freedom from fever is far from being understanding! Frozen-to-death spirits I do not believe. Whoever cannot lie does not know what truth is.

*   *   *

10

If you want to rise high, then use your own legs! Do not let yourselves be *carried* up, nor sit upon the backs and heads of others!

But did you mount a horse? Do you now ride swiftly up toward your goal? Very well, my friend! But your lame foot is sitting on the horse too!

When you reach your goal, when you jump down from your horse: precisely at your *height*, you superior human—will you stumble!

*   *   *

11

You creators, you superior humans! One is pregnant only for one's own child.

Do not let yourselves be persuaded or talked into anything else! For who is *your* neighbour?* And even if you act 'for the neighbour'—you still do not create for him!

So please unlearn this 'for', you creators: it is precisely your virtue that will have you do no thing 'for' or 'in order to' or 'because'.* Against such false little words shall you shut your ears fast.

This 'for the neighbour' is only a virtue of the little people: with them there is only talk of 'birds of a feather' and 'one good turn':— they have neither the right to nor the strength for *your* selfishness!

In your selfishness, you creators, is the prudence and providence of those who are pregnant! That which no one has ever laid eyes on, the fruit: that is what your entire love shelters and protects and nourishes.

Where your entire love is, with your child, there is your entire virtue too! Your work, your will, is *your* closest 'neighbour': let no false values persuade you otherwise!

*   *   *

12

You creators, you superior humans! Whoever has to give birth is sick; but whoever has given birth is unclean.*

Ask the women: one does not give birth because it is pleasurable. The pain makes hens and poets cackle.

You creators, there is much that is unclean about you. That is because you had to be mothers.

A new child: oh how much new filth has come into the world with it! Go aside! And whoever has given birth shall wash his soul clean!

* * *

13

Do not be virtuous beyond your strength! And will nothing from yourselves against probability!

Follow in the footsteps made by the virtue of your fathers! How could you want to climb high if the will of your fathers did not climb with you?

But whoever wants to be a firstling, see to it that he does not become a lastling too!* And where the vices of your fathers are, there you should not want to count as saints!

He whose forefathers consorted with women and with strong wines and wild boars: how would it be if he wanted chastity from himself?

It would be folly! Verily, it seems to me a lot for such a man to be the husband of one or two or three women.

And if he founded monasteries and wrote above the door, 'The Way to the Holy'—I would say: What of it! it is a new piece of folly!

If he founded for himself a new house of correction and refuge: much good may it do him! But I do not believe in it.

In solitude there grows whatever one brings to it, the inner beast as well. For this reason is solitude inadvisable for many.

Has there been anything more filthy on earth so far than desert-saints? *Around them* not only the Devil was loose—but also the swine.

* * *

14

Shy, ashamed, awkward, like a tiger whose leap has failed: thus, you superior humans, have I often seen you slink away. A *throw* you made had failed.

But, you dice-players, what does it matter! You have not learned to play and mock as one must play and mock. Do we not always sit at a great mocking- and gaming-table?

And if something great fails you, does that mean you yourselves are—failures? And if you yourselves are failures, does that mean—the human being is a failure? But if the human being is a failure: well then! come now!

*   *   *

15

The higher its kind, the more rarely a thing succeeds. You superior humans here, have you not all—failed?

Be of good courage: what does it matter! How much is yet possible! Learn to laugh at yourselves, as one has to laugh!

No wonder then that you failed and only half succeeded, you half-broken creatures! Does there not throng and press in you—the human's *future*?

The farthest in the human, the deepest, star-highest, its enormous strength: does that not all froth against itself in your pot?

No wonder that many a pot shatters! Learn to laugh at yourselves, as one has to laugh! You superior humans, oh how much is yet possible!

And verily, how much has already turned out well! How rich is this earth in small good perfect things, in what has turned out well!

Place small good perfect things around you, you superior humans! Their golden ripeness heals the heart. What is perfect teaches hope.

*   *   *

16

What has been the greatest sin here on earth so far? Was it not the word of him who said: 'Woe unto those who laugh now!'*

Did he himself find no grounds on earth for laughter? Then he simply did not look. Even a child can find such grounds here.

He—did not love enough: else he would also have loved us who laugh! But he hated and scorned us: weeping and gnashing of teeth he promised for us.*

Must one straightway curse where one does not love? That—seems to me bad taste. But that is what he did, this unconditional man. He came from the mob.

And he himself simply did not love enough: else he would have been less angry that he was not loved. All great love does not *want* love:—it wants more.

Get out of the way of all such unconditional men! That is a poor sick kind, a mob-kind: they look at life sadly; they have the evil eye for this earth.

Get out of the way of all such unconditional men! They have heavy feet and sultry hearts:—they know not how to dance. So how could the earth be light for such as them!

* * *

17

Crookedly do all good things approach their goal. Like cats they arch their backs, and purr inwardly at their imminent happiness—all good things laugh.

The gait betrays whether one is truly striding along one's *own* path: so watch me walking! But whoever is approaching his goal— dances.

And verily, I have not become a statue, nor do I stand here stiff, stumpy, stony, like a pillar;* I love the swiftest running.

And if there are also swamps and dense misery on earth: whoever has light feet even runs over mud and dances as upon well-swept ice.

Lift up your hearts, my brothers, high! higher! And do not forget your legs either! Lift up your legs too, you fine dancers, and better still: even stand on your heads!

* * *

18

This laugher's crown, this rose-wreath-crown: I myself have set this crown upon my head; I myself have pronounced my laughter holy. No other could I find today who was strong enough.

Zarathustra the dancer, Zarathustra the light, who beckons with his wings, one ready for flight, beckoning to all birds, ready and prepared, and blissfully light-hearted:

Zarathustra the soothsayer, Zarathustra the soothlaugher, not impatient, not unconditional, but one who loves leaps and side-leaps; I myself have set this crown upon my head!

* * *

19

Lift up your hearts, my brothers, high! higher! And do not forget your legs either! Lift up your legs too, you fine dancers, and better still: even stand on your heads!

Even in happiness there are heavy beasts, and clumsy-footed from the beginning. Wondrously they toil away, like an elephant that tries to stand on its head.

But it is still better to be foolish from happiness than foolish from unhappiness; better to dance clumsily than to walk lamely. So learn from me this piece of wisdom: even the worst thing has two good verso-sides—

—even the worst thing has good dancing legs: so learn from me yourselves, you superior humans, to stand on your own proper legs.

So unlearn for me trumpeting of misery and all mob-mournfulness! Oh how mournful do even the mob's buffoons seem to me today! But this today belongs to the mob.

* * *

20

Do for me as the wind does, when it rushes out from its mountaincaves: to its own piping it wants to dance, and the seas tremble and leap under its foot-taps.

That which gives asses wings to fly, which milks lionesses, praised be such a fine and wayward spirit, which comes to all todays and all the mob like a storm-wind—

—which is an enemy of thistle-strippers and hair-splitters and of all withered leaves and weeds: praised be this fine wild free storm-spirit, which dances on swamps and gloominess as on meadows!

Which hates the mob's wasting-dogs and all failed and gloomy breeds: praised be this spirit of all free spirits, the laughing storm that blows dust in the eyes of all who are dark-seeing and dark-tissued!

You superior humans, the worst about you is: that none of you has learned to dance as one has to dance—dance away beyond yourselves! What does it matter that you have failed!

How much is yet possible! So just *learn* to laugh away beyond yourselves! Lift up your hearts, you fine dancers, high! higher! And do not forget to laugh well too!

This laugher's crown, this rose-wreath crown: to you, my brothers, I throw this crown! Laughter I have pronounced holy; you superior humans, *learn* from me—to laugh!*

*　　*　　*

14. The Song of Melancholy

I

As Zarathustra gave these speeches he was standing near the entrance to his cave; but with the last words he slipped away from his guests and fled for a short while into the open air.

'Oh pure fragrances about me!' he cried. 'Oh blissful silence about me! But where are my animals? Come here, come here, my eagle and my serpent!

'Tell me now, my animals: these superior humans altogether—do they perhaps not *smell* good? Oh pure fragrances around me! Only now do I know and feel how much I love you, my animals.'

—And Zarathustra spoke once more: 'I love you, my animals!' And the eagle and the serpent came up close to him as he spoke these words, and looked up at him. In this way the three of them stood still together, sniffing and sucking in the good air together. For the air outside here was better than among the superior humans.

*　　*　　*

2

But hardly had Zarathustra left his cave before the old sorcerer stood up, looked slyly around, and said: 'He has gone out!

'And already, you superior humans—if I may tickle you with this

praise- and flatter-name, just as he does—already my wicked spirit
of deceit and sorcery assails me, my melancholy Devil,

'—who is an adversary* of this Zarathustra from the ground up:
forgive him this! Now *will* he do some sorcery for you, this being
precisely *his* hour. In vain I wrestle with this evil spirit.

'To all of you, whatever honours you may confer on yourselves
with words, whether you call yourselves "the free spirits" or "the
truthful men" or "the penitents of the spirit" or "the emancipated"
or "the great yearners",

'—to all of you, who like me suffer from *the great disgust*, for
whom the old God has died and no new God lies as yet in cradles and
swaddling clothes—to all of you is my evil spirit and sorcery-Devil
well disposed.

'I know you, you superior humans, I know him—I also know this
fiend, whom I love against my will, this Zarathustra: he himself
often seems to me like a beautiful holy-man's mask,

'—like a new and wondrous masquerade in which my evil spirit,
the melancholy Devil, takes pleasure:—I love Zarathustra, it often
seems to me, for the sake of my evil spirit.—

'But *he* assails me already and compels me, this spirit of melancholy, this evening-twilight Devil: and verily, you superior humans,
he has the desire—

'—just open your eyes!—he has the desire to come *naked*, whether
male or female, I do not yet know: but he is coming, he is compelling
me, woe! open up your senses!

'The day is fading, to all things now the evening comes, even
to the best things: now hear and see, you superior humans, which
Devil, whether man or woman, this spirit of evening-melancholy is!'

Thus spoke the old sorcerer, looked slyly around, and then took up
his harp.

*   *   *

3

In recently cleared air,
When dew's consolation
Already falls to earth,

Invisible, and unheard too—
For the consoling dew
Wears softened shoes like all mild consolers—:
Remember then, remember, heated heart,
How once you thirsted there,
For heavenly teardrops and drippings of dew
All parched and weary you thirsted,
While there, on yellow paths of grass,
Malicious rays of evening sunlight
Fell through darkened trees about you,
Blinding glowing sunlight-glances, gloating?

'A suitor of *truth?* You?'—thus they scoffed—
'No! A mere poet!
A beast, a cunning and quiet-prowling beast of prey,
One that must lie,
Must knowingly, willingly always lie:
Lusting after prey,
Colourfully masked,
To itself a mask,
To itself its prey—
That—is a suitor of truth?
No! A mere fool! A mere poet!
Speaking mere motley,
Colourfully crying out from masks of fools,
Clambering about on mendacious word-bridges,
On colourful rainbow-arcs,
Between deceptive skies
And deceptive earths,
Roaming about, hovering round—
A *mere* fool! A *mere* poet!

'*That*—is a suitor of truth?
Not still, stiff, smooth, cold,
Become an image,
A pillar of God,
Not posted up before temples,
The gate-guard of a God:
No! Bitter enemy to such truth-statues,
In any desert more at home than in temples,

Full of cat-wilfulness,
Jumping through every window
Quick! into every coincidence,
Sniffing at every jungle,
Sniffing addicted-yearningly,
That you might run in jungles
Among variegated beasts of prey
Sinning-healthy and colourful and fine,
Run with lustful lips,
Blissful-scornful, blissful-hellish, blissful-bloodthirsty
After prey, furtive and mendacious:—

'Or else, like the eagle, who looks long,
Long-staring into abysses,
Into *his* abysses:— —
Oh how they spiral down here
Downward and inward,
Into deeper and deeper depths!—
Then,
Suddenly, arrow-straight,
In quivering flight,
They pounce upon *lambs*,
Headlong down, hot-hungry,
Lusting for lambs,
Hating all lambs' souls,
Grimly hating whatever looks
Sheepishly, with lambs' eyes, curly-wooled,
Grayly, with lamb's sheep's wellwishing!

'Thus, then,
Eagle-like, panther-like
Are the poet's yearnings,
Are *your* yearnings behind a thousand masks,
You fool! You poet!

'You who have now seen man
As God and sheep—:
To *tear apart* the God in man,
As the sheep in man,
And, while tearing, *to laugh*—

'*That, that* is your blissfulness!
A panther's and an eagle's blissfulness!
A poet's and a fool's blissfulness!'— —

In recently cleared air,
When the moon's thin sickle
Slides green and envious
'Twixt purple twilights:
—hostile toward day,
With every step secretly
Reaping away at hanging
Roses, till they fall, pale now,
And sink down in the pit of night:—

Thus did I myself sink once
Away from my truth-madness,
Away from my day-yearnings,
Weary of the day, sick from the light,
—sank downward, evening-ward, shadow-ward:
Thirsty and scorched
By a single truth:
—do you recall, recall still, heated heart,
How much you thirsted then?—
That I be banished
From every truth,
Mere fool!
Mere poet!

*   *   *

15. On Science*

Thus sang the sorcerer, and all who were present drifted unawares like birds into the nets of his cunning and heavy-hearted voluptuousness. Only the conscientious in spirit was not caught up by it: he quickly snatched the harp away from the sorcerer and cried, 'Air! Let some good air in! Let Zarathustra in! You are making this cave sultry and poisonous, you wicked old sorcerer!

'You are seducing us, you false and subtle man, to unknown

desires and wildness. And woe when such as you makes much talk and ado about *truth!*

'Woe to all free spirits who are not on guard against *such* sorcerers! It is all over with their freedom: you teach and lure them back into prisons,

'—you old heavy-hearted Devil, from your lament there sounds a decoy-whistle; you are like those whose praise of chastity secretly invites to voluptuousness!'

Thus spoke the conscientious in spirit; but the old sorcerer looked around him, enjoying his victory, and for its sake he swallowed the annoyance the conscientious one had caused him. 'Be quiet!' he said in a modest voice. 'Good songs want to resound well; after good songs one should be quiet for a long time.

'They are all doing so, these superior humans. But you have perhaps understood little of my song? In you there is little of the spirit of sorcery.'

'You praise me,' replied the conscientious man, 'by distinguishing me from yourself. Very well! But you others, what do I see? You are all still sitting there with lustful eyes—

'You free souls, where has your freedom gone? You are almost, it seems to me, like men who have long been watching wicked naked dancing girls: your souls themselves are dancing!

'In you, you superior humans, must there be more of that which the sorcerer calls his wicked spirit of sorcery and deception:—we must certainly be different.

'And verily, we talked and thought enough together, before Zarathustra came home to his cave, for me to know: we *are* different.

'We are also *seeking* different things up here, you and I. For I am seeking more *security:* for that I came to Zarathustra. For he is still the most stable tower and will—

'—today, when everything is tottering, when all the earth quakes. But you, when I see the eyes you make, you almost seem to me to be seeking *more insecurity,*

'—more horror, more danger, more earthquakes. You desire, it almost seems so to me, forgive my presumption, you superior humans—

'—you desire the severest most dangerous life, which frightens *me* the most; you desire the life of wild beasts, forests, caves, steep mountains and labyrinthine gorges.

'Nor is it those who lead *away* from danger that you like best, but rather those who induce you to leave all paths, the seducers. But even if such desire is *actual* in you, it nevertheless seems *impossible* to me.

'For fear—that is the feeling which is inherited and fundamental in the human being; in fear lies the explanation of everything, original sin as well as original virtue. Out of fear grew also *my* virtue, which is called: science.

'Fear of wild beasts has been bred into humans the longest— including fear of the beast they harbour within themselves and fear:—Zarathustra calls it "the inner beast".

'This long and ancient fear, finally become refined, spiritual, intel- lectual—today, it seems to me, it is called: *science.*'—

Thus spoke the conscientious one; but Zarathustra, who was just coming back into his cave and heard and divined this last speech, threw the conscientious man a handful of roses and laughed at his 'truths'. 'What!' he cried. 'What did I just hear now? Verily, it seems to me, you are a fool or I myself am one: and your "truth" I turn straightway upside-down on its head.

'For *fear*—is the exception with us. Rather courage and adventure and pleasure in uncertainty, in the unventured—*courage* seems to me the entire prehistory of the human.

'The wildest and most courageous beasts they enviously robbed of their virtues: only thus did they become—human.

'*This* courage, finally become refined, spiritual, intellectual, this human courage with eagle's wings and serpent's cleverness: *this*, it seems to me, today is called—'

'*Zarathustra!*' they all cried, who were sitting together, as from a single mouth, and burst into uproarious laughter; though it rose from them like a heavy cloud. The sorcerer laughed, too, and said cleverly: 'Well then! It has gone, my evil spirit!

'And did I myself not warn you against him, when I said that he was a deceiver, a spirit of lies and deception?

'Especially, you see, when he shows himself naked. But what can *I* do about his tricks! Was it *I* who created him and the world?

'Well then! Let us be good again and in good spirits! And though Zarathustra is looking angry—just look at him! he bears me a grudge—

'—before night comes he will learn again to love and laud me, for he cannot live long without committing such follies.

'*He*—loves his enemies:* this art he understands better than anyone I have seen. But he takes revenge for it—upon his friends!'

Thus spoke the old sorcerer, and the superior humans applauded him: so that Zarathustra went around and shook his friends' hands with wickedness and love—like one who had to make amends and apologize to everyone for something. But when he thereby came to the entrance to his cave, behold, he again had a desire for the good air outside and for his animals—and he wanted to slip outside.

*   *   *

16. Among Daughters of the Desert

I

'Do not go away!' the wanderer then said, who called himself Zarathustra's shadow. 'Abide with us*—else the old gloomy misery might assail us again.

'That old sorcerer has already regaled us with his worst, and behold, the good pious pope there has tears in his eyes and has embarked once again onto the sea of heavy spirits.

'These kings here may well put on a good face for us: for *they* have learned that today better than any of us! But had they no witnesses, I wager that with them too the wicked play would begin again—

'—the wicked play of drifting clouds, of damp heavy spirits, of overcast skies, of stolen suns, of howling autumn winds,

'the wicked play of our howling and cries of need: stay with us, O Zarathustra! There is much hidden wretchedness here that wants to speak, much evening, much cloud, much muggy air!

'You nourished us with strong man's fare and forceful maxims: do not permit us to be assailed for dessert by soft effeminate spirits again!

'You alone can make the air around you strong and clear! Have I ever found on earth such good air as with you in your cave?

'For I have seen many different lands, my nose has learned to test and appraise many kinds of air: but in your home my nostrils taste their greatest pleasure!

'Except for—except for—oh, forgive me an old memory! Forgive me an old dessert-song that I once composed among daughters of the desert:—

'—for among them there was equally good clear Oriental air; there was I farthest away from damp and cloudy heavy-hearted Old Europe!

'In those days I loved such Oriental maidens and another blue realm of Heaven in which no clouds and no thoughts hovered.

'You would not believe how politely they sat there when they were not dancing, deep, but without thoughts, like little secrets, like beribboned riddles, like dessert-nuts—

'colourful and foreign indeed! but without clouds: riddles that let themselves be guessed: for love of such maidens I then composed a dessert-psalm.'

Thus spoke the wanderer and shadow; and before anyone could answer him he had already grabbed the harp from the old sorcerer, crossed his legs, and looked calmly and wisely around him:—and then his nostrils inhaled the air slowly and enquiringly, like one who in new lands tastes new and foreign air. Thereupon he began to sing with a kind of lowing.

*   *   *

2

The desert grows: woe to him who harbours deserts within!

—Ha! Solemnly!
Solemnly indeed!
A worthy beginning!
Africanly solemn!
Worthy of a lion,
Or a moral roaring-ape—
—but nothing for you,
My very dearest women-friends,
At whose feet I am now
For the first time
A European under palm-trees,
Permitted to sit down. Selah.*

Wonderful verily!
Here I sit now,
Near the desert, and yet
Again so far from the desert,
In nothingness deserted:
All swallowed down, you see,

By this smallest of oases—:
—it simply unlocked, yawning,
Its quite delightful mouth.
The sweetest smelling of all little mouths:
Then I fell right in,
And down, and through—among you,
My very dearest women-friends! Sclah.

Hail, hail to that great whale
When he let his unfortunate guest
Fare so well!—you understand
My very learned allusion?*
Hail to his belly,
If it was as
Delightful an oasis-belly
As this is: which I now want to put in doubt,
—for that have I journeyed from Europe,
Which is more doubt-addicted than any
Elderly married women.
May God make it better!
Amen!

Here I sit now,
In this smallest of oases,
Like a little date,
Brown, all sweet, oozing gold, lusting
For the rounded mouth of a maiden,
But even more so for maidenly
Ice-cool and snow-white and sharp-biting
Incisors: for teeth such as those
Does the heart of every warm date yearn. Selah.

Similar, all-too-similar,
To these same southern fruits,
Do I lie here, surrounded
By winged beetles
Playing and sniffing at me,*
And also by even smaller
More foolish and sinful*
Wishes and ideas—

Besieged by you,
You speechless and most ominous
Maiden-kittens,
Dudu and Suleika,*
—*ensphinxed*, if I may cram one
Word with many feelings:
(—May God forgive me
this linguistic sin!)
—I sit here, sniffing the finest air,
Paradisal air indeed,
Light and shining air, laced through with gold,
As fine air as ever
Floated down from the moon—
Whether by chance,
Or did it happen by exuberance?
As the ancient poets relate.
But a doubter such as I am
Raises doubts, and for that have I journeyed
From Europe,
Which is more doubt-addicted than any
Elderly married women.
May God make it better!
Amen!

Drinking in this finest air,
My nostrils distended like goblets,
Without future, without reminiscences,
Thus I sit here, you
Dearest of all women-friends,
And contemplate the palm-tree,
Which like a slender dancing girl
Bends slowly, bows slowly, sways at the hips,
—one does this too, if one looks for long!
Like a dancing girl, who, as it seems to me,
Has stood too long, dangerously long
For ever on only a single leg?
—so she thereby forgot, as it seems to me,
The other leg?
In vain, at least,

I searched for the missing
Twin-jewel
—that is, the other leg—
In the sacred neighbourhood
Of her dearest and most delicate
Fanlike and fluttering and spangled little skirt.
Yes, if you now, my dearest women-friends,
Believe me wholly:
She has lost her leg!
It is gone!
Gone for ever!
The other leg!
What a pity about this dearest other leg!
Where—might it be now, forsaken and mourning?
That lonely leg?
Afraid perhaps of an
Angry blond curly-maned*
Lion-monster? Or else perhaps
Gnawed away, nibbled away—
How pitiful, woe! woe! nibbled away! Selah.

Weep not for me,
You tender hearts!
Weep not for me, you
Date-hearts! Milk-bosoms!
You little liquorice
Heart-purses!
Weep no more,
Pale Dudu!
Be a man, Suleika! Courage now!
—Or else would perhaps
Something strengthening, heart-strengthening,
Be more in place here?
An unctuous maxim?
A solemn exhortation?—

Ha! Up now, dignity!
Virtue-dignity! European dignity!
Now blow, now blow again,
Great bellows of virtue!

Ha!
To roar once again,
To roar morally,
As a moral lion
Before the daughters of the desert!
—For virtue-howling,
You dearest of all maidens,
Is more than anything
European ardour, European hot-hunger!
And here I stand now,
As a European,
I can do no other, so help me God!
Amen!*

The desert grows: woe to him who harbours deserts within!

*   *   *

17. The Awakening

I

After the song of the wanderer and shadow the cave was all at once filled with uproar and laughter; and since the assembled guests were all speaking at once, and even the ass was unable to stay quiet in the face of such encouragement, Zarathustra was overcome with slight ill-will and scorn for his visitors, even though he was happy at their cheerfulness. For this seemed to him a sign of convalescence. So he slipped out into the open air and spoke to his animals.

'Where has their need gone now?' he said, already breathing a sigh of relief from his slight disgust. 'In my home they have unlearned, it seems, their need-crying!

'—if not also, alas, their crying.' And Zarathustra stopped up his ears, for just then the Yea-Ah of the ass was blending wondrously with the noisy jubilation of the superior humans.

'They are merry,' he began again, 'and who knows? perhaps at the expense of their host. And if they have learned from me how to laugh, it is nevertheless not *my* laughing that they have learned.

'But what does it matter! They are old people: they convalesce in their own way, and they laugh in their own way; my ears have surely endured worse noise without becoming morose.

'This is a day of victory: he is retreating already, and fleeing, *the Spirit of Heaviness*, my old arch-enemy! How well will this day end, which began so badly and heavily!

'And end it *will*. Evening is approaching already: over the sea he rides, the skilful rider! How he sways, blissfully, returning home, in his purple saddle!

'The Heavens look clearly on, the world lies deep: oh, all you wondrous men who have come to me, living with me is indeed worthwhile!'

Thus spoke Zarathustra. And then the screaming and laughing of the superior humans again issued from the cave: so he began again.

'They are biting, my bait is working, even their enemy the Spirit of Heaviness is retreating from them. They are already learning to laugh at themselves: do I hear aright?

'My man's fare is working, my sap-filled forceful maxims: and verily, I did not nourish them with bloating vegetables! But with warrior's fare, with conqueror's fare: new desires have I awakened.

'There are new hopes in their arms and legs; their hearts are stretching out. They are finding new words, and soon their spirits will breathe wilfulness.

'Such fare, to be sure, may not be for children, nor for yearning little females, old or young. Their entrails are persuaded in a different way; their physician and teacher I am not.

'The *disgust* is retreating from these superior humans: well then! that is my victory. In my realm they become secure, all stupid shame disappears, they are unburdening themselves.

'They are unburdening their hearts, good hours return to them, they celebrate and ruminate—they are becoming *thankful*.

'*This* I take as the best sign: they are becoming thankful. Before long they will be planning festivals and erecting monuments to their former joys.

'They are *convalescents!*' Thus spoke Zarathustra joyfully to his heart and gazed out; but his animals pressed close to him and respected his happiness and his silence.

*   *   *

2

But suddenly Zarathustra's ear was startled: for the cave, which had up to then been full of tumult and laughter, became all at once deathly quiet—but his nose smelled a fragrant smoke and incense, as if from burning pine-cones.*

'What is happening? What are they doing?' he asked himself and crept up to the entrance, that he might observe his guests without being noticed.* But, wonder of wonders! what a sight he had to see there with his own eyes!

'They have all become *pious* again, they are *praying*, they have gone mad!'—he said, and was amazed beyond measure. And indeed! all these superior humans, the two kings, the retired pope, the wicked sorcerer, the voluntary beggar, the wanderer and shadow, the old soothsayer, the conscientious in spirit, and the ugliest man: they were all on their knees, like children and devout little old women, and were praying to the ass. And just then the ugliest man began to gurgle and snort, as if something inexpressible wanted to come out of him; but when he was actually able to bring it to words, behold, it was a strange and pious litany to glorify the adored and incense-surrounded ass. And this litany rang out thus:

'Amen! And praise and honour and wisdom and thanks and glory and strength be unto our God, from eternity to eternity!'*

—But the ass in response brayed Yea-Ah.

'He bears our burdens, he took upon himself the form of a servant,* he is patient of heart and never says Nay; and whoever loves his God chastens him.'

—But the ass in response brayed Yea-Ah.

'He does not talk: except that to the world that he created he always says Yea: thus he praises his world. It is his cunning that does not speak: thus he is seldom found to be wrong.'

—But the ass in response brayed Yea-Ah.

'Inconspicuously he goes through the world. Gray is the body-colour in which he veils his virtue. If he has spirit, he conceals it; but everyone believes in his long ears.'

—But the ass in response brayed Yea-Ah.

'What concealed wisdom it is that he wears long ears and says only

Yea and never Nay! Has he not created the world in his own image,* that is, as stupid as possible?'

—But the ass in response cried Yea-Ah.

'You walk straight and crooked ways; it concerns you little what we humans think is straight or crooked. Beyond good and evil is your kingdom. It is your innocence not to know what innocence is.'

—But the ass in response brayed Yea-Ah.

'Behold then, how you push no one away from you, neither beggars nor kings. The little children you suffer to come unto you, and if naughty boys entice you,* you simply say Yea-Ah.'

—But the ass in response cried Yea-Ah.

'You love she-asses and fresh figs, and are no despiser of food. A thistle tickles your heart whenever you feel hunger.* Therein lies the wisdom of a God.'

But the ass in response brayed Yea-Ah.

* * *

18. The Ass Festival*

I

At this point in the litany Zarathustra could control himself no longer, himself brayed Yea-Ah even louder than the ass, and leaped into the midst of his deranged guests. 'What on earth are you doing, you human-children?' he cried, pulling the worshippers up from the ground. 'Woe, if anyone other than Zarathustra were to see you:

'Everyone would judge that with your new faith you were the worst blasphemers or the most foolish of all little old women!

'And you of all people, you old pope, how does it sit with you that you worship an ass as God like this?'—

'O Zarathustra,' replied the pope, 'forgive me, but in matters of God I am even more enlightened than you. And that is as it should be.

'Better to worship God thus, in this form, than in no form at all! Reflect upon this maxim, my exalted friend: you will see at once that in this maxim there is wisdom.

'He who said, "God is Spirit"*—he took the greatest step and leap on earth so far toward unbelief: such a word is on earth not easily made good again!

'My old heart leaps and prances at the fact that there is still on earth something to worship. Do forgive, O Zarathustra, a pious old pope's heart!—'

—'And you,' said Zarathustra to the wanderer and shadow, 'you call and think yourself a free spirit? And yet you engage in such idolatry and clericolatry?

'Even wickeder, verily, is your behaviour here than with your wicked brown maidens, you wicked new believer!'

'Wicked enough,' answered the wanderer and shadow, 'you are right: but what can I do about it! The old God lives again, O Zarathustra, you may say what you will.

'It is all the fault of the ugliest man: he is the one that woke him up again. And if he says that he once killed him: *death* in the case of Gods is always a mere prejudice.'

—'And you,' said Zarathustra, 'you wicked old sorcerer, what were you doing! Who, in this free age, shall believe in you any more, if *you* believe in such asinine Gods-nonsense?

'What you did, that was stupidity; how could you, being so clever, commit such stupidity!'

'O Zarathustra,' answered the clever sorcerer, 'you are right, it was stupidity—it has weighed heavily enough on me too.'

—'And even you,' said Zarathustra to the conscientious in spirit. 'Just consider and lay your finger on your nose! For does nothing here go against your conscience? Is your spirit not too cleanly for this praying and the miasma of these devotees?'

'There is something in this,' answered the conscientious one and laid his finger on his nose, 'there is something in this spectacle that actually does my conscience good.

'Perhaps I may not believe in God: but what is certain is that God in this form seems to me most worthy of belief.

'God is supposed to be eternal, according to the testimony of the most pious; whoever has so much time takes his time. As slowly and as stupidly as possible: *this way* can such a one still bring things very far along.

'And whoever has too much spirit may well become infatuated with stupidity and folly. Just think upon yourself, O Zarathustra!

'You yourself—verily! even you could become an ass through overabundance and wisdom.

'Does a consummate wise man not gladly walk the crookedest ways? Appearances teach this, O Zarathustra—*your* appearance!'

—'And you yourself,' finally, said Zarathustra and turned to the ugliest man, who was still lying on the ground, his arm raised toward the ass (for he was giving him wine to drink). 'Speak, you inexpressible creature, what have you been doing!

'You seem to me transformed, your eyes are glowing, a mantle of the sublime lies about your ugliness: *what* have you done?

'Is it really true what they say, that you woke him up again? And why? Was he not killed off and done away with for good reason?

'You yourself seem awakened to me: what have you done? why did *you* reform? Why did *you* convert yourself? Speak, you inexpressible creature!'

'O Zarathustra,' answered the ugliest man, 'you are a rogue!

'Whether *he* still lives or lives again or is thoroughly dead—which of us two knows that best? I ask you.

'But one thing I know—from you yourself I learned it once, O Zarathustra: whoever would kill most thoroughly, *laughs*.

' "Not with wrath but with laughter does one kill"—thus you spoke once. O Zarathustra, you concealed one, you annihilator without wrath, you dangerous holy man—you are a rogue!'

*   *   *

2

But then it happened that Zarathustra, amazed at such a series of roguish responses, leaped back to the door of his cave and, turning to all his guests, cried in a loud voice:

'Oh you buffoons, all of you, you jesters! Why do you disguise and conceal yourselves from me!

'How the heart of each one of you wriggled with pleasure and wickedness over the fact that you finally became as little children again, namely pious—

'—that you finally did as children do, namely prayed, folding your hands and saying "Dear God"!

'But now leave *this* nursery, my own cave, where today all childishness is at home. Come outside and cool your overheated child's exuberance and heart's noise!

'To be sure: except ye become as little children, ye shall not enter into *that* Kingdom of Heaven.' (And Zarathustra pointed upward with his hands.)

'But then we do not want to enter the Kingdom of Heaven at all: we have become men—and *so we want the Kingdom of Earth*.'

* * *

3

And once again Zarathustra began to speak. 'O my new friends,' he said—'You wondrous ones, you superior humans, how pleased I am with you now,

'—since you became joyful again! You have truly blossomed all of you: for such flowers as you are, it seems to me, *new festivals* are needed,

'—a little brave nonsense, some divine service and ass-festival, some joyful old Zarathustra-fool, a rushing wind to blow your souls clear.

'Do not forget this night and this ass-festival, you superior humans! *This* you invented here with me, which I take as a good omen—such things only convalescents invent!

'And should you celebrate it again, this ass-festival, do it for love of yourselves; do it also for love of me! And in remembrance of *me*!'

Thus spoke Zarathustra.

* * *

19. The Drunken Song*

I

In the meantime one after the other had stepped out into the open air and the cool and contemplative night; but Zarathustra himself led the ugliest man by the hand, that he might show him his night-world and the large round moon and the silvery waterfalls by his cave. There at last they stood together silently, old people all of them, but with consoled and valiant hearts and amazed in themselves that on earth they felt so well; but the secrecy of the night came closer and closer to their hearts. And again Zarathustra thought to himself: 'Oh how pleasing they are to me now, these superior humans!'—but he did not say this aloud, for he respected their happiness and their silence.—

But then something happened that was the most astonishing thing of that astonishing long day: the ugliest man began once again and for the last time to gurgle and snort, and when he finally managed to put it in words, behold, a question leaped round and pure from his mouth, a good deep clear question that moved the hearts of all who were listening.

'My friends, all,' said the ugliest man, 'what do you think? Thanks to this day—for the first time am *I* content to have lived the whole of my life.

'And that I declare this much is still not sufficient. Living on the earth is worth while: one day, one festival with Zarathustra, has taught me to love the earth.

' "Was *that*—life?" I will say to death. "Very well! One more time!"

'My dear friends, what do you think? Will you not, like me, say to death: Was *that*—life? For Zarathustra's sake, very well! One more time!'— —

Thus spoke the ugliest man; and it was not long before midnight. And what do you think happened after that? As soon as the superior humans heard his question, they all at once became aware of their transformation and convalescence, and who had granted them these. They thereupon rushed up to Zarathustra, thanking, revering, caressing, kissing his hands, each after his own fashion: such that some were laughing, some were crying. But the old soothsayer was dancing for joy; and even if, as some storytellers believe, he was at that point full of sweet wine,* he was certainly even more full of sweet life and had renounced all weariness. There are even those who say that the ass danced at that time: for it was not in vain that the ugliest man had earlier given him wine to drink. Now it may have been this way or otherwise; and if in truth the ass did not dance that evening, yet greater and stranger wonders occurred than the dancing of an ass would have been. In short, as Zarathustra's saying has it: 'What does it matter!'

*   *   *

2

But Zarathustra, when this happened with the ugliest man, stood there like a drunken man: his gaze was extinguished, his tongue babbled, his legs swayed. And who could guess what thoughts were then coursing across Zarathustra's soul? But apparently his spirit retreated and flew away and was in far distances and, as it were, 'on a high ridge, as it is written, between two seas,

'—wandering between past and future as a heavy cloud.'* Gradually, however, as the superior humans held him in their arms, he came to himself somewhat and fended off with his hands the crowd of admirers and concerned parties; yet he did not speak. But all at once he quickly turned his head, for he seemed to hear something: then he put his finger to his lips and said: '*Come!*'

And thereupon it became still all around and mysterious; but from the depths there slowly arose the sound of a bell*. Zarathustra hearkened to it, as did the superior humans; but then he put his finger to his lips a second time and said again: '*Come! Come! It is close to midnight!*'—and his voice had been transformed. But he still did not move from the spot: and it became stiller and more mysterious, and everything hearkened, even the ass, and Zarathustra's honourable animals, the eagle and the serpent, as well as Zarathustra's cave and the great cool moon and the night itself. Then Zarathustra put his hand to his lips a third time and said:

'*Come! Come! Come! Let us now wander! The hour is here: let us wander into the night!*'

*　　*　　*

3

You superior humans, it is close to midnight: now I want to say something in your ears, just as that ancient bell said it in my ear –

—as secretly, as terribly, as heartily, as that midnight-bell speaks it to me, which has experienced more than any human has:

—which has already counted off your fathers' heart-pains' beats—ah! ah! how she sighs! how in dreams she laughs! the ancient deep, Deep Midnight!

Still! Still! Now many a thing is heard that may not be audible by day; but now, in cool air, when all noise in your hearts, too, is stilled—

—now it speaks, now it is heard, now it slips into nightlike over-wakeful souls: ah! ah! how she sighs! how in dreams she laughs!

—do you not hear her, how she secretly, terribly, heartily speaks to *you*, the ancient deep, Deep Midnight?

O man, take care!

* * *

4

Woe is me! Whither has time gone? Have I not sunk into deep wells? The world sleeps—

Ah! Ah! The dog howls, the moon shines. Rather will I die, rather die than tell you what my midnight-heart is thinking.

Now I have died. It is over. Spider, what are you spinning around me? Do you want blood? Ah! Ah! The dew falls, the hour is nigh—

—the hour when I shiver and freeze, which asks and asks and asks: 'Who has heart enough for it?

'—Who shall be lord of the earth? Who will now say: *Thus* shall you run, you great and small rivers!'

—the hour is nigh: O man, you superior human, beware! this speech is for subtle ears, for your own ears—*What does Deep Midnight now declare?*

* * *

5

I am carried away, my soul is dancing. Day's work! Day's work! Who shall be lord of the earth?

The moon is cool, the wind silent. Ah! Ah! Have you all flown high enough yet? You have all danced: but a leg is still no wing.

You finest dancers, now is all pleasure gone: wine became lees, every goblet unsound, the graves are stammering.

You have not flown high enough: now the graves are stammering, 'Redeem all the dead! Why is it night for so long? Does the moon not make us drunken?'

You superior humans, now redeem the graves, and awaken all the corpses! Ah, why does the worm still burrow? It is near, the hour is nigh—

—the bell now booms, the heart is still rasping, the woodworm, heart's-worm still burrowing. Ah! Ah! *The world is deep!*

* * *

6

Sweetest lyre! Sweetest lyre! I love your tone, your drunken, toad-croaking tone!—from how long ago, from how far off comes to me your tone, over great distances, from the ponds of love!

You ancient bell, you sweetest lyre! Every pain has torn into your heart, father-pain, fathers'-pain, forefathers'-pain; your speech has become ripe—

—ripe as golden autumn and afternoon, as my solitary's heart—now you speak: The world itself became ripe, the grape turns brown,

—now will it die, die of happiness. You superior humans, do you not smell it? An odour is secretly welling up,

—a fragrance and odour of eternity, a rose-blissful brown gold-wine-odour of ancient happiness,

—of drunken midnight-dying happiness, which sings: The world is deep, *deeper than day had been aware!*

* * *

7

Leave me! Leave me! I am too pure for you. Do not touch me! Did my world not just now become perfect?

My skin is too pure for your hands. Leave me, you stupid loutish gloomy day! Is midnight not still brighter?

The purest shall be lords of the earth, the most unrecognizable, strongest, the midnight-souls, who are brighter and deeper than any day.

O day, you grope for me? You fumble for my happiness? To you I seem rich, lonely, a treasure-pit, a gold-chamber?

O world, you want *me?* To you I am worldly? To you I am spirit-ual? To you I am godlike? But day and world, you are too clumsy—

—have cleverer hands, reach for deeper happiness, for deeper unhappiness, reach for some kind of God, reach not for me:

—my unhappiness, my happiness is deep, you wondrous day, but yet I am no God, no God's Hell: *deep is its woe*.

* * *

8

God's woe is deeper, you wondrous world! Reach for God's woe, not for me! What am I! A sweet and drunken sweet lyre—

—a midnight-lyre, a bell-like toad that no one understands, but which *must* speak, before the deaf, you superior humans! For you understand me not!

Gone! Gone! Oh youth! Oh noon! Oh afternoon! Now evening and night and midnight have come—the dog howls, the wind:

—is the wind not a dog? He whimpers, he yelps, he howls. Ah! Ah! how she sighs! how she laughs, how she rattles and wheezes, the Midnight Hour!

How she speaks soberly now, this drunken poetess! Perhaps she over-drank her drunkenness? she became over-awake? she ruminates?

—on her woe she ruminates, in a dream, the ancient Deep Midnight, and even more on her joy. For joy, even if woe is deep: *Joy is deeper still than misery*.

* * *

9

You grape-vine! Why do you praise me? I have cut you after all! I am cruel, you are bleeding—what means your praise of my drunken cruelty?

'What has become perfect, all that is ripe—wants to die!' thus you speak. Blessèd, blessèd be the vintner's knife! But all that is unripe wants to live: woe!

Woe says: 'Be gone! Away, all woe!' But all that suffers wants to live, that it may become ripe and joyful and full of yearning,

—yearning for what is farther, higher, brighter. 'I want heirs,' says all that suffers. 'I want children, I do not want *me*.'—

But joy does not want heirs, nor children—joy wants itself, wants eternity, wants recurrence, wants all-eternally-self-same.

Woe says: 'Break, bleed, heart! Wander, leg! Wing, fly! Onward! Upward, pain!' Well then! Come now! Oh my old heart: *Woe says, 'Be gone!'*

*   *   *

10

You higher humans, what do you think? Am I a soothsayer? A dreamer? Drunkard? A dream interpreter? A midnight-bell?

A drop of dew? A haze and fragrance of eternity? Do you not hear it? Do you not smell it? Just now my world became perfect, midnight is also midday—

Pain is also a joy, curse is also a blessing, night is also a sun—be gone! or you will learn: a wise man is also a fool.

Did you ever say Yes to a single joy? Oh, my friends, then you said Yes to *all* woe as well. All things are chained together, entwined, in love—

—if you ever wanted one time a second time, if you ever said 'You please me, happiness!* Quick! Moment!' then you wanted *it all* back!

—All anew, all eternally, all chained together, entwined, in love, oh then you *loved* the world—

—you eternal ones, love it eternally and for all time: and even to woe you say: Be gone, but come back! *For all joy wants—Eternity!*

*   *   *

11

All joy wants the eternity of all things, wants honey, wants lees, wants drunken midnight, wants graves, wants graves'-tears consolation, wants gilded evening-glow—

—*what* does joy not want! She is thirstier, heartier, hungrier, more terrible, more secret than all woe, she wants *herself*, she bites into *herself*, the ring's will wrestles in her—

—she wants love, she wants hate, she is overrich, bestows, throws away, begs for someone to take her, thanks the taker, she would gladly be hated—

—so rich is joy that she thirsts for woe, for Hell, for hate, for disgrace, for the cripple, for *world*—this world now, you know it well!

You higher humans, it is for you that she yearns, this joy, intractable, blissful—for your woe, you that have failed! For failures does all eternal joy yearn.

For all joy wants herself, thus she wants misery too! Oh happiness, oh pain! Oh break, heart! You higher humans, do learn this: Joy wants eternity,

—Joy wants *all* things' eternity, *wants deepest, deep Eternity!*

* * *

12

Have you now learned my song? Have you guessed what it means? Well then! Come now! You higher humans, now sing for me my roundelay!

Now sing yourselves the song whose name is 'One More Time', whose sense is 'to all eternity!' Sing, you higher humans, Zarathustra's roundelay!

> *O man! Take care!*
> *What does Deep Midnight now declare?*
> *'I sleep, I sleep—*
> *From deepest dream I rise for air:—*
> *The world is deep,*
> *And deeper than day had been aware.*
> *Deep is its woe—*
> *Joy—deeper still than misery:*
> *Woe says: Be gone!*
> *Yet all joy wants Eternity—*
> *—wants deepest, deep Eternity!'*

* * *

20. The Sign

In the morning after this night, however, Zarathustra jumped up from his pallet, girded up his loins, and came out of his cave, glowing and strong, like a morning sun coming out of dark mountains.*

'Greetings, Great Star,' he said, as he had said before, 'you deep happiness-eye. What would all your happiness be, had you not *those* whom you illumine!

'And if they stayed in their chambers while you are already awake and come and bestow and distribute: how your proud modesty would be angry!

'Well then! they are still asleep, these higher humans, while *I* am awake: *they* are not my rightful companions! Not for them am I waiting here in my mountains.

'To my work will I go, to my day: but they do not understand what the signs of my morning are, my step—is for them no reveille.

'They are still asleep in my cave, their dreams still drink from my drunken songs.* Yet the ear that hearkens after *me*—the *obeying* ear is lacking in their limbs.'

—This Zarathustra had said to his heart as the sun was rising: then he looked enquiringly into the heights, for he heard above him the sharp call of his eagle. 'Well then!' he cried, 'thus does it please and suit me well. My animals are awake, for I am awake.

'My eagle is awake and, like me, he honours the sun. With eagle's talons he grasps for the new light. You are my rightful animals; I love you.

'But my rightful humans are still lacking!'—

Thus spoke Zarathustra; but then it happened that he suddenly heard himself surrounded as by innumerable birds swarming and fluttering around—and the whirring of so many wings and the thronging about his head was so great that he closed his eyes. And verily, like a cloud it descended upon him, like a cloud of arrows that shakes itself out over some new enemy. But behold, here it was a cloud of love, and over a new friend.

'What is happening to me?' thought Zarathustra in his astonished heart, and let himself down slowly onto the large rock that lay beside the exit of his cave. But as he felt with his hands around and above and beneath him, warding off the affectionate birds, behold, something even stranger happened to him: for he found himself with his hand unwittingly in a thick warm mane; and at the same time a roar came forth before him—a soft long lion's roar.

'*The sign is nigh*,' said Zarathustra and his heart was transformed. And in truth, as it became light before him, there lay at his feet a powerful yellow animal and nestled its head against his knee and did not want to leave him for love, and it was like a dog that finds his former master again. But the doves were no less eager in their love than the lion; and every time a dove flitted by the lion's nose, the lion shook his head and was amazed and laughed.*

To all this Zarathustra said only one thing: '*My children are near, my children*'—then he fell completely silent. But his heart was loosened, and from his eyes tears dripped down and fell upon his hands. And he no longer heeded anything and sat there, unmoving and without warding off the animals any more. Then the doves flew to and fro and perched on his shoulders and caressed his white hair and did not tire of their tenderness and rejoicing. But the strong lion kept licking the tears that fell upon Zarathustra's hands, roaring and growling bashfully as he did so. Thus did these animals behave.—

All this lasted a long time, or a short time: for, properly speaking, there is for such things on earth *no* time—. But meanwhile the superior humans in Zarathustra's cave had woken up and were arranging themselves into a procession, that they might go before Zarathustra and offer him a morning-greeting: for they had found when they awakened that he was no longer among them. But when they reached the door of the cave, with the noise of their footsteps preceding them, the lion started violently, turned all at once away from Zarathustra, and leaped with a wild roar toward the cave. When the higher humans heard him roar they all raised a cry, as if from a single mouth, fled back, and in a flash had disappeared.

Zarathustra himself, looking stunned and distant, rose from his seat, looked about him, stood there amazed, questioned his heart, reflected, and saw that he was alone. 'What did I hear?' he at last said slowly. 'What just happened to me?'

And then his memory returned and he realized all at once everything that had happened between yesterday and today. 'Yes, here is the rock,' he said, stroking his beard. 'It was *here* that I sat yesterday morning; and here the soothsayer came up to me, and here I first heard the cry that I heard even now, the great cry of need.

'Oh you superior humans, it was of *your* need that the old soothsayer prophesied yesterday morning—

'—to your need he wanted to tempt and seduce me: "O Zarathustra," he said to me, "I come to seduce you to your ultimate sin."

'To my ultimate sin?' cried Zarathustra and laughed angrily at his own words: *What* was it that was saved up for me as my ultimate sin?'

—And once more Zarathustra sank into himself and sat down on the large rock again and meditated. Suddenly he sprang up—

'*Pity! Pity for the superior human!*' he cried out, and his visage was transformed into bronze. 'Well then! *That*—has had its time!

'My suffering and my pitying—what does that matter! Am I striving then for *happiness?* I am striving for my *work!*

'Well then! The lion came, my children are near, Zarathustra has ripened, my hour has come:—

'This is *my* morning, *my* day is beginning: *Rise up now, rise up, you Great Midday!*'— —

Thus spoke Zarathustra and left his cave, glowing and strong, like a morning sun coming out of dark mountains.

* * *

The End of *Thus Spoke Zarathustra*

EXPLANATORY NOTES

The following abbreviations are used in the Notes:

B   *Friedrich Nietzsche: Sämtliche Briefe, Kritische Studienausgabe*, ed.
         Giorgio Colli and Mazzino Montinari, 8 vols. (Munich, 1986)
EH   *Ecce Homo*
GM   *On the Genealogy of Morals*
W   *Friedrich Nietzsche: Sämtliche Werke, Kritische Studienausgabe*, ed.
         Giorgio Colli and Mazzino Montinari, 15 vols. (Munich, 1980)

FIRST PART

9 *tire of them*: cf. Hellwald's account of the Persian prophet Zarathustra:
   'Zarathustra . . . was born in the town of Urmi on the lake of the same
   name. In his thirtieth year he left his home and went east to the province
   of Aria, and there he spent ten years in the solitude of the mountains
   working on the *Zend-Avesta*. After some time had passed he made his
   way to Balkh, where he proclaimed his new teachings' (Friedrich von
   Hellwald, *Culturgeschichte in ihrer natürlichen Entstehung* (The History of
   Culture in its Natural Development) (Augsburg, 1874), 128). Cf. Luke 3:
   23, where Jesus is said to be 'about thirty years of age' after his baptism
   and the descent upon him of the Holy Ghost. According to the account
   in Hermann Oldenberg's *Buddha: His Life, His Doctrine, His Order*, tr.
   William Hoey (Delhi: Indological Book House, 1971; German edn.
   1881), a book that Nietzsche knew well and made notes on while working
   on *Zarathustra* (*W* 11: 26 [220–5]), the Buddha was 29 when 'he left his
   home in order to lead a spiritual life', and 'went from his home into
   homelessness' (*Buddha*, 103, 105).

   whom you illumine!: Hellwald writes that, for the historical Zarathustra,
   'fire and the sun are seen in their purity as a symbol of God, and so in
   offering prayer one turns one's face to the fire or the sun' (*Culturgeschichte*, 130). Nietzsche's Zarathustra evinces a modern sensibility by
   addressing the sun using the familiar form of the second-person pro-
   noun, *du*, a form that is impossible to mark in English without recourse
   to the archaic-sounding 'thou'. (In this he follows Hölderlin's Hyperion,
   who addresses the sun as *du* in the second letter of *Hyperion*.) Zarathustra thereby sets the tone for the anti-Platonic argument of the book:
   whereas for Socrates the sun stands for the transcendent Idea of the
   Good, which is 'beyond Being', for Zarathustra it is a familiar that he
   claims is dependent for its being what it is on the response of him and his
   animals. And whereas in the famous image of Plato's *Republic* (514–18)
   the cave is a place of ignorance deep within the earth, in *Zarathustra* it is
   a place of enlightenment high in the mountains. Zarathustra's greeting

also recalls a passage in Ralph Waldo Emerson's *Essays*, which Nietzsche knew well, where Emerson suggests that a sunset needs human beings in order to be fully what it is: 'The sunset . . . wants men' (*Essays and Lectures* (New York: The Library of America, 1983), essay 1, 'Nature').

to receive it: cf. Plato's *Ion*, 534a, where poets are said to 'cull their songs from honey-dropping founts in certain gardens and glades of the Muses—like the bees'.

overrich star!: cf. Hölderlin, *The Death of Empedocles*: 'auch du musst untergehen, | Du schöner Stern!' (even you must go down, | You beautiful star!) (first version, 1, 38–9).

human again: Zarathustra's talk of 'going down to human beings' and 'becoming human again' is prefigured in several letters Nietzsche wrote around the time he was composing *Zarathustra* (*B* 8 Sept. 1882; 20 Dec. 1882; 27 Apr. 1883).

10 *awakened . . . among sleepers?*: the 'awakened one' is *Erwachter*, a common epithet for the Buddha (the Pali and Sanskrit root *buddh-* means 'awake') that Nietzsche encountered in Oldenberg's *Buddha*.

11 *to his heart*: Zarathustra often speaks 'to his heart', and in this he resembles figures in the Homeric epics (Odysseus especially), who frequently talk to their 'hearts' and other psychical centres within them, and in the Bible (where the locution is 'spoke in his heart'), as well as Hölderlin's *Hyperion*, who addresses his heart at the end of the first letter of the book.

a rope-dancer: 'rope-dancer' is a literal translation of *Seiltänzer*, and is preferable to the more idiomatic 'tightrope-walker' because of the importance of the dance (*Tanz*) as Zarathustra's preferred *modus agendi*. The 'rope-dancer' echoes the holy man's saying that Zarathustra walks 'like a dancer', suggesting an affinity between this figure and Zarathustra himself. What is more, an unpublished note from the period reads: 'Zarathustra himself [is] the jester who jumps over the poor rope-dancer' (*W* 10: 16 [88]).

than any ape is: the allusion here may be (rather than to Darwin) to a passage in a dialogue attributed to Plato, *Hippias Major*, 289a–b: 'the saying of Heraclitus that "the most beautiful of apes is ugly in comparison with the race of humans" . . . [does it not mean that] the wisest of humans, in comparison with a God, will appear an ape?'

13 *the lightning*: alludes to the god Dionysus, who was born after his mother Semele was consumed by a bolt of lightning, and perhaps also to the famous fragment of the pre-Socratic Greek philosopher Heraclitus: 'A lightning bolt steers all things.'

14 *preserve himself*: cf. *Hyperion*: 'With squandering love my soul poured itself out, to fill up all the gaps' (1. 1. 9); also Luke 17: 33: 'Whosoever shall seek to save his life shall lose it; and whosoever shall lose his life shall preserve it.'

14 *chastens . . . his God*: cf. Hebrews 12: 6: 'For whom the Lord loveth he chasteneth, and scourgeth every son whom he receiveth' (Luther).

forgets himself: a passage in the notebooks reads: 'I am too full: thus I forget myself, and all things are in me, and beyond all things there is nothing more: where have *I gone*?' (*W* 10: 5 [1] 238). This is the first intimation of an experience that becomes crucial to Zarathustra's understanding of the world, a quasi-mystical state of the soul's expansion in which the 'I' undergoes dissolution (fully depicted in the chapters 'At Midday' and 'The Drunken Song' below, 4. 10 and 4. 19).

entrails of his heart: in his notebooks Nietzsche quotes Napoleon as saying: 'The heart belongs to the entrails' (*W* 10: 3 [1] 130).

15 *with their eyes?*: cf. Isaiah 6: 10: 'Make their ears heavy, and shut their eyes; lest they see with their eyes, and hear with their ears.'

16 *then blinks*: there is an assonance between the *blinzelt* (blinks), which alludes to the short attention-span that has become so characteristic of the modern age, and the *Blitz* (lightning) associated with the Overhuman, which signifies by contrast a genuine flash of illumination or insight.

one herd!: cf. John 10: 16: 'And there shall be one herd and one herdsman' (Luther).

17 *market-square and the people*: this incident seems to be based on a passage near the beginning of Wagner's autobiographical *Mein Leben*, where Wagner recounts seeing as a child 'performances by a troupe of acrobats who appeared on a rope stretched from tower to tower over the square'; as noted by Roger Hollinrake, *Nietzsche, Wagner, and the Philosophy of Pessimism* (London and Boston, 1982), 12.

18 *catch of fish*: cf. Matthew 4: 19, where Jesus says to Simon (called Peter) and Andrew, 'Follow me, and I will make you fishers of men.'

19 *On you go then!*: 'Nun wohlan!' The *wohlan* is an interjection that Zarathustra uses frequently and which is also very common in the Luther Bible (the King James Version has 'Come on' or 'Behold' or 'Go').

20 *who all at once sees land*: a passage in the notebooks reads: 'I discovered a new land within the human being | where the soul boils over' (*W* 10: 4 [234] 179).

sheepdog to a herd!: cf. Plato, *Republic*, 440, where the rulers of the imagined city are likened to 'shepherds', the auxiliaries (military class) to 'obedient dogs', and the common people (moneymakers) to sheep.

21 *breaks their tablets of values*: cf. Exodus 32: 19, where Moses in anger breaks the tablets of the law.

harvest . . . ears of corn: cf. Matthew 9: 37: 'The harvest truly is plenteous, but the labourers are few'; and 12: 1: 'At that time Jesus went on the sabbath day through the corn; and his disciples were an hungred, and began to pluck the ears of corn, and to eat.'

22 *eagle . . . serpent*: cf. Homer, *Iliad*, 12. 230–9, where an eagle, 'clutching a monstrous bloody serpent in both talons', appears as a fatal omen high above the beleaguered city of Troy.

23 *becomes a camel*: Hellwald remarks that the name 'Zarathustra' originally meant 'possessing valiant camels', and that the earlier, much grander derivation 'golden star' has been found to be specious (*Culturgeschichte*, 128).

tempt the tempter?: cf. Matthew 4: 8, where Satan tempts Jesus on 'an exceeding high mountain'.

great dragon: cf. Revelation 12: 9, where Satan is referred to as 'the great dragon, the old serpent'.

24 *scaly beast*: cf. the description of the Leviathan in Job 41: 15: 'His scales are his pride, shut up as with a close seal.'

Innocence the child is: cf. Hölderlin's *Hyperion*: 'That one can become as children, that the golden time of innocence recurs (*wiederkehrt*)' (1. 2. 2).

its own will . . . its own world: this imagery is reminiscent of Hegel's discussion, near the beginning of the Preface to the *Phenomenology of Spirit*, of the way a new world of the spirit (*Geist*) supervenes: 'The spirit has broken with the world of its previous existence . . . As with the child the first breath breaks off the gradual process of growth . . . and the child is born' (sec. 11).

Thus spoke . . . Motley Cow: 'Thus spoke Zarathustra' is an echo of the refrain at the end of many of the accounts in the Buddhist sutras of the Buddha's sermons: 'Thus spoke the Sublime One' ('Also sprach der Erhabene'). The refrain occurs after every time Zarathustra speaks, up to 'The Stillest Hour' at the end of the Second Part (2. 22). At the end of the three songs (2. 9–11) it is changed, appropriately, to 'Thus sang Zarathustra'. Another favourite locution of Zarathustra's, 'O Brüder' ('O brothers'), also appears in German translations of the sutras. 'The Motley Cow' ('die bunte Kuh') is a translation of the name of a town Kalmasadalmya, which the Buddha is said to have visited on his wanderings. See Freny Mistry, *Nietzsche and Buddhism* (Berlin and New York: de Gruyter, 1981), 17.

25 *A wise man*: it is strange that the second chapter in the only one of the book's four parts to bear a title, 'The Speeches of Zarathustra', should contain a speech by someone *other* than Zarathustra. One implication of this might be that the character who delivers the speech, 'a wise man', is to be regarded as an aspect of Zarathustra's own multifaceted psyche.

false witness . . . adultery . . . maidservant?: cf. the Ten Commandments, Exodus 20: 14, 16, 17.

crooked authority!: cf. the epigraph to Romans 13: 'Admonition to obedience to authority' (Luther).

26 *greenest pasture*: cf. Psalms 23: 1–2, where the Lord as shepherd is said to make the psalmist 'to lie down in green pastures'.

26 *Blessèd are they*: cf. Matthew 5: 3, where the poor in spirit are said to be 'blessed'. Nietzsche was himself a frequent and tortured sufferer from insomnia.

28 *with broken wings*: cf. Plato, *Phaedrus*, 246d–248b, where the souls subject to divine madness are likened to winged horses: when insufficiently nourished on beauty, wisdom, and goodness, 'many wings are broken'.

an earthen head: cf. Plato, *Timaeus*, 44d–e, where the divine craftsman creates the human head as 'the most divine part' and supplies it with a trunk and limbs so that 'it should not go rolling upon the earth'.

29 *redemptive drops of blood*: cf. 1 Peter 1: 18–19, where redemption is said to take place 'with the precious blood of Christ'.

'thing-in-itself': 'Ding an sich', an allusion to Kant's notion, in his *Critique of Pure Reason* (1781), of the noumenal, unknowable ground of phenomena.

complete and four-square: 'vollkommne und rechtwinklige' (literally, 'right-angled'), an allusion to Aristotle, *Rhetoric*, 1411b, 26–7: 'to say that a good man is "four-square" (*tetragônon*) is a metaphor, for both the man and the square are complete and perfect.'

30 *lies the Self*: in an unpublished note Nietzsche calls the Self in the body *terra incognita*, or 'undiscovered country' (*W* 10: 5 [31]).

33 *The wheel of grounds*: the term *Grund* means 'ground' or 'reason' (for something), and figures prominently in the German philosophical tradition. It will usually be translated as 'ground', since Nietzsche generally emphasizes the literal meaning.

35 *Write with blood*: in a letter to his friend Franz Overbeck, who was a colleague of Nietzsche's when he taught at the University of Basel, Nietzsche writes about how much it cost him to write the First Part of *Zarathustra* the previous winter: 'Who knows whether *such great* torment was necessary in order to induce me to the blood-letting that this book constitutes? You know there is a great deal of blood in this book' (*B* 17 Apr. 1883).

will stink: an unpublished note reads: 'Another century of newspapers— and all words will stink' (*W* 10: 3 [1] 168). For Nietzsche's polemic against the popular press for the damage it does to language, see 'On the New Idol' (1. 11).

from summit to summit: cf. Emerson: 'The poet gives us the eminent experiences only,—a god stepping from peak to peak, nor planting his foot but on a mountain' ('Poetry and Imagination', in *Letters and Social Aims* (Boston, 1876), 9). Nietzsche read the German translation, *Neue Essays* (Stuttgart, 1876).

36 *the Spirit of Heaviness*: 'der Geist der Schwere'. Cf. Faust's relation to Mephistopheles in Goethe's *Faust*, who announces himself as 'the spirit that always negates' ('der Geist, der stets verneint') (*Faust I*, 1338).

38 *This tree . . . human and beast*: in a letter to his friend Carl von Gersdorff,

Nietzsche had written: 'Much weather and bad weather has broken over our heads (and our hearts), and many a layer of bark had to be split— but in spite of all that we two, like good old trees, have *grown into the heights*—who knows how high!' (*B* 18 Dec. 1881).

the first lightning?: cf. *Hyperion*: 'We want to grow upward, and to spread out up there our branches and twigs, and yet soil and weather bring us what they may; and if the lightning should fall upon your crown and cleave you down to the very roots, poor tree—what does it matter to you?' (1. 1. 7).

bark ... in their cellar: a note from the period reads: 'I still have all these wild dogs within, but in my cellar. I don't want to hear them barking' (*W* 10: 4 [86]; 5 [1]).

39 *Yellow ones ... black ones*: perhaps an allusion to the ochre robes worn by Buddhist monks and the black worn by Christian priests.

40 *invalid ... old man ... corpse*: Oldenberg recounts how the Buddha was prompted to leave home by the sight of invalids, old men, and corpses (*Buddha*, 123).

41 *war ... for your own thoughts!*: a passage in the notebooks from the time confirms that Zarathustra is talking not about literal war but about wars of ideas—or, as here, of *Gedanken* (thoughts): 'War (but without gunpowder!) between different thoughts! And their armies!' (*W* 10: 16 [50]). Service as a medical orderly in the Franco-Prussian War in 1870 dispelled Nietzsche's youthful fantasies about the glories of real war.

43 *finger of God*: cf. Exodus 8: 19, where the magicians, in response to the plague of lice visited upon the land of Egypt, tell Pharaoh: 'This is the finger of God.'

44 *worship it*: cf. Matthew 4: 9, where Satan says to Jesus: 'All these things will I give thee, if thou wilt fall down and worship me.'

lonesome and the twosome: an apt coinage of Walter Kaufmann's for 'Einsame und Zweisame'—a parallel wordplay to the 'Einsiedler und Zweisiedler', 'solitaries and dualitaries' earlier (Prologue, 9).

45 *play-actors*: as becomes clear in one of Nietzsche's last works, *The Case of Wagner*, the 'play-actor' (*Schauspieler*) here is an allusion to Wagner.

46 *poisonous flies*: cf. Emerson: 'The smallest fly will draw blood, and gossip is a weapon impossible to exclude from the privatest, highest, selectest' (*The Conduct of Life*, 'Worship'—in *Essays and Lectures*).

48 *perfect ... as beasts!*: an unpublished note reads: 'One must also be perfect as a beast if one wants to become perfect as a human being' (*W* 10: 4 [94]).

entered into swine: cf. Matthew 8: 28–32, where Jesus drives out the devils possessing two men into a herd of swine.

heat of the soul: cf. 1 Corinthians 7: 9: 'But if they cannot contain, let them marry: for it is better to marry than to be in heat' (Luther).

49 *I and Me*: an unpublished note reads: 'I and Me are always two different persons' (*W* 10: 3 [1] 352). This is a typical expression of Nietzsche's understanding of the duality—and beyond that the multiplicity—within the individual.

one's envy: an unpublished note makes the meaning of this sentence clearer: 'In loving a person one wants to get over one's envy of that person' (*W* 10: 3 [1] 204).

enemy in one's friend: cf. Emerson: 'Let [your friend] be to thee for ever a sort of beautiful enemy, untamable, devoutly revered' (*Essays 1*, 'Friendship').

50 *loosen his own chains*: one of Nietzsche's most personal and poignant notes reads: 'There is a false saying: "Whoever cannot save himself—how could he save others?" But if I have the key to your chains, why should your and my lock be the same?' (*W* 10: 5 [1] 92).

you cannot have friends: cf. Plato, *Republic*, 576a, where Socrates says of tyrannical types: 'They live their whole life without ever being friends of anyone, always one man's master or another man's slave'; also Aristotle, *Nicomachean Ethics*, 1161a33: 'In a tyranny, friendship has little or no place.'

51 *On the Thousand Goals and One*: the title of this chapter, as Laurence Lampert (*Nietzsche's Teaching: An Interpretation of 'Thus Spoke Zarathustra'* (New Haven and London, 1986), 59) has pointed out, indicates its main theme by emphasizing the one goal to come over the thousand goals there have already been ('Von tausend und Einem Ziele' instead of 'Von tausendundeinem Ziele'). It is also an allusion to the *Thousand and One Nights* (*Tausend und eine Nacht*), in which fantastic tales and intricate fabrications issue from the human imagination driven by the desire to prevail.

as its neighbour evaluates: an unpublished note reads: 'Valuations (*Wertschätzungen*) enter into all activities of the senses. Valuations enter into all functions of the organic being' (*W* 11: 26 [72]). The *schätzen* is related to *Schatz*, meaning 'treasure', which accounts for the association between 'valuing and treasure' later in this chapter.

excel over others: cf. Homer, *Iliad*, 6. 208 and 11. 784, where Glaucus and Peleus give the first part of the quotation as advice to their respective sons.

bow and arrow well: cf. *Ecce Homo*, 'Why I Am a Destiny', 3: 'To tell the truth and *shoot arrows well*, that is the Persian virtue.' Hellwald remarks on the prime importance of telling the truth in Persian culture (*Culturgeschichte*, 131). Cf. also Herodotus: '[The Persian boys] are taught three things only: to ride, to use the bow, and to speak the truth' (*The Histories*, 1. 136).

honour father and mother: this refers to the Jews. See Exodus 20: 12: 'Honour thy father and thy mother; that thy days may be long upon the land which the Lord thy God giveth thee.' (Cf. also Ephesians 6: 2.)

another people: both Kaufmann and R. J. Hollingdale take this as referring to the Germans, but I agree with Lampert (*Nietzsche's Teaching*, 62) that it is more plausibly an allusion to the Romans as depicted in Virgil's *Aeneid*.

52 *origin of the herd*: in his notebooks Nietzsche writes this about the relation of the I to the herd: 'The I first in the herd. The opposite: in the *Overhuman* the Thou of the many I's from millennia has become one. (thus *individuals* have now become one' (*W* 10: 4 [188]); 'Once the I was hidden in the herd: and now the herd is still hidden in the I' (*W* 10: 5 [1] 273).

of this beast?: cf. Plato, *Republic*, 588c–590b, where the desires of the lowest part of the soul are imagined as 'a many-headed beast' that is 'terrible, great, and many-formed'—and so needs to be kept in check by the human and the lion above it.

53 *love of the neighbour . . . yourselves*: cf. Leviticus 19: 18, Matthew 22: 39, and Mark 12: 31, where it is written: 'Thou shalt love thy neighbour as thyself.'

of the farthest!: *Nächstenliebe* ('love of the neighbour') could also mean 'love of the nearest', and this is the basis for the play between 'Nächsten-Flucht' ('flight from the neighbour/the nearest') and 'Fernsten-Liebe' ('love of the farthest'), the latter turning out at the end of the speech to be love of the Overhuman.

. . . when one has none: when this saying appears in the notebooks it is followed by the words: '—said Timon' (*W* 10: 3 [1] 302), probably a reference to the legendary misanthrope Timon of Athens.

56 *your own flame*: cf. *Hyperion*: 'Now I singed myself in my own flame no more' (1. 1. 9).

57 *under your cloak?*: cf. Plato, *Phaedrus*, 228d, where Socrates asks Phaedrus whether he is hiding under his cloak the text of the speech about love that he has offered to summarize.

to my soul: the little old woman's speech is distinguished by being addressed to Zarathustra's soul, to a deeper part of his psyche than his everyday personality, which otherwise only Zarathustra himself addresses.

58 *world became perfect!*: the theme of the world's becoming perfect assumes great importance in 'At Midday' (4. 10).

no thing is impossible?: cf. Luke 1: 37, where the angel Gabriel says to the Virgin Mary: 'For with God no thing is impossible' (Luther).

don't forget the whip!: note that the infamous 'whip' remark is not made by Zarathustra, but is a little truth given to him by the little old woman. By the time of 'The Other Dance-Song' (3. 15. 1) it becomes clear that Zarathustra has followed her advice, insofar as he uses his whip to try to make the figure of Life dance to his measure.

59 *an adder . . . in pain*: cf. Genesis 3: 1–7, where Adam and Eve, prompted by the serpent, lose their innocence in the vicinity of a fig-tree. Also Acts 28: 1–6, where Paul is bitten by a snake but is unharmed.

59 *with the cursing!*: cf. Matthew 5: 44, where Jesus says: 'Love your enemies, bless them that curse you, do good to them that hate you'; and also Romans 12: 14: 'Bless them which persecute you: bless, and curse not.'

60 *kill him too!*: probably an allusion to Machiavelli's recommendation that, if one is going to injure someone, it is best to employ sufficient force to preclude retaliation (*The Prince*, ch. 3).

61 *limps up . . . join together!*: the heavenly net and limping god are allusions to the story of Hephaestus, Aphrodite, and Ares in Book 8 of the *Odyssey*, while the joining together comes from Matthew 19: 6: 'What therefore God hath joined together, let not man put asunder.'

62 *beautiful festivals*: cf. *Hyperion*: 'But one alone holds his festivals among you; and that is Death' (1. 1. 11); also Herodotus (*The Histories*, 1. 31), where Solon tells the story of Cleobis and Biton, young men who die after pulling their mother in an ox-cart to the festival of Hera.

die thus . . . great soul: a variation on 'the wisdom of Silenus', companion of Dionysus, first mentioned by Nietzsche in *The Birth of Tragedy* (sec. 3): 'What is best of all is for you quite unattainable: not to be born . . . But the second-best for you is—to die soon.' Cf. the chorus in *Oedipus at Colonus* by Sophocles: 'Not to be born at all is best, far best that can befall. Next best, when born, with least delay to trace the backward way' (1. 1225, quoted as the epigraph to vol. 2 of Hölderlin's *Hyperion*).

a thief . . . as Lord: cf. 1 Thessalonians 5: 2, where Paul writes: 'For yourselves know perfectly that the day of the Lord so cometh as a thief in the night' (Luther). In *The Phenomenology of Spirit* (VI. A. a) Hegel refers to death as 'the Lord' of the individual.

63 *the Hebrew Jesus*: 'Jesus' is the only personal proper name other than 'Zarathustra' to occur in the entire text (aside from a mention of 'Noah's ark').

65 *coiled around the sun*: cf. Exodus 4: 2–4, where the Lord transforms the staff of Moses into a serpent and back again, and the opening scene of the *Iliad*, where the priest Chryses carries a golden staff wound with the wreaths of Apollo. The *ringelte* ('was coiled') tightens the connection between the serpent and the *ring* of eternal recurrence.

cats and wolves?: this is the first time that Zarathustra addresses his 'disciples' as such. A note from the period reads: 'What do you have in common with wolves and cats? which always only take and never give and would rather even steal than take?' (*W* 10: 4 [100]).

66 *called necessity*: there is a play here between *Wende aller Not* ('turn of all need') and *Notwendigkeit* ('necessity'), one that recurs in the Third Part in connection with Zarathustra's will ('On Old and New Tablets', 3. 12. 30) and his soul ('On the Great Yearning', 3. 14). In a letter to his friend Malwida von Meysenbug, Nietzsche writes of his solitude as his *Not*—a word with many meanings: need, difficulty, danger, deprivation, anguish, distress, trouble. He then writes: 'In this way I am trying to "turn around" (*wenden*) all my necessities (*Notwendigkeiten*)' (*B* 1 Feb. 1883).

The idea is that when the will realizes itself fully as 'will to power' it can turn its distress into its necessity, into something that—although it may seem 'negative'—it needs in order to be fully itself. For a helpful discussion of this idea, see Keiji Nishitani, *The Self-Overcoming of Nihilism*, trans. Graham Parkes with Setsuko Aihara (Albany, NY, 1990), ch. 4, sec. 3.

67 *heal thyself*: cf. Luke 4: 23, where Jesus says: 'Ye will surely say unto me this proverb, Physician, heal thyself.'

a chosen people grow: cf. Isaiah 43: 20, where the Lord, as 'creator of Israel', refers to 'my people, my chosen'.

68 *Alone I go . . . alone*: this section in based on John 13: 36, where Jesus says to Peter: 'Whither I go, there thou canst not follow me now'; and John 16: 32, where he says to his disciples, 'Ye shall be scattered, every man to his own, and leave me alone'.

a statue fall and kill you!: cf. Aristotle, *Poetics*, 1452a7–10, where he mentions the incident where 'Mitys' statue at Argos killed the murderer of Mitys, by falling on him as he looked at it'.

return to you: cf. Matthew 10: 33, where Jesus says to his disciples: 'But whosoever shall deny me before men, him will I also deny before my Father which is in Heaven.'

Dead are all Gods: in an unpublished note Nietzsche writes: 'The first book as a *graveside eulogy* on the death of *God*' (*W* 9: 12 [21]).

SECOND PART

69 *[epigraph]*: in a letter to his friend Heinrich Köselitz (who composed music under the name of 'Peter Gast'), Nietzsche writes of the epigraph: 'From this motto there emerge—it is almost unseemly to say this to a musician—different harmonies and modulations from those of Part One. The main thing was to *swing oneself up to the second level*—in order from there to reach the *third*' (*B* 13 July 1883).

71 *cast forth his seed*: cf. Matthew 13: 3–9, where Jesus tells the multitude the parable of the sower.

called wheat!: cf. Matthew 13: 24–30, where Jesus tells the parable of the tares, where 'an enemy' secretly plants weeds in the field where a man had sown 'good seed' for wheat.

72 *toward rising and setting*: cf. Psalms 50: 1, where the Lord calls to the world from the 'rising' of the sun to its 'setting' (Luther).

way to the sea!: cf. *Hyperion*, 1. 1. 7, where Hyperion likens his soul and his friend Alabanda's to 'two streams rolling down from the mountain' that are eventually 'united in a majestic river on their way to the far sea'.

the Isles of the Blest: referred to in Hesiod, *Works and Days*, 166 f.; Pindar, *Olympian Odes*, II 70 ff.; and Plato, *Republic*, 519c–d. In a letter to Köselitz, Nietzsche laments the fate of Ischia, a small island off the coast from Naples that had been devastated by an earthquake shortly before: 'That island has always stayed with me: when you have read the whole of *Zarathustra II* it will be clear to you *where* my "Isles of the Blest" lie' (*B* 16 Aug. 1883).

72 *The spear that I hurl . . . is raging over their heads*: cf. Wagner's *Parsifal*, Act II, where Klingsor hurls the spear at Parsifal and it remains hovering over his head.

73 *Upon the Isles of the Blest*: the title of this chapter ('Auf den glückseligen Inseln'), like that of the previous one, is distinguished from the titles of the chapters in the First Part by not beginning with the preposition *Von* (On). To mark this distinction I have used 'In' rather than the more natural 'On'.

ripe figs: cf. Mark 11: 12–14, where Jesus and his disciples, being hungry on their way from Bethany to Jerusalem, come across a fig-tree which Jesus curses because it is not yet bearing fruit.

74 *. . . mere allegory!*: a parodic inversion of the famous couplet at the beginning of the Chorus Mysticus that concludes Goethe's *Faust*: 'All impermanence | is a mere parable' (*Faust II*, 12104–5).

a hundred souls . . . final hours: an upublished note makes it clear that Zarathustra is not speaking here of reincarnation across a series of lives, but rather of deaths and rebirths within one and the same lifetime: 'One must want to pass away in order to be able to arise again—from one day to the next. *Transformation* through a hundred souls—let that be your life, your fate: And then finally: to will this entire series over again!' (*W* 10: 5 [1], 227).

75 *red cheeks*: cf. Emerson: 'The cool disengaged air of natural objects, makes them enviable to us, chafed and irritable creatures with red faces' (*Essays* 1, 'Nature').

76 *blessèd in their pitying*: cf. Matthew 5: 7, where Jesus says, in the Sermon on the Mount: 'Blest are the merciful: for they shall obtain mercy.'

gnawing worm: cf. Emerson: 'We do not quite forgive a giver. The hand that feeds us is in some danger of being bitten' (*Essays* 1, 'Gifts').

77 *foolishness . . . who pity?*: cf. the main theme of Wagner's *Parsifal*: 'Made wise by pity, | the pure fool.'

my neighbour like me: cf. Matthew 22: 37–9, where Jesus says to the lawyer: 'Thou shalt love thy neighbour as thyself.'

78 *from their redeemer!*: Nietzsche often writes of the need to be redeemed from the redeemer with respect to Wagner, playing off the final words of *Parsifal*: 'Redemption to the Redeemer!' See also his letter to Köselitz of 11 Aug. 1888; *W* 13: 14 [52], 35, 20–7; and *The Case of Wagner* (Postscript).

79 *on your knees, ye sinners!*: in a letter written in Rome to Overbeck, Nietzsche mentions his amazement at seeing the faithful 'going up the sacred steps on their knees' (*B* 20 May 1883).

80 *my shield*: an unpublished note makes it clear that Zarathustra uses beauty as a 'shield' to defend himself against those who are virtuous in the conventional sense (*W* 10: 9 [17]).

82 *just avenged!*: in German the words for 'just' (*gerecht*) and 'avenged' (*gerächt*) sound the same.

to abase others: cf. Luke 18: 14, where Jesus ends the parable of the Pharisee and the publican by saying: 'For every one that exalteth himself shall be abased; and he that humbleth himself shall be exalted.'

84 *with closed ears*: in his letters Nietzsche often writes of his fondness for living in countries (such as Italy) where he is less than fluent in the language.

85 *snowflakes in June!*: a letter to Overbeck makes it clear that passages like this refer to meteorological conditions around Sils-Maria when Nietzsche was working on the manuscript there (*B* 18 July 1884).

neighbours to the sun: two variant passages in the unpublished notes have 'nearness to death' instead of 'neighbours to the sun' (*W* 10: 10 [22]; 13 [9]).

88 *tie me fast . . . whirlpool of vengeance!*: cf. Homer, *Odyssey*, 12: 158 ff., where Odysseus has his crewmen bind him to the mast so that he will be able to hear the song of the Sirens without succumbing to it. The 'whirl-pool' is an allusion to Charybdis, which they pass not long after their encounter with the Sirens.

89 *the voice of God*: an allusion to the adage, *Vox populi, vox dei* (the voice of the people is the voice of god).

90 *into which he gazed*: an allusion to Oedipus in Sophocles' *Oedipus at Colonus*, for Nietzsche the archetypal 'wise man'—blinded by his attempt to 'stare into the sun' and 'the terrifying interior of nature' in pursuit of 'Dionysian wisdom' (*The Birth of Tragedy*, sec. 9).

to move mountains: cf. 1 Corinthians 13: 2: 'And though I have all faith, so that I could move mountains, and have not charity, I am nothing'; cf. also Matthew 17: 20.

lukewarm: cf. Revelation 3: 16: 'So then because thou art lukewarm, and neither cold not hot, I will spue thee out of my mouth.'

91 *The Night-Song*: Nietzsche worked on 'The Night-Song' in May of 1883 while living in lodgings on the Piazza Barberini in Rome, overlooking the famous 'Tritone' fountain. At the end of his career he would refer to 'The Night-Song' as 'the loneliest song that was ever composed': 'at that time a melody of indescribable melancholy would always be with me, whose refrain I found again in the words "dead from immortality . . ."' (*EH*, 'Why I Write Such Good Books', *Thus Spoke Zarathustra*, 4). In the same work he cites 'The Night-Song' in its entirety (except for the 'Thus sang Zarathustra' at the end) as a prime example of the Dionysian dithyramb (ibid. 7).

blessèd than taking: cf. Acts 20: 35, where Paul quotes Jesus as saying: 'It is more blessed to give than to receive.'

93 *little god . . . eyes closed*: in the letter to Köselitz about Ischia mentioned above, Nietzsche writes: ' "Cupido dancing with the maidens" is immediately understandable only in Ischia . . . No sooner did I finish my poetic composition than the island collapsed in on itself' (*B* 16 Aug. 1883). On Ischia, see note to 'Isles of the Blest' above (p. 297).

'Lord of the world.'—: cf. Ephesians 6: 12: 'For we wrestle not against flesh and blood, but against principalities, against powers, against the Lords of the world who rule in the darkness of this world, against evil spirits under heaven' (Luther).

that Zarathustra sang: Zarathustra's interaction with Life in the following section is reminiscent of Hyperion's relations with Diotima, a beautiful woman of superior wisdom, especially as depicted in *Hyperion* 1. 2. 17.

94 *between two pairs of eyes*: *unter vier Augen* (lit. 'among four eyes') is an idiom meaning 'in confidence', but it is important not to lose the 'eyes' in the translation.

95 *visions and apparitions*: the word translated as 'visions', *Gesichter*, can also mean 'faces'. There is also a play, which recurs in this section and several times later in the text, between *Blicke* ('glances') and *Augenblicke* ('moments': literally, 'eye-glances/looks'). The theme of the moment culminates in 'On the Vision and Riddle' (3. 2) with the first full presentation of the idea of eternal recurrence.

96 *'Divine shall all beings be to me'*: this saying, as well as 'All days shall be holy to me', is adapted from a passage from Emerson's *Essays* of which Nietzsche was especially fond, and which he used for the epigraph to *The Joyful Science* (1882). The original reads: 'To the poet, to the philosopher, to the saint, all things are friendly and sacred, all events profitable, all days holy, all men divine' (*Essays 1*, 'History'). In a letter to Overbeck written on the Christmas after the painful foundering of his relationship with Lou Salomé, Nietzsche writes: 'I have here the most beautiful opportunity to demonstrate that "all experiences are useful, all days holy, and all human beings are divine" to me !!!!' (*B* 25 Dec. 1882).

omens from birds: Nietzsche uses the term *Vogelzeichen* (literally, 'bird-signs') in connection with his relationship with Lou Salomé, whom he took at first to be 'an eagle' (letter to Köselitz, and a fragment addressed to Salomé, *B* 4 Aug. 1882).

97 *disgusts him*: in the Colli–Montinari edition the *ekelt* ('disgusts') has been replaced by *ekelte* ('disgusted').

hurting them the most: in a letter to Jacob Burckhardt accompanying a copy of the newly published book, Nietzsche writes about *Zarathustra*: 'At some point one empties one's heart and the *benefit* that he does himself is so great that he can hardly comprehend *how much pain* he is thereby inflicting on all other people' (*B* 1 May 1833).

How could I bear it?: 'Wie ertrug ich's nur?' A quotation from Wagner, *Tristan und Isolde*, Act II, which was for many years Nietzsche's favourite opera.

only in the heel: this condition makes Zarathustra a kind of anti-type to the hero Achilles, who could be wounded only in the heel.

98 *resurrections.*—: cf. Matthew 27: 51–3: 'And the earth did quake, and the rocks rent; and the graves were opened; and many bodies of the saints which slept arose, and came out of the graves after his resurrection' (Luther).

99 *the way of all the living*: I follow Lampert in translating the term *Art*, which also means 'kind' or 'species', as 'way' here and in the next sentence: see his discussion of the issue (*Nietzsche's Teaching*, 112–14).

tell to me: this secret is addressed to Zarathustra alone, as indicated by the singular form of the imperative 'Behold', whereas in the next sentence Life uses the plural form in 'you call it will to procreate'. She reverts to the singular five paragraphs later, to single out Zarathustra when she says: 'And even you, who understand.'

100 *to solve the riddle of your hearts*: Zarathustra's rhetorical situation here is comparable to that of Socrates in Plato's *Symposium* (212b), after he has told his fellow guests what the wise priestess Diotima taught him about the true nature of human love and life.

overflowing of your souls: 'overflowing' (*Überwallen*) echoes Hölderlin's *Hyperion*: 'And he wished to pour out the overflowing soul, like sacrificial wine, into the abyss of life' (2. 6).

a creator: here *Schöpfer* (as in 'God the creator') rather than *Schaffender*, which is Zarathustra's preferred term for 'creator'.

101 *taste and tasting!*: an allusion to the adage, *De gustibus non est disputandum*, 'there's no arguing about taste'. Judgements of taste and the sublime are the main topics of the first half of Kant's *Critique of Judgement* (1790). In an early, unpublished work Nietzsche makes the connection between the Greek for 'wise' (*sophos*) and 'to taste' (*sapiô*), arguing for taste as being central to the philosophical enterprise (*Philosophy in the Tragic Age of the Greeks*, 3. 2; also *Assorted Opinions and Maxims*, 170).

102 *powerful one . . . self-overpowering*: one would normally want to translate *Gewaltiger* as 'violent one' to distinguish it from the *Macht* (power) just referred to, but 'powerful one' replicates the play between *Gewaltiger* and *Überwältigung* ('overpowering').

103 *shudder with godlike desires*: 'vor göttlichen Begierden schaudern', an allusion to the Roman philosophical poet Lucretius, whose reaction to a mystical opening up of the natural cosmos is 'a sort of godlike delight and a shuddering' (*De rerum natura*, 3. 28 f.). Cf. also Goethe's Faust: 'Shuddering is the human being's best part' (*Faust II*, 6272).

abandoned her . . . the over-hero.—: an unpublished note from the period reads as follows: 'Dionysus on a tiger: the skull of a goat: a panther.

Ariadne dreaming: "Abandoned by the hero [Theseus] I dream of the overhero." Not to mention Dionysus!' (*W* 10: 13 [1], p. 433).

103 *On the Land of Culture*: *Bildung* ('culture') also means 'education'. Cognates such as *Bild* (image) and *bilden* (to form, mould) figure prominently in this chapter.

colourfully sprinkled!: 'Buntgesprenkeltes', perhaps an allusion to Greek *poikilos*, the word Socrates uses in Plato's *Republic* to characterize democracy as the most motley and multicoloured of regimes (557c).

104 *a day-labourer in the underworld*: Zarathustra again appears as the opposite of Achilles (*Odyssey* 11, 488–91), who tells Odysseus that he would rather be a hired labourer on earth than a king in Hades.

'Everything is worthy of perishing': almost a direct quotation of Mephistopheles's words to Faust in Goethe's *Faust I* (1339–40).

105 *to make . . . a little female!*: cf. Genesis 2: 21–2, where the Lord removes a rib from the sleeping Adam and makes Eve from it.

from all father- and mother-lands: Nietzsche became stateless when he left Germany to take up a professorship in Switzerland at the age of 24. Although Basel was a more cosmopolitan place than any he had lived in before, he eventually found the society there dull and stifling.

On Immaculate Perception: 'Von der unbefleckten Erkenntnis'. I have translated *Erkenntnis* as 'perception' here in an attempt to reproduce the play on *unbefleckte Empfängnis* ('Immaculate Conception'). The main point of the chapter is that 'pure understanding', in which one chastely backs away from the object in order to avoid all contact except through the eyes, is barren—just as the moon is barren and merely reflects borrowed light. This is contrasted with the 'solar love' of the one who truly understands, whose rich overflow brings out the heart of the object by nourishing its life. The grammatical genders of moon and sun in German are masculine and feminine respectively, and at the climax of the chapter the 'creator-desire' of the sun is imagined as a thirst that elicits the emergence of a thousand wave-breasts from the (grammatically neuter) sea.

107 *Loving and going-under . . . for eternities*: 'Lieben und Untergehn' do not actually rhyme very closely in German.

you habitual liars?: cf. Matthew 12: 34, where Jesus says: 'O generation of vipers, how can ye, being evil, speak good things? For out of the overflow of the heart the mouth speaketh' (Luther).

under the table: cf. Psalms 119: 141: 'I am tiny and despised: yet do not I forget thy precepts'; and Luke 16: 20–1, where the beggar Lazarus is said to desire 'to be fed with the crumbs which fell from the rich man's table'. Cf. also Matthew 15: 27, Mark 7: 28.

ringworm has crawled: cf. *Hyperion*, where Alabanda asks the protagonist: 'Shall the God in us, to whom the path of infinity lies open, stand and wait until the worm crawls out of his way?' (1. 1. 7) The word translated by 'mask', *Larve*, also means 'larva', which anticipates the ringworm imagery.

109 *the stockings of the spirit!*: an allusion to Hegel's dictum to the effect that, in the realm of spirit (as self-consciousness), a darned sock is not better than a torn one: 'Ein geflickter Strumpf besser als ein zerrissener; nicht so das Selbstbewußtsein.'

110 *inside my dovecote*: an allusion to the image of the remembering mind as an aviary in Plato's *Theaetetus*, 197–200.

belief in me: cf. Mark 16: 16, where Jesus says: 'He that believeth and is baptized shall be blessed' (Luther).

The Eternal Feminine: a translation of Goethe's 'das Ewig-Weibliche', Nietzsche's quotation of which here echoes his use of *Weibchen* in the previous two sentences, the diminutive suffix (*-chen*) of which has a pejorative connotation (hence 'female'). Goethe's famous dictum, 'Das Ewig-Weiblich zieht uns hinan' (*Faust* II, 12111), is alluded to a few lines below, when Zarathustra says: 'Verily, we are drawn ever upward.'

111 *... themselves dream!*: cf. 'There are more things in Heaven and earth than are dreamed of in your philosophy' (*Hamlet*, I. v. 166).

112 *... a stone*: cf. Matthew 7: 9, where Jesus asks: 'Or what man is there of you, whom if his son ask bread, will he give him a stone?'

fire-mountain: Nietzsche uses here the term *Feuerberg* ('fire-mountain') rather than the more usual *Vulkan* (volcano), which tends to confirm C. G. Jung's claim that several elements in this episode derive from a story recounted in Justinus Kerner's *Blätter aus Prevorst* (Karlsruhe, 1833). Jung suggests, quite plausibly, that the young Nietzsche came across this text in the library of his maternal grandfather, and that the *Zarathustra* passage derives from a case of 'cryptomnesia', where Nietzsche reproduced many of the details of the story without consciously remembering their source (C. G. Jung, *Collected Works*, trans. R. F. C. Hull (New York: Pantheon Books, 1957), i. 82–4 and 101–5). The first paragraph of 'On Great Events' echoes these two questions in Kerner's text: 'Is there a connection between this fire-Hell and our volcanoes? . . . Are the craters of fire-mountains gates to this flaming hell?' (*Blätter aus Prevorst*, 48–61, 52 f.). The dramatic setting of the chapter also derives from the six months Nietzsche spent in a villa in Sorrento with a view of Vesuvius (see his letters from Oct. 1876 to May 1877), as well as from his memories of visiting Mount Etna in Sicily (1882).

113 *way to Hell!'*—: Kerner reproduces a passage from the log of a ship named *Sphinx* which was sailing in the Mediterranean in 1686. Four English captains and a merchant go ashore on the island of Mount Stromboli to shoot rabbits. To their amazement they see two men fly over them and into the crater of the volcano. One of the captains recognizes one of the flying men as his close neighbour, Mr Bootty, from Wapping (in England). When they get back to port in Gravesend on the Thames, the captain's wife greets him with the news that old Mr Bootty

has died. The captain replies immediately: 'We all saw him going down to hell!'

113 *this skin has diseases*: cf. Schopenhauer's grim characterization of the place of life in the universe: 'In infinite space there are countless shining spheres, and around each one revolve a dozen or so smaller, illuminated ones, which are hot within and covered by a hardened, cold skin, on which a mouldy coating has engendered living and knowing beings' (*The World as Will and Representation*, 2. 1, 3). Speculating in a similarly unanthropocentric vein on the insignificance of the tiny 'drop of life' in the vast universe, Nietzsche surmises that the number of stars at the centre of systems capable of supporting life is 'a mere handful by comparison with the infinite number that have never had an exudation of life or have long since recovered from it' (*The Wanderer and His Shadow*, 14).

114 *drink . . . from the sea*: cf. the description of the Behemoth in Job 40: 23: 'Behold, he drinketh up a river, and hasteth not.'

mud close by: cf. Job 40: 21, on the Behemoth again: 'He lieth under the shady trees, in the covert of the reed, and the mud' (Luther).

115 *from wrath and envy*: cf. the description of God's great power in the Leviathan in Job 41: 19–21, 33—'Out of his mouth go burning lamps, and sparks of fire leap out. | Out of his nostrils goeth smoke, as out of a seething pot or cauldron. | His breath kindleth coals, and a flame goeth out of his mouth . . . Upon earth there is not his like.'

earth is of gold: cf. *Hyperion*: 'When all was still, as in the depths of the earth, where gold mysteriously grows' (1. 2. 17).

116 *all has been!'*: the words of the preacher in the first chapter of Ecclesiastes (1: 10), where he asks: 'Is there any thing whereof it may be said, See, this is new?' and answers: 'It hath been already of old time, which was before us.' The soothsayer is clearly a portrait of Nietzsche's erstwhile mentor Schopenhauer, a fact that becomes especially obvious when the soothsayer returns in the Fourth Part.

117 *Alpa! . . . ashes up the mountain?*: a note dating from 1880 or 1881 reads: '*Dreams*: eating the toad.—"Alpa Alpa, who is carrying his ashes to the mountain?"—the blood-coloured moon' (*W* 9: 10 [B26]). A good friend of Nietzsche's makes the following report in the course of a reminiscence of their friendship: 'Nietzsche told me with a laugh that in a dream he had had to climb up an endless mountain path; high up, below the mountain-peak, he had been about to walk past a cave when out of the dark depths a voice called to him: "Alpa, Alpa—who is carrying his ashes up the mountain?" ' Reinhard von Seydlitz, *Wann, warum, was und wie ich schrieb* (Gotha, 1900), 36.

118 *a colourful pavilion*: the term translated by 'pavilion', *Gezelt*, occurs in Luther's Bible (e.g. Psalms 27: 5 and 76: 3), in places where the King James Version has 'tabernacle'.

with a strange look: cf. Plato, *Phaedo*, 60b, where Socrates sits upright on his bed and comments to his friends on how strange a phenomenon pleasure is.

119 *cripples and beggars surrounded him*: cf. Matthew 15: 30: 'And great multitudes came unto him, having with them those that were lame, blind, dumb, crippled, and many others, and cast them down at Jesus' feet; and he healed them' (Luther).

cripples believe in Zarathustra!: cf. Matthew 11: 5, where Jesus says: 'The blind receive their sight, and the lame walk, the lepers are cleansed, and the deaf hear, the dead are raised up, and the poor have the gospel preached to them.'

120 *I call such beings*: cf. Emerson: 'Among the multitude of scholars and authors, we feel no hallowing presence . . . their talent is some exaggerated faculty, some overgrown member, so that their strength is a disease' (*Essays* 1, 'The Oversoul').

An ear as large as a human being!: Nietzsche was probably familiar with the well-known cartoon of Wagner that appeared in *L'Éclipse* in Paris on 18 April 1869, portraying him as not much more than a gigantic ear.

fragments . . . no human beings!: this imagery echoes Schiller's concern (in the sixth letter of *On the Aesthetic Education of Man*) with a pernicious fragmentation of individuals that he sees as characteristic of the modern age. Cf. also Hölderlin's devastating criticisms of the Germans for being prone to lose their humanity through over-specialization: '[One sees] no human beings—is it not like a battlefield where hands and arms and limbs of all kinds lie dismembered in heaps' (*Hyperion*, 2. 2. 7). And Emerson again: 'The state of society is one in which the members have suffered amputation from the trunk, and strut about so many walking monsters—a good finger, a neck, a stomach, an elbow, but never a man' ('The American Scholar').

121 *composing and striving*: a translation of 'Dichten und Trachten', an idiomatic expression meaning 'thoughts and endeavours' (or 'meditations and musings') which is used memorably by Luther (Genesis 6: 5). *Dichten* (to write, compose poetry) echoes the *Dichter* (poet) of a few lines above, but there are also overtones here of its other meanings (to compress, condense, thicken), which I have tried to convey by translating *Dichter* as 'composer' in the next sentence. The musical connotation is apt, since *Tondichter* means a composer of music.

cannot roll away: cf. Luke 24: 2, where after the Resurrection the women 'found the stone rolled away from the sepulchre'.

122 *deserves to pass away!*: what madness preaches is: 'Alles vergeht, darum ist Alles wert zu vergehn.' Cf. Mephistopheles, just after announcing himself as 'the spirit that constantly negates': 'denn alles, was entsteht, | Ist wert, dass es zu Grunde geht' ('for all that arises deserves to perish'; *Faust I*, 1339–40).

devour its children: an allusion to the decision of Kronos to devour his children as soon as they are born, in order to prevent their usurping his kingly rule (Hesiod, *Theogony*, 459 ff.). Cf. also the extant fragment from the pre-Socratic Greek philosopher Anaximander on the destruction of things, which happens 'according to necessity; for they pay penalty and retribution to each other for their injustice according to the assessment of time (*chronos*)'. Nietzsche discusses this fragment at the beginning of section 4 of the unpublished *Philosophy in the Tragic Age of the Greeks*.

123 *want back*: the term *Zurückwollen* can also mean 'willing backwards', but I have chosen 'wanting back' in order to emphasize the allusion to the willing of eternal recurrence. Cf. the recurrence of this verb at the end of section 10 of 'The Drunken Song' (4. 19).

to his disciples?: cf. Matthew 13: 10–11, where Jesus, after telling to 'great multitudes' the parable of the sower and the seed, explains to his disciples why he speaks otherwise to them than to the multitudes.

124 *Come on, old heart!*: 'Wohlauf, altes Herz!' The *wohlauf*, from now on a common interjection of Zarathustra's, is also used in Luther's Bible (though not as often as *wohlan*), where the King James Version has 'Come ye' or 'Arise'.

125 *twelve shoes wide and three months long!*: Gustav Naumann suggests that these two expressions come from archaic German legal language (*Zarathustra-Commentar* (Leipzig, 1899–1901), ii. 165).

have good hunting!: insofar as Nietzsche is always, like Zarathustra, on the hunt for insights and flashes of understanding, he follows in the footsteps of Plato and Socrates. Cf. especially the trilogy, *Theaetetus*, *Sophist*, and *Statesman*, where the hunts are for 'knowledges' imagined as wild birds, the nature of the sophist, and the distinctive features of the statesman, respectively. (On this topic, see my *Composing the Soul: Reaches of Nietzsche's Psychology* (Chicago and London, 1994), 215–19.)

soar into different futures: cf. Plato's description of a thinker gripped by the fourth kind of divine madness, erotic *mania*: 'when he sees beauty on earth, remembering true beauty, he feels his wings growing and longs to stretch them for an upward flight, but cannot do so, and, like a bird, gazes upward and neglects the things below' (*Phaedrus*, 249d).

126 *The Stillest Hour*: Plato, *Sophist*, 263e, where thought is said to be 'the soul's conversation with itself without sound'.

the clock of my life drew breath: cf. Goethe's *Faust*, where Mephistopheles says, 'The clock stands still—' and the Chorus replies, 'Stands still! It is silent as midnight. | The clock-hand falls' (*Faust II*, 11593).

127 *moves valleys and lowlands*: cf 1 Corinthians 13: 2; 'And though I have the gift of prophecy, and understand all mysteries, and all knowledge; and though I have all faith, so that I could remove mountains, and have not charity, I am nothing.'

dew falls . . . most silent: cf. Deuteronomy 32: 1–2, where Moses says: 'My doctrine shall drop as the rain, my speech shall distill as the dew, as the small rain upon the tender herb, and as the showers upon the grass.'

for commanding: in the Colli–Montinari edition the word *allem* has been added between *zu* and *Befehlen*: 'I lack the lion's voice for any commanding.'

doves' feet direct the world: cf. Emerson, 'But real action is in silent moments. The epochs of our life are not in the visible facts of our choice of a calling, our marriage, our acquisition of an office, and the like, but in a silent thought by the way-side as we walk; in a thought which revises our entire manner of life, and says—"Thus hast thou done, but it were better thus" ' (*Essays* 1, 'Spiritual Laws'). Zarathustra's expression *Taubenfüssen* ('doves' feet') is also used to mean 'quote-marks', which may suggest the special power that great thoughts have when they are quotable.

128 *more to give to you!*: cf. John 16: 12, where Jesus says to his disciples: 'I have yet many things to say unto you, but ye cannot hear them now.'

THIRD PART

131 *one experiences only oneself*: cf. Emerson, in one of the young Nietzsche's favourite essays: '[A man] thinks his fate alien, because the copula is hidden. But the soul contains the event that shall befall it, for the event is only the actualization of its thoughts ... A man will see his character emitted in the events that seem to meet, but which exude from and accompany him' ('Fate', *The Conduct of Life*).

132 *what makes hard!*: in a letter to Overbeck, Nietzsche writes: 'I believe that you know what Zarathustra's admonition "Become hard!" means in relation to myself. My sense of how to do justice to each individual, and to treat precisely what is basically most hostile *to me* with the greatest mildness, is *overdeveloped* and brings one danger after another, not only for me but also for my task. Here a hardening is necessary and, for the sake of education, occasional cruelty' (*B* 30 Apr. 1884).

butter and honey—flow!: cf. Exodus 3: 8, where the Lord says he will deliver his people to 'a land flowing with milk and honey', and Isaiah 7: 15: 'Butter and honey shall he eat, that he may know to refuse the evil, and choose the good.'

out of the sea: cf. *Hyperion*: 'They must arise, they must come forth, like young mountains from out of the sea, when their subterranean fire drives them' (1. 2. 19).

133 *wept bitterly*: cf. Matthew 26: 75, where Peter, after denying Jesus thrice, 'wept bitterly'.

134 *searchers, tempters, experimenters*: there is a play here between *Sucher* (searchers, seekers) and *Versucher* (tempters, experimenters): I have used both 'tempters' and 'experimenters' to translate *Versucher*, since Nietzsche often refers to his own philosophy as *versucherisch* in the dual

sense of 'experimental' (in the spirit of Montaigne and Emerson, something to be tried out or tested in the reader's own experience) and also 'seductive' (above all in its poetic style).

134   *half dwarf, half mole*: there is a parallel between Zarathustra's encounter with the dwarf and Siegfried's encounter with the dwarf Mime in Wagner's *Siegfried*.

135   *philosopher's stone*: 'Stein der Weisheit'—literally 'stone of wisdom' (usually 'Stein der Weisen').

ringing play: 'klingendes Spiel', alludes to the ringing of the blade (*Klinge*) of a sword in combat, but also has a connotation of the sound of a military band.

One more time!: an allusion to the thought of recurrence: see the presentation of the idea in *Beyond Good and Evil*, aphorism 56.

let him hear.—: cf. e.g. Matthew 11: 15, Mark 4: 9, Luke 8: 8, 14: 35: 'He that hath ears to hear, let him hear!'

138   *bear to die right now!—*: cf. Tristan's 'Yearning! Yearning—to yearn in dying, not to die from yearning!' and Isolde's 'How did I bear it then? How can I bear it still?' in Acts III and II of Wagner's *Tristan und Isolde*.

clear sky and open sea: in a letter to his mother and sister from Genoa, Nietzsche writes: 'When the sun shines I always walk to a lonely rock by the sea and lie there in the open under my parasol, like a lizard; that has cured my headache on several occasions. Sea and clear sky!' (*B* 8 Jan. 1881).

140   *burrowing . . . no longer tremble?*: there is a play here between *graben* (burrowing) and the *Gräber* (graves) of a few lines earlier. Several months after being struck by the thought of eternal recurrence in August of 1881, Nietzsche writes to his friend Köselitz: 'I am not yet ripe enough for the elemental thoughts that I want to convey in these final books [projected as supplements to *Dawn of Morning*]. There is one thought among them that will in fact take "millennia" to come into its own. Where can I find the courage to express it!' (*B* 25 Jan. 1882).

I see no end: cf. the Wanderer in Act III of Wagner's *Siegfried*: 'I summon you: up! up! . . . Dreaming see my end!'

142   *Yea- and Amen-saying*: cf. 2 Corinthians 1: 20, where Paul writes: 'For all the promise of God in him are Yea, and in him Amen, unto the glory of God by us.'

143   *azure bell and eternal security*: cf. this passage from Emerson: 'In childhood, we fancied ourselves walled in by the horizon, as by a glass bell, and doubted not, by distant travel, we should reach the baths of the descending sun and stars. On experiment, the horizon flies before us, and leaves us on an endless common, sheltered by no glass bell. Yet 'tis strange how tenaciously we cling to that bell-astronomy, of a protecting domestic horizon' (*The Conduct of Life*, 'Considerations by the Way').

Lord Contingency: 'Von Ohngefähr'. The phrase means 'by chance', but Nietzsche is playing on the use of the prefix *von* to indicate nobility (as in the name Johann Wolfgang von Goethe).

for the sake of folly . . . into all things!: there is an inversion here of the universe described by Plato in the *Timaeus*, where the Divine Craftsman 'sows' souls into the stars (41d–42d), and where the universe is ruled by reason (*nous*) except for that minimal force of irrational recalcitrance known as the 'errant cause' (*Timaeus*, 48).

145 *Take the children away!*: cf. Luke 18: 15, where Jesus is rebuked by his disciples when children are brought to him.

146 *the first servant!*: cf. the dictum of Frederick II of Prussia: 'A prince is the first servant and first magistrate of the state.'

149 *for fire!*: cf. *Hyperion*, where Alabanda cries, 'Oh let someone light for me a torch, that I may burn the weeds from the heath!' (1. 1. 7).

tongues of flame: cf. Isaiah 5: 24, concerning the fate awaiting the unjust: 'Therefore as the fire devoureth the stubble, and the flame consumeth the chaff, so their root shall be as rottenness, and their blossom shall go up as dust.' Also Acts 2: 3, on the apostles' coming together on the day of Pentecost: 'And there appeared unto them cloven tongues as of fire.'

Upon the Mount of Olives: cf. e.g. Matthew 21: 1, where Jesus enters Jerusalem via the Mount of Olives.

pot-bellied fire-idol: in letters written during winter from Genoa, Rapallo, and Nizza, Nietzsche often writes about how much he suffers from the cold since he cannot afford to buy a heating stove.

151 *like a little child!*: an allusion to Luke 18: 16, where Jesus says: 'Suffer little children to come unto me, and forbid them not: for of such is the kingdom of God.'

152 *pity on your feet!*: cf. Matthew 10: 14, where Jesus says to the twelve apostles: 'And whosoever shall not receive you, nor hear your words, when ye depart out of that house or city, shake off the dust of your feet.'

153 *the God of armies*: 'Gott der Heerscharen', cf. Psalms 103: 21: 'Bless ye the Lord, all ye his armies; ye ministers of his, that do his pleasure' (Luther). *Heerscharen* occurs rarely in the Luther Bible; the corresponding term in the King James Version is 'armies'.

spittle trickle down: cf. Isaiah 45: 8, where the Lord says: 'Trickle down, ye heavens, from above, and let the skies pour down righteousness' (Luther).

154 *Woe unto this great city!*: cf. Revelation 18: 16, where on the destruction of Babylon by fire the merchants cried, 'Woe, woe, the great city!' (Luther).

pillar of fire . . . consumed!: cf. Exodus 13: 21, where the Lord guides the Israelites out of Egypt and toward the Red Sea: 'And the Lord went before them by day in a pillar of cloud, to lead them the way; and by night in a pillar of fire, to give them light.'

155 *crawling toward the Cross*: cf. *Nietzsche contra Wagner*: 'Richard Wagner, apparently most triumphant, but in truth a decaying and despairing decadent, suddenly sank down, helpless and broken, before the Christian cross' (10. 1).

like a whale?: cf. Matthew 12: 40: 'For as Jonas was three days and three nights in the whale's belly; so shall the Son of man be three days and three nights in the heart of the earth.'

156 *wild hunt*: the *wilde Jagd* is a motif from Germanic folklore in which spectral horsemen with hounds course through the night.

157 *little children again*: cf. Matthew 18: 3, where Jesus says to his disciples: 'Except ye be converted, and become as little children, ye shall not enter into the kingdom of Heaven.'

cross-spider: the young Nietzsche will have come across the term *Kreuzspinne* (cross-spider, garden spider) in his German edition of Emerson's *The Conduct of Life*, where in this sentence from the essay 'Worship' the word 'caterpillars' is rendered as *Kreuzspinnen*: 'Men as naturally make a state, or a church, as caterpillars a web.'

spirits to come to him: Nietzsche appears to have been interested in spiritualism from an early age, as evidenced by his having read Kerner's *Blätter aus Prevorst* (see n. to p. 112, above). But in October 1882 he attended a séance in Leipzig that was supposed to be 'very important for the history of spiritism' but was a complete fiasco—'a miserable piece of deception'. See the letters to Köselitz of 2 and 3 Oct. 1882.

belief in him: cf. Mark 16: 16, where Jesus appears to the apostles after the Resurrection and says: 'He that believeth and is baptized shall be saved; but he that believeth not shall be damned.'

158 *'twilight' death*: an allusion to the last part of Wagner's *Ring* cycle, *Twilight of the Gods*.

no other God before me!: cf. Exodus 20: 3–5, where the Lord introduces the Ten Commandments by saying: 'Thou shalt have no other Gods before me . . . for I the Lord thy God am a jealous God.'

159 *blessèd still than receiving?*: cf. Acts 20: 35, where Paul quotes Jesus's saying: 'It is more blessèd to give than to receive.' I have translated *nehmen* as 'receiving' here rather than 'taking' in order to preserve the allusion to the King James Version of the Bible.

160 *In caring and pitying . . . lain*: a note from the period reads: 'Pitying: my weakness, which I am learning to overcome. It is good if the most detestable *abuse* of my sympathy and indulgence eventually teaches me that I have *nothing* to do in this area' (*W* 11: 25 [498]). In a letter to Overbeck in which he discusses the difficulties he has been having with his relatives, Nietzsche writes: 'This is the mistake that I perpetually make: that I imagine the suffering of others to be much greater than it is. From my childhood on, the proposition 'my greatest dangers lie in *pitying*' has confirmed itself again and again. . . . It will be enough if, through the

bad experiences I have had with pitying, I am stimulated to make a theoretically interesting alteration in the *esteem* that pitying enjoys' (*B* 14 Sept. 1884).

162 *as if a tree . . . my foothills:*—: cf. Emerson: 'Wherever we begin, thither our steps tend: an ascent from the joy of a horse in his trappings, up to the perception of Newton, that the globe on which we ride is only a larger apple falling from a larger tree; up to the perception of Plato, that globe and universe are rude and early expressions of an all-dissolving Unity,—the first stair on the scale to the temple of the Mind' (*The Conduct of Life*, 'Beauty'). On trees waving: 'The greatest delight which the fields and woods minister, is the suggestion of an occult relation between man and the vegetable. I am not alone and unacknowledged. They nod to me, and I to them. The waving of the boughs in the storm, is new to me and old. It takes me by surprise, and yet is not unknown' (*Nature*, ch. 1; in *Essays and Lectures*).

163 *thorn and stake . . . and delusion*: cf. 2 Corinthians 12: 7, where 'the messenger of Satan' is said to be 'a thorn in the flesh'; and 1 Corinthians 1: 20, where Paul writes, 'Hath not God made foolish the wisdom of the world?'

164 *into my gardens!*—: a letter to Köselitz (*B* 3 Aug. 1883) confirms that this is an allusion to the philosopher Epicurus and his garden in Athens.

whited sepulchres: cf. Matthew 23: 27, where Jesus denounces the scribes and Pharisees as 'whited sepulchres, which indeed appear beautiful outward, but are within full of dead men's bones, and of all uncleanness'.

165 *pseudo-wisdom*: a somewhat bowdlerized translation of 'After-Weisheit', where the *After* is a pejorative prefix with connotations of 'behind' in the sense of 'arse'. When the philologist Ulrich von Wilamowitz-Moellendorf published a scathing review of Nietzsche's first book, *The Birth of Tragedy*, his friend Erwin Rohde replied with a scathing response to Wilamowitz's review entitled *Afterphilologie* ('Arse-philology').

166 *much be revealed!*: cf. Luke 2: 35: 'Yea, a sword shall pierce through thy own soul also, that the thoughts of many hearts may be revealed.'

168 *this world is even the best*: cf. Leibniz, *Theodicy*, sec. 209, where the 'law of the best' dictates that 'everything resolve itself into the greatest perfection'.

169 *set up tabernacles*: cf. Exodus 40: 1–2, where the Lord instructs Moses to 'set up the tabernacle of the tent of the congregation'.

170 *On Old and New Tablets*: 'That decisive chapter bearing the title "On Old and New Tablets" was composed during the difficult climb from the station to the magnificent Moorish rock-fortress at Èze [near Nizza]' (*EH* 'Why I Write Such Good Books', *Thus Spoke Zarathustra*, 4).

Here I sit . . . inscribed tablets: 'Here I sit' are the first three words of the last stanza of Goethe's poem 'Prometheus' (1773), which was a favourite of the young Nietzsche's (who wrote a one-act play titled *Prometheus* when he was 14). Cf. Exodus 34: 1, where the Lord says to Moses: 'Hew thee two tables of stone like unto the first: and I will write upon these tables the words that were in the first tables, which thou shattered' (Luther).

172 *hearts of flesh?*: cf. 2 Corinthians 3: 3, where Paul speaks of the epistle of Christ as 'written not with ink, but with the Spirit of the living God; not in tablets of stone, but in the fleshy tablets of the heart' (Luther).

173 *gratis . . . least of all life*: cf. Revelation 22: 17: 'And whoever will, let him take the water of life gratis.' The word translated as 'gratis' (*umsonst*) also means 'in vain'.

a firstling is always sacrificed: cf. Genesis 4: 4, where Abel brings as an offering to the Lord 'the firstlings of his flock and of the fat thereof'.

old idol-statues: cf. Ezekiel 40: 39 ff., where in his vision of the temple Ezekiel sees 'tables . . . to slay thereon the burnt offering . . . whereupon they slew their sacrifices'.

174 *all science*: I have translated *Wissen* here as 'science', to try to convey the play between *Gewissen* (conscience) and *Wissen* (knowing).

Everything is in flux: the word translated as 'flux' is *Fluss*, which is otherwise translated (as in the previous clause) as 'river'. The entire section is an extended allusion to the debate between philosophers (like Parmenides) who argue that evanescence is illusory and that ultimate reality is fixed, permanent, and stable, and those who (like Heraclitus and Nietzsche) believe that flux is universal ('Everything flows') and stasis is a fiction. Cf. Heraclitus as cited in Plato, *Cratylus*, 402a.

everything stands still: cf. the pre-Socratic philosopher Parmenides, fragment 8, for whom Being, as the ultimate reality, is 'uncreated and imperishable, entire, immovable, and without end'.

175 *through all the streets!*: cf. Jeremiah 11: 6, where the Lord says: 'Proclaim all these words in the cities of Judah, and in the streets of Jerusalem.'

took off one's shoes: cf. Exodus 3: 5, where the Lord speaks to Moses from the burning bush: 'Put off thy shoes from off thy feet, for the place whereon thou standest is sacred ground.'

176 *with the grandfather time stops*: the idea of time's stopping with the grandfather occurs in an unpublished note from 1881, where it is preceded by an expression of Nietzsche's desire to become acquainted with 'the family tree of [his] spirit' through history: 'Without this we are all mayflies and rabble' (*W* 9: 15 [70]).

177 *for being children of your fathers*: cf. Exodus 20: 5, where the Lord says: 'For I the Lord thy God am a jealous God, visiting the iniquity of the fathers upon the children unto the third and fourth generation of them that hate me.'

surely be muzzled!: cf. Deuteronomy 25: 4: 'Thou shalt not muzzle the ox when he threshes' (Luther).

178 *all things are pure*: cf. Titus 1: 15: 'Unto the pure, all things are pure: but

unto them that are defiled and unbelieving is nothing pure.' Also Gurnemanz's pronouncement in Act III of Wagner's *Parsifal*: 'Be blessed, you pure one, by what is pure!'

180 *dogs lick . . . languish*: cf. Luke 16: 21, where Lazarus is laid at the rich man's gate and 'the dogs came and licked his sores'. See also Diogenes Lacrtius, *Lives and Opinions of the Philosophers*, 9. 4, on the death of Heraclitus.

by the hair: cf. Ezekiel 8: 3, where the prophet recounts how the hand of God 'took me by the hair of mine head; and the spirit lifted me up between the earth and the heaven' (Luther).

182 *A prelude . . . my example!*: there is a play here on the element of 'play' (*Spiel*) in the words *Vorspiel* (prelude) and *Beispiel* (example). Cf. John 13: 15: 'For I have given you an example, that ye should do as I have done unto you.'

185 *not a 'contract'*: an allusion to Rousseau's idea of the social contract.

They are Pharisees: cf. Matthew 5: 20: 'For I say unto you, That except your righteousness shall exceed the righteousness of the Pharisees, ye shall in no case enter into the kingdom of heaven.' See also the parable of the Pharisee and the publican in Luke 18: 9–14.

188 *you sleepy worm*: the 'worm' is an allusion to the dragon (referred to as a *Wurm* rather than a *Drache*) that Siegfried confronts in Act II, scene 2 of Wagner's *Siegfried*.

—sleep on!: this is a parody of the brief appearance of Erda in Act III, scene 1 of Wagner's *Siegfried*: 'A whole act with *no* female voice—that won't do! But the "heroines" are not free right now. So what does Wagner do? He emancipates the oldest woman in the world, Mrs Erda: "Up, old grandmother! You have to sing!" Erda sings. Wagner's intention is fulfilled. He gets rid of the old lady again immediately. "Why did you come here after all? Off you go! Please go back to sleep." ' (*The Case of Wagner*, 9).

the advocate . . . of the circle: in a contemporary letter to Overbeck, Nietzsche reports having undergone one of his worst bouts of illness ever, but immediately adds : 'No! *This* life! And I am the advocate of life!' (*B* 22 Feb. 1883).

189 *rose-apple . . . delightful*: Oldenberg recounts the story of the Buddha's spending 'four periods of seven days each' in meditation leading up to his enlightenment, and also paraphrases a Buddhist text that describes how the Buddha as a boy used to spend time on the estate of his father 'sunk in contemplation in the cool shadow of a fragrant rose-apple (Jambu) tree' (*Buddha*, 137 f. and 121).

let me listen to you!: just as Siegfried was able to understand the song of the birds in the forest after slaying the dragon, so Zarathustra is able to understand the speech of his animals after confronting the thought of eternal recurrence.

190 . . . *the ring of Being*: cf. the penultimate paragraph of *Hyperion*: 'Reconciliation is in the midst of strife and all that is separated finds itself again' (2. 2. 8).

centre is everywhere: an allusion to the (pseudo-)Hermetic idea of God as 'an infinite sphere of which the centre is everywhere and the circumference nowhere', first found in a treatise by the twelfth-century theologian Alain de Lille, and subsequently taken up by Nicholas of Cusa, Giordano Bruno, and Blaise Pascal. Jorge Luis Borges traces a brief history of the idea in his essay, 'The Fearful Sphere of Pascal'.

a hurdy-gurdy song of it all?: Zarathustra has just called his animals 'barrel-organs' (*Drehorgeln*), and he now complains that they are making 'a hurdy-gurdy song' (*Leier-Lied*) of his recent affliction. As well as meaning 'the same old story', *Leier* originally means 'lyre', and so there is an allusion to Apollo in his complaint that the animals are making a caricature of the (Dionysian) thought of eternal recurrence.

193 *a Great Year*: the Great Year (also called 'Platonic Year'): a period of time in which the stars and constellations return to their former places in relation to the equinoxes (approx. 26,000 years).

194 *On the Great Yearning*: the original title of this chapter, which reflects the abundance of Dionysian imagery it contains, was 'Ariadne'.

your round-dance: the word translated by 'round-dance,' *Reigen*, is common in Luther's Bible, and especially in Psalms. Cf. e.g. Psalm 149, which begins, 'Sing unto the Lord a new song', and later says, 'Let them praise his name in the dance (*Reigen*)'. Psalms 102 and 103 begin, as does the present chapter, with an apostrophe to the soul: 'Bless the Lord, O my soul.'

195 *the bark floats . . . frolic*: this image alludes to the representation of Dionysus crossing the sea on his boat surrounded by dolphins, in the black-figure painting on a *kylix* by Exekias (6th cent. BCE).

196 *The Other Dance-Song*: in a letter to Overbeck, Nietzsche writes that his friend Heinrich von Stein is enough of a poet to be deeply affected by 'The Other Dance-Song' and has even learned it by heart: 'For whoever is not compelled by precisely the serenity of Zarathustra to shed tears, such a one is still very far from my world, from me' (*B* 14 Sept. 1884).

198 *noise murders thoughts*: cf. Schopenhauer's remarks, in 'On Din and Noise', where he deplores the fact that the cracking of whips is permitted: 'This sudden, sharp, brain-laming sound cuts off all reflection and murders all thoughts' (*Parerga und Paralipomena*, vol. 2, ch. 30).

200 *The Seven Seals*: cf. Revelation 5: 1: 'And I saw in the right hand of him that sat on the throne a book written within and on the backside, sealed with seven seals.'

Never yet . . . O Eternity!: cf. Diotima's speech to Socrates concerning the lover's ultimate union with divine and eternal Beauty, which results in the generation of true virtue or excellence (Plato, *Symposium*, 212a).

shattered tablets: cf. Exodus 32: 19, where Moses, on seeing the people dancing around the golden calf, 'was very wroth, and he cast the tablets out of his hands, and shattered them beneath the mount' (Luther).

202 *... space and time sparkle*: these lines echo an eight-line poem that Nietzsche wrote as a dedication to Lou Salomé which he inscribed in a copy of *The Joyful Science* that he presented to her, the second half of which reads (in a literal, non-rhyming translation, to show the similarity): 'The one he loves he gladly lures | Far out into space and time— | Above us sparkles star upon star, | About us roars eternity.' See Lou Andreas-Salomé, *Friedrich Nietzsche in seinen Werken* (Frankfurt, 1983), 169.

my Alpha and Omega!—: cf. Revelation 1: 8: 'I am Alpha and Omega, the beginning and the ending, saith the Lord, which is, and which was, and which is to come, the Almighty.'

FOURTH AND LAST PART

207 *honey in my veins . . . tranquil*: one of the myths concerning Dionysus is that, to protect him as a young child, the Maenads hid him in a cave and nourished him with honey.

208 *golden fishing-rod . . . humans' abyss!*: Matthew 4: 19, where Jesus says to the fishermen Simon and Andrew, 'Follow me, and I will make you fishers of humans' (Luther).

Become the one you are!: cf. Pindar, *Pythian Ode*, 2. 72: 'Become such as you are, having learned what that is', tr. W. R. Race, *Pindar I*, Loeb Classical Library (Cambridge, Mass., and London, 1997).

'endureth': this word in quotes, *duldet*, may refer to its only occurrence in Luther's Bible, in 1 Corinthians 13: 7, where Paul writes of love, or charity, that it 'endureth all things'. Nietzsche was certainly familiar with this passage, since he chose the next line, 'Love never ceases' ('Charity never faileth'), as the epitaph for his father's gravestone.

209 *Our great hazar . . . a thousand years*: an unpublished note from the period reads: 'I had to grant Zarathustra, a *Persian*, the honour: the Persians were the first to *think* history as a great whole. A series of developments, with a prophet presiding over each. Every prophet has his *hazar*, his reign of a thousand years' (*W* 11: 25 [148]). Cf. the frequent mentions of thousand-year periods in Revelation 20.

my in-and-for-me: the 'in-and-for-me' is an allusion to the notion of the 'in-and-for-itself' (*an-und-für-sich*) in Hegel.

211 *The superior human . . . for you!*: in an unpublished note Nietzsche writes of 'the *fate of the superior humans* in the present age, the way the species seems *condemned to extinction:* it comes as a great cry for help to Zarathustra's ears. All kinds of insane degeneration of superior natures (e.g., nihilism) comes up to him' (*W* 11: 27 [23]).

212 *caves he would surely find*: in a letter to Resa von Schirnhofer, Nietzsche writes: 'Well—I shall show you Nizza and also, as far as it goes, myself, since you say you want to "make the acquaintance of" the old solitary. However, every solitary has his cave, in himself, and sometimes behind the cave another cave and yet another . . .' (*B* 30 Mar. 1884).

213 *a strange procession*: cf. the processions of the knights to the Gralsburg in Wagner's *Parsifal*. For an excellent summary of the parody of *Parsifal* in the Fourth Part, see Hollinrake, *Nietzsche, Wagner, and the Philosophy of Pessimism*, 166–71.

 a laden ass: cf. Matthew 21: 5: 'Behold, thy King cometh unto thee, meek, and sitting upon an ass, and a colt the foal of an ass.'

214 *—and yet must appear to be*: an unpublished note emphasizes the necessity of making clear 'to what extent the slave has now become master, without having the virtues of the master/nobility without the foundation of heritage and purity/monarchs without being *first among men*' (*W* 11: 25 [246]).

215 *the Sibyl*: name of the first oracle at Delphi, which came to be applied to all virgin priestesses with the gift of prophecy in the cult of Apollo.

 Rome became a whore . . . too: cf. Isaiah 1: 21, and the description in Revelation 17: 1–6 of the Whore of Babylon.

216 *sun of peace . . . shameful*: in a notebook from the period Nietzsche quotes the motto to Emerson's essay 'Heroism' (in Essays 1): 'Paradise is under the shadow of swords' (*W* 11: 25 [3]). Where Emerson has 'Mahomet' after the quotation, Nietzsche has 'Orient.[alisch'.

219 *want to be blind*: several notes from the period characterize the 'will to blindness' as deriving from the eye's inability to see when one's honesty comes to an end (*W* 10: 4 [176], 12 [5], 13 [7]).

 The Sorcerer: in a letter to Heinrich Köselitz, Nietzsche refers to Wagner as 'der alte Zauberer', 'the old sorcerer' (*B* 1 Aug. 1882), and this figure is just as clearly intended as a portrait of Wagner as the soothsayer is of Schopenhauer.

220 *to wail thus*: this song is one of the poems in the posthumously published *Dionysus Dithyrambs*, where it bears the title 'Ariadne's Lament'—so that the unknown God the poem addresses would be Dionysus.

 Strike . . . this heart!: cf. Amfortas in Act III of *Parsifal*: 'Drive your swords deep—deep, up to the hilt! Up, you heroes!'

223 *you play-actor!*: in an unpublished note Nietzsche writes: 'Everything I said about Wagner is wrong. I felt that in 1876: "everything about him is ungenuine; what is genuine is concealed or decorated. It is all play-acting, in every bad and good sense of the word" ' (*W* 11: 26 [22]).

225 *a frog . . . bursts*: cf. the fable by Aesop, 'The Frog and the Ox'.

227 *a hidden God*: cf. Isaiah 45: 15: 'Verily thou art a hidden God, O God of Israel, the Saviour' (Luther). The notion of *deus absconditus* (hidden God) is central to Luther's theology.

228 *this potter*: cf Isaiah 45: 9 and Romans 9: 20–1.

229 *The Ugliest Man*: cf. W. E. H. Lecky, *History of the Rise and Influence of Rationalism in Europe* (New York and London, 1925), i. 245, where a note on the tradition of the deformity of Christ remarks that Cyril of Alexandria held that Christ had been 'the ugliest of the sons of men'. Nietzsche read the translation of 1866.

230 *this valley 'Serpents' Death'*: cf. *The Thousand and One Nights*, 'The Second Voyage of Sinbad the Sailor', where Sinbad describes finding himself in the Valley of Serpents: 'a great, wide valley, surrounded by mountains on all sides . . . In the valley were a large number of snakes, as long and thick as a large date palm.'

revenge on this witness!: an unpublished note reads: 'Defiance in self-abasement, going so far that it demands deadly revenge on the witness/therefore God must *die!*' (*W* 10: 17 [54]).

232 *I—am the truth*: cf. John 14: 6, where Jesus says to Thomas: 'I am the way, the truth, and the life: no man cometh unto the Father but by me.'

233 *the one who does, learns*: an unpublished note reads: 'Not to your ears, but to your hands do I direct my teaching. Do as I do: only the doer learns: and only as a doer shall I become your teacher. Better that you emulate me poorly, than that you let your hands rest and pray!' (*W* 10: 13 [1]).

234 *cows . . . warmed his heart*: in *Ecce Homo* Nietzsche writes: 'In such a condition [of extreme susceptibility to small stimuli during periods of creativity] I once sensed the presence of a herd of cows, through the return of milder, more philanthropic thoughts, even before I saw it: *that* is something with warmth' (*EH* 'Why I Write Such Good Books', *Thus Spoke Zarathustra*, 5). Nietzsche was accustomed to frequent encounters with herds of real cows during his walks in the countryside around Sils-Maria.

sermonizer on the mount: there are several allusions in this chapter to Christ's Sermon on the Mount (Matthew 5–7).

the Kingdom of Heaven: cf. Matthew 18: 3, where Jesus says to his disciples: 'Except ye be converted, and become as little children, ye shall not enter into the kingdom of Heaven.'

235 *what is he profited!*: cf. Matthew 16: 26, where Jesus asks: 'For what is a man profited, if he shall gain the whole world, and lose his own soul?'

But they received him not: cf. John 1: 11: 'He came unto his own, and his own received him not.'

237 *eat of it!*: cf. Proverbs 25: 16: 'If you find honey, then eat of it so much as is sufficient for thee' (Luther).

no longer of this world: cf. John 18: 36, where Jesus says to Pilate, 'My realm is not of this world' (Luther).

238 *I have feared no prohibition*: cf. Ovid, *Amores*, 3. 4. 17: 'we always strive for what is forbidden.'

239 *'Nothing is true, everything is permitted'*: a saying attributed to Hassan i
     Sabbah, the first Grand Master of the Order of Assassins in 11th-century
     Persia. Nietzsche repeats the saying as the motto of the Order of Assas-
     sins in *GM* 3. 24.

     . . . their new security: cf. Francis Galton, *Inquiries into Human Faculty
     and its Development* (London, 1882), 61: 'Scenes of heartrending despair
     are hardly ever witnessed among prisoners; their sleep is broken by no
     uneasy dreams—on the contrary, it is easy and sound.' A note of
     Nietzsche's suggests that the reason is that they have no 'pangs of
     conscience' (*W* 11: 25 [18]).

240 *One thing is more necessary than another*: Nietzsche's sister Elisabeth
     writes that this saying was a favourite of their grandmother's (*The
     Young Nietzsche*, trans. Anthony Ludovici (London: Heinemann, 1912),
     ch. 4).

241 *the world . . . become perfect?*: cf. Emerson: 'There are days . . . wherein
     the world reaches its perfection . . . The day, immeasurably long, sleeps
     over the broad hills and warm wide fields' (*Essays* 1, 'Nature'). In an early
     letter to his friend Carl von Gersdorff, Nietzsche writes of days, 'like
     those beautiful summer days that spread themselves out so broadly and
     comfortably across the hills, as Emerson so excellently describes: then
     nature becomes perfect, as he says' (*B* 7 Apr. 1866).

     a seventh day . . . at midday?: a note for this passage reads 'blissful and
     weary, like every creator on the seventh day' (*W* 11: 31 [40]). Cf. Genesis
     2: 3, where God is said to have 'rested on the seventh day from all his
     work which he had made'.

246 *'coarse, solid German'*: this passage, with its play between *deutlich* (clear)
     and *Deutsch* (German), lampoons a piece of etymology proposed by
     Wagner: 'The word "German" is to be found again in the verb *deuten* [to
     explain, indicate]: "German" is therefore what is clear [*deutlich*] to us'
     (*Bayreuther Blätter* 2 (Feb. 1878), 30).

247 *The Last Supper*: (the German for which is simply *Abendmahl*, 'evening
     meal'). The diners at this 'last supper' number twelve, if one includes
     Zarathustra's eagle and serpent and the ass. Cf. Matthew 26: 20–9.

248 *by bread alone*: cf. Matthew 4: 4, where Jesus, having fasted for forty days
     and forty nights, says to the Devil: 'Man shall not live by bread alone, but
     by every word that proceedeth out of the mouth of God.'

     prepared with spices and sage: cf. Exodus 12: 3–9, on the preparation of the
     lamb for Passover.

249 *On the Superior Human*: in a contemporary note on 'the superior human',
     Nietzsche writes: 'During the period when *contentment of the mob* rules,
     disgust is the mark of the superior human' (*W* 11: 29 [52]).

250 *the mountain . . . go into labour*: cf. Horace, *Ars poetica*, 139: 'mountains
     will be in labour, a ridiculous mouse will be born.'

251 *greatest number*: an allusion to the basic principle of Utilitarianism—'the

greatest happiness of the greatest number'—as represented by Jeremy Bentham and John Stuart Mill.

252 *bore man's sin*: cf. John 1: 29, where John says of Jesus: 'Behold the Lamb of God, which takes upon himself the sin of the world!' (Luther).

253 *convinces through gestures*: a note from the period reads: 'Wagner addresses himself to those who are suspicious of reasons but can be convinced by sublime gestures' (*W* 10: 11 [6]).

254 *who is your neighbour?*: cf. Luke 10: 29, where the lawyer, having been told to love his neighbour as himself, asks Jesus: 'And who is my neighbour?'

. . . *or 'because'*: a note from the period emphasizes that 'every thing should be done for the sake of that thing itself and for love of it', and that purpose by contrast 'desecrates' things (*W* 10: 17 [61]). This attitude toward things was described in 'Before Sunrise' (3. 4), where Zarathustra 'redeemed things from their bondage under purpose'.

whoever has given birth is unclean: cf. the instructions for the purification of women made 'unclean' by childbirth in Leviticus 12.

255 *a firstling . . . a lastling too!*: cf. Genesis 4: 4, where Abel brings to the Lord 'the firstlings of his flock and of the fat thereof'; also Mark 9: 35, where Jesus says to his disciples: 'If any man desire to be first, the same shall be last of all, and servant of all.'

256 . . . *who laugh now!*: cf. Luke 6: 25, where Jesus says to his disciples: 'Woe unto you that laugh now! for ye shall mourn and weep.'

gnashing of teeth . . . for us: cf. Matthew 8: 12, where Jesus says: 'But the children of the kingdom shall be cast out into outer darkness: there shall be weeping and gnashing of teeth.'

257 *like a pillar*: a note from the period confirms that the pillar is another allusion to a stylite, or 'desert-saint' (*W* 11: 31 [64]).

259 *learn . . . to laugh!*: cf. Wagner's *Siegfried* where the hero's task is to 'learn fear', and *Parsifal* where it is to 'learn pity'.

260 *who is an adversary*: cf. 1 Peter 5: 8: 'Be sober, be vigilant; because your adversary the Devil, as a roaring lion, walketh about seeking whom he may devour.'

263 *On Science*: the German word *Wissenschaft* has a broader range of meaning than our 'science', which nowadays tends to suggest the natural sciences. *Wissenschaft* has the broader sense of human knowledge, learning, scholarship, and so forth. There is an assonance in German between *Wissenschaft* and its proponent in this chapter, *der Gewissenhafte* (the conscientious man).

265 *loves his enemies*: cf. Matthew 5: 44, where in his Sermon on the Mount Jesus says: 'But I say unto you, Love your enemies, bless them that curse you, do good to them that hate you, and pray for them which despitefully use you, and persecute you.' An unpublished note of Nietzsche's reads: 'Enmity has never been a serious problem for me. In the heat of the

moment, admittedly, and especially under the pressure of an overcast sky, I could easily kill someone—and have sometimes been amazed that I didn't. But I then laugh again too soon for any enemy to have much to make amends for. Besides I am utterly convinced that I have more to thank my hostile feelings for than friendly ones' (*W* 11: 25 [15]).

266 *Abide with us*: cf. Luke 24: 29, where the apostles say to Jesus: 'Abide with us: for it is toward evening, and the day is far spent.'

267 *A European under palm-trees . . . Selah*: in Goethe's *Elective Affinities* (2. 7), an entry in Ottilie's journal concerning travellers to exotic lands reads: 'No one wanders under palm-trees unpunished.' The 'Selah' is a common refrain in the Psalms.

268 *great whale . . . learned allusion?*: cf. Jonah 2: 1 and Matthew 12: 40 for the story of Jonah and the whale.

sniffing at me: in the Colli–Montinari edition the verb *umschnüffeln* ('sniff at') has been replaced by *umtänzeln* ('skip around').

More . . . sinful: in the Colli–Montinari edition the *sündhafteren* ('more sinful') has been replaced by *boshafteren* ('more wicked').

269 *Dudu and Suleika*: Dudu is an odalisque who figures prominently in Byron's *Don Juan* (Canto VI), which was one of the young Nietzsche's favourite works; similarly with Suleika in Goethe's *West-östlicher Divan*. The scene is a parody of the flower-maidens scene in Wagner's *Parsifal*.

270 *Angry blond curly-maned*: in the Colli–Montinari edition the word *gelben* ('yellow') has been added after the 'Angry'.

271 *I can do no other . . . Amen!*: an allusion to Luther's famous pronouncement before the Diet of Worms in 1521: 'Here I stand. I can do no other. So help me God! Amen!'

273 *. . . burning pine-cones*: cf. the account by Georg Christoph Lichtenberg (1742–99), an author Nietzsche knew well, of the 'Ass-Festival' that arose during the thirteenth century (*Vermischte Schriften* (Göttingen, 1867), v. 326 f.).

without being noticed: cf. the way Parsifal appears in the Hall of the Grail 'without being noticed' (*unvermerkt*) in Act III of *Parsifal*.

. . . from eternity to eternity!: cf. Revelation 7: 12. Nietzsche here quotes Luther's version verbatim, except for the omission of the word *Kraft* (strength, power) between *Preis* (praise) and *Stärke* (might).

bears our burdens . . . a servant: cf. Psalms 68: 19, where God is said to 'load us with a burden, but also to help us'; Philippians 2: 7, where Paul says of Jesus that he 'took upon him the form of a servant'; and Hebrews 12: 6.

274 *his own image*: cf. Genesis 1: 27, where God creates man 'in his own image'.

if naughty boys entice you: cf. Proverbs 1: 10: 'My son, if naughty boys (*bösen Buben*) entice thee, follow them not' (Luther).

figs . . . feel hunger: cf. Matthew 7: 16: 'Ye shall know them by their fruits. Do men gather grapes of thorns, or figs of thistles?'

The Ass Festival: in an earlier manuscript this chapter bears the title 'The Old Faith and the New', an allusion to the book by D. F. Strauss that Nietzsche had criticized in the first of his *Untimely Meditations*.

'God is Spirit': cf. John 4: 14: 'God is a Spirit: and they that worship him must worship him in spirit and in truth.'

277   *The Drunken Song*: in the Colli–Montinari edition this chapter is entitled *Das Nachtwandler-Lied* ('The Night-Wanderer Song'), according to a later version of the manuscript.

278   *full of sweet wine*: cf. Acts 2: 13, where mockers say of the apostles, filled with the Holy Ghost: 'These men are full of new wine.' Nietzsche follows Luther in using the adjective *süss* (literally, 'sweet').

279   *. . . a heavy cloud*: a repetition from 'The Seven Seals' (3. 16), sec. 1.

    the sound of a bell: cf. *Human, All Too Human*, 628: 'In Genoa I once heard at dusk a long peal of bells coming from a tower: it did not want to end and rang out, as if insatiable for itself, over the noise of the streets into the evening sky and the sea air, so ghastly, so childlike at the same time, so full of melancholy.'

283   *you please me, happiness!*: cf. Faust's challenge to Mephistopheles: 'If I should say to the moment (*Augenblick*) | "Do stay! You are so fine!" | Then may you put me in chains | Then gladly will I perish (*zu Grunde gehn*)' (Goethe, *Faust I*, 1699–1700). This is also where *zurückwollen* is used to mean 'want . . . back' as a counterpart to 'will backwards' (as in 2. 20, 'On Redemption').

284   *girded up his loins . . . dark mountains*: cf. e.g. 1 Kings 18: 46: 'And the hand of the Lord was on Elijah; and he girded up his loins, and ran before Ahab to the entrance of Jezreel'; also *Hyperion*: 'Yes! a sun is the human being, all-seeing, all-transfiguring, when he loves' (1. 2. 18).

285   *. . . drunken songs*: in the Colli–Montinari edition the *trinkt* ('drink') has been replaced by *käut* ('chew') and the *trunknen Liedern* by *Mitternächten*: 'their dreams still chew on my midnights.'

286   *the lion . . . laughed*: cf. Goethe's *Novella*, in which an escaped lion is charmed into submission by a young boy: 'If it were possible to think that the features of so fierce a beast, the tyrant of the forests and despot of the animal kingdom, could display an expression of friendliness and grateful contentment, then it happened in this case.' Shortly before his mental collapse, Nietzsche wrote: 'The *Lion-Novella*, which was strangely the first thing by Goethe that I encountered, gave me once and for all my conception or my *taste* for "Goethe." A purely transfigured autumnal tone to enjoying and ripening—to waiting, October sun all the way to the most spiritual heights; something golden and sweetening, something mild, *not* marble—*that* is what I call Goethean' (*W* 13: 24 [10]).

INDEX

I, the 28, 31, 33, 172, 218, 224, 228, 235, 247

ice 17, 55, 60, 92, 100, 134, 140, 151, 175, 220, 222, 230, 257

idol 43, 44, 89, 149

ill 16, 94, 153, 167, 210, 211, 215, 224, 229, 249; ill-will 121, 215, 249, 271

image 27, 33, 34, 71, 74, 75, 87, 89, 98, 106, 207, 215, 239, 246, 261, 274

impatience 71, 72, 107, 162, 166, 197, 208, 209, 226, 231, 234, 258

injustice 47, 50, 56, 82

innocence 46, 48, 75, 96, 97, 106, 141, 151, 161, 163, 166, 173, 197, 239, 274

island 67, 89, 112, 113, 131, 154, 159, 198; *see also* Blest, Isles of the

jealous 33, 46, 51, 81, 86, 102, 106, 141, 150, 158, 162, 198, 221

jester 17, 18, 19, 46, 155, 172, 276

Jesus 63

Jew 214, 215, 238

joy 32, 34, 74, 75, 92, 113, 121, 122, 150, 199, 201, 202, 278, 282–4

jubilation 72, 271

judge 33, 34, 55, 59, 60, 86, 99, 228, 274

justice 35, 59, 82, 86, 87, 88, 109, 122; *see also* righteous: righteousness

kill 32, 33, 36, 40, 46, 55, 60, 68, 96, 175, 220, 231, 275, 276

king 114, 169, 183, 213–16, 243–6, 248, 249, 266, 273, 274

knife 34, 282

knowledge 66, 90, 101, 175, 223; *see also* understanding

ladder 51, 131, 169, 181, 221

lake 9, 72, 197, 207

lame 103, 109, 119, 134, 156, 254

land 10, 17, 20, 51, 103, 105, 132, 144, 177, 185, 186, 210, 216, 229, 241, 245

laugh 10, 11, 13, 15, 17, 19, 25, 26, 30, 35, 36, 48, 61, 62, 64, 75, 80, 88, 91, 96, 98, 112, 113, 116, 126, 128, 129, 133, 135, 144, 147, 149–53, 158, 159, 165, 166, 169, 174, 180–4, 186, 188, 189, 201–8, 211, 212, 214, 227, 229, 231, 233, 240, 243, 245, 249, 251, 252, 260, 266, 270, 272, 273, 277, 278; laughter 17, 36, 71, 88, 98, 112, 126, 144, 153, 159, 173, 176, 179, 182, 206, 221, 223, 236, 252

law 31, 51, 55, 99, 114, 122, 249

lazy 17, 40, 81, 93, 180, 181, 236, 242

lead (metal) 34, 134

leaf 100, 107, 156, 241, 258

learn 15, 28, 30, 35, 36, 62, 64, 73, 76, 82, 84, 90, 96, 101, 102, 111, 112, 115, 120, 122, 125, 131, 132, 139, 142, 143, 145, 146, 150, 154, 157–62, 167–9, 172, 174, 177, 178, 179, 183, 185, 186, 188, 191, 192, 196, 197, 208, 216, 218, 231, 233–5, 241, 245, 249, 250, 252, 253, 255, 258, 259, 265, 266, 268, 271, 272, 276, 283, 284

liberate 38, 51, 75, 117, 121, 179; liberator 74, 121

lie (falsehood) 26, 27, 40, 43, 46, 53, 60, 61, 74, 81, 106, 107, 110, 113, 124, 136, 137, 146, 150, 158, 161, 163, 167, 168, 181, 186, 188, 189, 190, 197, 203, 207, 215, 223, 224, 239, 240, 252, 253, 260, 261, 265, 276

life 12, 14, 16, 18, 26, 27, 31, 33, 36, 39–45, 49, 62–4, 66, 67, 74, 79, 81, 83, 84, 87, 88, 90, 98, 101, 104, 106, 108, 114, 117, 118, 122, 124, 126, 135, 139–41, 148, 150, 161, 167, 168, 170, 173, 175, 179, 181, 188, 191, 193, 216, 217, 219, 239, 247, 257, 264, 275, 276, 278; Life (feminine figure) 94, 95, 99, 100, 196, 198, 199

light (opp. of dark) 9, 19, 20, 26, 36, 37, 50, 57, 62, 78, 81, 86, 88, 91, 92, 107, 111, 116, 136, 138, 139, 142, 155, 156, 160, 167, 169, 171, 184, 189, 194, 195, 200, 202, 203, 212, 249, 252, 257, 263, 285

lightning 13, 15, 18, 38, 50, 149, 164, 200, 201, 224, 252

lonely 11, 18, 67, 71, 73, 85, 95, 111, 117, 131, 135, 149, 159, 164, 217, 222, 234, 270, 281

longing 92, 164, 181, 215; *see also* yearning

lord 23, 26, 46, 146, 183, 215, 250, 251, 280, 281; *see also* master

love 10, 13, 14, 15, 16, 20, 22–4, 31–3, 35, 36, 38, 39, 41–3, 45, 48–54, 56–8, 60–6, 68, 69, 71–4, 77, 79, 81, 82, 87, 91, 94, 95, 97, 99, 100, 102, 105–8, 111, 113, 118, 124, 131, 133, 139–41, 147–50, 154, 155, 158, 159, 162–4, 167–9, 172, 173, 177, 180–2, 184, 190, 191, 194,

The Oxford World's Classics Website

www.worldsclassics.co.uk

- Information about new titles
- Explore the full range of Oxford World's Classics
- Links to other literary sites and the main OUP webpage
- Imaginative competitions, with bookish prizes
- Peruse the Oxford World's Classics Magazine
- Articles by editors
- Extracts from Introductions
- A forum for discussion and feedback on the series
- Special information for teachers and lecturers

www.worldsclassics.co.uk

American Literature

British and Irish Literature

Children's Literature

Classics and Ancient Literature

Colonial Literature

Eastern Literature

European Literature

History

Medieval Literature

Oxford English Drama

Poetry

Philosophy

Politics

Religion

The Oxford Shakespeare

A complete list of Oxford Paperbacks, including Oxford World's Classics, Oxford Shakespeare, Oxford Drama, and Oxford Paperback Reference, is available in the UK from the Academic Division Publicity Department, Oxford University Press, Great Clarendon Street, Oxford OX2 6DP.

In the USA, complete lists are available from the Paperbacks Marketing Manager, Oxford University Press, 198 Madison Avenue, New York, NY 10016.

Oxford Paperbacks are available from all good bookshops. In case of difficulty, customers in the UK can order direct from Oxford University Press Bookshop, Freepost, 116 High Street, Oxford OX1 4BR, enclosing full payment. Please add 10 per cent of published price for postage and packing.